AUSTRALIA AT THE POLLS

AEI'S AT THE POLLS STUDIES

The American Enterprise Institute
has initiated this series in order to promote
an understanding of the electoral process as it functions in
democracies around the world. The series will include studies
of at least two national elections in more than twenty countries
on five continents, by scholars from the United States and
abroad who are recognised as experts in their field.
More information on the titles in this series can
be found at the back of this book.

AUSTRALIA AT THE POLLS

The national elections of 1980 and 1983

Edited by Howard R. Penniman

George Allen & Unwin   Sydney   London   Boston
American Enterprise Institute   Washington D.C.   London

Distributed to the Trade by National Book Network, 15200 NBN Way, Blue Ridge Summit, PA 17214. To order call toll free 1-800-462-6420 or 1-717-794-3800. For all other inquiries please contact the AEI Press, 1150 Seventeenth Street, N.W., Washington, D.C. 20036 or call 1-800-862-5801.

National Library of Australia
Cataloguing-in-Publication entry:

Australia at the polls.

Includes index.
ISBN 0 86861 086 0 (pbk.)

1. Australia. Parliament—Elections, 1980–
Addresses, essays, lectures. 2. Elections—
Australia—Addresses, essays, lectures. 3. Australia
—Politics and government—1976- —Addresses,
essays, lectures. 4. Australia. Parliament—
Elections, 1983—Addresses, essays, lectures.
I. Penniman, Howard R. (Howard Rae), 1916–
II. American Enterprise Institute for Public Policy
Research. (Series: At the polls series).
(Series: AEI studies; 369).

324.994'063

Library of Congress Cataloging in Publication Data
Main entry under title:

Australia at the polls, 1980.

(AEI studies; 369)
Includes index.
1. Australia. Parliament—Elections, 1980—Addresses,
essays, lectures. 2. Elections—Australia—Addresses,
essays, lectures. 3. Australia—Politics and government—1945-   —Addresses,
essays, lectures.
I. Penniman, Howard Rae, 1916–   II. Series.
JQ4094.A79 1982   324.994'063   82-73669
ISBN 0-8447-3506-X (pbk.)

AEI Studies 369

Set in 10 on 12 pt Palatino by Graphicraft Typesetters Limited, Hong Kong

Contents

Preface

Australia at the Polls, 1980 and 1983 is another in the series of national election studies in selected democratic countries published by the American Enterprise Institute for Public Policy Research (AEI). The series has been supported because AEI believes that scholars and practitioners can better understand their own democratic institutions by developing a greater knowledge of electoral rules and practices in other modern democracies.

The first study of Australian elections included in this series described the dramatic and divisive elections of 1975 that followed a constitutional crisis brought about when the opposition-controlled Senate blocked passage of the Labor government's Budget. To break the parliamentary deadlock, the Governor-General ousted the Labor government; Parliament was dissolved, and elections were called to select all members of both chambers. The election resulted in a resounding victory for the Liberal-National Country Party coalition (L-NCP), which won ninety-one seats to Labor's twenty-seven in the House of Representatives and the first absolute senatorial majority for any party in a decade.

The Australian national elections of 1977 were called by Prime Minister Fraser a year early in order to preserve the coalition's control of the Senate for at least another three years and to confront the Labor Party at the polls before it could replace Gough Whitlam whose leadership, Fraser believed, was Labor's greatest handicap. The L-NCP retained a large, though slightly reduced, majority in the House of Representatives and a slim majority in the Senate. In fact, the Liberal Party itself won a clear majority of the House seats just as it had in 1975. Also, as in 1975, Cabinet positions were shared with the National Country Party whose leader, Doug Anthony, was again named deputy leader of the parliamentary coalition. [In October 1982, motivated by a desire to broaden its electoral appeal, the NCP decided to drop 'Country' from its name, and became the National Party (NP).]

In his chapter on the electorate, Don Aitkin says that voting "swings have tended to go in the same direction for two elections [in Australia], and then to reverse.... This phenomenon has been quite regular since 1963". The four Australian elections covered in the *At the Polls* studies fit neatly into the pattern Aitkin describes. After its very successful elections of 1975 and 1977, the coalition's popular support declined sharply in 1980 and 1983, as did its membership in the House of Representatives and the Senate. Labor cut the coalition's margin in the House to twenty-three seats in 1980 and took control of that body in 1983, winning 60 percent of the seats. In the Senate, where members are chosen by the single transferable vote system (a form of proportional representation), the same change has been clear if less dramatic. The coalition lost its Senate majority in 1980 and its membership dropped to only twenty-eight in 1983. Labor won thirty seats leaving the balance of power in the hands of five Australian Democrats and a single independent.

Fraser and the Liberal-National Party coalition have faced three quite different Labor leaders in the four Australian elections covered in the *At the Polls* series. In the 1975 election study Patrick Weller and R. F. I. Smith said, "Whitlam's activities compelled attention. His errors were as impressive as his successes. His was a brittle leadership—brilliant, industrious, and enthusiastic, but also infuriating, headstrong, and tactless." Weller described Bill Hayden, who succeeded Whitlam after Labor's defeat in 1977, as a man who consulted widely, listened to alternatives, who was erudite, careful, and adequate if not inspiring. Nonetheless, he led a vigorous and relatively successful campaign in 1980.

Hawke, who replaced Hayden as party leader, literally only hours before the dissolution of Parliament and the beginning of the 1983 campaign, is described as a man with "formidable" qualifications. For twenty years he was a leader in the Australian Council of Trade Unions—ten of those as president. He held numerous positions on governmental and quasi-governmental boards and commissions. His reputation as a negotiator and his record of settling industrial disputes were extremely high. His bitterest enemies in general have come from the socialist left as his own views have become increasingly moderate. As leader of the Labor Party, he may be expected to play a decisive role in Australian national politics for a decade or more.

The enfranchisement of eighteen-year-olds in 1974, according to Aitkin, may have been responsible for a lessened stability of the national vote in recent years and the "weaker structuring effect of partisanship". The youth vote may have had a somewhat greater impact in Australia than in most other democracies, where the absence of compulsory voting rules has often meant that young people contributed more to the decline in voter turnout than to a general destabilization of voting patterns.

Australian women, as Anne Summers points out, now support Labor candidates more frequently than in the past. Evidence of a similar leftward shift is to be found in some other democracies, including the United States. Summers states that whatever their ideological positions, "a record number of women candidates contested the [1980] elections and a record number was elected". Three women were elected to the House and ten to the Senate. In 1983 women set new records when they doubled their membership in the House and slightly increased their number in the Senate. As in other democracies, one may expect more female candidates and more successes in the future.

The Contributors

With the exception of David Butler of Nuffield College, Oxford, who contributed the introductory chapter, all other authors writing for this volume are Australian scholars or journalists. Don Aitkin analyzes the Australian electorate; Patrick Weller, Martin Rawlinson, Keith Richmond, and John Warhurst provide chapters on the campaigns of the Labor Party, the Liberal Party, the National Country Party, and the place of minor parties and pressure groups; Anne Summers describes the changing role of women in Australian politics; Murray Goot discusses the media's coverage of the campaign; and Colin Hughes, as in previous volumes, offers an overall look at the 1980 campaign, its results, and some perspective on the future of Australian politics. Colin Hughes and Patrick Weller kindly agreed to prepare a supplementary discussion of the 1983 elections that were called shortly before the 1980 volume was to go to press. The appendix contains a description of Australia's procedures for casting and counting ballots and the 1980 election returns by Richard M. Scammon. Professor Hughes provides the 1983 returns.

Howard R. Penniman

1
Introduction

David Bulter

The Australian people went to the polling-booths on October 18, 1980 and elected Malcolm Fraser's Liberal-Country Party coalition to a further three-year term. In times to come, the 1980 election may appear utterly unimportant, a trivial milestone in another protracted Liberal ascendancy. The contest may come to be likened to those tedious elections in 1958 and 1963, so predictably won by Sir Robert Menzies in the middle of the long years from 1949 to 1972 when Labor was kept continuously in opposition.

It is therefore important to record that, at the finish of the 1980 campaign, there was, for the first time in fifty years, real doubt about who would win. On the morning of the vote, the opinion polls were forecasting a Labor victory. Some, it is true, indicated a close outcome and Labor pessimists, inured to defeat, could not quite accept the evidence of the polls; like the public service establishment and the world of business, they assumed that, in the end, the Liberals would get back. However, no one was betting on a government majority as large as the one that transpired. As the campaign ended the general verdict was the Bill Hayden and Labor had scored a clear victory on points and that the Liberals had done much to throw away the advantage of being the incumbent government. Thus, even if the 1980 election cannot yet be given its final place in history, there is much about it that challenges explanation.

Perhaps the 1980 election shows how wise Prime Minister Fraser had been to call the 1977 election a year early. Ostensibly he did so in order to get Senate elections into phase with House elections.[1] But in practice it seems almost certain that he was trying to anticipate Bill Hayden's replacement of Gough Whitlam. In 1977 the Liberals ran against the Labor record of 1972–75, embodied in the towering arrogant personality of Gough Whitlam, and, contrary to all expection, they managed to repeat their 1975 landslide victory. In 1980 Gough Whitlam was not there. Bill Hayden proved himself more formidable as a party leader than anyone had expected. Labor made a major advance. More seats changed hands than in most recent elections. Although the swing was not enough to give victory to the Labor Party, it was on a scale that was exactly in line with the expectations that had been held during the campaign of 1977. The Labor recovery came three years late—and it was still not enough for victory.

Yet it was enough to take away the government's Senate majority and to open up the prospect of more exciting politics than had been possible with the deadeningly large parliamentary majorities of the previous five years. The government won twenty-three more seats than the opposition but there were no fewer than twelve government seats where Labor came within 1.3 percent of victory. In the new situation where a nationwide swing of only 1.3 percent would turn the Coalition majority of twenty-three into a Labor majority of one, it was plain that the 1983 election would cast a powerful shadow over the Parliament.

The period from 1977 to 1980 had been without triumphs or disasters. Australia had shared in the world recession and the world inflation but it had fared less badly than many other nations. The inflation rate had drifted up from 8 percent to 11 percent and unemployment from 6 percent to 8 percent. Production had been stagnant, though high tariffs had saved industry from some of the dumping that occurred elsewhere. But the sturdy agricultural sector and the continued expansion of mining kept the economy going. New finds of coal, uranium, diamonds, allumina and lodes of diverse metals were reported and their development produced boom areas in Western Australia and Queensland and drew in plenty of foreign capital. Oil searches proved disappointing but enough new natural gas, shale-oil and coal was discovered to check anxiety about future energy supplies. Despite the slump, Australia (whose population passed 15 million in 1980) still had the feel of a growing nation.

Malcolm Fraser's government met with some vicissitudes. There were isolated incidents leading to the dismissal or resignation of ministers. The New Federalism policy of giving more financial freedom to the States hardly worked; Canberra continued to monopolize income tax and to dominate, in a much criticized way, the share-out at the Annual Premiers' Conference. John Howard survived as an unexciting Treasurer. He had twice to bring in Supplementary Budgets in May in his efforts to keep the economy in balance and, though gift tax and inheritance taxes were ended, he was not able to bring down the general level of taxation despite a limited, if premature, give-away of small benefits six months before the election. The monetarist policies of the government were very mild and there was no great success in the efforts to bring down expenditure, though Labor's Medibank system of health care was abolished, as was the indexation of means tests for welfare benefits. Meanwhile, symbolic of a dominant and free-spending central government, the peripatetic Australian High Court settled down in a magnificent permanent home in Canberra and ground was broken for a vast new building to house the Federal Parliament in time for the 1988 Bicentennial.

At the State level the Liberals stayed in control in Victoria and Western Australia while Labor held on in Tasmania and New South Wales. South Australia in 1979 slipped from Labor to Liberal but in Queensland the strident Country Party Premier, Joh Bjelke-Petersen, continued firmly in power, infuriating Labor and embarrassing his Liberal allies, in Brisbane and in Canberra, by his outbursts against Aboriginal rights and on law and order and federal–State relations

The parties nationally survived the period without undue incident. There was increased sniping against Fraser but his dominance over the government and the Liberal Party was not seriously challenged; there was no acceptable alternative to him. On the Labor side, Bill Hayden, who had swiftly and easily taken over from Whitlam, managed the party competently but so unostentatiously that, when the charismatic leader of the Australian Council of Trade Unions, Bob Hawke, announced that the he planned to enter Parliament, speculation about his taking over the leadership naturally developed. However, despite troubles in the Queensland and Victorian branches, the Labor Party entered the election in notably good order.

After the contest, some fundamental questions were asked about the Australian electoral system and the nature of the Australian political battle. Later chapters deal with many of these questions in detail. The following pages can only touch on a few of them. On election night some people—including Hayden—expressed bewilderment that the apparent 7 percent increase in the Labor vote was not producing a Labor victory—they had been told that a 6.1 percent swing was all that was needed. The immediate reaction was to suggest that something had gone wrong with the Australian electoral system and that the relationship between seats and votes had changed.

But in fact the 1980 election went according to established form. The system worked in its familiar and predictable way. A 4 percent

3

swing in the "preferred" vote (the vote that the main parties would have got when all the minor party votes had been reallocated between them) produced a net switch of thirteen seats, almost exactly the number that past experience would have suggested.[2] Public confusion arose because, while Labor's share of first preference votes went up by 6 percent, the government's only fell by 2 percent. Thus the average of Labor gain and government loss (that is, the net movement between the main forces in Australian politics) was in fact just 4 percent, well short of the 6 percent needed to put Labor in. The asymmetry of the change in the major party votes was due to the 4 percent fall in support for other parties.

One of the remarkable features of Australian politics is their nationwide homogeneity. In a federal country that is a continent, with hundreds of miles between its main centres of population and with six distinct State political systems, party support is distributed with singular evenness. In 1980 the most Labor State (Victoria) divided 51:49 in the party's favour and the least Labor State (West Australia) 53:47 against—the narrowest spread in party strength between States ever recorded.

It was not only the absolute level of party strengths that was uniform across the nation; the diversity in the movement of party support from 1977 to 1980 was equally small. The swing was in Labor's direction in every State; it was also in Labor's direction in 120 of the 125 constituencies. New South Wales and South Australia did swing appreciably less than Victoria and Western Australia but State variations from the national movement were lower than in most previous elections. For a far-flung federal society Australia showed itself, to a remarkable degree, one nation politically.

The Public Opinion Polls

The public opinion polls had their worst election yet in Australia and committed the ultimate sin of indicating the wrong winner. For pollsters, Australia in 1980 will join those great disasters, Britain in 1970 and the United States in 1948. Yet it is important to keep the error in perspective. Morgan Gallup, which produced the best of the final forecasts, suggested a 51:49 division of the vote in favour of Labor. That was only 1.4 percent away from the actual result. It is worth remembering that the Morgan poll acquired its enviable reputation for accuracy in the 1950s and 1960s in a period when, for four elections in a row, its predictions were over 3 percent in error. A 3 percent error is comparable to the deviations of the McNair poll in

1980 which forecast a 53:47 division of the vote in favour of Labor, and to the ANOP survey in marginal seats which indicated a similar outcome. The worst forecast came from the poll that had had the best record through the 1970s. Irving Saulwick's *Age* poll suggested that the vote would divide 54:46 in favour of Labor, an error of 4.4 percent, the greatest yet recorded in Australia by a serious polling organization.

The poll predictions had been notably accurate in the previous four elections and there is no reason to suppose that in 1980 their methods were less professional or conscientious than before. The pollsters themselves inevitably jumped to "late swing" as the explanation for their error. Most forecasts were based on interviews conducted on October 11 and 12. The *Age* and ANOP made telephone callbacks to respondents a day or two later but no one checked on how opinion was moving in the last three days before the vote at a time when the Liberals were putting on a great advertising blitz in the newspapers.

The polls themselves may have had a significant impact. For two weeks there had been fully publicized reports of Labor's lead. As the forecasts of a Labor victory struck home, there may well have been some swing back to the Liberals by cautious voters who did not wish to risk a change of government. In Britain there has been good reason to suppose that the polls have had a self-falsifying quality in recent elections, with a significant number of people switching their vote in order to cut down on the majority of the party which the polls show to be ahead. It is plausible that this also happened in Australia in 1980.

But, despite the disaster, the polls are certainly not finished in Australia. In one way, the 1980 election may be remembered for the impact of the polls as much as for their error. During the campaign they had an overwhelming influence on the style of reporting and on the stance of politicians. They certainly helped to give Bill Hayden the confidence he so impressively displayed and they caused visible flurries in the Liberal camp. An observer who probed in the head-quarters of either of the parties for their evidence about what the public was thinking inevitably found that they hardly ever cited local reports with anything like the respect they accorded to the polls.

The fact that the polls got the 1980 result wrong will not mean that they are abandoned next time. Newspapers may be a bit more sceptical about commissioning them and readers will read them with greater hesitation. But Australian polls are unlikely to be damaged by this disaster any more than the American polls were damaged by an even greater disaster in 1948. The simple fact is that there is nowhere else to turn. Politicians and journalists want to know how the mass public is thinking and how opinions are moving. They cannot trust their taxi driver surveys or the reception they get on the doorstep. They know that every "informed source" is liable to be corrupted by wishful thinking or by leaning too far backwards to avoid wishful thinking.

The reaction of the pollsters was, of course, to set about reexamining their own operations, looking critically at their fieldwork and at the way in which their findings were presented. They were also spurred to look at new techniques. In America and Canada, where telephone saturation is over 90 percent, telephone surveys have been shown to offer quicker and more reliable findings than can be derived from doorstep interviews. In Australia telephone ownership is due to reach into over 80 percent of homes by 1983. It may well be that, with suitable weighting for the non-telephone owners, voting surveys will be more accurate and final predictions more up-to-date.

This is not an apologia for the polls. To point to their inevitability is not to endorse their activities or to advocate them as constructive adjuncts to democracy. There is no doubt that the 1980 election would have been a very different affair in its conduct, and probably in its result, if there had been no opinion polls. Certainly the reception of the outcome would have emphasised the Liberal loss of seats rather than the Labor disappointment. But, in the aftermath of this poll disaster, it is worth stressing one fact of twentieth-century democratic life. Nowhere in the world has a debacle for the polls diminished their use in subsequent elections.

The Political Campaigns

The election was, on the whole, a fair one. There were no major scandals during the campaign. Neither side grossly over-reached the rules of decency. There were some complaints about details of party advertising. The Governor-General appeared in one Liberal advertisement and the National Country Party got into trouble with its "How to Vote" card in Queensland. Labor also complained about Liberal advertisements which suggested that Labor would tax increases in private house values. However, in March 1981 the High Court unanimously rejected a Labor attempt to invalidate particular results because of misleading propaganda from the government side.

A more serious complaint could be made about the general level of argument and reporting. Australia's major problems received less than adequate attention. Yet great issues are seldom lucidly discussed during elections. It is probably unreasonable to blame Malcolm Fraser for his prudent refusal to debate with Bill Hayden on the costs of the party program; the leader of a nation is unwise if he invests his opponent with the aura of his office by appearing on equal terms with him.

The press was reasonably fair in its coverage. The front page headlines of the Murdoch mass circulation papers were absurdly loaded but it did not seem that the news columns departed far from an acceptable equilibrium. Any imbalance in the press and on television came from the much greater sums of money spent by the Liberal side. It is possible to argue that the late swing back to the government, if there was one, was induced by the heavy advertising in the final days with its strident arousal of fears about capital gains tax on house ownership. Yet by world standards of democratic fair play, no one could suggest that this was an election in which money or governmental influence upset the will of the people.

The Liberals tried to rerun their successful 1977 campaign. But the attempt misfired. In 1980 the target presented by the opposition was very different. Hayden, discreetly supported by Bob Hawke and by Neville Wran, the Premier of New South Wales, in a supposed triumvirate, was not Gough Whitlam. The effort to contrast Malcolm Fraser, the big man, with his lesser challenger misfired; Hayden justifiably earned a better and better press as the campaign progressed.

With remarkable candour, Fraser observed that the Liberals had made a mistake by handing out their tax-relief goodies in the Budget in August so that they were forgotten by the time of the campaign. The Liberal list of promises in the election policy speech seems to have cut little ice.

The promises in the Labor policy speech were probably equally unimportant. However, the Labor Party, with its studious moderation, put on a competent campaign, notably free from the muddles and mutual contradictions of previous contests. It offered a well orchestrated attack on Fraser's past record and his current remarks.

What was notable about the Labor and the Liberal campaigns was the increasingly subtle exploitation of the media. The time of the leaders was largely devoted to events that would produce televisual material in time for the news bulletins or that would catch the housewife audience listening to talk-in radio shows. The traditional speeches on the hustings were an ever smaller feature of the election.

Yet in one respect the election was like past contests; the policy speeches were full of relatively uncoordinated promises, and they were supplemented by extra statements and clarifications day by day throughout the campaign. Each side still seemed to be working with an image of the voter as a rational cost accountant, assessing what was in it for him or her in the rival lists of goodies on display. Every academic survey suggests that the voter has far less exact responses and on the whole, far less materialistic.

The Senate Result

One result of this election was that the government lost its majority in the Senate.[3] The situation was not a new one. From 1964 to 1974 the presence of Senators from the breakaway Democratic Labor Party meant that no government had a Senate majority. This did not matter much, at least until 1973, because the DLP hated the Labor Party much more than the Liberal government. To some extent indeed the DLP contingent may have stiffened the resolve of right-wing coalition Senators. In 1975 the Labor government was brought down because it lacked a majority in the Senate and could not get a vote of Supply. Since July 1, 1981, when the balance of power has been held by five Australian Democrat Senators, dissident Liberal Senators may be increasingly encouraged in their recalcitrance about some aspects of the Fraser regime.

But there was surely no question of a repetition of 1975 occurring during the 1980–83 Parliament. Senator Chipp, the leader of the Australian Democrats, promised that he and his colleagues would never vote to block Supply. But they might well frustrate specific parts of the government's legislation. It was even conceivable that a situation might arise where Fraser would be forced to call their bluff by invoking a double dissolution. That might lose them one or two seats (although they would probably be in a position to pick up the tenth seat in almost every State).

One irony of the Senate election lay in the working of proportional representation. Senator Chipp's party secured, on average, 9 percent of the Senate vote yet it found itself near to getting a seat in five out of the six States because the other parties were split so evenly. In fact it won three and only just missed out in the other two. If its national vote had even been 1 percent more, the Australian Democrats would have got 17 percent of the Senate seats with only 10 percent of the vote. Proportional representation does not always produce strictly proportional results.

Labor parties in Australia and Britain have a brawling tradition. Ideologues and power brokers let their views be known very bluntly. But the Labor campaign in 1980 was the most notably united and harmonious affair that Australia had seen for thirty years. Nobody in their moderate parliamentary leadership put a foot out of step.

It is worth considering how the act was got together. A lot of Labor people had come to make Gough Whitlam, with his brilliant, ebullient personality, the scapegoat for their setbacks in 1975 and 1977: they were delighted to do anything needed to secure power under the banner of the less abrasive Bill Hayden. It was nonetheless remarkable that, in his platform and in his speeches, Hayden was able to go so far in watering down any proposals of the Labor Party which might worry middle Australia. It became a Tweedledum and Tweedledee election; yet, surprisingly, no significant protest was heard from those on the left who undoubtedly believed that a Labor Party has the duty to offer a radical alternative to the establishment. What Labor presented was state capitalism with a human face; they offered good administration and an end to Malcolm Fraser. In orchestrating this prudent campaign Hayden's achievement was extraordinary. He kept in line—and was positively supported by— such very different State secretaries as Graham Richardson of NSW and Robert Hogg of Victoria as well as by that formidable duo, Bob Hawke and Neville Wran.

Chapter 4 expands on that delicate and harmonious convergence, as well as on the way in which the campaign leaders and Hayden's own personal staff developed new skills in administration and public relations. What was offered was a peculiar miracle of centralized cooperation and timing.

It is always difficult to say what issues stir the bulk of the electorate or have the power to switch their votes. What is plain is that the politicians in the 1980 election gave low priority to matters that the outsider might think would disturb Australians. There was no discussion of foreign affairs (except for marginal references to the derecognition of the Pol Pot regime). There was no debate on what Australia's defence posture should be (with the bleak alternative of D.J. (Jim) Killen or Gordon Scholes as Defence Minister). There was remarkably little reference to uranium mining, or to the development of national resources, or to the problems of foreign capital and multi-nationals.

All these were matters on which the future of Australia might be said to depend. But the contestants adjudged them to be issues on which there was no party difference, or none that could be deployed before the voters in a way that would interest enough of them to waste air time or advertising space on.

The choice before Australians was a relatively narrow one. It was hard to believe that in terms of economic indicators, or of social policy, Australia would be a very different place by 1982 after two years of Fraser or of Hayden government. People were, it seems, voting on personality, choosing between the unloved but known Malcolm Fraser and the liked but unproved Bill Hayden. They were expressing a general verdict about the handling of national affairs.

What Labor did in 1972–75 had passed on into the land of myth, for good or for ill. But it had left some Australians a bit frightened. The Liberals' accomplishments in 1975–80 were not outstanding in terms of employment, or industrial output, or the control of inflation but the continuance of a Liberal administration did not seem too threatening to ordinary Australians. It is indeed a lucky country that can have so good humoured an election in which so little is at stake.

Notes

1 The Australian Constitution allows a maximum of three years between elections and twenty-two of the thirty-one Parliaments since 1901 have lasted virtually their full term. On four occasions only the Parliament has ended with a double dissolution of both House and Senate. Following the double dissolution of 1975 when the full Senate was reelected (half for three-year and half for six-year terms), half the Senators would have had to face reelection by July 1, 1978, at least six months before the full three-year term of the House ended in December 1978.

2 Since 1918 Australia has used the alternative vote in single member constituencies. Voters must number all candidates in order of preference. The votes for the weakest candidate are redistributed to the next preference until one candidate has an absolute majority. But for convenience of analysis Malcolm Mackerras and other psephologists have continued the distribution of preferences, by a process of estimation, so that every vote can be allocated to government or opposition. In fourteen constituencies the two government parties, taking advantage of the preferential system, invited the voters to decide between Liberal and National County Party candidates. There were in fact only six seats where the final distribution of preferences changed the outcome from what it would have been under first-past-the-post counting.

3 Since 1949 the Senate has been elected by the single transferable vote system of proportional representation. Every three years, five of each State's ten senators come up for reelection: in normal circumstances government and opposition can be sure of two seats each. It is the fate of the fifth seat that is at issue.

2

The Changing Australian Electorate

Don Aitkin

Some nine million citizens were eligible to vote on October 18, 1980 in the thirty-second elections for the House of Representatives which were combined, as had been the case on twenty-one previous occasions, with elections for one-half of the Senate. Much was known about the nine million, and much more could be accurately guessed: the steady flow of opinion polls, together with two comprehensive academic analyses of the electorate that appeared in the late 1970s,[1] made the task of party strategists and commentators somewhat easier than in the past. Yet, as always, the outcome was not an open-and-shut matter—indeed few early predictions proved to be close to the mark. Two months before the poll the coalition government led by Malcolm Fraser was generally seen as an easy winner; yet as the campaign progressed there were periods when the composition of a Hayden government was more than a fantasy exercise over drinks, and the coalition's eventual victory was in fact a narrow one. The 1980 elections were to provide the first electoral test of the staying power of the Australian Democrats (AD), the centre-party formation that had secured nearly 10 percent of the popular vote in the 1977 elections, and might be moving to occupy and enlarge the middle ground. And 1980 was to see, almost certainly, the entry into Parliament of Bob Hawke, recently retired as President of the Australian Council of Trade Unions (ACTU), Federal president of the ALP from 1973 to 1978, and arguably the most popular figure in Australian politics for some years.

Other chapters follow up each of these themes. This chapter explores the nature and structure of the Australian electorate at the end of the 1970s, concentrating on the changes which had occurred over the twelve years since its first comprehensive exploration in

1967.[2] Such an exploration is the more timely because of the growing scholarly interest in electoral volatility, and in the possibility that Western party systems, for so long frozen in the shapes they adopted in the 1920s or even earlier, were beginning to crack, and to re-form in unexpected ways.[3] The sudden rise of the Australian Democrats seemed, on the face of it, evidence of volatility, as had the sharp change in support for Labor in 1974/75. Was Australia undergoing the same process? And in either case, what were the causes?

A Volatile Electorate?

In one account, politics for Australians has been partisan, practised, but somehow peripheral. Three generations at least of native-born Australians have known only party politics, whose temper is often high and whose style is usually rough; they take their own partisanship from parents, or, if theirs were not obvious, from social milieux; political debate is not so much the rational discussion of alternatives (though that does occur) but the confrontation of "my party, right or wrong"; elections are frequent, and serve as occasions for the registration of partisanship—but between-times the electorate gets on with its own life, and leaves politics to the politicians. Inherited partisanship is the sheet-anchor of the system's stability, providing replacement supporters as older generations pass out of the electorate, restricting the possibility of change, and preventing Poujadist outbreaks. If Australia were becoming more volatile, something would be happening to partisanship, and thus to the political outlook of Australians. Kemp's work, showing a progressive decline in the power of the connection between some aspects of social structure and partisanship, points to a potential line of enquiry, and to a fascinating puzzle. But are there hints in the record of election results?

The Aggregate Data

Table 2-1 sets out the party shares of the formal first preference vote at elections for the House of Representatives from the first postwar election in 1946 to the election of 1980.[4] The most immediate message of the table is the regularity of the performance of the major parties: Labor secures between 40 and 50 percent, the Liberals between 32 and 42 percent, the National Country Party between 8 and 11 percent. The only sustained linearity is the decline in the vote of the splinter Democratic Labor Party after 1961. Some elections are, in their broad results, almost replicas of other elections.

12

There have not been continuous movements in support towards or away from either of the major parties, and in fact there were swings (in two-party terms: the average of Labor gains and coalition losses) equal to or greater than 5 percent in only three years—1949, 1969 and 1975. Swings have tended to go in the same direction for two elections, and then to reverse. Thus 1946 and 1949 saw swings away from Labor, 1951 and 1954 swings toward; this phenomenon has been quite regular since 1963.

Australia knew a pure two-party system for only a very short time, the nine years after 1910. In 1919 the emergence of the Country Party brought about a three-party system in country electorates as well as in Parliament; a pact in 1923 between the non-Labor parties meant that a kind of two-party system operated thereafter, though from time to time subject to small explosions when the coalition partners quarrelled. Since 1955, when a section of the Labor Party hived off to form the DLP, it has been sensible to see a four-party system, in which the four parties which have some kind of parliamentary representation are attended by a number of very small parties and electoral pressure groups which do not. The number of parliamentary candidates has tended to increase over this period (1949: 349; 1958: 407; 1969: 493; 1980: 502), which is in part a consequence of the greater number of

TABLE 2-1
Party shares of the formal first preference vote in elections for the Australian House of
Representatives, 1943–80
(in percentages)

Election Year	Labor	Liberal	Country Party[a]	Minor Party	Others
1946	50	33	11	—	6
1949	46	39	11	—	4
1951	48	40	10	—	2
1954	50	39	8	—	3
1955	45	40	8	(DLP) 5	2
1958	43	37	9	9	2
1961	48	34	8	9	1
1963	45	37	9	7	2
1966	40	40	10	7	3
1969	47	35	8	6	4
1972	50	32	9	5	4
1974	49	35	11	1	4
1975	43	42	11	1	3
1977	40	38	10	(AD) 9	3
1980	45	37	9	7	2

Note: Succession in office: Labor 1941–1949, L-CP 1949–1972, Labor 1972–1975, L-NCP 1975–
[a] Since 1975 the Country Party at the Federal level has called itself the National Country Party.
Source: Don Aitkin, Stability and Change, p. 4 (updated).

parties and groups; it may also be due to greater affluence and a greater interest in politics.

The evidence so far does not point to a notable volatility in the later 1970s. Indeed, if volatility is to be found in Australia one would need to describe it as 'cyclical', and explain it as the concomitant of short periods of turbulence in the affairs of one or other of the major parties which follow long periods of comparative calm. In the last fifty years such turbulence has occurred in 1930–31, 1944–45, 1954–55 and 1975–77. The Australian Democrats are clearly not unique as a challenging fourth party; nor is their central position along the left-right continuum. The DLP, despite its claim to be radical and the true inheritor of the Labor tradition, was generally portrayed by the cognoscenti as well to the right of the centre,[5] but the small Australia Party of 1969–75 did claim the middle ground, though with only tiny success. And if quantitative precision is desired, Rae's "fractionaliza-tion index" provides a simple measure of the postwar impact of challenging parties:[6] for the periods 1946–54 (pre-DLP), 1955–69 (DLP) and 1972–80 (the 1970s) the average scores are .61, .65 and .64 respectively, and the variation is very slight.

Finally, there has been no steady erosion of the position of the "governing parties", such as Crewe, Sarlvik and Alt have diagnosed for Britain, where between 1951 and 1974 the share of the enrolled electorate commanded by the Conservative and Labour Parties fell from 80 percent to 56 percent.[7] To be sure, compulsory voting in Australia guarantees a near-maximum turnout, but in fact the sup-port of the *voting* electorate for the coalition-plus-Labor has fallen below 90 percent only twice since 1946—in 1958 and 1977—the years of greatest challenge from fourth parties. Neither the DLP nor the AD has managed to win 10 percent of the vote at a House of Representa-tives election, and there seems no reason to suppose that the Democrats will be able to do so in the future.

The Survey Evidence

Our focus must be mostly on party identification, because it is here that observers elsewhere have perceived striking changes over time. The most powerful evidence of a decline in party identification was pointed to by Nie, Verba and Petrocik, in a re-analysis of American S.R.C. data: from 1952 to 1974 the proportion of "Independents" increased from 23 percent to 38 percent, virtually matching the decline in the proportion of strong partisans—37 percent to 26 percent.[8] Crewe, Sarlvik and Alt found that partisanship in Britain remained high between 1964 and 1974, but that, as in the USA,

14

strength of partisanship seemed to have declined. Moreover, partisanship seemed no longer as effective in "structuring" the vote as had once been the case—that is, people might still think of themselves as Conservative while voting Labour, or Liberal or something else.[9] They found evidence, as Kemp had done in Australia, of a weakening of the class-party link.

There was, then, something to look out for: reductions in partisanship, in the strength in which that partisanship was held, and in the strength of the links between partisanship and social structure.

The evidence for the first two possibilities is contained in Figure 2-1, which presents a comparison of partisanship and its strength in three national samples twelve years apart.[10] It is important to note that the 1979 survey was deliberately a replication of the first one, so far as technical details were concerned, and that both were carried out in what for Australia were periods of electoral calm; for the 1969 post-election survey the 1967 respondents were re-interviewed and their number was increased by an appropriate sample of those who had come on to the rolls since 1967. Figure 2-1 contains no evidence of a slide in partisanship in the 1970s: if there has been any change it is in the slight strengthening of the proportion of "fairly strong" partisans at the expense of the "not very strong".[11] So far, the survey evidence confirms the impression gained from a reading of the aggregate data, that volatility—at least to a noticeable degree—was not present in Australia.

FIGURE 2-1
Strength of Party Identification, 1967, 1969 and 1979.

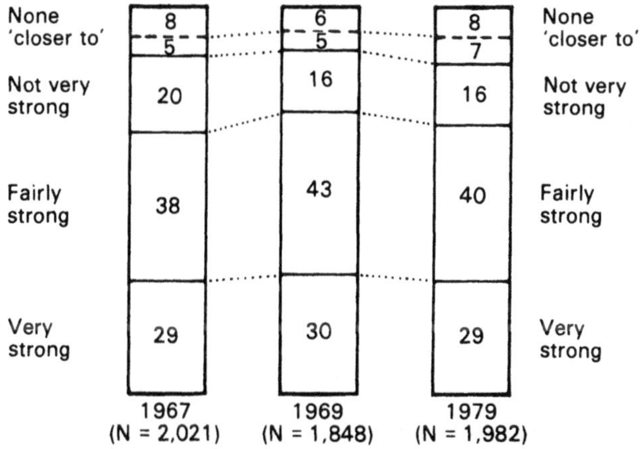

Source: 1967 ANU Survey, 1969 ANU Survey, 1979 Macquarie Survey.

15

Partisanship and the Vote

Confirmation comes from an investigation of the extent to which party identification "structured" voting. Clearly the impact of partisanship on the outcome of elections would be less, notwithstanding a continued preparedness of people to give themselves party labels, if the party label came to be worn as carelessly as, say, denominational labels often are. Crewe, Sarlvik and Alt estimated that the proportion of British voters *not* voting in accordance with their party identification increased from 14 percent in 1964 to 23 percent in October 1974.[12] The comparable Australian data are set out in Table 2-2, which in one respect speaks as eloquently as any table can: the 1966 and 1977 columns are identical. But why the abrupt change in 1969? The answer almost certainly lies in the fact that in 1969 respondents were reporting a vote cast days before, whereas the gap between interview and reported vote in 1967 and 1979 was many months in each case. In 1969 there was a strong move to the Whitlam-led ALP by many Liberal and Country Party partisans,[13] and at the time of interview such respondents were still coming to terms with their vote. In 1967 and 1979, it may be argued, sufficient time had elapsed for party-identification to have been brought into line with vote in many cases. The data of Table 2-2 may contain puzzles, but they offer no support to the view that party identification is losing its impact on voting.

A further demonstration of the continued utility of partisanship—this time in conditions of uncertainty—is offered by Figure 2-2. Here

FIGURE 2-2
Uncertainty and party identification, 1967 and 1979

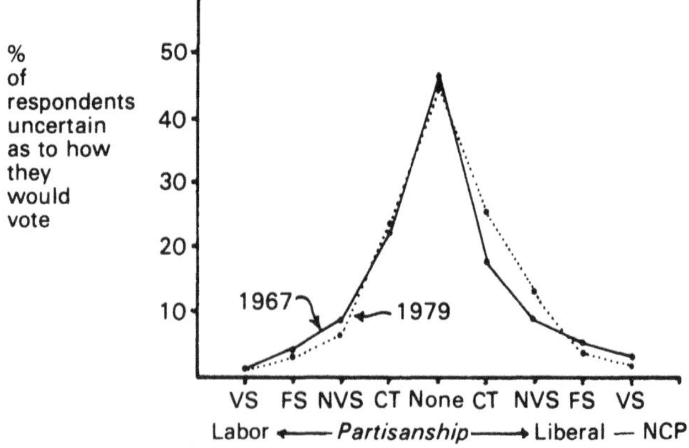

% of respondents uncertain as to how they would vote

VS = Very strong, FS = Fairly strong, NVS = Not very strong, CT = 'closer to'
Source: 1967 ANU Survey, 1979 Macquarie Survey

are plotted the responses to the question "If a federal election were held tomorrow, which party would you vote for?" The 1967 and 1979 curves are very similar indeed, even to the slightly greater certainty of Labor partisans compared with their Liberal and National Country Party counterparts.

Has nothing changed at all? The answer is that there has been less *stability* in party support than was true in the 1960s, despite the high levels of party identification. Table 2-3 presents the evidence, by comparing responses to the question "Since you have been voting in federal (state) elections, have you always voted for the same party, or have you voted for different parties?" (This question followed a series exploring voting behaviour in some past elections.) The proportion reporting having voted for different parties was rather higher in 1979 than in 1967, and the increase was greater in the Federal arena. At the same time, stable Labor voting showed no decline—indeed, it very slightly increased; it was the coalition supporters who, on the face of

TABLE 2-2
Party identification and voting in elections, 1966, 1969 and 1977 (%)

Proportion who . . .	Election Year		
	1966	1969	1977
voted in agreement with party identification	93	86	93
voted, but not in agreement with party identification	5	12	5
didn't vote/don't know	2	2	2
(N)	100	100	100
(proportion of total sample)	80	89	83

Note: The analysis is confined to Labor, Liberal and [National] Country Party identifiers, the latter being grouped. Data obtained in 1967, 1969 and 1979 respectively; party identification applies to these years.
Source: 1967 ANU Survey, 1969 ANU Survey, 1979 Macquarie Survey.

TABLE 2-3
Stability in voting, 1967 and 1979 (%)

	Federal Elections		State Elections	
	1967	1979	1967	1979
Always voted Labor	32	33	35	36
Always voted Liberal/Country Party	36	27	35	30
Always voted other party	1	*	1	1
Voted for different parties	28	39	24	31
Don't know	3	1	5	2
Total	100	100	100	100
(N)	(1,924)	(1,934)	(1,876)	(1,879)

Notes: Excludes respondents who had voted once only.
　*　= less than 0.5 percent.
Source: 1967 ANU Survey, 1979 Macquarie Survey.

it, had been most ready to move. These data are consistent with the view that Labor partisanship is in some sense more deeply held, more strongly felt, than partisanship for the Liberal or National Country Parties, and that Labor's core support is therefore more solid.[14]

Figure 2-3 provides a further dimension to this puzzle by comparing the extent to which strength of partisanship was associated with stability in voting in 1967 and in 1979. While the effect of increasing degrees of partisanship was even more apparent in 1979 than in 1967, the effect was somewhat less powerful, and at every level.

There may be a variety of causes for the rather weaker stability of vote and the weaker structuring effect of partisanship apparent in the data drawn from the late 1970s. But one quite likely cause is the reduction of the voting age to eighteen, which took effect for the Federal elections of 1974. Young voters are less secured by habit and experience to the party of their choice, and they are more likely to be affected by the political events of their time.[15] It happens that not only was the electorate suddenly enlarged with young voters in 1974, but the three years thereafter were unusually turbulent. The conditions for more than normal instability in voting were certainly present. A full exploration cannot be undertaken here, but it seems very likely that much of the greater instability of the late 1970s is directly attributable to the voters under 25, a necessarily much larger proportion of the 1979 sample than of the 1967 sample. The young were more likely to have switched between 1975 and 1977, more likely to be uncertain as to how they would vote in 1979, more likely to have

Figure 2-3
Strength of Identification and Stability in Voting, 1967 and 1979.

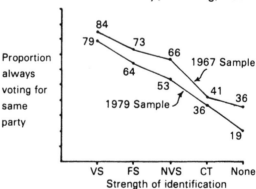

VS = Very strong, FS = Fairly strong, NVS = Not very strong, CT = Closer to (respondents who said that they felt "closer to" one party rather than others, though without accepting a party label), None = No Party identification.

Source: 1967 ANU survey, 1979 Macquarie survey.

voted out of sympathy with their identification in 1977, and more likeky to have split their House and Senate votes in 1977 and their House and Senate voting intentions in 1979. The differences were not remarkable in any case, but because the young were such a high proportion of the sample (those who entered the electorate in the 1970s made up three voters in every ten) they could have a considerable effect on the behaviour of the sample as a whole.

Party and Society

That the Western party system is not simply an outgrowth of social structure has become increasingly clear, as survey research in country after country has demonstrated that when account has been taken of social structure (at least as social science is able to measure it) there is much left to explain. In Australia contemporary social structure is particularly weak as an explanation either of the shape of the party system or of the distribution of partisanship. Rose's 1974 cross-national comparison placed Australia twelfth of fifteen Western democracies in the extent to which social-structural characteristics reduced the variance in predicting partisanship, and the thrust of more recent work is that the links between social structure and the party system in Australia are getting progressively weaker.[16] It is not uncommon for a party system to have its roots in historic political events rather than in social structure—Ireland's is one such—but there is something paradoxical in the steady erosion of the links with social structure of a party system like Australia's with the parties themselves apparently almost unaffected. Tentative responses to this paradox are now being offered:[17] the following discussion centres on four aspects of social structure in which important political changes have occurred since 1967.

Class

Aitkin's finding that measures of class explained little of the distribution of partisanship, and Kemp's finding that the importance of class had in any case been declining in the postwar years prompted a good deal of criticism, especially from those who felt that class and class conflict were the essential ingredients in Australian political history.[18] To a large extent the criticisms overshot their mark. To say that measures of class no longer provide much explanatory power in accounting for people's party preference is not to say that "class" does not exist. The distinctions and tensions between haves and have-nots, powerful and weak, and the looked-up-to and looked-down-upon are probably inescapable concomitants of social life, and wax and wane according to circumstances. The problem is, that whatever "class" may be, it is not easily defined (in which it is like most other indispensable concepts in social science), or, having been defined, built into a useful measure.

A tendency to equate class with occupation, graded according to some schema, has developed for a number of straightforward reasons. First, occupation is what is referred to in the term "working class", the most salient of class terms; second, it is what is suggested by the Marxian test of "relationship to the means of production"; third, alternative measures are no better. Compound measures, involving occupation, income, education, trade-union membership and the like can be constructed, but in Australia at least they do not greatly improve explanatory power, while they multiply boundary problems and complicate theory. It is possible, of course, that the declining explanatory power of occupational grade could be masking the rise of a better measure of class. But so far no-one has elaborated it; the blessings of social science await the elaborator. Until his or her appearance, we must conclude, on the basis of the evidence, that class, as measured by occupation, is not as powerful as it used to be in determining party preference.[19]

This point has been made most effectively by David Kemp, in his chapter in the preceding volume in this series. In what follows we consider the message of the most recent data, collected in 1979.

(1) "Subjective" class (people's own self-description in class terms) has been shown to be of dubious validity, partly because the labels commonly do not make much sense, given the respondent's occupation, and partly because many respondents switch to another label at small provocation.[20] In 1979 the tendency of people to describe themselves as "middle class" was even greater than in 1967, 56 percent compared with 43 percent. Forty percent of manual workers called themselves middle class, while among manual *trade-unionists* the "working-class" proportion declined from 71 percent to 64 percent. It is hard to doubt that "middle class" is becoming a term that is almost empty of meaning. These self-descriptions proved no more stable in 1979 than they had been in 1967.

(2) The continuing weakening of the class-party link is confirmed by Table 2-4, which compares the 1967 and 1979 male samples, using the manual/non-manual occupational distinction as the measure of class.[21] The general increase in Labor identification for the entire sample between 1967 and 1979 was 5 percent: the increase was actually smaller than this among manual workers, but it was more

than three times greater among non-manuals. Alford's class-voting index, a simple summary measure, shows scores of +33 for 1967 but +26 for 1979, a decline of a fifth.[22] Table 2-4 is very similar in its shape to Kemp's Table 2-3 in the previous volume, though this relied on class self-placement as the measure.

(3) Finally, the conventional image of trade unions as radicalizing agents operating on behalf of the Labor Party, a view already under suspicion,[23] no longer appears tenable. Although union membership increased substantially, from 50 percent of the workforce in the late 1960s to 60 percent in the late 1970s, the growth represented the continuing unionization of white-collar and female workers rather than a growth of radical spirit in the workforce. Moreover, there is abundant survey evidence that unions themselves declined steadily in public esteem during the period, and that union links with the Labor Party were decreasingly welcomed. Paradoxically, Labor identification increased much more sharply outside union ranks than it did within them, as Table 2-5 demonstrates. And the proportion of trade-unionist Labor partisans who claimed a "very strong" partisanship declined from 46 percent to 40 percent over the twelve years. Trade unionism, like the Labor Party itself, has been changing its shape.

TABLE 2-4
Party identification and occupational grade among men 1967 and 1979 (%)

| Party Identification[a] | Occupational Grade | | | |
| | Non-Manual | | Manual | |
	1967	1979	1967	1979
Liberal + NCP	66	55	32	31
Labor	30	40	63	66
Other Party	4	5	5	3
Total	100	100	100	100
(N)	(431)	(424)	(493)	(426)

Note: [a] Of those with some party identification.
Source: 1967 ANU Survey, 1979 Macquarie Survey.

TABLE 2-5
Labor identification and unionism, 1967, 1969 and 1979 (%)

Proportion identifying with Labor	1967	1969	1979
among unionists	61	62	63
among non-unionists	34	38	43

Source: 1967 ANU Survey, 1969 ANU Survey, 1979 Macquarie Survey.

Women

In 1967 women were more likely than men to prefer one or other of the non-Labor parties, no matter what their social location, age or birthplace. The differences were not large in absolute terms—they ranged commonly between 5 percent and 15 percent—but their universality pointed to very general causes indeed, rather than to simple consequences of social structure. Twelve years later the political conservatism of women was a good deal less marked, as Table 2-6 reveals. While women were still more likely than men to prefer the Liberal or National Country Parties, the gap between the sexes had narrowed appreciably, from 12 percent to 7 percent. The 1967 sample contained, as it ought to have done, a majority of non-Labor supporters, while the 1979 sample was properly more evenly balanced. And the change from 1967 to 1979 was much more marked among women. The swing to Labor between the two time-periods (defined as the average of Labor gains and Liberal plus National Country Party losses) was 4.5 percent among men, but 9 percent among women, twice as large.

Not only had women become rather less conservative, they had also become rather more strongly partisan. In 1967, men were more likely than women to describe themselves as "very strong" partisans and much less likely to describe their partisanship as "not very strong"; by 1979 sex differences in this area had completely disappeared: the enthusiasts, the lukewarm and the entirely nonpartisan were in identical proportion in each sex.

It is too early to say either that the change is a permanent one, or

TABLE 2-6
Party identification by sex, 1967 and 1979 (%)

Party identification	Men		Women	
	1967	1979	1967	1979
Liberal	38	36	48	43
Labor	44	49	33	42
[National] Country Party	6	4	8	4
DLP [1979: AD]	3	3	3	3
Other	1	*	*	*
None[a]	8	8	8	8
Total	100	100	100	100
(N)	(1,011)	(952)	(1,033)	(1,044)

Notes: [a] Respondents who claimed no current partisanship, and said that they were not now, nor had ever been, closer to one party than another.
       * = less than 0.5 percent.
Source: 1967 ANU Survey, 1979 Macquarie Survey.

that the movement towards Labor among women has finished. But there can be no doubt of its importance. It is connected with what might be called "the politicization of women", a change discussed in a later section of this chapter.

Religion

Religious denomination once provided an important political cleavage in Australian society, and the memory lingers on in the composition of the parliamentary parties and the shades of emphasis in party platforms. But the Catholic=Labor, Protestant=non-Labor equations have been declining for a long time, and Kemp has measured that decline for the thirty years after World War II.[24] In the 1970s two related social changes in this area had unmistakable force. One was a decline in the authority of churches in temporal matters, as measured by the liberalization of the laws regarding abortion, homosexuality, censorship and related matters. The second, a direct response to the first, was the establishment of conservative pressure groups, like the Festival of Light, linking regular churchgoers of all denominations in an attempt to stem what was seen as a secular, humanist tide. These changes reflected changes in the body politic, some of which are reported here.

The most impressive shift of all in the nature of the 1979 sample was in the preparedness of its members to declare themselves to be without a religion. This was not an unexpected development. The 1971 and 1976 censuses showed a sharp increase in the proportion of Australians claiming not to have a religion.[25] The design of the 1979 questionnaire took some account of this trend, and respondents were first asked whether they thought of themselves as having a religion.

Exactly 25 percent did not. Twelve years before, only 3 percent had claimed to have no religion, although on that occasion the question presumed the contrary.[26] Something must be put down to question-wording, of course. Even so, the proportion claiming no religion or a total non-attendance at church doubled, from 20 percent in 1967 to 40 percent in 1979, which suggests that the contribution of question-wording was slight.

Churchgoing seems, in fact, to have fallen substantially. Table 2-7 shows that attendance at church declined between 1967 and 1979 both for men and for women, and for two broad categories of attender, the regular and the occasional. Women continue to make up nearly two-thirds of the regular attenders (63 percent in both 1967 and

1979) but the size of that group has shrunk from a little more than a third of the electorate to a little more than a quarter.

The partisan accompaniments of the change have been predictable enough: it is the Labor Party that has benefited. Nearly six in every ten of those who had no religion or never attended church identified with Labor, and the proportion was exactly the same for men and women. In 1967 the Labor Party did just as well from those without a church but their number, as we have seen, was only half as great. The secularization of Australian society, if that is what it is, carries with it some important costs and benefits for the political parties.

Denomination alone, on the other hand, has no such potent changes to reveal. The conservative Presbyterian and rather less conservative Methodist Churches formed the "Uniting Church" in 1977, although a minority of their adherents stayed outside the new formation. The decline and near-disappearance of the DLP removed a powerful competitor to the ALP for the Catholic vote—which, in any case, was increasingly affected by the growing presence of Italian Catholics in what had traditionally been an Irish-Catholic church. Marriages contracted outside a single denomination continued to grow (from 36 percent in 1967 to 48 percent in 1979). And the greater tendency of Catholic men as against Protestant men to find themselves in manual occupations finally disappeared by 1979, when that proportion was 43 percent in each case. In terms of partisanship these trends moved in many directions, and the outcome can be seen in Table 2-8, which compares the Labor identification of the major denominational groupings over the two time-periods.

Labor identification increased in all groups save "Other Protestants", where it remained low. The largest gain was among those with no religion, a very much larger group in 1979 than had been the case in 1967. And some straightforward arithmetic shows that, assuming no important intervening factors, the move to an explicit non-religious stance occurred most frequently among Protestants; by and large the Catholic Church kept hold of its own.

Migrants

In 1967 migrants had "adopted a very low posture" in politics.[27] They were less involved than the native-born, had less use for party labels, and were surprisingly indifferent to the claims of the ALP, given that they were rather more likely to have manual jobs. Mistilis has argued persuasively that the explanation is a simple one: migrants become socialised into Australian politics and political culture as adults, the native-born as children and adolescents. So for migrants the process has to begin much later, and it is only when new settlers are middle-aged or older that they "catch up" with their native-born fellow citizens.[28]

The Mistilis argument, based on a re-analysis of the 1967 and 1969 data, was buttressed by the plain fact that in the late 1970s migrants —at least in groups—had begun to adopt a high posture. To some degree governments had encouraged the mobilization of ethnic communities. There were Ethnic Affairs Committees or Councils in all States and nationally, and government departments or sections for whom these organizations were clients, while a good deal of government money was available for activities, programs or research which focussed on the migrant presence in Australian society. Migrants were much more visible in the party organizations, and were increasingly being elected to municipal councils and State Parliaments. In 1980 Dr Andrew Theophanous, a college lecturer, was elected from

TABLE 2-7
Churchgoing, by sex, 1967 and 1979 (%)

Frequency of Churchgoing[a]	Men		Women	
	1967	1979	1967	1979
Regular	27	21	44	32
Occasional	49	30	42	36
Never	24	49	14	32
Total	100	100	100	100
(N)	(997)	(960)	(1,023)	(1,051)

Note: [a] Regular = at least once a month; Occasional = less than once a month; 'Never' includes those with no religion.
Source: 1967 ANU Survey, 1979 Macquarie Survey.

TABLE 2-8
Denomination and Labor identification, 1967 and 1979 (%)

Denominational Grouping	Proportion Labor[a]			
	1967	(proportion of sample)	1979	(proportion of sample)
Anglican	42	37	44	25
Catholic	51	25	55	22
Other Protestant	35	31	35	23
Other religions[b]	41	4	49	5
No religion	53	3	62	25
All	42	100	49	100
(N)		(1,867)		(1,831)

Notes: [a] Of those with some party identification
[b] Principally Orthodox
Source: 1967 ANU Survey, 1979 Macquarie Survey.

the safe Labor seat of Burke (Victoria), a selection which owed something to the importance of Greeks within the State Labor Party organization. There had, beyond question, been substantial changes since 1967.

Two aspects of that change need recording here. First, the gap between migrants and the native-born in terms of political awareness and involvement has closed substantially, as it ought to have done if Mistilis were right. This was especially true in the case immigrants from outside Britain (Table 2-9).

Second, there has been a swing by immigrants toward the ALP, a movement reported by Kemp in 1977,[29] and confirmed by Table 2-10. The 1979 data are broadly similar to those discussed by Kemp, although the preference for Labor was a good deal stronger in 1979, among all categories, than it had been two years previously. The movement to Labor was not simply an exchange. While the coalition parties were relatively less popular among migrants in 1979 than had

TABLE 2-9
Political awareness and involvement, native-born and foreign-born, 1967 and 1979 (%)

Proportion who . . .	Australian-born		British-born		Foreign-born	
	1967	1979	1967	1979	1967	1979
care a good deal which party wins a general election	61	74	61	72	44	71
know *neither* the name *nor* the party of their Federal MP	27	28	38	39	56	40
think that what the Federal Government does makes any difference to how well off they are	56	76	60	79	40	64

Source: 1967 ANU Survey, 1979 Macquarie Survey.

TABLE 2-10
Party identification by birthplace, 1979 (%)

	Voter's Birthplace				
Party identification	Australia	Britain	Southern Europe	Eastern Europe	Northern Europe
Liberal-National Country Party	45	34	29	50	55
Labor	44	52	57	37	33
Democrat/Other party	3	3	4	2	7
None/Don't know	8	11	10	11	5
Total	100	100	100	100	100
(N)	(1,596)	(200)	(49)	(46)	(42)

Source: 1979 Macquarie Survey.

been the case twelve years before, the more important cause was the development of party identification among migrant citizens who had formerly been outside the party system. In 1967, 21 percent of Southern Europeans and 25 percent of Eastern Europeans had disclaimed any Australian political partisanship, even the most tenuous. In 1979 those proportions had dropped to 10 percent and 11 percent respectively, and in this basic aspect of political life Southern and Eastern Europeans now hardly differed from the native-born or the British-born.

The politicization of the immigrants during the 1970s occurred relatively quietly. It is hardly likely that the quiet will continue. As political choices become more difficult migrants will increasingly discover that they have more political capacity than they presently realize, if only because immigrants and those of the native-born who have at least one immigrant parent now represent nearly half of the Australian population. Future volumes in this series are likely to devote much larger space to their efforts.

The New Awareness

The picture of a rather apathetic, uninvolved Australian electorate did not accurately portray the polity of the 1970s. The election of the Whitlam Labor government in 1972 introduced a period of heightened political activity that reached its climax in the months that led up to that government's dismissal by the Governor-General in November 1975. Even when the new coalition government led by Malcolm Fraser had been confirmed in office by the elections of December 1975, the public interest in politics did not wane quickly. Perhaps part of the cause lay in the continuing presence of the three principals of the "constitutional crisis", for it was not until the end of 1977 that Gough Whitlam and Sir John Kerr separately bowed out. Perhaps it had something to do with the continuation of hard times: unemployment and inflation soon banished the euphoria and complacency of the 1960s.

Whatever the cause, there can be no doubt that at the end of the 1970s the Australian electorate was a good deal more politically aware than had been the case in the late 1960s. Table 2-11 makes the comparison, using some simple measures. It is important to remember that the 1967 and 1979 surveys were carried out in periods of comparative political quiet. The level of political awareness of 1979, indeed, is comparable to that of an election period in the 1960s.

Tempting as it is to ascribe the new political awareness to "the events of 1975'' it has to be said that the 1979 data do not offer much supporting evidence. Respondents had many opportunities to bring forward such memories, and in an unforced way, but few did so. Certainly the mood of the sample was critical and anxious, and its concentration on the economy as the source of its woes was unmistakable. But the bad times came after the election of the Whitlam government, and were first apparent in its last year, whereas political awareness and involvement seemed to be growing even before that government's election. Two additional hypotheses deserve more sustained examination: that the increase in political awareness flowed mainly from the entry into the electorate of a large body of young voters who came of age in the strife-ridden 1970s, and that the cause was the politicization of women.

Young Voters

Between 1967 and 1979 the electorate grew by some 40 percent, from 6.3 million to 8.8 million, and of the 1979 electorate perhaps 5.5 million, or 63 percent, had been citizens in the earlier year. Most of the new voters were young, especially because from 1974 the voting age dropped from twenty-one to eighteen, and if they were distinctive—that is, more deeply interested and more active in politics—their sheer weight in numbers must have affected the general characteristics of the electorate.

Yet the data suggest otherwise. In 1979, as had been the case in 1967, young voters were *less* likely to take an interest in politics than those older. In fact, the evidence suggests that there occurred a general increase in political awareness across all age-groups. Cohort analysis provides the best demonstration, by monitoring the increase in each of several age-cohorts, that is, groups of respondents defined

TABLE 2-11
Political awareness, 1967 and 1979 (%)

Proportion who . . .	1967	1979
followed politics on the radio	17	32
talked much about politics with others	31	45
followed politics on television	34	60
followed politics in the newspapers[a]	41	51
claimed at least "some" interest in politics	55	70
(N)[b]	(2,054)	(2,016)

Notes: [a] First newspaper mentioned.
[b] Total sample size; the base of each percentage is the proportion giving a substantive answer to the question, usually 95 percent or more.
Source: 1967 ANU Survey, 1979 Macquarie Survey.

by age who appear in both surveys but at different positions in the life-cycle. Those aged 21 to 33 years in 1967, for example, were 12 years older in 1979, and comprised the group of those aged 33 to 45 years. Similarly, those aged 34 to 48 years in 1967 were 46 to 60 years old in 1979, and so on. Table 2-12 provides the *increases* in political awareness, measured by the variables used in Table 2-11, for each of four large age-cohorts; the method of analysis necessarily excludes the oldest group in 1967 and the very youngest in 1979. It is clear that the increase was general, perhaps a little greater in the youngest cohort, and certainly least among the oldest. What occurred in Australia, then, was a general increase in the levels of political awareness. But was it more pronounced among women than among men?

The Politicization of Women

There are good grounds for arguing that levels of political awareness should have been more pronounced among women than men. The 1970s saw the emergence of the women's liberation movement as a force in Australian politics and society, the establishment of the very successful Women's Electoral Lobby, the recognition by governments of both political persuasions that women's issues had to be taken seriously, and the success of female candidates in lower house elections.[31] These changes themselves suggested a profound change in the extent to which women saw politics as important to them.

Table 2-13 shows that indeed the increase in awareness of politics was greater among women than men, and for each activity. The increase was slight with respect to television, where there had been

TABLE 2-12
Increase in political awareness, by cohort, 1967 to 1979 (%)

	Cohort 1	Cohort 2	Cohort 3	Cohort 4
Age in 1967	21–33	34–48	49–60	61–83
Age in 1979	34–45	46–60	61–72	73–95
Increase in Proportion who ...				
followed politics on the radio	20	21	20	12
followed politics on television	34	30	23	26
followed politics in the newspapers[a]	17	18	16	5
talked about politics to others	20	16	15	4
claimed at least "some" interest in politics	24	22	15	7

Notes: Each cell contains the arithmetic difference, for a given cohort, between the proportions displaying a given behaviour in 1979 and in 1967. All signs are positive, since there was an increase in all cells.
[a] First newspaper mentioned.
Source: 1967 ANU Survey, 1979 Macquarie Survey.

no real gap in 1967 in any case (35 percent of men had reported following politics *via* television, compared with 34 percent of women) —probably because television-watching is largely a family affair. There remain three areas in which women scored appreciably lower than men: in talking politics with others (men 52 percent, women 37 percent), in following politics in the press (men 57 percent, women 45 percent), and in claiming at least "some" interest in politics (men 78 percent, women 64 percent). There is no reason to suppose that these gaps will not continue to lessen.

What factors produced the new interest in politics among women? Surprisingly enough, going to work does not seem to have been a major one. Scores on the measures of awareness do not vary much among women in full-time work, in part-time work or out of the workforce completely, save that the last group scores lowest in terms of talking about politics with others, which is predictable enough.

Although a complete analysis cannot be offered here, it seems that there were two major causes. The first was education: there was a pronounced increase between 1967 and 1979 in the proportions completing secondary education and going on to university and college,[32] and women benefited from this more than men did because the proportions of girls in higher education had been generally much lower than the proportion of boys. The second was the "women's politics" factor, which drew women into the political world rather than men. Again, there is no reason to suppose that these movements have ceased, though it is true that the "women's movement" has to some extent been institutionalized. Anyone speculating on the likely distribution of interest in politics at the end of the century would have good grounds for arguing that sex differences will by then have become slight indeed.

TABLE 2-13
Increase in political awareness, 1967 to 1979 (%)

Increase in proportion who . . .	Men	Women
followed politics on the radio	79	107
followed politics on television	71	74
followed politics in the newspapers[a]	12	32
talked about politics to others	30	76
claimed at least "some" interest in politics	22	39

Note: Each cell contains the percentage difference between the proportions of a given sex reporting a given activity in 1967 and in 1979. All signs are positive as there was an increase in each cell.
    [a] first newspaper mentioned.
Source: 1967 ANU Survey, 1979 Macquarie Survey.

Conclusion

Movements in political awareness, in education, in social composition all have considerable potential for political change. The puzzle must be why these quite perceptible movements in Australia had so little impact on the party system. Of course, parties and party systems have a robustness and an elasticity that compel the respect of anyone who studies them. But in the face of changes to the basis of party systems elsewhere we are entitled to wonder why the Australian party system remained relatively unscathed. One part of the answer must lie in the formal rules governing parliamentary and electoral politics—the bi-cameral system whose upper house has a power and visibility shared by few counterparts elsewhere, a proportional representation rule that gives challenging parties some possibility of a foothold in Parliament, and the still widely supported institution of compulsory voting[33] which compels the citizen to choose rather than abstain and opt out. But isolating the contribution of these well-established (and sometimes overlooked) aspects of Australian political life requires another essay.

Notes

1 Don Aitkin, *Stability and Change in Australian Politics* (Canberra: Australian National University Press, 1977, reprinted 1978), and David A. Kemp, *Society and Electoral Behaviour in Australia* (St Lucia Qld: Queensland University Press, 1978). There is a useful summary in Kemp's chapter "The Australian Electorate", in Howard R. Penniman, ed., *The Australian National Elections of 1977* (Washington, D.C.: American Enterprise Institute, 1979). See also Don Aitkin, "Electoral Behaviour", in H. Mayer and H. Nelson, eds, *Australian Politics: A Fifth Reader* (Melbourne: Longman Cheshire, 1980).
2 Financial support from the Australian Research Grants Committee allowed the replication of the 1967 survey in 1979; the results are reported at some length in the second edition of Aitkin, *Stability and Change*, published in 1982.
3 A conference at Lancaster University in March/April 1981 organized by the European Consortium for Political Research heard papers describing electoral volatility in more than a dozen countries. The "freezing" metaphor was first used by S.M. Lipset and S. Rokkan in the celebrated introductory chapter to their *Party Systems and Voter Alignments* (New York: The Free Press, 1967).
4 A similar record from 1901 to 1980 can be found in Aitkin, *Stability and Change*, p. 4.
5 A position favoured by its own partisans. See Aitkin, *Stability and Change*, pp. 76–86. The DLP's supporters were mostly churchgoing Roman

Catholics, its *rationale* was anti-Communism and its social policies were conservative, placing an emphasis on the family and morality. In all these respects the Australian Democrats are further to the left.

6 Douglas W. Rae, *The Political Consequences of Electoral Laws* (New Haven: Yale University Press, 1967), p. 56. To obtain the index of fractionalization for a given election one squares each party's decimal share of the vote, and subtracts the sum of these squares from 1.00. Very high scores would denote one-party dominance, while low scores reflect a multi-party situation, with a score of 0.50 indicating a pure two-party system.

7 Ivor Crewe, Bo Sarlvik and James Alt, "Partisan Dealignment in Britain 1964–1974", *British Journal of Political Science*, 7(2), April 1977, pp. 129–90.

8 Norman H. Nie, Sidney Verba and John R. Petrocik, *The Changing American Voter* (Cambridge: Harvard University Press, 1979), especially ch. 4. The question on which this measurement was based did not change throughout the twenty-two years: "Generally speaking, do you think of yourself as a Republican, a Democrat, an Independent, or what?"

9 Crewe, Sarlvik and Alt, "Partisan Dealignment", pp. 129, 142.

10 Partisanship and its strength were obtained through two questions: "Generally speaking, do you usually think of yourself as Liberal, Labor, Country Party or DLP?" and "Now, thinking of the Federal parties, how strongly [R's party] do you feel, very strongly, fairly strongly, or not very strongly?" In 1979 the options were: "Liberal, Labor, National Country or Australian Democrat". In Australia, as in Britain, the label "Independent" is sometimes applied to non-party candidates as a general category, but has little meaning applied to citizens, perhaps because the parties are not legal entities in the same important sense that they are in the USA, primary elections do not exist, and voters cannot "register" as Labor or Liberal supporters.

11 The 1977 survey conducted by Irving Saulwick and Associates and reported by Kemp ("The Australian Electorate", p. 31), provides estimates of strength of identification very similar to those obtained in 1979.

12 Crewe, Sarlvik and Alt, "Partisan Dealignment", p. 144.

13 Aitkin, *Stability and Change*, part III.

14 ibid., pp. 47–50. In both years Labor had a higher proportion of "very strong" identifiers than any of its rivals.

15 These are well-supported generalizations for Western politics in general; the Australian evidence is discussed in *Stability and Change*, ch. 6.

16 Richard Rose, ed., *Electoral Behaviour: a Comparative Handbook* (New York: The Free Press, 1974), p. 17. See also the recent work of Kemp, already referred to in these notes.

17 See Kemp's discussion of the role of values and beliefs in "The Australian Electorate", pp. 48–64. The whole question is addressed in the concluding chapter of the second edition of Aitkin, *Stability and Change*.

18 See, for example, the review of both authors by R.W. Connell and Murray Goot in *Meanjin*, 38(1), April 1979.

19 Nor is Australia unusual in this respect. Very similar findings have been reported for Great Britain by Richard Rose, *Class Does Not Equal Party* (Glasgow: Centre for the Study of Public Policy, 1980) and by Crewe, Sarlvik and Alt, "Partisan Dealignment".

20 Aitkin, *Stability and Change*, pp. 126–9.

21 Males were chosen in order to preserve comparability: in 1967 women were categorized according to their husbands' occupations, if they were married, but in 1979 according to their own occupation whatever their marital status. The change in procedure reflected the near-parity in male and female employment at the end of the 1970s.

22 To obtain scores, subtract the proportion of non-manuals supporting Labor from the proportion of manuals doing so. The index has a sensible range of 0–100, with 0 representing a situation in which the parties of the left and of the right gain supporters equally from the two classes. R. Alford, *Party and Society* (London: John Murray, 1964), pp. 79–80.

23 Aitkin, *Stability and Change*, pp. 138–42.

24 Kemp, *Society and Electoral Behaviour*, ch. 6.

25 After 1921 the census question on religious affiliation ceased to be compulsory, and in the five censuses between 1933 and 1966 there was little change in the proportions declining to answer the question (between 10 percent and 13 percent) or claiming to have no religion (less than 1 percent). In 1971 these proportions were 6 percent and 7 percent respectively, and in 1976 12 per cent and 8 per cent respectively.

26 In 1967 respondents were asked first "What is [was] your father's religion?" and "And your mother's religion?" before the question "And what is your religion?". In 1979 the order was "Do you think of yourself as having a religion?", "How often do you go to Church?", "What is your father's religion" etc. In 1979 rather higher proportions reported their fathers as having no religion on (8 percent, compared with 2 percent in 1967) and their mothers likewise (4 percent, compared with 1 percent in 1967).

27 Aitkin, *Stability and Change*, p. 156.

28 Nina Mistilis, "The Political Participation of Immigrant Electors", *Politics*, vol. XV (1), May 1980, pp. 69–70.

29 Kemp, "The Australian Electorate", pp. 42–3.

30 See Aitkin, *Stability and Change*. Table 16.1, p. 257.

31 The literature on women in Australia grew very quickly in the decade, and some books, notably Anne Summers' *Damned Whores and God's Police* (Melbourne: Penguin, 1975) were best-sellers. Women had been elected to the Senate, and to some of the State Legislative Councils, but the first woman to win a seat in the House of Representatives in her own right (that is, without some previous family connection in the seat, as when Dame Enid Lyons or Mrs Blackburn won seats formerly held by their husbands) was Miss Kay Brownbill (Kingston, SA) in 1966. It was generally agreed that had the Liberal-Country League expected to win the hitherto safe Labor seat of Kingston Miss Brownbill would not have secured the endorsement. The endorsement of female candidate in winnable seats became much more common during the 1970s, and in 1980 three women won seats for their parties, while others came close to doing so.

32 A summary of the change is as follows (1967 percentage first): Primary education or less (33:15), Some secondary (31:26), Full secondary or technical college (30:45), Some tertiary (6:15). The rapidity of the change is due, of course, to the replacement factor: those dying are less well-educated than those entering the electorate.

33 In 1979 68 percent supported compulsory voting, a proportion a little lower than the 74 percent of 1967, but still very comparable to other approving proportions in the past. See Aitkin, *Stability and Change*, pp. 30–3.

The author would like to thank Dennis Rose and Vance Merrill for research assistance and the Australian Research Grants Committee for financial support of the 1979 Macquarie survey.

3
The Liberal Party

Martin Rawlinson

The Fraser Government 1977–80, and the Liberal Campaign

In retrospect, the 1977 general election which swept the L-NCP coalition back into office with the second largest majority since Federation may come to be seen as the high point of Malcolm Fraser's political career. Unlike 1975, the election itself was not an issue; some of the bitterness of the events of two years earlier had dissipated. Fraser was in firm control of his party and the government possessed the enthusiasm of those new to office. It could point to some successes on the economic front and had the enviable political challenge of attacking an opposition which could not escape the memories of its recent past.

The economy had been the central issue of the 1977 election and the outcome was, in large measure, determined by public perception of the parties' capacity for national economic management. After two years in office the coalition was able to claim some credit for improved economic performance in Australia. Inflation had fallen, growth in government expenditure slowed, and the money supply reduced. On the debit side, economic growth remained sluggish and unemployment continued to side.

The coalition campaign in 1977 had promised a continuation of existing policies. Achieving "sustained economic growth through the private sector" required further economic restraint, though this was sweetened with the promise of tax cuts early in 1978.

In a political climate where the economy was the central issue the Australian Labor Party had faced an unenviable task. It was shackled with the legacy of having recently presided over one of the most difficult periods in Australia's economic history, and its then leader,

Gough Whitlam, provided a constant reminder of past troubles—
something which the coalition did not let the electorate forget during
the course of the 1977 campaign.

The coalition had clearly signalled to the electorate in 1977 that
economic management would be its major preoccupation for the
immediate future, and that it would expect to be judged on its
performance in that area at the next election. If the coalition was
successful in setting the political agenda for the immediate future it
was, perhaps, less than successful, subsequently, in meeting the
expectations it had raised during the 1977 campaign.

Taxation—The Government's Achilles Heel

The government's lack of success was particularly in evidence in the
area of personal taxation where over the ensuing three years, the
claims of the coalition in the taxation area had lost ground. In
February 1978 the personal tax scales were restructured and the
marginal rates reduced, providing substance to the political rhetoric
of the 1977 campaign. However, some six months later, when the
government presented the 1978–79 Budget, it announced increases in
personal taxes, big increases in excise tax on beer and spirits, and the
pricing of domestic crude oil at world parity levels. It also announced
further changes to national health insurance and, in a particularly
niggardly move, decided to bring children's income to account in the
payment of family allowances. This last decision, which became
popularly known as "the newsboys tax", was reversed a month or so
later, but when coupled with the rise in personal tax, set in train
progressive erosion of the claims of the coalition of being a low-tax
government.

The taxation issue was given a further airing over the following
months as the government publicly canvassed views about the
possible introduction of a broad-base indirect tax as a means of
redressing the balance of taxation in Australia away from personal to
indirect taxation. While the government decided in January 1979 not
to proceed with new indirect taxes the spectre of future changes could
not be ruled out.

In May 1979 the Treasurer, John Howard, in a major economic
statement to Parliament, announced that the reintroduction of full tax
indexation (a method by which the tax rate scales are indexed to
inflation movements) would be postponed and that the personal tax
surcharge imposed in the 1978–79 Budget would be maintained until
December 30, 1979. Also announced in May were further increases in
the levy on crude oil and another round of changes to health
insurance arrangements.

In March 1980—election year—the Treasurer gave some comfort to tax payers with the announcement that half-indexation would apply from July 1, 1980 and that there would be a significant increase in the dependent spouse rebate. However, any political credit the government might have gained from these initiatives was lost later in the year when the Treasurer become engaged in a long-running battle with mining companies and unions over the taxation treatment of subsidized employee accommodation in remote areas. While not a major issue in itself, it did little to help the government restore credibility in the taxation area.

Crude Oil Pricing—Rhetoric and Revenue

The difficulties the government faced in the 1977–80 period on the taxation front were exacerbated by the decision in the 1978–79 Budget to price all Australian oil at world parity levels. The rapid increases in the price of fuel which flowed from this decision was claimed by the government to be an important step in the conservation of fuel, the promotion of exploration and the development of alternative fuel supplies. Its impact on the government's revenue was substantial, raising some $2.2 billion in revenue in 1979–80 alone—an increase of 85 percent on the previous year. The electorate, however, was less than convinced of the merits of the argument for world parity pricing, seeing it essentially as a new method of government revenue-raising.

The Economy: Doing Better than the OECD Average

While the government was becoming increasingly vulnerable on the issues of taxation, petrol pricing and health insurance, by 1980 it could look to the performance of the economy with a degree of satisfaction. Unemployment remained high but growth in employment was particularly strong throughout 1980. Inflation had nudged up from the low levels achieved in 1978, but as the government was constantly to point out, Australia's performance was better than the majority of OECD countries. It could also point to modest economic growth performance, and a dramatic improvement in the fortunes of the rural sector. Although of doubtful impact on the average elector, the 1980–81 Budget achieved a domestic surplus of some $39m—the first since 1973–74.

The Resources Boom

Supporting the government's view of an optimistic economic future was the emerging "resources boom" especially in such areas as natural gas, uranium and coal which had taken on new significance in the wake of the oil crises of the 1970s. In the 1977 election the coalition had claimed some $6 billion worth of development projects were in the pipeline. By 1980 this had risen to some $29 billion.

Personality Politics

Any political gains made by the government in its approach to economic management after the 1977 election were to a degree overshadowed by a series of events which were to damage the image of the government.

A decision in February 1978 to appoint a former and controversial Governor-General, Sir John Kerr, to the post of Ambassador to UNESCO, which had been previously closed down as an economy measure, was a serious political misjudgement.

In April 1978 a Queensland Liberal backbencher, Don Cameron, made allegations before the Parliament claiming irregularities in the 1977 electorate redistribution in Queensland. Subsequently, a Royal Commission was established and found that Reg Withers, the leader of the government in the Senate, who was also Minister for Administrative Services and a key "numbers man" in the Liberal Party, had committed "an impropriety" in seeking to influence the distribution commissioners. The minister was duly dismissed and, unlike other ministers who had been stood down for a period, was not to return to the ministry.

Some six months after the dismissal of Withers, the Finance Minister, Eric Robinson, resigned abruptly, only to return to the ministry a couple of days later. It was evident that the style of the Prime Minister's leadership was one factor in the Robinson decision, while another was undoubtedly the prolonged friction between Fraser and Robinson over whether there should be a joint Senate ticket with the National Party or a separate Liberal Senate ticket in Queensland at the next election. This issue was perhaps one of the most bitter within the Liberal Party during the 1977–80 period with the Queensland division determined to have separate tickets. In the end Fraser was to gain a pyrrhic victory when separate tickets saw only two coalition Senators out of five being returned from the State of Queensland.

Running through this period was another potentially damaging issue. In 1978 it was revealed that the Primary Industry Minister, and deputy leader of the National Country Party, Ian Sinclair, was under investigation by the NSW Corporate Affairs Commission because of alleged irregularities in the operation of his family companies. In September 1979 Sinclair resigned from the ministry to defend criminal charges laid against him. The fact that Sinclair was being prosecuted in NSW with a Labor government inevitably gave the issue a strong partisan tone. Subsequently he was acquited of all charges and promptly reinstated to the ministry in August 1980. Sinclair's reappointment undoubtedly reinforced the belief amongst critics of Malcolm Fraser that National Country Party ministers received preferential treatment over their Liberal colleagues.

Politics and Sport

As 1980 progressed the economy was pushed further into the background in the wake of Australia's response to the Russian invasion of Afganistan. In early January the government announced a series of trade sanctions against the Soviet Union. This was followed later in the month by a request from the government to the Australian Olympic Committee not to participate in the forthcoming Olympic Games in Moscow.

The ensuing period witnessed a particularly acrimonious public debate over the Olympics issue with the government placing heavy pressure on the AOC. Athletes were called upon to forgo a once-in-a-lifetime opportunity while trade relations between Australia and the Soviet Union, in major commodities such as wheat and wool, were to proceed largely as normal. In May the government suffered a severe rebuke when the AOC decided to send a team to Moscow. Even when the Olympic Games were a *fait accompli* the government was unrelenting and initially refused to give public acknowledgement of the performance of the Australian team.

The Olympic Games issue was highly divisive for a period of months, although it is doubtful whether it had any significant effect on the election.

Defense: The Wild Card

The Russian invasion of Afganistan did, however, raise the specter of defense playing a role in the 1980 election campaign. In May 1980 the government announced a $17 billion forward defense program, including the politically significant move of upgrading Australia's defense presence in the Indian Ocean and ground facilities in Western Australia. The outbreak of the Iraqi–Iran war in September 1980 offered a further prospect of defense playing a major role—but in the final analysis defense was perhaps one of the least significant issues in the 1980 campaign.

As the government moved closer to the opening of the 1980 campaign, published opinion polls gave grounds for confidence in the Liberal camp. The Morgan Gallup poll published in the *Bulletin* on September 23 showed support for the government at 47 percent and the ALP at 45 percent, with the Prime Minister and opposition leader roughly level-pegging in approval ratings.

Pre-Campaign Research

The importance of quantitative and qualitative research as a method of opinion monitoring and as strategic input to policy development and campaign planning is well recognized by the Liberal Party's Federal Secretariat. In keeping with earlier practice, a three-year forward research program involving both quantitative and qualitative research had been developed following the 1977 election. Mid-term quantitative research conducted in 1979 pointed to unemployment and inflation as the major policy issues of concern to the electorate, with welfare assistance, income tax, education, health insurance and defense also featuring. Significantly, fuel costs did not rate strongly, although there was little evidence of community understanding of the concept of world parity pricing and evidence of strong opposition to the policy which had been introduced in the 1978–79 Budget.

As a pointer to difficulties in the 1980 campaign, research showed the government to be gaining little recognition for performance, with the exception of its anti-inflationary policy. Initiatives taken between 1975–77 had long since been forgotten. Criticism of the government centred on unemployment and "broken promises"—a shorthand reference to past predictions or commitments which had proven wrong or had failed to be honoured.

Against the background of the 1979 quantitative research, a major qualitative study was conducted amongst swinging voters early in 1980. This research pointed to problems for the government, particularly in relation to health insurance and fuel pricing. On the positive side, defense, in the wake of Afghanistan, appeared to have potential. With regard to the key issue of leadership, the Prime Minister's image was clearly perceived, in contrast to continuing uncertainty about the capability of the opposition leader, Bill Hayden.

On the issues of economic management and resource development the Liberals had the edge over Labor, although "development", which had played a major role in the 1977 campaign, raised questions about the distribution of benefits and foreign ownership.

Further quantitative research conducted in July 1980 showed unemployment to be of declining importance to the electorate, but the long dormant issue of defense was increasing sharply. The significance of inflation had also declined although it, rather than unemployment, remained as the major barometer of the "man-in-the-street" perceptions of the state of the economy. In this context it pointed to some community recognition of Australia's improved economic performance.

Further questioning of attitudes on fuel pricing showed an inten-sification of community opposition to the world parity pricing policy. More importantly, and despite the government's rhetoric, the policy was clearly seen as a method of revenue raising. Fortunately for the government the level of concern about health insurance had declined as several months had elapsed since the last changes to policy had been put in place. The research also showed evidence of a decline in pressure for income tax relief although it indicated at the same time that government initiatives in the area would be well received: a fact that was not to be ignored by the ALP. It also showed the govern-ment to have a strong edge over Labor in terms of its capacity for economic management: a fact that the ALP also clearly recognized in the development of its own campaign. Responses to resource de-velopment prompted a mixed reaction; on the one hand it achieved little spontaneous recognition, although on the other, it was an area of Liberal strength.

In anticipation of Labor's campaign focussing on living standards, the research indicated that, at least to mid-1980, Labor's claims of declining living standards had made little impact on the electorate. On the key issue of leadership, both Fraser and Hayden could claim similar approval levels, the major difference in community perception being continued indecision about the capability of the opposition leader.

The Liberal Party moved into the final stages of campaign prepara-tion with a comprehensive research base complemented by extensive political input from the ministry, backbench, key committees and the party orgainzation.

Strategy and the Advertising Campaign

Since the introduction of "national campaigning" in 1974 the Federal Secretariat had placed high priority on maintaining close dialogue with its advertising agency. In the lead up to the 1980 election, regular meetings to discuss political developments were held in 1978 and 1979 with the level of contact and planning intensifying in the early stages of 1980.

While the relationship with the agency covered the widest

ambit and the professional expertise of both groups of participants was respected, the final responsibility rested with Federal
director, Tony Eggleton, and the campaign committee, which was
charged with approving campaign strategy and its advertising
support.

As 1980 advanced and planning progressed, the party's Federal
Executive was regularly briefed on progress in the development of
strategy, concepts and advertising techniques and its political input
constantly sought. This process culminated in a meeting of the
campaign committee which gave its seal of approval to the strategy.
Subsequent meetings involving the Prime Minister, senior ministers,
key organizational and professional staff were held with the agency
for the purpose of "fine tuning" advertising and strategy as the
campaign opening approached.

Election planning focussed on both the development of the government's campaign and, importantly, anticipation of ALP strategy and
tactics as well as that of the Australian Democrats. From an early
stage it was clear that the ALP would place heavy emphasis on claims
of declining living standards for families, with special reference to
petrol prices, interest rates, and health insurance costs. It was
correctly anticipated that the "negative" side of Labor's campaign
and advertising would involve a personal attack on the Prime
Minister and make strong reference to the "broken promises" of the
government. What was not clear was the priority Labor would assign
to its various policy commitments.

From the Liberal's perspective it was evident that the ALP's
spending proposals would be an area of vulnerability and, accordingly, two major television commercials were developed on this issue. In
addition, evidence on the standing of the Prime Minister *vis-à-vis* ALP
leader, Hayden, suggested that the contrast between the two leaders
should be drawn out in advertisements. Only in retrospect was it
possible to question this approach. The performance of Hayden in the
campaign caught the Liberals by surprise and pointed to "dynamics"
in a campaign which could not be predicted beforehand.

Research had also pointed to the potential of defense as an issue
and again advertisements on this topic were developed. In anticipation of the ALP's attack on living standards, and the need to project
economic progress, the Liberals adopted a comparative approach,
developing a series of advertisements which featured "returning
travelers" discussing the benefits of living in Australia in contrast to
the cost of living overseas. These advertisements also addressed the
fuel cost issue, albeit indirectly, by reference to the price of petrol in
other countries. More dramatic advertisements on petrol pricing were

developed but never went to air as the issue lost impetus in the campaign.

The major Liberal advertising innovation in 1980 was the use of ten-second television commercials featuring statements from the Prime Minister on a wide range of issues. This approach had several benefits: forceful presentation of the Prime Minister in addition to low production and placement costs, crispness and flexibility.

While Liberal strategy and its supportive advertising campaign was geared to the election for both the House of Representatives and the Senate, the importance of seeking to retain a government majority in the Senate required special attention. The appropriate strategy for countering the Australian Democrats was the subject of much discussion. In the end it was decided to develop a series of advertisements drawing attention to both the voting record of Democrat Senators and the need for consistency of voting behaviour in both the House of Representatives and the Senate as a means of ensuring stable government.

In most instances, Liberal television commercials were complemented with newspaper and radio advertisements. In addition, a series of specially produced programs were developed separately for the segments of "free" time made available by the national public television network, the Australian Broadcasting Commission (ABC).

In its final form the Liberal campaign and its advertising support reflected a strategy which focussed on Australia's economic performance, the government's record, leadership qualities and on the consequences of the ALP's proposed expenditure commitments and its "capacity" for economic management. In the subsequent evolution of the campaign it was necessary to make tactical adjustments requiring, in particular, new advertising treatment of the inflation issue and Labor's capital tax commitments which became the centrepoint of the government's campaign in the last few days before the election.

Liberal Policy Development

In the lead up to the 1980 election a quite complex structure of policy development machinery was activated within the Liberal Party and the government. The Joint Standing Committee on Federal Policy (JSCFP) is the major policy committee within the party organization, drawing its membership in equal numbers from organizational representatives and leading backbenchers. Under the chairmanship of

43

John Howard, the Federal Treasurer, JSCFP met regularly throughout 1980 examining potential policy issues and initiatives. In many instances preparatory work was undertaken within a small group known as the Platform and Policy Review Sub-Committee, under the chairmanship of the president of the Australian Capital Territory division of the party, Margaret Reid. This subcommittee, established in 1979, had taken on the role of a ginger group with its membership carefully selected to create a "think-tank" capability.

With the two committees working in close conjunction, "check lists" of potential initiatives were developed and forwarded to the ministerial Forward Planning Committee (FPC). FPC was established in February 1980 for the purpose of coordinating policy input from all sources—ministers, party organization, backbench committees, pressure groups, etc. Created by the Prime Minister, and chaired by the deputy leader of the parliamentary party, Sir Phillip Lynch, FPC was designed to streamline the policy development process in election year. It also had a responsibility for coordinating input to the Budget and between March and July concentrated on preparing advice for the Budget Cabinet. In essence the FPC became a "political" subcommittee of Cabinet and at each meeting an assessment was made of the current political climate, with appropriate advice being forwarded to the Prime Minister as the need arose.

Ministers and backbench committees were requested to submit ideas for possible policy initiatives to FPC, prior to submission of a final list of potential initiatives to the co-ordination committee of Cabinet in mid-September 1980.

In support of its political role and to provide a perspective on policy development, results of the party's commissioned opinion polls and qualitative research material were presented to the committee at various stages throughout 1980. Discussion of policy initiatives was undertaken against a background of economic restraint—with a constant check being made on the costs of proposals. The ultimate decision of the co-ordination committee not to propose any major expenditure commitments was taken against a background of three key factors: first, after three years of restraint, expensive election promises would damage the government's credibility for economic management; second, it would limit its capacity to attack ALP spending proposals; and thirdly, the prospect of re-election in view of the government's existing majority, appeared reasonable.

Consciously, a decision was made for the government to "run on its record", with a policy speech offering small inducements to a number of sectors within the community, but lacking any initiative which would generate widespread electoral appeal. The more significant policy initiatives included a decision to maintain half tax indexation, a commitment to proceed with the Darwin–Alice Springs Railway, modification to the Home Savings Grant Scheme, the introduction of an international standard sports facility program, and increases in spending on education. The catalogue of election promises provided newspaper copy in quantity if not quality, but after initial reporting by the media at the time of the policy speech, the promises (except for their cost) were to play little part in the government's campaign.

Campaign Headquarters

The Liberal Party campaign headquarters, a rather dingy ex-insurance building in King Street, Melbourne, was activated on Sunday, September 21. A national campaign headquarters is a recent phenomenon for the Liberal Party, which until the 1974 election had run "national" campaigns on a State basis. With the defeats of 1972 and 1974, however, pressure mounted for the appointment of a national campaign director and central coordination of Federal campaigns. Electoral success in 1975, and again in 1977, reinforced party and prime ministerial support for the centralized approach which had been adopted in 1975.

Logistics basically determined Melbourne as the nerve centre of the Liberal campaign. The party's advertising agency was located there, it was the hub of the Prime Minister's campaign itinerary, thus giving the campaign director, Tony Eggleton, traveling with the Prime Minister, maximum opportunity for meeting with the strategy committee. Importantly, Melbourne gave access to four (as opposed to Canberra's two) network television stations for monitoring purposes.

At the core of the campaign headquarters operation was a twice daily meeting of the strategy committee. The committee met at about 6.00 am and again at 8.30 pm, with its main tasks being to provide the campaign director with a summary of media coverage and appropriate tactical advice for the Prime Minister and his staff. Such advice might include new themes for speeches and suggested responses to initiatives or actions of the ALP and the Australian Democrats.

The most significant innovation in the operation of campaign headquarters in 1980 was establishing daily telex contact with all candidates. In earlier elections individual candidates had been provided with "speaker notes" by the Federal Secretariat, prior ot the campaign, but subsequent contact between candidates and the national campaign headquarters had been virtually non-existent. For the most part, the candidate was forced to rely on the media as his or her major source of political information. Telex provided the only practical method of direct contact, and in close consultation with Telecom, a national telex network linking all candidates was established by the time the campaign opened. Through the telex it was thus possible to provide candidates on a daily basis with extracts from major ministerial speeches, "quotable quotes" from the opposition, suggested speech drafts and prior notification of new advertisements.

Coordinating ministerial movements was a further key role of campaign headquarters. In 1980, former approaches to ministerial coordination were significantly modified in an attempt to reduce traveling demands, and to tailor programs for ministers which made best use of individual talents. Accordingly, and with an eye to the key issues of the election, some ministers undertook extensive traveling programs while others remained largely within their own States, principally for the purpose of generating maximum local media exposure in addition to providing their party organizations with strong support.

Campaign headquarters was also responsible for the party's private research program, plus the close monitoring of the published opinion polls. A planned program of regular telephone polling supplemented by qualitative research was set in train shortly before the opening of the campaign. Research results provided a key input to the strategy committee with assessment and advice being forwarded to both the campaign director and Prime Minister throughout the campaign.

A further function of campaign headquarters was maintaining close liaison with the State divisions of the Party. While central control of Federal campaigns has resulted in significant changes in the role of the State divisions they remain responsible for a wide range of essential activities. Prior to the election they are closely involved in the preselection of candidates, while during the campaign their responsibilities include monitoring of the State political climate, organization of ministerial functions, State how-to-vote information, and the tailoring of "national" advertising to State requirements.

A myriad of other functions including the provision of a tape service for radio stations, media liaison, and media monitoring, rounded out the role of the headquarters as the nerve centre of the Liberal campaign.

The Liberal Campaign

The Liberal campaign opened with the Prime Minister's policy speech to a gathering of the faithful at the Moorabbin Town Hall, Melbourne,

---

on Tuesday, September 30. Because the government had made a deliberate choice to restrict new policy commitments the speech was inevitably long on rhetoric, punctuated with references to the more substantial of a limited range of initiatives. The Prime Minister structured his speech around five challenges: responsibility in economic affairs, a coordinated program of national development, adequate assistance to those in need, the encouragement of excellence and safeguarding national security. It was the speech of a government standing on its record, calling forth in the traditional rhetoric of liberalism the values and aspirations the government had sought to cultivate over the previous five years.

By contrast, Hayden's policy speech, delivered on October 1 and televised the following evening, was a more lively and spontaneous affair with Neville Wran and Bob Hawke also featuring prominently. Much of what Hayden actually said in his speech was not new. Labor had followed a schedule of announcing policy proposals over the months prior to the election. The policy speech focussed on priorities and expanded on detail. It was carefully constructed to emphasize the ALP's claims of being responsible economic managers, while announcement of the key policy initiatives provided the highpoints.

The decision to provide a tax cut of $3 a week by raising the tax threshold and to freeze the price of petrol for a year were the most electorally attractive of the ALP's promises. A job creation program, a revamped housing scheme, free health care in certain circumstances and a means-tested family income supplement rounded out the total package. Revenue to fund Labor's program was to come from abolition of the investment allowance to business, the introduction of a resource or excess profits tax and by taking further action to eliminate tax avoidance. The ALP achieved some useful headlines from the speech: "Hayden bids for the family vote"[1] said the Australian, while the Melbourne Sun's front page announced "Hayden: Its $3 tax cut".[2]

Costing Promises

From previous experience the ALP had realized it would be vulnerable to the question so commonly leveled by the Liberals: "where's the money coming from?" This time the ALP was prepared, and turned the argument back on the government using the "authority" of a NSW Treasury paper to claim that the promises of the coalition were "close to $2000m, not the $225m claimed by the Prime Minister".

The Liberals were also prepared for the costing battle and in the months preceding the election had been costing each new ALP policy commitment as it was announced. Expenditure in the major policy areas was estimated at $2500m with some 281 uncosted promises.

Carefully laid Liberal plans to provide the media with details of Labor's spending commitments coincided with ALP plans to do the same to the Liberals. The result was a barrage of words—as the *Age* commented: "A paper war over promises".[3]

While the costing battle may have ended in a "nil-all draw" for the Liberals, it did have the virtue of distracting attention from the ALP's initiatives and its obviously electorally attractive commitment to cut taxes. Policy issues were pushed even further into the background towards the end of the first week when polls were published showing the ALP to be in a strong position. The *Age* poll, published on October 4, was regarded with a degree of disbelief by the Liberals, although private polls taken on October 4–5 also showed the ALP's position to be strengthening rapidly, with strong endorsement of their taxation initiatives.

By the first weekend of the campaign the media were beginning to file stories of increasing difficulties in the Liberal campaign. A story in the Sydney Paper, the *Daily Telegraph*, for example, was entitled: "Fraser finding poll life is not so easy".[4]

In the Liberal camp there was concern about the progress of the campaign although, prior to the campaign, there had never been any doubt that the performance of the ALP would show a strong improvement on 1977. In contrast to research findings prior to the campaign, private research now indicated that Bill Hayden had emerged as a highly credible politician, ably supported and strengthened by the campaign presence of Neville Wran and Bob Hawke. As the first week of the campaign progressed, therefore, it became increasingly apparent that the campaign was more a Fraser–Hayden/Hawke/Wran contest rather than a Fraser–Hayden contest. On the critically important evening television news programs, film of the Prime Minister frequently had to compete with lengthy footage of the ALP "triumvirate" in action.

Sharpening the Campaign

The strong performance of the ALP in the first week, combined with private and published opinion poll results, sharpened Liberal tactics. Flexibility was a key axiom in Liberal campaign planning. While a broad strategy could be developed beforehand, against the background of research evidence, policy and political input, the party, and especially the campaign team, saw "fine tuning" of strategy as an essential element of the campaigning process.

The difficulties the Liberal campaign was facing at the end of the first week were confirmed in private, qualitative research conducted by the party amongst groups of swinging voters in Melbourne on October 6. While Labor's capacity for economic management was still suspect, its commitment to reduce taxation was seen by swinging voters as most appealing. By contrast the Liberals were promising more of the same, with no apparent "light at the end of the tunnel". After five years of "austerity" it was believed that the community should get something back in return—especially as government coffers were perceived to be "flowing over" with revenue from the oil levy. While the leader of the opposition was still seen as lacking strength, the research highlighted the credibility of the Labor "triumvirate". Thus, both the qualitative and quantitative research confirmed the "gut feelings" of the Liberal campaign team that Labor had got off to a good start and a close evaluation of the Liberal campaign was required.

Monday, October 6 was not, however, without some good news, with published polls showing an overwhelming majority of voters believing that the government would be returned to office.[5] Fraser had moved into the second week firing strongly and taking the opinion polls head on. At a rally at Pakenham in outer Melbourne he claimed that if the polls were correct Australia would have a Labor government—"a socialist government whose stated objective would be to recycle the Whitlam policies".[6]

Further opinion polls published on October 7,[7] which showed Hayden's standing increasing further, added credibility to Hayden's claims that the government was beginning to find the going very tough: "I think that you are now seeing the beginning of some panic in the Government camp.... They are starting to thresh about", Hayden was quoted as saying in the Sydney Morning Herald.[8]

Attempts by the government to put Labor on the defensive were not immediately successful. Developing his "socialist" attacks on the ALP the Prime Minister singled out the influence of the socialist left on ALP foreign policy when he campaigned in Perth, Western Australia. Against the background of Afghanistan and the outbreak of the Iran-Iraq war just prior to the campaign, the Liberals had hoped to gain some advantage from defense. Hayden, however, was quick in his attempt to defuse the issue, claiming that "In fact there is no difference between them and us on defence".[9]

In the middle of the second week, attempts by both parties to gain the ascendency in the media reports on issues, failed again when Labor's attempts to focus on tax avoidance degenerated into a tussle between the two leaders over their willingness (in the case of

Hayden) and unwillingness (on the part of the Prime Minister) to make their tax returns public. The Liberal campaign was further diverted when the Prime Minister reopened the 1975 constitutional crisis in response to questions at the Sydney Journalists Club. Asked if he might block supply, the Prime Minister was quoted as saying: "If circumstances existed as existed in 1975 I would do everything I could to get rid of the Government of that day".[10]

In response to research evidence which indicated that support for the Government was slipping badly in Victoria, the Prime Minister amended his itinerary and returned to Melbourne, rather than proceeding to the far north of Queensland. Coupled with the return south was a decision to give the Prime Minister greater opportunity for community functions—rallies, street walks—something which had been notably absent in the earlier part of the campaign.

As the second week progressed some optimism returned to the Liberal camp. A drop in share prices, in anticipation of an ALP victory, lifted Liberal morale, especially when coupled with headlines such as: "Mums and Dads hit hardest say brokers: Millions lost in new plunge".[11] The release of new opinion polls showed some closing of the gap between the two parties and was a welcome boost to the Liberal campaign, although privately commissioned polls were much less optimistic.

Although it was not necessarily recognized in the Liberal camp at the time, the latter part of the second week proved in many ways to be the turning point. While Hayden had been providing the media with comments on such matters as the likely size of his ministry and legislative priorities of an ALP government,[12] the Prime Minister was refining and intensifying his attack on the ALP.

The Liberal campaign team took little comfort from stories about the future structure of a Labor government, but in retrospect it appears that buoyed up by the polls, Labor was showing perceptible signs of easing back. By contrast, and by necessity, the Liberal campaign was intensifying, with the focus now firmly fixed on the inflationary consequences of the ALP's spending proposals and the implications of its capital tax commitments. Decisions to concentrate on these aspects of Labor's program were made at a strategy meeting at campaign headquarters on October 7. Following a detailed review of campaign progress and assessment of private and published research there was a clear consensus that the Liberal campaign lacked "bite". The ALP's triumvirate had proved successful, giving depth to Labor's leadership and taking the edge off the Liberals' emphasis on the strong leadership qualities of the Prime Minister. Research showed that the ALP's promised tax cut was attracting strong support. In the absence of a similar Liberal initiative, and against the background of the polls, the options were clear: either a new initiative or intensification of the "negative" campaign against Labor.

A series of ideas for countering Labor's tax cuts were canvassed. It was recognized, however, that such a course of action had drawbacks: firstly, a major expenditure commitment could bring into question the government's credibility as economic managers; secondly, it could be interpreted as a sign of panic. Intensifying the "negative" campaign against the ALP also was seen to have drawbacks. Pointing to the inflationary consequences of Labor's spending proposals raised questions of credibility and salience. Capital taxation, on the other hand, was a difficult concept to deal with, especially in advertising. Moreover, a heavy emphasis on negative campaigning was likely to produce adverse reaction amongst party members.

Despite reservations, a decision was made to develop a new series of advertisement on inflation, and Labor's capital taxation proposals, but with a "positive" advertisement designed to provide some balance to the new thrust of the advertising campaign. The attraction of attacking Labor's capital gains tax proposals was that the ALP had been consistently vague about the specifics, thus leaving considerable potential for interpretation. Moreover, in a country with one of the highest levels of home ownership in the world, the issue appeared to have strong potential.

The last week of the campaign showed a consistency of Liberal strategy in a way which had been absent at the launch. Against the background of a heavy advertising campaign on the inflationary consequences of Labor's policy commitments and its capital gains tax proposal, the Prime Minister further refined these themes in speeches and interviews. Press stories and comment, however, followed different paths, with opinion poll results dominating the headlines in the final week. Monday gave results showing the popularity of both leaders had increased during the campaign. On October 15, further polls were published, in one case showing Labor comfortably in the lead; in another, calling a close finish.[13]

The last card played by the government was the announcement, on October 16, that it would return to the community additional revenue from the oil levy through tax cuts or increased family allowances. This type of initiative had been canvassed by the campaign review on October 7 and subsequently discussed at a ministerial meeting at Kiribilli House (the Prime Minister's official Sydney residence) on the last weekend of the campaign. The announcement of a new initiative so late in the campaign clearly pointed to the dilemma the party was

in over the last two weeks of the campaign and the inevitable uncertainty as to whether the heavy "negative" advertising campaign
in the last ten days or so would reverse the trend of the opening
week.

It is difficult to assess what impact this late announcement might
have had on voters, although against the background of earlier
qualitative research some benefit might have been expected. Moreover, with the privately commissioned polls continuing to run against
the party, and with differing results in the published polls, the
government had little to lose in the final stages of the campaign.

In retrospect, the last week of the campaign saw the Liberals wrest
the initiative back from Labor. More strongly focussed advertising
coupled with consistency in speech themes and a last minute
announcement on taxation contrasted sharply with a wound-down
ALP campaign which had difficulty in sustaining any issue and
appeared, in light of the polls, preoccupied with the anticipated
transfer of power.

Conclusion

Unlike the elections of 1975 and 1977, the Liberals arrived at polling
day in a state of uncertainty as to the outcome of the election. The
published opinion polls which pointed in different directions contributed to the uncertainty, as did the party's private research which, at
best, called a close result. Indeed, it was to be many hours into
election night before the Prime Minister could claim victory in the
House of Representatives, where the government was returned with
a twenty-three-seat majority. It was some weeks before the outcome
of the Senate election was known. Here the government lost its
majority and the Australian Democrats gained the balance of power
by increasing their representation from two to five Senators.

Labor had required a swing of over 6 percent to win; in the final
analysis it gained 4.1 percent and increased its numbers in the House
of Representatives by thirteen seats. While the Liberal Party lost
fourteen seats, of which seven were in Victoria, the primary vote for
the party declined by less than 1 percent.

Many commentators saw the result as disappointing for the
government—against expectations of an easy win prior to the
campaign—but, in fact the Government's majority was still the sixth
largest since Federation.

No one factor can account for electoral victory or loss, the outcome
normally being the result of a mix of factors; at best an assessment can

only place priority on those factors considered significant. The ALP demonstrated a quality and depth to its leadership which had been absent prior to the campaign. Bill Hayden could claim much of the credit for the swing to Labor, having established, in a little more than two weeks, an image and reputation which had eluded him for the two years since he had attained the Labor leadership. By contrast with 1977, Labor's advertising campaign was polished and the blend of positives and negatives, underscored with moderation, enhanced its appeal. Promised tax cuts struck a responsive chord in the electorate as Liberal research clearly indicated.

The ALP campaign did, however, exhibit considerable inflexibility which worked to the government's advantage. While advertising throughout the campaign appeared to conform to a predetermined strategy, an inability or unwillingness by the ALP to cope with the government's sharpened attack on inflation and capital taxation allowed the government to dominate the latter stages of the campaign.

The opinion polls, too, appeared to lull the ALP into a false sense of security. While private Liberal research showed Labor to be in a commanding position as the campaign moved into its final week, preference for Labor on a range of policy issues was beginning to decline, pointing to a loss of impetus at a time when the Liberals had at last achieved a sense of direction and purpose.

The Liberal campaign strategy was a calculated gamble to run on the government's record, while emphasizing the contrast in leadership styles of the Prime Minister and opposition leader. It is doubtful whether the Liberals will again go into an election without an initiative of widespread electoral appeal, although the final result might have suggested that the Liberal attempts to scale down public expectations of government largesse had been successful. The Liberal emphasis on leadership as an election issue claimed many detractors, but as research throughout the campaign showed, the Prime Minister did not lose ground; rather, the stature of Bill Hayden increased dramatically.

Much will ultimately be written about the Liberal attack on Labor's capital tax proposals and its possible influence on the outcome of the election. The 6.2 percent swing to Labor in Victoria, compared with the 2.8 percent swing in New South Wales might suggest that this aspect of the campaign, against a background of buoyant property values in Sydney and depressed prices in Melbourne, was significant.

In the final analysis, however, factors outside the immediate influence of the major protagonists may have been of most influence. The dramatic falls in share prices in response to opinion polls confidently predicting an ALP victory may have created doubts in the minds of many voters about the ALP's capacity for national economic management. Irrespective of their impact on the stock market, the same polls, considered in isolation, must have given some voters cause to reflect in more than usual depth about their decision on polling day. If this were true, it suggests that the Liberals succeeded in maintaining their credibility in the key area of national economic management, while Labor failed to make a clean break from the memories of economic conditions between 1972 and 1975.

It is possible, however, that any explanation based on the campaign is of less significance than the realignment of political support which is likely to take place in circumstances where a government has achieved unusually high levels of support in the recent past. In 1975 and 1977 the government was returned with record majorities in circumstances when it was able totally to dominate the political agenda. In the face of a resurgent ALP and with the consequences of the passage of time, a blurring of the agenda was perhaps inevitable in 1980, and the pendulum swung accordingly.

Notes

1 *Australian*, October 2, 1980.
2 *Sun*, Melbourne, October 2, 1980.
3 *Age*, Melbourne, October 3, 1980.
4 *Daily Telegraph*, Sydney, October 5, 1980.
5 *Age*, Melbourne, October 6, 1980.
6 ibid.
7 ibid., October 7, 1980.
8 *Sydney Morning Herald*, October 7, 1980.
9 *Sun*, Melbourne, October 7, 1980.
10 *Age*, Melbourne, October 8, 1980.
11 *Daily Telegraph*, Sydney, October 9, 1980.
12 *Mercury*, Hobart, October 9, 1980.
13 *Herald* and *Age*, Melbourne, October 15, 1980.

4
Labor in 1980

Patrick Weller

If a survey of the leaders of the Labor Party had been held in July 1980, it would have been difficult to find more than one or two people who seriously believed that their party could win the election. The pessimism engendered by the second shattering defeat in a row, in 1977, had continued throughout the ensuing parliament. Hayden's leadership, by far the best available to the parliamentary party, was still considered inadequate. The only expectation was that the party must surely pick up some seats at the next poll, although how many was open to dispute.

Yet throughout much of the period the Labor Party was leading in the opinion polls—not by much, it is true, but it had seldom dropped far behind either. The common belief was that when faced with the reality of an election the voters would drift back to the Liberals and that the perceived innate conservatism of the electorate would once again prevail. In a much-noticed article in the *Australian Financial Review*, Anne Summers asked:

> Can Labor win this year's Federal election? The question has barely been raised in Canberra, among media commentators or political observers?
>
> Nor is it given serious consideration in business, round the stock exchanges or in other sensitive indications of movements of political sephyrs.
>
> Even many parliamentary members of the Labor Party tend to talk about the election after next—rather than this year—as the one to be won ...
>
> This perception gap between the data provided by the polls and the expectations of professional observers of the political

process is one of the more extraordinary facets of Federal politics this year.[1]

The degree of pessimism among the Labor ranks needs to be explained. It was in part the legacy of 1977, in part due to the internal problems of the party and in part a response to the party's leadership. But underlying it all was the feeling of the normalcy of opposition that has become basic to Labor in Federal politics. With only nineteen years in office since the formation of the Commonwealth in 1901, and that in seven different spells, the party had stayed in office for more than three years on only one occasion—between 1941 and 1949. While the conservative parties believed they should govern as a matter of habit, Labor regarded office as an exceptional and unusual opportunity. The party members have yet to develop the attitude that they should be the natural governing party in their own minds, let alone among the electorate at large.

The size of the 1977 defeat had been shattering because everyone assumed that the pendulum would swing back from its 1975 position and that, to some extent, the party would be back within range of government. But it did not happen. Only one seat was actually won (two others were gained by changes caused by redistribution) and the swing was a mere 1 percent.[2]

Several lessons were drawn, not always accurately, from that result. People were supposed to be suspicious of big government, and Fraser's attempts to reduce the public's expectations of government were regarded as successful. Labor was tagged as the party of big government. Unemployment, at a higher level in 1977 than at any previous election since 1945, was said to be "no longer" an issue. People were concerned about it, but not to the extent that they were prepared to change their votes to Labor. Gradually, as memories of the Whitlam government became more distant, there had grown a tendency among Whitlam's colleagues to blame him for all their errors. That was grossly unfair. But it led to the impression that without him the problems of reaching and holding office might disappear. That was grossly naive.

State election results did not do much to reduce the pessimism. In New South Wales and Tasmania, Labor governments were indeed returned. But these were States with strong Labor traditions and the massively increased majority in New South Wales was due to the popularity of Premier Neville Wran. There was no guarantee that these results could be translated into Federal votes—in 1975 and 1977, while Labor easily retained the power in the State, the Liberals had won every seat in Tasmania. Elsewhere, the results in State elections had been uniformly unimpressive. In elections in Queensland, Western Australia and Victoria Labor won only a few seats, and never threatened to eject the incumbent conservative governments, despite the fact that, in Victoria at least, the government appeared tired and scandal-ridden. In South Australia where the party had governed for ten years under the charismatic Don Dunstan, it was ejected, to everyone's surprise, a mere nine months after his retirement in a snap election called by his successor.

Organization

The Labor party is a federation of six State and two Territorial branches, some of which were founded before 1900 and thus preceded the creation of the Commonwealth. The Federal parliamentary party, known as the caucus, was formed before the first meeting of the Commonwealth Parliament; the policy to which it was bound was decided initially by triennial Federal Conferences at which each of the six States had six representatives, as befitted a federal party. In the early days of Federation most of the issues of direct relevance to citizens concerned State governments and the Federal party was left to its own devices and to its limited platform. It first gained office with a full majority in 1910.

The power over machinery matters remained with the State branches. They controlled preselections at both Federal and State levels, maintained contacts with the unions which were affiliated to them and elected delegates directly to the State Conference, and had access to all the real resources of manpower and money. As long as the relations between State branches and their Federal representatives remained harmonious, the system worked. But the possible existence of clashes was one of the reasons for the creation of the Federal Executive in 1915.

After the great split of the party over conscription in 1915, the basic problem of a federal structure became obvious. If a State Executive could direct the Federal representatives elected from that State to follow policies that were opposed to those adopted by Federal caucus, or even in contradiction to Federal policy, then the Federal caucus would soon fragment into five or more units. It was essential, therefore, that Federal authorities had the power to make decisions on any matter that affected the "general welfare of the movement" or that transcended State boundaries. After all, for the Federal Executive to make a majority decision, the delegates of more than three branches had to vote in favour. The Federal authority was never separate from, nor independent of, the State branches.[3]

Gradually, and primarily in response to a series of challenges from the New South Wales branch, the Federal Executive painfully established its authority to intervene in the internal affairs of a State branch if they were conducted so badly that the welfare of the movement was threatened. One such intervention, in Victoria in 1955, led to the split in the party that helped form the Democratic Labor Party and assisted in keeping Labor in opposition. Another move, again in Victoria in 1970, removed the left-wing executive and allowed the party to win enough seats in that state to form a Federal government in 1972.

Invariably intervention occurred when a branch was electorally unsuccessful. Given the class, rather than the regional, basis of Australian political parties,[4] the Labor party cannot expect to win office unless it gains seats in every State. This was particularly true in the peripheral States: in Queensland, Western Australia and Tasmania, Labor won only four out of thirty-five seats in 1977. Improvements were required.

Of the State branches, two—the Victorian and Queensland ones —were notably unsuccessful. In Victoria the branch had broken into three almost independent factions which maintained their own organizations and fought bitterly for positions of power. The socialist left—outspoken, extreme, pro-Arab—was widely regarded as an electoral liability; some of its members used a local community radio station, 3CR, to air their extreme views and frequently to attack the moderates, particularly the ACTU leader and former national party president, Bob Hawke.[5]

In Queensland the situation was electorally worse. There a small group of trade union officials ran both the Trades Hall and the local branch of the Labor Party. They were impervious to criticism and vindictive to all opposition; minority voices were seldom given a chance. In a State colloquially and not inaccurately known as the "Deep North", the ruling clique of the Labor Party was almost as conservative as the coalition led by the peanut-farming Country Party leader, Jo Bjelke-Petersen. Electorally the party was unsuccessful. In the 1974 State election it had won only eleven seats in a house of eighty-two; in 1977 it had increased only to twenty-three; federally, the party won only one seat in 1975 (and that was Bill Hayden's) and three in 1977.

Federal action was taken in two stages. First, an inquiry was undertaken by the Federal officers and on their recommendations a series of changes in structure and the methods of representation were made. But, although supported initially by Hayden who argued that those minor changes were the best that could be expected, the reform group was far from happy. The changes indeed were not enough; the old guard still maintained full control. The complete takeover of the branch by the Federal Executive was considered. The New South Wales delegates argued against intervention in the fear that changes in the Queensland structure, and hence in its representation on the Federal Executive, would lead to an alteration in the balance of power there, and a tilt towards the left.

Nevertheless a decision to take control of all the affairs of the branch was made in early 1980. The old officials refused to give up its books or premises. But the new branch began to receive considerable support, and some unions affiliated to it; throughout the year recriminations continued and, even at the launching of the Federal campaign in Brisbane, the two groups ostentatiously sat at separate tables. It was scarcely a picture of party unity, although it seems that Labor's divisions were overshadowed by the even more public bickering at State level between the two State government coalition partners.

Elsewhere divisions continued to show. In South Australia disputes about the control of the branch by the unions' use of a card vote simmered. In Tasmania a preselection panel put the Deputy Premier and Federal president, Neil Batt, in a vulnerable fourth position in a State by-election run on the basis of proportional representation. (But he topped the poll and confounded his critics.)

The Labor Party was well aware of the problems created by its organizational structure and of the weaknesses that had to be overcome if it was to regain office. Directly after the 1977 defeat, a national committee of inquiry was established, with Hayden and Hawke as joint chairpersons. The membership of the committee included three professors, two Members of Parliament (one of them an ex-professor), three union representatives and two branch members. The committee advertised for submissions and also commissioned ten discussion papers on organizational topics such as the composition of the National Conference, the role of the local branch and the position of women in the party, electoral strategies, the impact of the relationship which the party had with the unions and issues of social change and regionalism. These discussion papers were bravely published; so was the final report.[6]

Many of the committee's proposals were far-reaching. It recommended a new communications policy, a policy of affirmative action in favour of women, better liaison with ethnic committees and trade unions, and a reconstructed and more representative organizational structure. The National Conference was to consist of 124 delegates elected directly by each of the Federal electorates; 124 elected by affiliated trade unions; forty, as at present from the States; twenty Federal parliamentary delegates; and two from the Young Labor movement. The National Executive, too, was to be dramatically revised, with a more effective committee system.[7] If adopted, the committee's report would have led to a dramatic alteration of the historical methods and balance of the Australian Labor Party.

But changes come slowly in the ALP. To change the composition of the National Conference, for instance, needs the consent of the existing Conference. It would mean that the delegates of the small States who were as influential in votes as their counterparts from the larger States, would be required to vote themselves out of influence. Those proposals that needed change were largely shelved in 1979: to be considered again at the 1981 conference—after the election. The factional and historical factors that have moulded the party in the past ninety years are hard to shift. Nor does it seem likely that the federal nature of the party will be altered; the electoral impact of such a move in those smaller States where the party needs to win seats would be too great.

Yet the Federal party was not as divided as it had been in the past. Fights about internal positions are always in existence in the Labor Party. At Federal level, few of these tensions erupted; there were fewer open disputes and wrangles than in the past, and apparently less personal vindictiveness. Perhaps it was because the divisive presence of Whitlam was gone. Nevertheless, if the Labor Party nationally required unity and cohesion of purpose (to some extent, anyway) before it could win, there was little sign that it was likely to develop.

Preselection

The Labor Party's performance in office, or the potential team that it can present to the electorate as an alternative set of ministers, depends heavily on the people that it chooses for safe seats. Because of the history of the party and its tendency to suffer bad defeats (as in 1966, 1975 and 1977), those who keep their seats for long enough are quite likely to be elected to the shadow executive or, in the event of an election victory, the ministry. Even though the Cabinet is always larger than the Shadow Cabinet (in 1980 Hayden's Shadow Cabinet was twenty-three strong; his Cabinet was planned to be twenty-five), members elected to Parliament for the first time are unlikely to be elected to the ministry. If Labor had won in 1980 Hawke would have provided only the second occasion when a minister was elected directly after his first entry into Federal Parliament (assuming he was successful in the ballot).[8]

Therefore, the process of preselection must serve two distinct purposes. In safe seats—and that includes the first two on the Senate ticket since, under the system of proportional representation, these are certain to be elected—it consists of choosing the small pool from whom a Cabinet will be primarily elected. If, for instance, Labor were to win the election in 1983, the great majority of those who became ministers would come from those who entered Parliament in 1977 or before, and who were thus elected to the shadow executive after the 1980 election. The caucus would almost certainly stick by them—or most of them at least. In 1977 the Labor caucus consisted of thirty-eight members of the House of Representatives and twenty-six Senators—sixty-four in all. Since a few retire at each election, a few fall out of favor, a few have had their chance and a few never appear to be of ministerial calibre, it seems that a Cabinet elected in 1983 would be chosen from a pool of forty or less survivors of 1977, with one or two additions, like Hawke, elected in 1980. Therefore, the selection process in safe seats perhaps ought to be concerned with choosing people of ministerial calibre (however that may be judged, and it is very difficult to estimate in advance).

By contrast, in marginal seats the party needs candidates who can win seats and then hold them. When the swing in the different seats is not uniform, and a good sitting member has to be displaced, then attractive, energetic local candidates are needed. Once elected they have to nurse their electorates. Even if a candidate's personal vote may be worth no more than 1 or 2 percent, and a good local candidate would not, therefore, be immune from large national swings, that small amount may nevertheless be the means of holding on to the seat.

But the processes by which candidates are chosen invariably take many other factors into account. Factional alignment within the branches is often as important as personal calibre. The selection of Federal candidates is entirely the prerogative of the State branches. The Federal machine has no direct involvement and, therefore, does not have the capacity, so useful in Britain, to find safe seats for candidates of ability. There is no easy way into Parliament. Further, in every State all local members have to seek readoption before every election. This is not a mere formality: before the 1980 election two Federal Members of the House of Representatives were discarded and one Senator was placed third on the Victorian Labor ticket, a position in which she was given no chance of reelection. In factional terms it is not true that either the left or the right has gained. Often, old, tired or mediocre members have simply been replaced.

In each State the preselection process follows local rules. In Victoria candidates are selected by a panel consisting partly of local and partly of central representatives. The degree to which branches can be "packed" by supporters of one faction or individual, and thus the degree to which candidates and members can be removed, depends largely on the methods of choice. New South Wales is the one State where local branches are reputed to be stacked, leading in part to the choice of several undistinguished local members who are nonetheless able to maintain their position by consistent contact with their local branches, whose members are able to vote. In Tasmania choices are made by a specially convened State Conference. All candidates are required to sign a pledge to accept the decision of the ballot, and any member of the Labor Party standing against a nominated candidate is automatically expelled. Preselection is thus vital for a political career. It is not surprising that future ministerial calibre is not often an explicit, or even a major consideration. The one exception may be South Australia where two talented men, Mick Young and Neal Blewett, were in 1974 and 1977 respectively, shifted into seats previously held by nonentities.

For the 1980 campaign three particular cases—two strongly disputed, one unchallenged—deserve comment. In Tasmania the leader of the party in the Senate, Ken Wriedt, decided to give up his safe position at the top of the Senate ticket and his leadership position to contest the marginal seat of Denison. He argued that unless leading Labor personalities were prepared to take risks Labor could never expect to win. Perhaps, too, he was tired of opposition. Since Denison has been won by the party that was to form the government in every election since 1940, Wriedt could expect that if he won, so too might Labor. It was a quixotic gesture that failed.

In Victoria two preselections were hotly contested. In the safe seat of Wills the leading candidate was Bob Hawke, president of the ACTU since 1969, Federal president of the Labor Party from 1974 to 1978, a well-known conciliator, and a figure whose popularity rating was always higher than that of any other public figure. For some years Hawke had considered entering Parliament, but he was always loath to give up his position of considerable influence in the ACTU for the less certain parliamentary possibilities. He clearly wanted to be parliamentary leader and Prime Minister. His stature was such that his presence in Parliament was almost certain to be of benefit to Labor.

But internal divisions ensured that he was given no easy ride.

Hawke was an avowed enemy of the socialist left faction, which he believed was divisive. Its adherents in their turn were determined to stop him even reaching Parliament and put up an alternative candidate who was nationally unknown. Much of the argument presented by Hawke's opponents was specious and more vitriol was spilt than in the whole State election campaign a few months before. Hawke finally won by 38 votes to 29, but the spectacle of a small faction's attempting to prevent the selection of one of the country's most attractive figures was unedifying. It illustrated the diverse forces that often influenced preselections and the factors that have often given safe seats to local hacks whose parliamentary and ministerial contribution is certain to be limited.

The second major fight occurred over the Senate ticket in Victoria. Since it is chosen by a system of proportional representation each of the two main factions could expect one person in the safe positions at the top. Two senators were standing for reelection—one, the socialist left candidate, was put top of the list, but the second, Jean Melzer, was relegated to the third position. She had originally been elected as a member of the "Centre Unity" group, but in the Senate she had increasingly shown her sympathy with the socialist left. Her demotion, to a position that was expected to be—and was—unwinnable caused an outrage, particularly because she was one of Labor's very few women parliamentarians. (See also the section, "Preselection", in Chapter 7.) But despite several campaigns and considerable pressure no changes were made. The precedent of reopening preselection decisions, just because a faction did not like the result, was regarded as too dangerous.

In general two trends were noticeable in those selected by the Labor Party for those marginal seats that the Labor Party had to win if it were to take office. First, a larger number of women were chosen including Joan Child, the *only* women who had ever been elected for the House of Representatives as a Labor candidate. But none of these were safe seats. Second, a large number of those chosen for these seats were involved in education, either as school-teachers, university or college lecturers or administrative staff. Only a few—and most notably the former radical official of the Amalgamated Metal Workers' and Shipwrights' Union (AMW & SU) in South Australia—had the traditional working class/union background. In its Federal representation the embourgeoisment of the Labor Party continued apace.

At local level many of the candidates had been selected early and, by the time of the election, had campaigned regularly and extensively in their electorates. The belief in personal contact and in regular door-knocking continued. Some of the local committees surveyed opinion and adjusted their proposals accordingly, although most of these detailed pieces of politicking were lost to the media that concentrated almost exclusively on the leaders.

Leadership

In the Labor Party there is a strong egalitarian ethos. Control is supposed to be in the hands of the rank and file who can exert influence through State and Federal Conferences, whose decisions in policy are binding on MPs. Each MP signs a pledge to accept the party platform; he is in theory a delegate responsible for implementing the will of the Labor movement. The Federal party leader is elected by members of caucus; he has to stand for reelection after each general election; he is bound to accept decisions arrived at in caucus by majority vote. His independence is far more limited than that of his Liberal counterpart.

In practice he must be more influential than this picture of a mere chairman suggests. He has, in the first instance, gained the support of caucus in order to become leader; as long as he performs well and maintains his contacts with his parliamentary colleagues, he should be able to keep that support. No leader of the Federal Labor Party has yet been defeated in a leadership ballot. Further, the leader naturally has all the advantages that publicity can present. His view is sought more readily than his colleagues', his statements are given greater weight. What he does must always be news. In theory—and particularly in opposition—both Liberal and Labor leaders must take their parties with them in any important decisions.

Between 1967 and 1975 Whitlam had dominated the Labor Party by the sheer force of his personality and intellect. After the size of the 1975 defeat had become apparent, he was kept leader almost on sufferance; there was no alternative and Hayden did not want to stand then. When he did run in May 1977, Whitlam defeated him by only two votes. In the 1977 poll Whitlam's presence was regarded as one of the main reasons for Labor's dismal showing. He resigned the leadership with dignity on that election night and was replaced by Bill Hayden, then forty-five years old, a one-time policeman from Queensland who had been in Parliament since 1961 and whose reputation as a minister, both as the introducer of Medibank and later as Treasurer, was high. To become leader Hayden defeated the NSW member, Lionel Bowen, who then stood for and won the deputy leadership. Although some seemed to question Hayden's toughness (for, shattered by the 1975 result he had initially not even stood for reelection to the shadow executive), he was the best leader available to caucus by far.

The contrast between Hayden and Whitlam was vast. Whitlam's visions were grand; he picked up ideas from all over the place, fashioned them into a mosaic of reforms and assumed that they could be achieved within the economic structure. Hayden, learning from the bitter experiences of office, was concerned primarily with sound economic management. The more detailed reforms came later. Whitlam dominated his party, demanded allegiance and had a policy of "crash or crash through"; his public visibility was high. Hayden operated far more on a process of consensus, consulting widely, listening to alternatives; his was a low-key persona, the leader of a team, the sieve, not the originator of most ideas. Both men were intellectually curious; before he became leader Hayden was likely at times to appear as concerned with the career of Rosa Luxemburg as he was with recent events, and he must be one of the few Australian parliamentarians to quote St Thomas Aquinas in debate. Even had they faced similar conditions their styles of leadership would have always been different.

But the dramatic change in circumstances also meant that the grand visions were no longer viable. Labor leaders argued that cautious sound government was needed; they had had enough of the authoritarian style of leadership that Whitlam had imposed. So Hayden suited the mood of the party, as well as being the best available candidate within it.

Yet between his election in early 1978 and the election of 1980 he was not regarded as successful or dominant. His style was careful, often erudite; he was inclined to quote figures at length, and to sound carping on television even when presenting sound and logical criticism of government policy. He could be tough and determined; when his mind was made up he was reputed to be difficult to shift. At times he could be tactless; one or two of the changes in the distribution of responsibility within the shadow executive caused open dissension. But it was not long lasting. His parliamentary performances were adequate, but not inspiring. He could not dominate Parliament as a political arena in the way Whitlam had done. He was not regarded as a potential winner. As Michelle Gratten, chief political correspondent of the *Age*, gracefully conceded during the election campaign:

Whatever the outcome of this election it has demonstrated one fact; Bill Hayden is a much better campaigner than many of us thought he would be.

No one doubted that he was a strong leader within the party. But in the past few months many people in the ALP and the media (myself included) believed Mr Hayden was not coming across strongly enough, convincingly enough, to carry an effective campaign. Recent weeks have shown we underestimated him.[9]

That was fair comment, both on Hayden's reputation as a leader and of the media response to him.

In a sense that image made him appear vulnerable, because there were two dominant figures in the Labor movement whose popularity far exceeded Hayden's: Bob Hawke and Neville Wran. Wran was Premier of New South Wales, the most populous State of the Commonwealth. He had won office in 1976—a mere four months after Labor's 1975 debacle—ending eleven years of Liberal rule in what had for a long time been a traditional Labor State. He had massively increased that majority in 1978. While in office he reformed the State upper house, turning it from a nominated chamber to one that was directly elected by the voters. His style of government was generally moderate, conservative and cautious, although he was aided by a divided and ineffective opposition. Most important, Wran managed to appeal to almost all sections of the community; his relations with business were good and many middle-class voters found his approach palatable, as the 1978 election win illustrated. As a public speaker Wran was well presented, confident and articulate. Whether Wran had Federal ambitions was always questionable. He was five years older than Hayden and seemed firmly in power in New South Wales. Besides, he knew that a path to the Federal leadership would not be easy; as he frequently pointed out, nothing is given away free in the Labor Party and it is always a hard and bloody road to the top.

Hawke's ambitions were clearer. Once he decided to stand for Parliament he wanted to be leader and Prime Minister. His qualifications were formidable: a Rhodes scholar, ten years as industrial advocate of the ACTU, and then ten years as president. He had been a member of the board of the Reserve Bank and a member of the Jackson and Crawford Committees that examined the structure of manufacturing industry in Australia. While his party colleagues had been involved in the parliamentary battles, Hawke had roamed widely through the boardrooms and union offices of the country. His breadth of experience and knowledge of the power structures of the country were wide. His reputation as a negotiator and fixer was high;

his record of settling industrial dusputes unrivalled. As a politician he illustrated an instinct for the jugular that too often was missing among his colleagues. Yet at the same time his performances were sometimes intemperate; the occasional outburst did his reputation little credit and brought into question the type of leadership he might provide. Besides, Hawke had many enemies; the socialist left in Victoria were particularly determined to stop Hawke, who was strongly pro-Israeli, whose views had become more and more moderate, and whose greatest objective, as expressed in the rather patchy Boyer lectures,[10] was the reduction and settlement of conflict in society.

Neither Hawke nor Wran had been unequivocal in their support for Hayden. At the Federal Conference in Adelaide in 1979 Hawke and Hayden had clashed openly. Hawke had chaired the economic committee that proposed that a future Labor government would seek constitutional powers over wages and prices by referendum. The left wing unions opposed any idea of a referendum to control wages. Hayden sponsored a compromise amendment which dropped the reference to the referendum. Hawke was not consulted and, later that evening, vehemently expressed his views of Hayden's leadership. They were crude and far from complimentary. The rift between the two, emphasized at every turn by the media, appeared to continue. As a result Hawke's potential as a leader, and the possibility of an immediate challenge to Hayden if the election was not won, were often canvassed. Hawke did not deny his interest in the job, but probably realized that no newcomer to caucus could expect instant leadership. Wran was more quietly critical, describing the final economic policy as a bit of a hotch-potch. Wran had also been reported as saying, while on a trip to the USA, that Labor had no chance of regaining power before 1983—scarcely a vote of confidence in Hayden.

The important factor both Wran and Hawke was that both had their own power base; they were, during 1980, independent of the Federal party. Other Federal members were less noticeable. Mick Young on industrial relations, Ralph Willis on economic affairs, John Button on education and Don Grimes on social security were occasionally in the news; they argued their case well without making a dramatic impact. Neal Blewett, appointed to the shadow executive in mid-1980, made a rapid impression as a persuasive and articulate spokesman. But the most impressive member of the front bench was Paul Keating, the shadow spokesman for minerals and energy. A disciple of the former minister, Rex Connor, he was a hard worker, a rugged fighter and an effective numbers man. He produced a green paper on energy and minerals policy, with the aid of one assistant, faster and more efficiently than the government could with all its bureaucratic assistance. In debates with government spokesmen his toughness and undoubted mastery of his subject were daunting. Fraser shifted responsibility for minerals policy to a Senate minister to get it away from Keating's criticisms. Also Keating, as the recently elected president of the NSW State branch, had an important base in the party. Of all the shadow ministers, Keating was the one who had the most obvious leadership potential.

Ideology and Policy

The Labor Party's opponents call it socialist. The first plank of its objective commits it to achieve:

> The democratic socialisation of industry, production, distribution and exchange—to the extent necessary to eliminate exploitation and other anti-social features in those fields—in accordance with the principles of action, methods and progressive reforms set out in this Platform.[11]

The platform then goes on to interpret that objective and indicate the general (very general) means by which it might be achieved.

To the left these ideals are regarded as important. Purity of policy is often seen as more important than electoral victory. Thus one socialist left member, then an academic but now a Federal member, could write in 1979:

> Since to be socialist is to be opposed to the existing distribution of wealth and power which perpetuates these moral evils (of oppression, inequality, exploitation and injustice) the ALP has nothing to fear from an open espousal of its socialism.... For the socialist issue will not disappear. As the economic crisis deepens and the conservatives prove to be incapable of solving this crisis, the Australian people will become more receptive of new socialist ideas. This will prove an historic opportunity for the ALP.
>
> There are conservative governments in NSW, Tasmania and South Australia. What have they done to improve the lot of their people in the current economic and social crises? By refusing to take their own radical tradition seriously and seek substantive changes they may hold the government but at what price? There is a possibility that the ALP, in overcompromising to gain power, may change its own ideology to such a degree that it loses its own soul.[12]

He also accused the ALP leadership of "ideological incoherence".

Those views are probably held by many of the left. But they are historically inaccurate, politically suicidal, and patently unfair to three State Labor governments that have often achieved what they intended. In government the Labor party has never been radical; it has always been concerned with alleviating the worst impact of social conditions, of redistributing income to the less well-off and of managing the capitalist mixed economy more humanely. There was only one serious attempt in history to implement any step in the process of nationalisation—that was the legislation to take over the banks, introduced by Chifley in 1947–49 which was declared unconstitutional by the High Court. Thereafter the limitations of the Constitution and the expected electoral reaction have combined to bolster the natural caution of Labor leaders to remove such a tactic from the party's arsenal. It stays at the head of the platform at least in part because to try and remove it would cause more internal dissension than it would be worth.

Despite the vehemence of the official objective, the platform adopted in 1979 was more cautious. It reflected the views of the leaders. Whatever their personal differences, there is virtually no policy difference between Hayden, Hawke, Wran, Willis or Keating. As Hayden stated in his speech to the National Conference in 1979:

> First, and above all else, we must demonstrate beyond doubt that we are competent economic managers. That competence, and the public's recognition of it, is the absolute essential underpinning of everything we want to do. Without it, without an unqualified commitment to pursue responsible economic management, we might just as well pack up our bags and give the game away. I believe it is as crucial as that. While I admit that there are times when even my best friends seem irritated by my personal commitments to responsible economic management, it seems to me the alternative can only be irresponsible economic management. And that, of course, just is not on—not to me as national leader of our party and certainly not to the Australian people.[13]

He argued that economic management should be coupled with a sense of social and economic justice; but agreed that it would not be easy to achieve or to reduce unemployment. Grand visions he did not present.

Of course there were disputes about some of the details of the strategy; responsible economic management can be little more than a glib phrase. The argument between Hawke and Hayden over the pursuit of power by referendum to control wages was one such. But the general tone of the platform, as espoused by all the leaders, had two or three central themes. First, it was necessary to do only what was economically sensible. Reforms, however desirable, would be introduced only when the country could afford them. (The platform binds the Federal party; the caucus, or in effect a Labor Cabinet, decides when these items will be implemented). Second, reforms would be introduced gradually, after proper investigation and consideration of the alternatives. There would be none of the rush, bustle and excitement that characterized the early days of the Whitlam government. Third, the main emphasis would be on presenting a more humanitarian approach to social problems, less blaming of the dole-bludgers, more consideration of the problems of the unemployed, and particularly of the young unemployed where levels were particularly high.

At the same time Labor was concerned to ensure that links with the business community remained sound, and that contacts were made with US officials so that the misunderstandings that were said to occur under the Whitlam government were not repeated. Labor did not want to scare away foreign investment, even if it sought to maintain some control over its levels.

The approach demanded consultation—with the unions, with business, with the main groups in the community. Nor is there any immediate prospect of change. All the current leadership, and all the potential leaders throughout the next decade accept the convergence view of politics, the idea that the Labor Party must move ideologically into the middle ground if 'it wants to win and retain power. The example of Wran shows what might be done. The left is likely to remain noisy, electorally divisive and influential at State branch level, where its union connections may give it strength (but not exclusively so, since the union influence in New South Wales and Queensland has bolstered the right of the party).

But Federal leaders are anyway one step removed from direct union influence. The approach and policy adopted in 1980 is likely to continue. Internal disputes about policy objectives and particular programs will continue—as they must in any pluralist party, and particularly one on the left of centre. It is unlikely they will lead to a change in strategy.

The Campaign Structure

Since the 1980 election was the first poll since 1972 to be held after a Parliament had gone a full three years, it was the first time that the party had the opportunity to plan in advance. It did so. Its basic research, carried out by ANOP, was completed by September 1979. Thereafter the party polled intermittently to maintain contact with the electorate. For the Labor Party it was the most comprehensively researched campaign in its history. The results said, *inter alia*:

> The swinging voters are selfish, ignored and depressed. They know virtually nothing of Hayden. We must therefore give Hayden some profile in their minds, preferably one built in terms of things which affect them tangibly, and which offer them some concrete hope of improving their lot.
> They vote on instinct for superficial, ill-informed and generally selfish reasons.
> They think Fraser is a fair sort of all-round bastard.[14]

When these survey documents were leaked to the Liberals in November 1979, the Liberals tried to paint Labor as being very condescending to the voters. But these findings provided the basic thrust of the Labor campaign—the demand for an improvement in the living wages of families and the slogan "Raise the Standard."

Planning of the campaign had continued throughout the previous year. The national planning committee, under the presidency of Neil Batt, had met regularly and Batt's enthusiasm, at a time when it was a rare commodity, was important. The structure of the campaign itself was organized like that of 1977; David Combe, the national secretary, was based in Sydney as the central director of the party. Rod Cameron, the head of ANOP polls, was responsible for interpreting the results. Hayden was accompanied by two veterans of the press gallery, Alan Ramsey and Ken Randall, and by his principal private secretary, Clem Lloyd, who had been an adviser to Labor leaders and ministers for the previous fifteen years. Finally, he had as adviser a rich liquor and tea merchant and former journalist and public servant, Richard Farmer, who was described towards the end of the campaign as a decisive influence, bringing originality and flair to the presentation of Hayden. Farmer acted as the link between the secretariat and the leadership. Each morning, after an analysis of the morning press, Farmer and Lloyd were linked by phone to plan the final details of the day. The party's media centre in Sydney, under Tony Ferguson, was able to monitor the talk-back radio shows, and maintain close links with the advertising agencies and the pollsters.

Unlike many previous campaigns, the organization was efficient and smooth. In 1977 the Liberals had been able to issue lists of the contradictory statements made by Labor's economic spokesmen. That never happened in 1980. The party decided to make a virtue of having three leaders in the public eye. In July the Federal president of the party, Neil Batt, resigned to take up a United Nations post in Bangladesh. Initially it was regarded as another sign of Labor's pessimism. But then it was turned to the party's advantage. Neville Wran, even though recuperating from a throat operation that left his voice croaking and hoarse throughout the next six months, agreed to become Federal president. The party then decided to create a triumvirate to head their campaign, consisting of Hayden, Wran and Hawke. The Liberals immediately labelled it "the troika", a suitably Russian term (but never a "trinity"!). Hayden also appointed Hawke as party spokesman for industrial relations, a move that gave authority to his statements after he resigned as president of the ACTU and became merely the candidate for Wills. As a tactic it was a masterstroke, for it ensured that the activities of all three received media coverage.

Further, the organization ensured that tight controls on all speakers were kept. When Fraser stated he would be prepared to block supply again if the numbers in the Senate were available and the circumstances warranted it, most Labor spokesmen were instruted not to react. That was left to one or two specified individuals. In the last week or so all but eight spokesmen—the leading trinity plus Lionel Bowen, Paul Keating, Mick Young, Ralph Willis and Neal Blewett—were gagged at anything but local level so that contradictions would not occur. In the Victorian branch the administrative committee decreed that, on pain of explusion, local members should not make national pronouncements. This had the desired effect of effectively silencing people like Bill Hartley whose intemperate statements often lost the party votes. Divisions in the party were minimized and a smooth, coherent and professional campaign was run—the best since 1972 at least.

The advertising company, Forbes Macfie Mitchell and Hansen, was the same as in 1977 and took responsibility for all advertising, basing its plans on the ANOP research and the decisions of the national campaign committee in the previous year. The advertising concentrated on predeterminded themes—raising the standard of living, arguing that the average wage earner was $16 a week worse off than he had been in 1975 and attacking the excessive price of petrol. Regardless of the Liberals' actions the Labor Party stuck to its theme; perhaps too much so. After the election Wran argued that Labor should have stated its intentions about the capital gains tax more clearly. The Labor Party did say that the tax would not be introduced within the next Parliament, but over the years enough contradictory statements had been made to give some credence to the fear campaign the Liberals ran in the last week before the election. Paul

Keating commented after the election: "I think in the last 10 days of the campaign we failed to react enough to the vicious advertising campaign of the Liberal party. We could have responded aggressively to the tax question without moving away from our central strategy".[15]

Yet during the campaign the polls showed Labor well ahead, maintaining its adequate lead. It was not surprising that they stuck to a campaign strategy which appeared to be winning the election for them. Further, the party believed it should stick to the consistency of its message; it did not want to lose momentum in the last week, or to shift its ground. Throughout the party concentrated on the electronic media, believing it was far more influential to run shots there than to buy large advertisments in the national newspapers.

The great bonus throughout the campaign was Hayden's own performance. Far from overshadowing him, the creation of the troika seemed to increase his stature. The Labor Party initially planned to run the policy speech one night and then, in the televised version the next evening, to interweave messages into the program. But Hayden's presentation was so good that those proposals were scrapped and the whole program was taken up by the policy speech itself. Hayden gained in confidence as the campaign progressed. He may have made one or two tactical errors; since the prevention of tax evasion was one of the themes of Labor's campaign, he challenged Fraser to publish his recent tax return, agreeing that he would then publish his own. Yet most people probably think individual tax returns are private and disliked the implicit connotation that Fraser was trying to evade paying tax.

For the first time Hayden brought his family into public view. His wife, Dallas, joined him on the campaign trail. The picture presented of Hayden was that of a family man, modest, responsible, pleasant and above all in touch with the problems of the average man—in contrast to Fraser who simply "wouldn't understand". He was the man that sought consensus, not confrontation. Whereas Fraser's tactics in the last weeks were to hold street rallies in the hope of violent scenes from opponents, Hayden ostentatiously abandoned proposals for street campaigns at the first signs of such problems. He stated that he did not want to do anything that might provoke trouble. By the time of his Press Club luncheon in the last week of the campaign, Hayden was relaxed, humorous, in control of every situation. Although he was always cautious about the result, he was clearly buoyed up by the polls and was beginning to behave like the Prime Minister that the polls were predicting he would soon become.

The Labor campaign cost $1.5 million. One million dollars went on the media advertising. It was not an increased commitment from

1977; rather the costs had increased by about a third since then. The unions as usual provided donations; so too did big business. Initially the party seemed to be asking for funds from business on the grounds that the country needed a strong opposition. As one letter put it "I do not necessarily seek from you a commitment to the ALP but I do seek a commitment to the strength of democracy in Australia". But as the polls suggested that Labor might win, so the size, rather than the numbers, of business donations increased. Access to a potential governing party is essential. In that respect, even though resources for the Labor Party were far scarcer than for its opponents, the polls must have aided Labor funds.

Policy

Hayden's policy speech was deliberately a contrast in style to those of Whitlam. It was low key, limited in scope and presented to a quiet audience in the Greek Community Centre, a location that illustrated the party's commitment to the ethnic communities. In the months before the election the Labor Party had issued a series of detailed policies for specific areas. In his policy speech Hayden concentrated on the main themes—Labor's approach was to unite the country: "They are policies to bring Australians together, not drive them apart ... policies that unite our country ... policies that allow all Australians to share our national good fortune and to play their part in the development of our future.[16] But there were bound to be limitations on what the government could do:

> I don't pretend there are easy solutions. There are not. I don't suggest that a rash of election promises is all that's needed to meet these challenges. They won't ... and the record of the Fraser government proves that they won't.
>
> And I do *not* claim that a Hayden Labor Government can produce some magic formula overnight to correct all the mistakes, all the hardship, and all the disunity created since 1975. We can't.
>
> What we *do* offer ... What we *can* promise ... is a more equal, a fairer, and a better Australian society than all of us have known in the last five years.[17]

The details reflected this sombre approach. In his reply to the Budget a month before Hayden had indicated that Labor had been considering three possible methods for returning spending power to the electors: a small tax cut, a reduction in sales tax, or a three-cent-a-litre cut in petrol taxes. He now promised to implement the tax cut. He also promised to overhaul the tax structure, to make much greater efforts than the Liberals to reduce the high level of unemployment, to freeze the price of locally produced oil for twelve months and to move towards the reestablishment of a universal health insurance scheme. He expected that these steps would help to restore between $10 and $20 a week to the average living wage. Further, he argued that pensions should be raised to 25 percent of average weekly earnings. The charges were to be paid for by three measures: the introduction of a resources tax, the abolition of the investment allowance "under which machines are replacing jobs", and the prevention of tax avoidance. He argued that $1000 million a year was being lost to the government by tax avoidance schemes which would be outlawed retrospectively by legislation. In foreign affairs Hayden declared that a Labor government would immediately withdraw recognition of the Pol Pot regime in Kampuchea and that: "more broadly Australia is firmly allied with the United States as the result of a Labor Government's far sighted attitudes forty years ago".[18]

There were comparatively few changes to that initial speech during the campaign. Hayden promised that no wealth tax would be introduced in the next Parliament and that tariffs would not be reduced; *ad hoc* decisions were comparatively limited. The six basic themes—on taxes, housing, jobs, petrol and energy prices, family health care, and family allowances — were plugged consistently and, the polls seemed to suggest, successfully.

Labor made no attempt to react to the advertising campaigns conducted by the Liberals in the last week that emphasised the potentially dire consequences of a Labor victory, particularly in regard to inflation and the introduction of a capital gains tax. Money was short, and the party believed that such changes in tactics might be counterproductive. When the Liberal government published costings of the Labor Party's promises undertaken by the Federal Treasury, Labor reacted with costings of the Liberal promises by the New South Wales Treasury, and argued that they were much higher. The debate disappeared into mumbo-jumbo that was unintelligible to the average voter. The Liberals argued that a Labor government would soon have increased the inflation rate to 20 percent per annum, a figure that they admitted later had been plucked out of the air with the attempt to scare voters. In the face of such provocation Hayden remained cool; he refused to react or to make unwise prophesies. Nevertheless, after the election Labor did react. It launched appeals to the High Court against the Liberal victories in twelve marginal seats (just enough to overcome their minority of twenty-three if all results were reversed), arguing that the advertising campaign of the Liberals breached the electoral act.

Some issues never did surface. Although the Liberal Party made much of the resources boom that would bring prosperity to the country, Labor's existing policy ban on the export of uranium was seldom discussed. Foreign policy was relatively bi-partisan (despite Liberal attempts to raise the Communist threat). Education was not a theme, for once, on which the parties differed. Nor, despite the inconsistency of the Liberal policy towards medical insurance, was health. Throughout the campaign the Labor Party managed to determine the issues which were to be discussed. Their campaign was widely regarded as brilliantly executed—coherent, persuasive, well directed and presented, even if a mite cynical. But those judgements were made primarily on the eve of the poll.

Results and Implications

On polling day Labor's hopes were high, primarily because of the polls of which most still remained apprehensive. But as the votes were counted, it never really seemed likely that Labor would win. It did well in Victoria, winning seven seats: for the first time since the 1955 split it held a majority of seats in the State. The major reversal of previous performances was in McMillan, where the Democratic Labor Party, once the sworn enemy of Labor, directed its preferences to Labor. Surprisingly, they held tightly and Labor won the seat. One commentator even suggested that in Victoria women were now no longer more conservative than men. In New South Wales Labor won two seats and lost one country seat. Its comparatively poor performance there—given Wran's popularity it was expected to do much better—was attributed later to the Liberals' advertising on the possibility of a capital gains tax. Property values in Sydney are much higher than in the rest of Australia. The likelihood of a tax on capital gains from the sale of residences did, according to Labor spokesmen after the election, frighten off many of those young marrieds in the mortgage belts of suburbia whose votes were needed for Labor to win seats. In the four smaller States it won a mere four new seats (two in Queensland, two in Western Australia and, once again, none in Tasmania). It also won one seat in the Australian Capital Territory. In Queensland, Western Australia and Tasmania combined, Labor held eight out of thirty-five seats. In New South Wales, Victoria and South Australia, it held forty-one out of eighty-seven seats. It was the periphery that ensured that Labor was well short of office.

Labor's main problem was that it did not draw adequate votes from Liberal supporters of 1977. Its increase, especially apparent on election night, was at the expense of the Democrats. If it is to win, it is Liberal voters that it must convert.

Hayden's performance, so much more dominant than widely anticipated, ensured that the internal changes to the parliamentary party were small. In a caucus meeting on November 7, Hayden and Bowen were returned unopposed; Button was elected to the leadership in the Senate and in the only contested leadership position, Don Grimes became deputy leader in the Senate. In the choice of the shadow executive, Hawke was successful, as were three or four younger and talented members. The Labor front-bench looks stronger now than at any time in the past twenty years. As long as Hayden and his colleagues perform adequately, and no major split develops, there is unlikely to be any change before the 1983 election. If Hayden does not win then he, probably voluntarily, will vacate the leadership.

In policy terms no major change will occur; the centralist, economically conservative policies adopted by Hayden and Hawke will continue. The Labor party in 1983 will look similar to that of 1980. The fact that the party came so close to victory in gross percentage terms, and the small change of vote needed next time to push it into power, will probably mean that not many changes will occur in policy or organizational terms.

After the election, Labor supporters compared the result to that of 1969 when under Whitlam's leadership the party reduced the vast 1966 deficit and was within striking distance of power. No one compared it to the 1954 or 1961 elections when Labor came even closer to victory and then fell back. No one seriously argues that it is easier to win power in two stages. The unknowns are too considerable. The economy may improve, the Liberals could scarcely run a worse campaign, international events may create changed circumstances. The Labor Party may redevelop its internal problems. Whether it can keep the votes that it gained and attract more is the challenge. In the meantime the Labor party will continue on the same track. The analogies to the 1969 election were drawn partly as a means of consolation, partly in hope, partly as a method of finding some achievement in an election that turned out as everyone had expected in July but that had promised so much in the later stages of the campaign.

Notes

1 *Australian Financial Review*, July 10, 1980.
2 See Howard R. Penniman, ed., *The Australian National Elections of 1977* (Washington, D.C.: American Enterprise Institute, 1979), particularly ch. 2 and ch. 11.
3 For the development of the Federal executive, see the introduction to Patrick Weller and Beverly Lloyd, eds, *Federal Executive Minutes, 1915– 1955* Melbourne: (Melbourne University Press, 1978).
4 For a discussion of the class basis of Australian politics, see D.A. Aitkin *Stability and Change in Australian Politics* (Canberra: A.N.U. Press 1977), and David Kemp, *Society and Electoral Behaviour in Australia* (St Lucia, Qld: University of Queensland Press, 1979).
5 For details on Hawke, see below p.62 and p.66.
6 For a convenient source, see Australian Labor Party, National Committee of Inquiry, Discussion Papers (A.P.S.A. Monograph no 23).
7 Australian Labor Party, National Committee of Inquiry, *Report and Recommendations to the National Executive* (Canberra, 1979).
8 The only other person was Joe Lyons in 1929; and he had been a member of the State Parliament for twenty years and resigned the premiership of Tasmania to enter Federal politics.
9 *Age*, October 13, 1980.
10 R.J. Hawke, *The Resolution of Conflict*, Boyer Lectures 1979.
11 See *Australian Labor Party Platform, Constitution and Rules*, 1979, p. 3.
12 A. Theophanous, "The Labor Campaign: analysis & critique", in Peter Hay, Ian Ward, John Warhurst, eds, *Anatomy of an Election*, (Melbourne: Hill of Content, 1979), p. 59.
13 ALP, 33rd Biennial Conference, Adelaide 1979, Transcript, p. 351; for a wide ranging discussion of the future of the ALP, see J. North and P. Weller eds, *Labor: Directions for the Eighties*, (Sydney: 1980 Novak).
14 Quoted in *Age*, October 13, 1980.
15 *National Times*, October 24,' 1980.
16 Address by Bill Hayden to the Opening of Labor's Federal Election Campaign 1980, p. 1.
17 ibid., p. 2.
18 ibid., p. 11.

5

The National Country Party

Keith Richmond

The National Country Party (NCP)[1] remains a constant enigma in Australian politics. Since it was formed in 1920, the Federal party has helped to govern the nation for forty-three years.[2] As a rural minority party polling around 10 percent of the national vote in the most urbanized country in the world, it should enjoy little political success. But the NCP has persisted against every adversity: it maintains its capacity as a political force despite a declining electoral base and constant attempts at undermining its position of power by the urban-based political parties.

Yet the record of the NCP is impressive.[3] Since it first joined in a Federal coalition government as the minority partner in 1923, the party has grown used to the fruits of office. In government the NCP is granted the Deputy Prime Ministership and a brace of ministerial portfolios dear to the concerns of its supporters—Treasury (until the 1950s), Trade, Communications, Transport, Interior, and Primary Industry are usual. Moreover, its virtually permanent governing status since 1923 has allowed the NCP to have a significant impact on the administration of settled policies as well as the introduction and implementation of a range of other issues which have affected the face of Australian life.

Much of the NCP's dominance (and a sizable amount of the explanation for coalition governments enjoying so much time in office), can be explained in terms of the NCP's electoral strength. The party usually wins about twenty seats of a lower house total of approximately 125, leaving the Liberal and Labor Parties to share the other 105 or so. Further, the NCP usually contests only those seats it has a chance of winning (thus conserving its resources); it customarily offers good quality candidates; it is overwhelmingly pragmatic in its political methods—such as using multiple endorsement of candidates—and it is fortunate in having its electoral support concentrated in a limited number of electorates. The NCP has also been assisted in maintaining its political strength by the retention of particular measures including compulsory voting, preferential voting, and by legislating to ensure rural electorates have less voters than city electorates.

These factors have helped to give the NCP electoral stability. Federal representation, for example, has varied but little since the early 1920s. It held twelve seats out of seventy-five in 1922; in 1956 it held thirteen seats out of seventy-four; in 1958 it held nineteen out of a total of 122 seats; in 1977 it held twenty-three out of 127; and entering the 1980 elections, the NCP had nineteen out of a total of 124 House seats. Electoral volatility, it should be added, is more a feature of urban rather than rural politics; a basic conservatism dominates the rural political scene.

This is not to claim that the NCP is the only party capable of winning rural seats. But the NCP has been much more successful—because of its limited ambitions—in carving its niche as the specialist rural party. The Liberal and Labor Parties are urban based and, therefore, are suspect to many country dwellers. The Liberals are seen to side with the merchants and bankers, both traditional enemies of rural folk; while Labor has long talked of socializing the land, and of keeping high the cost of rural labor. The larger urban parties have tried to garner the rural vote but their efforts have been fragmentary and inconsistent. In contrast, the NCP has enjoyed remarkable (albeit limited in the wider sense) success for around sixty years.

If two features of the NCP can be said to characterize its success, these might be its electoral stability and its capacity for survival. For a party accustomed to joining in coalitions, both features have been necessary. A few of its State branches have found more success with a "support-in-return-for-concessions" strategy, while others—and including the Federal party—have worked toward a coalition approach. But the latter mode is not as genteel as the phrase infers. It implies a working relationship which depends for its success on particular benefits being awarded—and this is effectively a support-for-concessions strategy which can be called upon at any time when the minority partner is dissatisfied. By manipulating this relationship via the use of coercion and threats (customarily the threat is to leave the coalition and vote as independents), but overwhelmingly by offering valued support, the NCP has become an essential part of the nation's governance.

These remarks should not be taken to imply the NCP has few

difficulties in achieving its goals, and some of its problems have been canvassed above. Even at the Federal level the party is an effective force only in New South Wales, the Northern Territory and Queensland, with little strength in Victoria. But at the State level, the party is virtually nonexistent in South Australia and Tasmania, it has massive problems in remaining in coalition in Western Australia and Queensland, it is a weak force in Victoria, and only in New South Wales and the Northern Territory, can it claim any level of stability. In this mass of contradictions lies the amorphous body known as the NCP.

One of the little researched attributes of the Federal NCP is the particular style of its leaders and parliamentarians, which has contributed to its political success. We might consider the following. First, NCP leaders have been remarkably strong politicians—as witnessed by the popular images of Earle Page, John McEwen, Arthur Fadden, and Doug Anthony. These men have been—despite their faults—masterful pragmatists, opportunists, and hard negotiators. Secondly, senior NCP politicians have enjoyed a reputation for toughness under stress. Today's crop of Doug Anthony, Ian Sinclair, and Peter Nixon rank among the most astute, most professional and toughest parliamentarians-cum-platform performers in Australian politics. Many Federal NCP politicians seem to have a natural affinity with the brutish "if you see a head, kick it" style of politics. Thirdly, the Federal NCP is characterized by a smooth working relationship: limited objectives, a homogeneity of background, and shared ambition assists in molding a common identity. Fourthly, there is a dual theme of loyalty: NCP supporters give a very high level of loyalty to the party and expect benefits in return, while Federal NCP parliamentarians offer a high level of loyalty to their party leader and expect fidelity in return.

In sum, Federal NCP parliamentarians have been recognized over many years as superb horsetraders, opportunists, and pork barrel specialists. They are masterful proponents of a finely honed pragmatic style, who know when to push their nonlabor counterparts and when to accept what benefits have been gained. This capacity for toughness has occasionally been mixed with apparent naivete, but almost always it has been combined with amiability, country good manners, and charm.

NCP History and Organization

While the NCP came to prominence from about World War I, the seeds of the party's success were sown in the middle of the preceding century. Farmers believed they were engaged in a higher or elevated form of vocation and that they occupied a sanctified position in society. They also saw that they were underprivileged in relation to others. City merchants especially were seen as conspiring to prevent them from achieving their ambitions. Some form of political organization was recognized as being necessary to redress their grievances. Rural organizations of various forms were tried, with permanent rural pressure groups being established by the 1890s. Access to political structures was deemed crucial, and a "country party" offering economic and political salvation was seen as the answer.

Any new party, however, had many obstacles to overcome. The Labor Party talked of socializing the land; the urban dominance of the major parties worried many country people (especially as so few benefits were forthcoming to the country); and the party "fusion" of 1909 encouraged any new party to link itself with one of the dominant blocs. The years surrounding World War I provided a necessary impetus for party formation. Wheat farmers—supported by the rural pressure groups formed in the 1890s—with their concern over marketing and tariffs were in the forefront of political activity. Over a period of less than a decade (1914–22) the new party emerged at different times in all States; it was first formed at the Federal level in 1920. The NCP was allowed to have a significant impact on the political system because of the introduction of preferential voting at the Federal level in 1918. This device allowed nonlabor candidates to stand in a constituency—provided voters directed their preferences to the coalition partners—and be assured that the nonlabor vote was not split.

The party held office in various States from 1914. But it was not until the December 1922 elections that the new Federal party was placed in a situation of holding the balance of power. Following some very hard negotiations, the leader of the NCP, Earle Page, achieved a significant role for his party in a nonlabor coalition. More significantly, Page established the ground rules that the two parties have followed ever since in forming coalitions.

Since 1923, the Liberals and the NCP have grown to accept the benefits of a coalition government. The Liberals accept that NCP support is usually required in the lower house and almost always in the Senate. The Federal NCP realizes that without the Liberals, it is almost powerless to achieve its aims, for its members have little stomach for the style and philosophies of Labor, although many policies might be similar.

Whether the perspective is on simply staying in power, the

implementation or selling of policies, parliamentary performance or in election campaigning, there are very great advantages in maintaining a harmonious coalition. A cohesive team in easy to lead: it can offer solid policy initiatives and strong government, and it represents a formidable opponent. In elections, for example, the Liberals focus on the urban centers while the NCP concentrates on rural constituencies.

The theme of coalition is compromise—a true marriage of convenience. Harmony in a meeting of highly individualistic parties with a will to win is not easy to achieve. Any coalition will be confronted by a succession of problems, among them being the personalities and ambitions of the party leaders, the demands of parliamentarians and their supporters, and the basic attitude of the parties toward coalition (the latter becomes more important for the NCP in the State context). That the Federal coalition has lasted as long as it has is a tribute to the attitude of the leaders—and to their pragmatic political instincts for fostering coalition unity. But with the best intention possible, some notable coalition rifts have occurred, including the NCP's refusal to serve with some nonlabor leaders—W.M. Hughes, R.G. Menzies, and W.M. McMahon. Despite these examples, the Federal coalition has been maintained with a surprising level of amicability for a long period.

State coalitions are less secure. In Western Australia and Victoria the NCP on past occasions has joined in coalition with Labor; in both States a more independent mode is seen as normal behaviour. In the Northern Territory and New South Wales the coalition functions satisfactorily, while the party in recent years has been able to win but one seat in South Australia and seems unable to gain a foothold in Tasmania. In Queensland, owing to population distribution and electoral boundary drawing, the NCP has been the dominant coalition partner in the government since 1957. Coalition relations there are so acrimonious, however, that it appears to be only a matter of time until the coalition disintegrates and the nonlabor government is forced into opposition. But despite the differences among the State branches, the NCP everywhere represents a continuing theme of agrarian resentment against urban political dominance.

Policies of the party have changed but little in fundamentals since the movement towards "a country party" began in the last century. The linked themes of conspiracy by city interests and the belief that those living in the country are a worthy people, are still expounded. Party leader J.D. (Doug) Anthony said at the 1980 NCP Federal Conference: "We have policies specifically designed to try to meet the special needs of people who do not have the benefits and privileges enjoyed in our great cities where the preponderance of the Australian people and power lies".[4]

Party policies are tailored to satisfy these beliefs. Organized marketing schemes for primary producers, tariff protection, valuation of the Australian currency, defense policies, anti-communism— these are the foci on which the NCP builds its rural support. Some critics claim the NCP is a party of rural socialists, but Doug Anthony says that he prefers to describe the NCP as being "perhaps a little more pragmatic than the Liberals in terms of its attitude to government involvement in industry and commerce".[5]

NCP policy is very largely a mirror of dominant rural ideas. Matters of concern in the local farmers' organizations, local government circles, rural women's groups, ex-service groups, and community organizations will also be of concern to the NCP. Sometimes this means that the same people are prominent in both the NCP branch structure and other community groups. But it is more probable that regional political culture is best represented in the NCP forum.

NCP policy is channeled through the branch structure to electorate councils—regional bodies focussing on State or Federal electorates. These structures are usually responsible for selecting parliamentary candidates, endorsing sitting members, raising necessary finance, and planning election campaigns. At State Conferences, policy is further refined.[6]

The State NCP bodies are both powerful and virtually autonomous, accepting little direction from the Federal organization. The Federal structure, in contrast, has more capacity for offering advice than for determining events, and recent revamping has done little to change its toothless image. Party leader Anthony has tried to introduce, *inter alia*, Federal Conferences for supporters, and a management committee to streamline administration, but little benefit has been apparent from these changes.

The NCP is supported by a predominantly rural-based bloc of people. Most have links with the land (including farmers, graziers, farm employees) and the productivity of the land (stock and station agents, shop owners, rural professionals, or white-collar workers employed in the towns). Generally the NCP member will be uninterested in his party provided he can attend to his employment free of unwarranted intrusions. Usually NCP meetings are poorly attended and branch executive positions are filled with extreme reluctance— yet paradoxically, this is a sign of supporters' contentment with the performance of their party.

Despite these favorable features, NCP leaders have long worried over the party's future. The possibility of coalition with the Liberals is raised sporadically but comes to little. In the 1960s party leader John McEwen widened the base of the party to include the mining and extractive industries. From the early 1970s Doug Anthony tried his hand: he advocated joining with the now virtually defunct Democratic Labor Party in order to gain an urban base (voters rebelled against the alliance); and he caused the party's name change to the *National Country Party* (largely a symbolic move), complete with wider platform and policy. As part of this stratagem some suburban seats were contested, especially at State level in Queensland, but with little real success. The urban Australian voter saw through these ploys and rejected them: the NCP is seen to represent the rural voter, and to do this well, but it cannot claim to be a true national party.

The NCP, 1977–80

Within the Liberal-NCP coalition government from 1977 to 1980, the NCP had to bide its time while the Liberals had overwhelming parliamentary support (sufficient indeed to govern alone). In 1980 the pendulum was sure to swing, leaving the NCP in a balance of power position again. While the NCP suffered its defeats—including the defection of Northern Territory Senator Bernie Kilgariff to the Liberals in March 1979—its constant aim was to support the coalition and expect to achieve a greater level of control later. And the NCP's way was not easy. Owing to the Liberals's majority, the NCP was not in a good bargaining position to exact concessions, although the usual ministerial portfolios were forthcoming. Moreover, Prime Minister Fraser was an irritant to the NCP because he represented a rural constituency, and he often preempted the NCP in agrarian policy matters.

The NCP was placed in an invidious position. On the one hand, it was outgunned by Fraser and the Liberals, and the NCP was often accused of being powerless to extract benefits for its supporters. Yet because the senior NCP men and Fraser were on good personal terms, many Liberals were worried that the NCP was able to distort Liberal policies and orient them in directions more receptive to NCP plaudits.

From 1977 to 1980 the NCP encountered a range of problems. The first issue concerned deputy NCP leader, Ian Sinclair. Deficiencies were found in financial returns of funeral companies with which the Sinclair family was associated. Sinclair requested an investigation be held into the missing funds, and a New South Wales Corporate Affairs Commission report accepted there was no wrong doing on his part. The Labor Party sensed the possibility for revenge for Sinclair's role in the Labor downfall of 1975. Sinclair was subjected to torrid criticism focussing around his capacity to hold public office: any criticism of this able and astute minister could be projected as a general failing of a tired and corrupt government.

The New South Wales Labor Attorney-General, Frank Walker, then claimed he had uncovered new evidence, and a special inspector—Michael Finnane—was appointed under the State Companies Act to review the matter. Finnane subsequently tabled a report in State Parliament which contained sufficient evidence so that Malcolm Fraser required Doug Anthony to relieve Sinclair of his (Federal) parliamentary offices in September 1978. Eventually the case came to trial in the State Supreme Court: following a twenty- three-day hearing, Sinclair was found not guilty of nine charges involving forgery, uttering and wilfully making false statements. Sinclair was restored to Cabinet, his parliamentary positions, and to deputy leadership of the NCP, in August 1980.[7]

In the same year—1978—that Sinclair came under heavy Labor criticism, another problem plagued the NCP. A faction emerged in the parliamentary party which became known as "the young Turks". (Factions in other parties are commonplace, but most unusual in the Federal NCP.) These younger NCP men—allegedly including Lusher, Fisher, McKenzie, and Lloyd—were irritated especially over their prospects in the party. They saw that, being comparatively young men in their thirties and early forties, they would be likely to languish on the backbench for years while the "elder" NCP statesmen (Sinclair, Anthony, Hunt, Nixon), only a few years more senior, governed the country. The "young Turks" offered a show of strength in defeating the long-serving NCP man, Phil Lucock, for the post of chairman of committees and deputy speaker in early 1978: Lucock was replaced with the comparatively unknown Clarrie Millar.[8]

State coalition wrangles—largely arising because of rivalries between Liberals who wish to rule alone, and NCP members demanding concessions for remaining in coalition—are of concern to their Federal counterparts because of the spill-over effect which undermines the image of stability that is cultivated. In New South Wales the NCP has long accepted the role of a fairly conservative and dutiful junior coalition partner. Two events (both of which are of minor importance as issues) highlight the tension under the surface calm. First, when the State Labor government announced plans for an electoral redistribution, the Liberals suggested that the electorate of the NCP leader, Leon Punch, be abolished. Secondly, Labor Premier Neville Wran suggested that he would contemplate asking the parliamentary speaker to declare which of the leaders of the near-equal nonlabor parties would become the opposition leader. The level of rancour evident in both cases from the coalition partners illustrates that the harmonious facade hides a surprising quantity of bitterness.[9] With the redistribution completed and with Labor's hold on the State apparently secure for a generation, there will be ample opportunity to watch the opposition parties work out a formula for survival.

In Victoria, the NCP has traditionally been a rebel party. As a general rule, the NCP and Liberals cooperate adequately at the Federal level, but at the State level the relations are acrimonious. A spill-over occurred in 1979 when sections in the State Liberal party decided to stand a candidate against Federal NCP minister, Peter Nixon. While eventually rejected, such moves are contrary to the agreement in the State which denies the right of one coalition party to stand candidates against a minister from the other coalition party.[10] Attempt such as the one to oppose Nixon are hardly remarkable in the Victorian context. At the last State election the NCP refused to direct its preferences—thus denying any automatic flow-on to the Liberals—and Labor directed some preferences to the NCP. Moreover, at their 1979 State Conference, the Liberals supported moves to contest all State seats, and to offer a separate Senate ticket. The proposed Senate ticket was eventually amended so that the NCP was given the unwinnable third coalition position.

In Western Australia the NCP has long pursued a radical approach to politics. It has entered into coalitions with both Labor and Liberals, but it seems most comfortable being fiercely independent, even when it is in coalition with the Liberals as in recent years. Three-cornered contests among the NCP, Liberals, and Labor have become an accepted part of electoral competition. The NCP has not held a Federal seat for some time and it is unlikely to do so in the near future. At the State level the NCP usually forms part of a coalition government with the Liberals; but the relationship between the partners is inevitably marked by mistrust and bitterness: over the past few years the NCP and Liberals have split publicly on a number of occasions.

Some evidence of the difficulties faced in the West is seen in the split within the NCP in 1978. Following a series of public wrangles, the NCP parliamentary and organizational wings divided into the NCP and the National Party.[11] Amusingly enough, the Liberals hold more parliamentary rural seats than either of the splinters, so it is the Liberal Party that can best claim to be rural-based.

In Queensland since 1957, the NCP—not the Liberals as elsewhere—have led a coalition government; the Liberals have been junior coalition partners since the mid-1930s. This galling position of Liberal subservience has helped to make coalition problems in Queensland the worst anywhere. At the heart of the problem is the electoral arrangement. Queensland is characterized by having its greatest population in the southeast corner, and in a small number of provincial cities scattered along the coast—the inland is sparsely populated. The coalition has divided the State into four population zones: the southeastern zone (forty-seven electorates averaging 16,400 voters); provincial cities zone (thirteen electorates averaging 16,000 voters); western, far western, and far northern zone (six seats averaging 8,600 voters); and the country zone (fifteen seats averaging 11,500 voters). Of the 22 undersized seats in 1980, the NCP held twenty-one and the Liberals none.

The coalition has ruled since 1957. Current Premier, Johannes Bjelke-Petersen ("Joh" to everybody), is the longest-serving Premier in the history of the State. While the Liberals resent the dominance of Petersen and want to rule alone, they have no real desire to sit on the opposition benches for a generation.[13]

Coalition wrangles are legion. Three-cornered contests, bitterness, preselection battles, and public slanging matches are the stuff of Queensland coalition politics. Nor is the public debate confined to junior parliamentarians. During the late 1970s Liberal Senator Neville Bonner and Federal Minister for Finance, Eric Robinson, declared their support for separate tickets and the beginning of the long-heralded war of attrition against the NCP.[14]

In mid-1980 the State Liberals decided to run a separate Senate ticket to offer the voters a separate identity from the NCP. The NCP's response to this was typically brazen and contemptuous. After long hours of discussion—and not a little arm-twisting by the Premier— Florence (Flo) Bjelke-Petersen, wife of the Premier, was selected to lead the NCP Senate ticket. Flo Bjelke-Petersen had no previous political experience and was mocked constantly by sections of the media for her culinary skills (pumpkin scones and lamingtons) and homely manner. Second place on the ticket went to Senator Glen Shiel, and third place to the former ticket leader, Senator Ron Maunsell.[15]

For years critics had talked of Queensland as the "Flo and Joh show", of Flo's lamingtons and homespun philosophies: one placard at a subsequent NCP conference read "No matter how Joh's fortunes may ebb, there will always be a Flo". Perhaps Flo's charm was best captured in a paragraph (later widely circulated) which first appeared in the Queensland *Gold Coast Bulletin*: "Flo is as homely as a sponge cake with passionfruit icing, as comfortable as a squatter's chair on a shady verandah, as straightforward and practical as a yabby pump, as wholesome as a plump, ripe mango".[16] For all the cuteness of the political strategem, however, there was a serious problem in the choice of Flo. One southern journalist described her selection to the NCP's only safe Senate seat as the act only a party of "cretinous irresponsibility" would undertake.[17]

Issues and the 1980 Campaign

Entering the 1980 election period, the NCP realized it might lose significant support in the Senate poll. Victorian Senator Laurie Neal, an academic in his thirties appointed to complete Senator Webster's term, was in the virtually unwinnable third position on the Victorian coalition Senate ticket. Senator Maunsell in Queensland had only a remote chance of winning a seat—despite the efforts of many North Queenslanders to campaign for Maunsell first and Flo Bjelke-Petersen third—and even Senator Shiel was not in a favored position. In the lower house poll, the NCP boasted it would hold all its seats and pick up some more—Indi in Victoria, Riverina in New South Wales and the new seat of O'Connor in Western Australia.

Among the NCP's greatest difficulties was selling its domestic oil pricing policy. The coalition government—largely under the prompting of NCP leader Anthony—had adopted import parity pricing for oil. This meant that cheaply produced local oil was charged to the fuel-consuming public at world price: the public was forced to pay a heavy surcharge to make up the difference between domestic and overseas prices.

Anthony tried very hard to advertise the advantages of the oil pricing policy (which was intended to promote fuel conservation and stimulate further development and exploration). He claimed that under Labor rule there had been no oil or fuels policy and no guarantee that consumers would have access to fuel in future years. But the long-suffering motorist and farmer were far from convinced of the virtues of this artificial pricing policy. (Surprisingly, however, this issue seems not to have cost the coalition too many votes in the subsequent election.)

The Liberal-NCP government was vulnerable in other areas.[18] Elected on promises to mend the economy, the government was saddled with high inflation (over 10 percent) and unemployment (approaching 6 percent of the workforce). There was also the rising price of fuel and an array of broken promises—all of which led to a lowered standard of living, according to Labor.

Moreover, Labor had successfully personalized the coalition's failures by blaming almost everything on Prime Minister Fraser: Fraser was projected as arrogant, uncaring and aloof, and responsible for not mending the nation's ills.[19]

As far back as March 1980, the NCP had established two campaign bodies: a Federal committee to include parliamentary members and a coordinating committee to include State branches[20] (the importance of the organization at State level is evident by the use of this ploy). By the time the campaign had begun the NCP and Liberals had patched some of their differences at State level: it was decided that a no-poaching agreement would exist in both Victorian and Queensland Lower House seats.

The four senior NCP Ministers—Anthony, Sinclair, Hunt, and Nixon—concentrated on marginal electorates including Leichhardt, Calare, and Northern Territory, and the possible gains of Riverina, Indi, and O'Connor. The party was to spend some $300,000 at the Federal level on radio, television, and newspaper advertising. The figure of $300,000 was expected to be tripled by additional campaign spending in electorates.[21]

Television advertising was released to twenty-one channels throughout Australia. Featuring Doug Anthony, the commercials began with a general theme—the importance of rural Australia—then led into a range of issues focussing around the slogan "Keep Australia Strong". These issues included fuel policy, Australia's future, rural industry, the economy, leadership, free enterprise, defense, and the role of the NCP.[22]

Advertisements were taken out in the mass circulation *Australian Women's Weekly* for the first time, in an attempt to win the women's vote for Flo Bjelke-Petersen. The NCP secretariat planned to issue two press releases per day in the campaign as well as releasing additional material for rural newspapers.

Doug Anthony delivered the NCP policy speech at Tweed Heads (in Anthony's electorate) on October 1. As expected, the speech contained numerous promises, especially those designed to ease the resentment over rising fuel prices, including concessions for fuel storage facilities. There were also concessions for soil conservation, rural electricity generation, depreciation allowances for new agricultural machinery and so on.[23]

Farm lobby groups were pleased with the bounty: the Cattlemen's Union said farmers had done better from election promises than any other interest group.[24] Typically, the urban newspapers were scathing. The Melbourne *Age* headlined its edititorial: "There's still a Santa Claus" and spoke of the NCP approach as promising a "cornucopia of concessions, incentives and projects to the rural electorate". As the *Age* snidely remarked, Anthony's simplistic message "Keep Australia Strong" "made a change from seeing a socialist under every haystack".[25] The *Canberra Times* made criticism of the NCP's "wampum mentality".[26] But the NCP message was not aimed at the urban newspaper editors. It was directed at the traditional rural voter-those who responded to promises of future economic responsibility and strong leadership, and those who reacted to the idea of another era of disastrous Labor policies for the countryside.[27]

As opinion polls began predicting a likely Labor win, the NCP campaign found its stride. Voters were reminded of every scandal associated with the Whitlam era, of every rise in inflation, every unemployment shock, and Labor's "campaign of trickery that made Dr. Goebbels look like a beginner".[28]

Beyond the television advertisements and the exhausting campaigns of the leaders, much of the election was fought out in the local constituencies. It was here that the NCP strength lay: here also the irritations of the voters with issues such as rising fuel prices, inflation, and unemployment were clearly heard.

In seats as different as Leichhardt in north Queensland, Northern Territory, Riverina in western New South Wales, O'Connor in Western Australia, or Lyne in New South Wales, the most discussed issue was fuel prices. But next in importance were local concerns: defense and tourism in Leichhardt,[29] tax zone allowances and development in Northern Territory,[30] and drought aid in O'Connor,[31] Hume, and most other, parched electorates.

The NCP faced an uphill battle to retain a number of electorates. In Northern Territory and Lyne, sitting NCP members had resigned and their personal votes were lost. In Leichhardt, the margin needed to allow the seat to change hands was only 1 percent; it was 2.6 percent in Northern Territory. But the NCP had a few items in its favor too. The seat of Leichhardt was held by David Thomson, the first NCP member of a Federal ministry ever appointed from north Queensland; local chauvinism made the seat more difficult to lose. Riverina in New South Wales—while redistributed in Labor's favor in 1977—had lost its Labor incumbent and with only a 0.2 percent swing required, the NCP sensed a possible victory.[32] In addition, the NCP and Liberals had ended their differences over contesting each other's seats against the rules (the seat of McPherson might be an exception), and this level of harmony was desirable in any election.[33]

Two particular contests in Queensland caught the attention of the media: Flo Bjelke-Petersen's Senate campaign, and the campaign against Finance Minister Eric Robinson. Eric Robinson had a reputation for being anti-NCP. When the NCP decided not to run candidates against sitting Liberals, one branch member of the NCP, Lou Rowan, resigned from his party to contest Robinson's seat of McPherson. This was seen as a betrayal of good faith, especially when Premier Bjelke-Petersen endorsed Rowan's candidature and Rowan directed his preferences to Labor. While the NCP organization did not support Rowan, some of its members did so privately. One of the choicest quotes of the campaign came from Rowan, who said of Robinson: "He's a political submarine—he only shows up at election time".[34]

In her campaign for the Senate, Flo Bjelke-Petersen introduced the idea of a 20 percent flat rate tax. Labor leader Hayden scoffed at the plan, Liberal Treasurer John Howard was not impressed, and Labor's Bob Hawke said it made as much sense as the flat earth theory. Flo Bjelke-Petersen's concept had been approved by her party. It rested on two notions—that nontaxable income should be lifted to $6,000 and that a 20 percent flat rate income tax should be offered to those earning above $6,000. It promised significant savings (around 6 to 7 cents in the dollar) to most taxpayers—although the cost of introducing the scheme would most likely have been prohibitive. What Flo Bjelke-Petersen's articulation of the plan did demonstrate, however, was that Flo was not afraid of introducing new ideas; nor was she worried over attracting criticism.[35]

The Results—and the Aftermath

Most opinion polls predicted the wrong election winner. But the polls did predict the overall swing that occurred away from the government. Perhaps the findings of the polls released in the middle of the campaign urged the government to greater effort. Certainly the early complacency seemed to be replaced by near desperation as the Liberals (but particularly Prime Minister Fraser) focussed on the menace of socialism. Not that the NCP objected, for this allowed them to rerun their successful anti-Labor and anti-Whitlam campaigns of yore. It appears that the change of tactics by the coalition allowed them to consolidate their hold on government.

As noted earlier, the results of most federal elections have shown a surprising level of consistency in the NCP vote, and 1980 was little different. The NCP won twenty lower house seats, retaining all it had in 1977 and edging out Labor in Riverina after a close vote. It thus held Leichhardt, Calare, Lyne, and Northern Territory, but failed in its attempt to wrest O'Connor from the Liberals (the NCP still has no Federal representation in Western Australia). The overall NCP vote was 8.6 percent, down from 10 percent in 1977. The NCP vote dropped 4.4 percent in Queensland and 2.1 percent in Western Australia, largely because of the lesser number of seats contested.

The Senate poll offered few surprises. Senator Scott of New South Wales was favorably placed on the joint Senate ticket and was returned easily; Senator Laurie Neal of Victoria failed to retain his seat from the difficult third coalition ticket position; and Queensland Senators Maunsell and Shiel also failed to be returned. Perhaps the one surprise was Flo Bjelke-Petersen's ease in getting elected: she polled extremely well, receiving 252,783 votes. She was thus the second Senator elected for the State outpolling the popular Liberal Senator, Neville Bonner, who received a total of 242,884 votes. Flo Bjelke-Petersen effectively prevented the Liberal Yvonne McComb from being elected—but she did not gain sufficient votes to enable Senator Shiel to retain his position.[36] After July 1981 the NCP had three members only in the Senate, less than the Australian Democrats.

The NCP has cause for concern in the future. State coalition wrangles spilled over into some of the Federal campaigns—including the campaign in O'Connor, the effort to unseat Eric Robinson (where Lou Rowan reduced Robinson's majority by some 14,000 votes) and the selection of Flo Bjelke-Petersen—with the ramifications yet to be revealed. Joh Bjelke-Petersen's strategem worked in having his wife elected Senator, but what is likely to happen at the next Senate election? Can coalition differences be satisfactorily resolved, in that State especially?

Prime Minister Fraser's ministerial reshuffle following the election highlighted these and related questions. A Liberal Prime Minister's job in allocating portfolios is never easy. He has to take account of NCP demands and the need to balance State representation; and he has to recognize those parliamentarians with particular talents or support in the party (such as Andrew Peacock who requested and was given a demanding domestic portfolio).

The NCP demanded a higher proportion of ministries, but this bid failed. It was allocated six: Trade and Resources (Doug Anthony), the new Communications portfolio (Ian Sinclair), Primary Industry (Peter Nixon), Transport (Ralph Hunt), Science and Technology (David Thomson), and Housing and Construction (Tom McVeigh). Of the six, Anthony, Sinclair and Nixon are in the Cabinet. Ian Sinclair was back in favor and was given the tough area of Communications; Ralph Hunt was dropped from Cabinet ranking; and Queenslander Tom McVeigh replaced his State counterpart, Evan Adermann, in a low-ranking portfolio (Adermann was in Veteran Affairs).

But the most controversial action attributed to the NCP was the dumping from ministerial rank of Eric Robinson. Robinson was reportedly offered a demotion from Finance, to Business and Consumer Affairs. But he refused, so he was relegated to the backbench. Initial reports claimed Premier Bjelke-Petersen had demanded Robinson's sacking as retaliation for Robinson's role in attacking the Queensland NCP. Later stories stressed the resentment of Robinson by the Federal NCP bloc led by Anthony, and this has a greater level of credibility.[37]

Robinson's sacking needs to be seen in the context of coalition relations (and purely political questions such as the effect of disgruntled backbenchers on coalition stability will not be discussed here). First, to what extent should a Liberal leader succumb to minority demands, especially when this is at the expense of Liberal principles? Eric Robinson said on this: "An effective coalition requires a leader who strikes a proper balance between giving reasonable consideration to the views of the minority partner and at the same time giving loyalty to his own party and its parliamentary members.... It also requires a leader who is loyal to his party organization....''[38]

Secondly, and as a corollary, the question can be asked whether Malcolm Fraser listens more to the NCP than his own party. This question was raised in many quarters after the Robinson dismissal; one can be certain it will reappear on many occasions to come.[39] And thirdly, is it necessary to offer occasionally a sacrificial-cum-symbolic lamb—such as Robinson—on the altar of coalition relations? Over the past twenty years or so, the NCP and Liberals have differed on a range of issues and it was necessary that they be resolved before the coalition could continue. Thus, in 1962, Liberal Minister for Air, Les Bury, was forced to resign his ministry after he made statements that irritated NCP leader, John McEwen. As previously recounted, the NCP has refused to serve under a number of nonlabor leaders. Such examples demonstrate that the case of Eric Robinson is not unique—but it is a serious obstacle for the coalition nonetheless.

It is ironic that the closing remarks on the NCP must focus on the level of acceptance of the Liberal Party and its leaders to NCP demands. For all the electoral stability and political resilience of the NCP, it requires constant reexamination of its mode of operation if it is to survive. Being a minority partner in a long-standing coalition arrangement is a game best played by horsetraders—and at this the NCP excels. But the NCP must take care lest its demands do not become too onerous. Its future might be determined by its capacity to modify claims on its Liberal patrons so that the good governance of the nation is not brought into question, as it has been on numerous occasions in the past.

The NCP might be a political enigma but it is highly successful nonetheless. It represents—particularly at the Federal level—one of the finest examples of minority party tactics within a coalition arrangement. Political answers have always been more important to the NCP than fussy philosophical debate—and this remains a major factor in its success.

Notes

1 To maintain consistency I have used *National* Country Party as the name of the party throughout this chapter, although until 1975 the Federal body was known (as were most State branches) as the *Country* Party. In October 1982, in an attempt to broaden its electoral appeal, the party was again to change its name—to the National Party.
2 This claim was made by J.D. Anthony: *Canberra Times*, June 1, 1980.
3 Numerous studies have been made of the NCP, including: D. Aitkin, *The Country Party in New South Wales: A Study of Organization and Survival* (Canberra: Australian National University Press, 1972); D. Aitkin, "The Australian Country Party", in H. Mayer and H. Nelson, eds., *Australian Politics: A Third Reader* (Cheshire: Melbourne, 1973); B.D. Graham, *The Formation of the Australian Country Parties* (Canberra: Australian National University Press, 1966); K. Richmond, "The National Country Party", in G. Starr, K. Richmond, and G. Maddox, *Political Parties in Australia* (Melbourne: Heinemann, 1978).
4 *Canberra Times*, June 1, 1980.
5 *Weekend Australian*, June 21–22, 1980.
6 See Richmond, *Political Parties in Australia*, pp. 125 ff for discussion of the party structure. Reference to the 1980 NCP Platform revisions may be seen in Melbourne *Age*, September 13, 1980.
7 *Canberra Times*, August 19, 1980 offers brief summary of events.
8 *National Times*, October 28, 1978. Dispute arose also over the NCP parliamentary party's not fighting against the Liberals' 1977 electorate redistribution proposals. This incurred the wrath of backbenchers and many supporters. See *Australian*, August 14, 1980.
9 *Australian*, June 25, 1980; *Sydney Morning Herald*, August 2, 1979.
10 Melbourne *Age*, August 14, 1980; *Australian*, July 24, 1980.
11 *West Australian*, July 7, 1980; July 29, 1980.
12 Melbourne *Age*, September 6, 1979. For an extended discussion on coalition problems in Queensland, the electoral system and the level of distortion with zoning, see C.A. Hughes, *The Government of Queensland* (St. Lucia: University of Queensland Press, 1980).
13 While the Liberals toy with the idea of joining with Labor to revise electorate boundaries, the results of such actions might not necessarily assist the Liberals: see *Canberra Times*, December 3, 1980, and Melbourne *Age*, December 26, 1980 (letters to editor).

14 *Australian*, September 18, 1979, and Melbourne *Herald*, September 27, 1980.
15 For some comments on this issue, see Melbourne *Age*, July 26, 1980; *Canberra Times*, July 26, 1980; *Australian*, July 28, 1980; *National Times*, July 27–August 2, 1980; and *Australian Financial Review*, July 28, 1980. Note that Flo Bjelke-Petersen's recognition level was a staggeringly high 97 to 99 percent, compared to Maunsell's at 12 to 35 percent: *Weekend Australian*, July 26–27, 1980.
16 Melbourne *Age*, August 2, 1980.
17 *Courier Mail*, July 28, 1980. The whole episode calls to mind revolving governorships in another style of steamy tropical politics, and includes figures such as George and Mrs Wallace of Alabama and Ma and Pa Ferguson of Texas.
18 A convenient listing of coalition problem areas is in *Australian Financial Review*, October 6, 1980.
19 Nor was the NCP seen as blameless for the mess: the peak rural lobby group, the National Farmer's Federation, was not impressed with the government performance (Melbourne *Age*, October 4, 1980) and a survey showed about 25 percent of rural coalition voters might switch sides (*Australian Financial Review*, October 6, 1980).
20 Melbourne *Age*, March 3, 1980.
21 *Australian Financial Review*, September 29, 1980.
22 *Canberra Times*, September 27, 1980.
23 J.D. Anthony, *Policy Speech*, October 1, 1980; published by the National Country Party secretariat, Canberra, 1980.
24 *Australian Financial Review*, October 2, 1980.
25 Melbourne *Age* October 3, 1980. Anthony stressed the safety of remaining with a strong coalition government; in the course of an eleven-page speech he used the word "strong" 17 times (12 on the first page), "security" 12 times (8 on the first page), and "safe" 3 times (2 on the first page).
26 *Canberra Times*, October 4, 1980.
27 As Doug Anthony expressed it, a Labor win would allow the advances made under the coalition to "go down the gurgle-hole"—*Australian*, October 10, 1980.
28 See *Australian*, October 6, 1980 and October 13, 1980.
29 *Sydney Morning Herald*, October 6, 1980.
30 *Northern Territory News*, September 8, 1980; September 12, 1980.
31 *West Australian*, October 9, 1980.
32 *Sydney Morning Herald*, October 3, 1980; *Canberra Times*, October 3, 1980.
33 *Sydney Morning Herald*, October 20, 1980 discusses the contest between the coalition partners in Lyne.
34 *Sydney Morning Herald*, October 8, 1980. Also see *Sydney Morning Herald*, October 20, 1980; *Courier Mail*, October 1, 1980; October 10, 1980.
35 *Courier Mail*, October 8, 1980; *Weekend Australian*, October 11–12, 1980.
36 The significant feature of the separate Senate tickets was that the coalition was likely to—and did—lose one seat. Under the previous arrangements, the result with a joint ticket would have been two seats NCP, one seat Liberal, two seats Labor. With a split ticket the result, predictably, became one NCP, one Liberal, two Labor and one to the Democrats—*Weekend Australian*, September 27–28, 1980.

37 *Australian Financial Review*, November 4, 1980; *Australian*, November 5, 1980; Melbourne *Age*, November 4, 1980.
38 *Australian Financial Review*, November 4, 1980.
39 Thus, in a discussion on interest rates, Senator Walsh abused Ian Sinclair for his "redneck economics" and suggested Prime Minister Fraser might follow the NCP financial as well as political directives—*Canberra Times*, December 1, 1980.

6

Minor Parties and Pressure Groups

John Warhurst

Minor parties and pressure groups do not usually occupy the center of the stage in Australian Federal elections, but they often play significant roles on the edges of the main drama. In the case of minor parties, for example, recent political history has seen the Democratic Labor Party (DLP) with sufficient support, under a State-wide system of proportional representation in elections for the Senate, for its members to be able to determine the fate of government legislation in the upper house for much of the period between 1955 and 1974.[1] Under the system of preferential voting in single-member electorates, for the House of Representatives, minor parties have not been able to win lower house seats but on a number of occasions have been able, by directing the second preferences of their supporters, to determine which of the major parties gained office. The second preferences of DLP voters were instrumental in denying the Australian Labor Party (ALP) office in the elections of 1961 and 1969, while the second preferences of Australia Party (AP) voters won the ALP office in both 1972 and 1974.[2] Similarly, numerous pressure groups have exercised influence in Federal election campaigns both directly in support of the major party of their choice or indirectly through ensuring that an issue favourable to one or the other major party was prominent in the election campaign. In addition to such general campaigns, pressure groups have chosen to exercise their influence selectively for or against individual major party candidates, and in the conventional wisdom, at least, have contributed to the downfall of senior politicians, such as Gordon Freeth, Minister for External Affairs in the Gorton government, in 1969, and Al Grassby, Minister for Immigration in the Whitlam government, in 1974.

Sectional and promotional pressure groups both have a history of intervention in Australian election campaigns.[3] The major sectional groups each have ties with the established parties—trade unions with the ALP, employers with the Liberal Party (LP) and farmers with the National Country Party (NCP). A majority of Australian trade unionists are members of trade unions formally affiliated with the ALP, although the national peak association, the Australian Council of Trade Unions (ACTU) is not. Employers' and farmers' associations are not formally affiliated with their respective parties (although some farmers' associations once were affiliated with the NCP). Their major national peak associations, the Confederation of Australian Industry and the National Farmers Federation, are, like the ACTU, formally unattached and apolitical. The same is true of equivalent peak associations at the State level.

Sectional pressure groups regularly intervene in election campaigns. Some of these are now celebrated occasions, such as the massive campaign by employers, led by the private banks, against the incumbent ALP government in 1949, or the public statements at successive elections in the 1950s by members of the Catholic hierarchy in thinly veiled support of the DLP and opposition to the ALP.[4] The trade union movement is always a major source of funds for ALP campaigns and often individual unions publicly urge their members to support the party. Other sectional associations such as teachers have campaigned against Liberal-NCP governments, particularly at the State level.[5] Participation in campaigns by sectional groups is not always explicitly partisan, but may be directed to promoting an issue for consideration by electors.

Group intervention in election campaigns is more often associated with promotional associations. Over the last two decades, prominent examples have included the Council for the Defence of Government Schools (DOGS), most active in the late 1960s and early 1970s, which opposed government funding for private schools; the various groups opposed to Australian participation in the Vietnam War; organizations opposed to liberal legislation on matters such as abortion, divorce and homosexuality, including the Right to Life Association (RTLA), and the Festival of Light (FOL); and feminist groups, particularly the Women's Electoral Lobby (WEL).[6]

The tactics of some pressure groups have on occasions blurred the distinction between these groups and the minor parties. Some have chosen to stand their own candidates in elections rather than rely on indirectly influencing the election result. Normally such a step is viewed by the group as a means of gaining publicity rather than a serious attempt to win office, although, through the distribution of their second preferences DOGS claimed some success in the 1969

Federal election, and at some State elections. The RTLA has also stood candidates, while FOL has done so at each election since 1974 under a pseudonym.[7] However, even when they choose to stand candidates, these organizations are rightly not regarded as political parties but remain pressure groups.

What should not be over-dramatized, though, is the distance between the parties and the pressure groups and between the sectional groups and the promotional groups. Each draws from the same pool of active members and supporters. The membership of promotional and sectional groups may overlap: DOGS and teachers organizations; the trade union movement and anti-Vietnam War groups; RTLA and FOL and the Christian churches. The same may be true of groups and parties, for example, RTLA and the DLP. Pressure groups may also work within parties, influencing the preselection of candidates for election. The Catholic Social Studies Movement (CSSM), the industrial organization from which the DLP later drew much of its strength, was active within the ALP in the late 1940s and early 1950s;[8] while both the LP and the NCP have been troubled in recent years by the influence within their ranks of extreme right-wing groups such as the Australian League of Rights.

Somewhat the same overlapping occurs between parties and groups and some independent candidates. Not a single genuine independent has been elected to the House of Representatives in the past thirty years, although a former ALP member retained his seat at the 1966 election. Naturally, independents, like minor parties, have benefited from proportional representation and have been more successful in elections for the Senate. Four independents have been elected to the Senate in that same period (three of them from Tasmania). Of these, Senator R.J. Turnbull, elected from Tasmania in 1961 and again in 1967, was a former member of the ALP who joined the Australia Party from July 1969 to March 1970 as its parliamentary leader.[9] Senator Brian Harradine, first elected from Tasmania in 1975, was a former member of the Federal executive of the ALP, who, it was alleged upon his expulsion from that body, not only was a former DLP member but was still associated with the successor to the CSSM, the National Civic Council.[10]

Minor Parties in 1980

Minor parties may be placed, for the purposes of analysis in several, not always clear-out, categories.[11] Some are primarily a segment of a major party which has broken away for reasons of principle or personalities. Some minor parties primarily draw their support from a particular geographical area, religious denomination or socioeconomic class and have little appeal to the wider electorate. Other minor parties are largely the expression of an intensely ideological view of politics which sets their supporters apart from the mainstream of society. Many parties contain elements of more than one category. In fact, this is the norm rather than the exception. Australian politics contains examples of each of these types of minor parties, and most stood candidates in the 1980 Federal election.

The DLP has been the most successful example of a breakaway party, though it clearly contained elements drawn from the other categories. The party's representation in the Senate was eliminated in the 1974 election, and since 1974 the party has stood candidates for the House of Representatives only in Victoria. Still, it received 5.3 per cent of the total vote for the House of Representatives in that State in 1977. Furthermore, it had maintained its ability to deliver the second preferences of its supporters to the LP and the NCP. Usually 80 percent or more of DLP second preferences were given to the coalition parties.[12] The DLP had dissolved itself in March 1978, but shortly after had been revived by a small number of former supporters. Not only did it stand candidates in a number of seats in the May 1979 Victorian State elections and maintain its support at about 5 percent, but, for the first time it chose to direct its second preferences to the ALP where the Liberal candidate was judged to be not sufficiently opposed to abortion. This was done in about half the seats the DLP contested and in these seats it was able to successfully redirect its supporters' second preferences to the ALP.[13]

At the 1980 Federal election the DLP stood candidates for eleven Victorian House of Representatives' seats and also for the Senate in that State. As it had in the previous State election, the DLP executive chose to allocate preferences to ALP candidates in seats where the LP candidate's attitude on issues such as abortion did not meet with its approval. The three electorates chosen included two where the sitting LP member was also opposed by the RTLA.

The NCP is the most significant example of a minor party in Australia based largely on a narrow section of the community, with its support restricted to rural electorates. It and the Australian Democrats (AD) were the most important minor parties standing candidates in the 1980 election. There were, however, a number of others which had maintained a presence in Australian politics for some time. Two, the Australia Party (AP) and the Progress Party (PP) were lights of other days. The AP, orginally based on discontented Liberals, had been weakened when many of its supporters chose to join the AD in 1977 and only a rump remained. The PP, formerly known as the Workers Party, highly ideological supporter of the free enterprise system, had also lost whatever momentum it had possessed since the 1977 election. Both parties concentrated their energies on the Senate: the AP in two States and the PP in three. The remaining minor parties standing were really single-issue pressure groups such as the Marijuana Party or independents. The exceptions were examples of ideological parties on the left: the Communist parties and factions. Of these parties the pro-Soviet Socialist Party of Australia (SPA) stood Senate candidates in four States, while both it and the independent Communist Party of Australia (CPA) contested some House of Representatives seats.[14] The Socialist Workers Party (SWP), a Trotskyist group, and the Socialist Labor League (SLL) also stood candidates. Generally, the left parties either stood in inner-city working-class seats, or in electorates where some publicity would ensue as in the Victorian electorate of Wills where former ACTU president, Bob Hawke, was opposed by the CPA, the SWP and the SLL.

The Australian Democrats

The AD is the most recently formed of the significant minor parties.[15] The party can be understood partly as a breakaway party, some of whose supporters and candidates were formally members of the LP, and partly as a middle-class party whose supporters share common characteristics. There remains, however, something of the essence of the party which still defies capture by commentators.

The AD was formed in mid-1977 by their present parliamentary leader, Don Chipp, a former LP parliamentarian who had resigned from the party in March 1977. Chipp had been a minister in L-NCP governments in the late 1960s and early 1970s, but had failed to be appointed to the ministry by Malcolm Fraser in December 1975. Not only had he been an active supporter of the previous Liberal leader, Bill Snedden, who had been deposed by Fraser earlier in 1975, but he and Fraser held radically different views. Paul Reynolds has written that "Fraser and Chipp were as far apart as it was possible to be while remaining within one party".[16] The new party drew to it people who had previously supported both the LP and the ALP, and many who had not supported either major party. To this was added a large number of former supporters of two earlier offshoots of the LP, the AP and the New Liberal Movement, the rump which remained of the Liberal Movement (LM) after the bulk of the latter had followed their leader, a former Premier of South Australia, Steele Hall, back into the LP.[17]

The Democrats stood candidates in State elections during 1977 with encouraging results. Then, in November 1977, Steele Hall resigned to contest a House of Representatives seat in Adelaide at the forthcoming December 1977 Federal election. The South Australian ALP Government, arguing that the AD were the identifiable heirs of the LM, for whom Hall had been elected in 1975, chose the Democrat's candidate, Janine Haines, to serve the remaining seven months of Hall's term.

The 1977 federal election was called before the AD had had time to build a party, much less consolidate their position:

> The Party had to face a major electoral test less than a year after its foundation and with its organization only a skeleton in most of the states. It was handicapped by a lack of money.... It had only one national figure in Don Chipp.[18]

Nevertheless, the general opinion of the party's first national test was that it had performed well. It stood Senate candidates in each State and Territory and polled an average of 11.1 percent. Chipp was elected to the Senate in Victoria with 16.2 percent of the vote, while a former Australia Party member, Colin Mason, was elected in New South Wales with the support of ALP second preferences, though polling less (8.3 percent) than AD candidates in most other States. The party narrowly missed winning the fifth Senate seat in both South Australia and Western Australia. In the House of Representatives the AD did not succeed in winning a seat, but won 9.4 percent of the national vote. The party's best result occurred in Chipp's former electorate of Hotham in suburban Melbourne, with the AD candidate polling 18.4 percent.

This encouraging performance was not enough to lead critics to predict a future for the party, bearing in mind the failure of other minor parties in the past. One success did not change Keith Richmond's June 1977 judgement of the party: "It possesses few resources, an untried support base, and its chances of attaining significant political representation are therefore limited".[19] The party was perceived as having two major weaknesses. The first weakness, common to all minor parties, was the absence of political resources, especially finance, which prevented the employment of full-time officers (over and above the staff allowed to the two parliamentary representatives) who could build and maintain a professional organization, and which prevented the mounting of elaborate media campaigns prior to elections. As mighty as this problem was, the party was seen to possess a greater weakness which would bring it undone in the end: the absence of an identifiable core of positive ideas and policies upon which support could be built. It was this which was later to lead Don Aitkin to speak of the "marshmallow-like substance" of the Democrats.[20] There appeared to be little about the party's support which did not depend upon phenomena which would be passing—such as the leadership of Don Chipp—or the confrontationist style of the major parties under the leadership of Malcolm Fraser and Gough Whitlam. Two prophecies of the AD's future hit upon this last point. Reynolds saw the destiny of the Democrats ". . . inextricably interwoven with those of the two main parties". Furthermore, "If the ALP is able to reshape its policy making, to present a more appealing image under its new leadership, and to rejuvinate its organization . . . then the Australian Democrats of 1977 could well be Labor supporters by 1980."[21] Katherine West's later conclusion was very similar: ". . . in the light of the 1977 result, the Democrats' best electoral hopes seemed to lie in an ineffective government and an unacceptable opposition".[22]

The Democrats in 1980

Had anything occurred by October 1980 to temper or radically alter the assessments of the party after the 1977 election? Nothing had occurred that was so dramatic as to either ensure the party's future or undermine the possibility of its winning a permanent place in the party system.

The party's performances in the State and Territory elections which occurred between the two Federal elections, while uneven, maintained the momentum which had been achieved in 1977. Each State, except Queensland, and both Territories, held elections during this period. Among the highlights for the Democrats were the winning of four more parliamentary seats to add to the two Senators elected in 1977, and the one member of the South Australian lower house, the House of Assembly, inherited from the New Liberal Movement. Two AD candidates were elected to the Australian Capital Territory's House of Assembly in June 1979. Under the proportional representation system for two nine-member electorates, one Democrat was elected in each electorate. At the South Australian State election in September 1979, a vote of 6.5 percent in the election for the upper house, the Legislative Council, won the party the eleventh and final place to be decided under a list system of proportional representation based on a single, State-wide electorate. Finally, in February 1980, the party polled 9.2 percent in a by-election for the Tasmanian State seat of Denison, and, under the Hare–Clark system of proportional representation, the Democrat candidate won the seventh and final seat in the multi-member electorate. The AD also polled well in situations where single-member electorates made it highly unlikely they could win. Noteworthy performances included a vote of 11.9 percent in a by-election for the Queensland State seat of Sherwood in November 1978, and 8.8. percent in seats contested (up to 15.2 percent in one electorate) in the May 1979 Victorian State elections. The most disappointing results were achieved by the party in New South Wales, in State and Federal by-elections, and in the October 1978 State elections where the introduction of a new electoral system based upon proportional representation for the State upper house, the Legislative Council, gave the party hopes of winning a seat. However, it polled only 2.7 percent, and failed dismally to do so. Overall, the party could, by October 1980, boast seven parliamentarians across the country. All but one of these had been elected under electoral systems based upon proportional representation, and the seventh was an established member who had been originally elected as LP candidate, and then as a representative of the LM before changing his allegience to the Democrats. Clearly the AD would be looking to the Senate in 1980 to increase their numbers in the national Parliament. Candidates for the House of Representatives would be put forward with the immediate purpose of "flying the flag" and ensuring the party's organization would be operating to support Senate candidates.

The sources of the AD's support and the reasons for voters choosing to support the party were not much clearer in 1980 than they had been in 1977. What the answers to these questions may be is suggested by the responses to a national survey conducted during 1979.[23] Those who identified with the Democrats represented a segment of the middle class who were disproportionately well educated (15.3 percent had completed university education compared with 8.2 percent of those who identified with the LP, and 7.0 percent of identifiers with the ALP), and disproportionately interested in politics (only 8.5 percent admitted to not much interest in politics compared with 21.0 percent of LP supporters and 24.7 percent of ALP supporters), but also disproportionately cynical (81.4 percent thought people in government looked after themselves compared with 77.1 percent of ALP supporters and 54.1 percent of LP supporters).

AD supporters were drawn fairly equally from ALP and LP or NCP backgrounds, with a minority from the ALP. Some of their likes and dislikes of the major parties were deeply rooted in the structure of those parties, while others were tied more to contemporary phe-

105

nomena. For example, AD supporters saw the LP acting in the interests of rich and powerful private business and the ALP as influenced by extremists to work in the interests of trade unions. They shared with LP supporters the view that trade unions had too much power, while at the same time joining with ALP supporters in believing also that big business had too much power.[24] Democrats also viewed the LP as dishonest and insincere, and possessed a particular dislike for the Prime Minister, Malcolm Fraser, who, in turn, was seen as personally dishonest (by 13.6 percent of AD supporters). These latter characteristics were ones which presumably meant that a change of LP leadership might weaken the opposition to that party of some Democrats.

Democrats, by way of contrast with extremist, confrontationist major parties, saw and liked their own party as not extreme, but moderate and in the center of the political spectrum. The second most popular characteristic of the party nominated by its own supporters was the leadership of Don Chipp. Chipp himself was identified with trustworthiness, honesty and sincerity (by 27.1 percent of AD supporters).

The responses to political issues revealed by the survey showed several areas where the Democrats held quite distinctive opinions. In particular, Democrats held more liberal views on most social issues than the supporters of both the major parties. This was true of attitudes to the legalisation of homosexuality, to the legalisation of marijuana for use and sale, and to easily obtainable abortion. Only in the case of censorship were the attitudes of ALP, but not LP supporters, more liberal than those of Democrats.[25] On some issues such as attitude to the mining and use of uranium, Democrats held a position quite different from the LP and shared the opposition of ALP supporters, but on others such as questions of taxation and social services, Democrats occupied a position very much in the center of the two major parties.[26]

As the 1980 election approached Don Chipp remained the party's only nationally recognized spokesman and financial resources were still meagre. Two things, though, had changed from 1977. The first was the change in the Labor Party's leadership. The ALP's new leader, Bill Hayden, was not identified with confrontation between the major parties as Gough Whitlam had been. The danger for the Democrats was that its supporters might now find the ALP more attractive. The second was the balance of power in the Senate. In 1977, such was the strength of the government in the Senate because of its overwhelming victory in 1975 that no feasible result in 1977 could challenge its majority in that house between 1977 and 1980.

Now the situation had altered. The government needed to win three of the five Senate places in three of the six States to maintain its control.

Estimates of AD support in opinion polls leading up to the election made clear that in each State, with the possible exception of Tasmania, where the situation was clouded by the candidature of Senator Harradine, an AD candidate might be elected to the Senate. The government was undoubtedly aware of this possibility. The national organ of the LP, the *Australian Liberal*, argued, in July 1980, under a front-page headline, "Keep the Senate Safe":

> The Senate election this year will be of critical importance to the Government—and to Australia.
>
> The task facing the party is the maintenance of the Coalition's majority in the Upper House.
>
> The Liberal Party is confident of meeting this challenge, and will be putting special emphasis on the Senate Campaign....
>
> The Federal Campaign Organization and the State Strategy Committees are making special plans to give maximum support to the Liberal Senate teams....
>
> At all levels of campaigning, the Party will be urging its supporters to promote and assist the Senate team as well as their own local members and candidates.[27]

Foreshadowing the type of attack by the LP on the Democrats in the campaign proper, the leader of the government in the Senate, John Carrick, argued:

> The two Democrat Senators for most of their time have voted with Labor to defeat Government motions.
>
> This is not sufficiently understood. Some Liberal supporters have voted for Democrats in the belief that the Democrat policies and philosophy are in close parallel with our own.
>
> That is not so. A vote for the Democrats is, for all practical purposes, a vote for Labor.[28]

Government worries were further increased when the draw for places on the Senate ballot paper was held after nominations closed. The Democrats drew the first place on the ballot paper in both Queensland and South Australia to strengthen its chances in those States. Sir Charles Court, Liberal Premier of Western Australia called the possibility of the Democrats' holding the balance of power in the Senate "nearly as disastrous as a change to a Labor government".[29] While the Liberal Party in five of the six States gave their own second preferences to the Democrats, the South Australian State executive chose to direct their preferences to the ALP rather than the number one Democrats' candidate, Janine Haines. The LP also stepped up its campaign to portray a vote for the Democrats as the equivalent of a vote for the ALP. To do this it used the raw figures of roll calls in the Senate to imply that the Democrats voted with the ALP most of the time. As the Democrats pointed out, these figures included "procedural matters, arising from the gag or guillotine to stifle debate" and were a misrepresentation.[30]

The Democrats made one major decision prior to the election's being called. The national executive decided, in July, not to direct the second preferences of its supporters as it had attempted to do in some electorates in the 1979 Victorian State election, but to issue two-sided how-to-vote cards, giving two alternatives to Democrat voters. A second major step was to have every AD number one Senate candidate swear a statutory declaration that, should the party hold the balance of power, they would not vote to block Supply to the government.

The emphasis of the Democrats in the campaign proper was shrewdly pitched to appeal to the known characteristics of Democrat supporters. It was assisted by the party's access, unlike 1977, to some free media exposure through the Australian Broadcasting Commission—one hour in each State, most of which was used for Don Chipp's policy speech. The theme of this speech was: keep the major parties honest by giving the Democrats the balance of power in the Senate. The Democrats would vote: "as each of us sees how the issues affect our electors: by obeying, not a combined trade-union monolith or a multi-national consortium or even a political party hierarchy, but you, the Australian people". And the emphasis on honesty, integrity and moderation was repeated:

> We are the only political party to refuse secret money: all substantial donations can be publicly disclosed and we owe favours to no one.
> We are not bound to the dogma of the left or the right, and we're the only party totally free from the influence of powerful vested interests—whether they be trade unions or big business. Very importantly, we believe no big problem is ever solved by confrontation.

Chipp's final plea to the electors returned to the central theme: "There needs to be a force in Canberra keeping politicians honest and preventing them from breaking their promises. We believe we are that force. Will you give us the chance?"[31] It was this message rather than specific policies which were the heart of the Democrats' appeal.

It came to be summed up informally in Chipp's own words on another occasion: "... We will keep the bastards honest".[32] Chipp's continuous attacks on his own arch-enemy, the Prime Minister, left little doubt as to whom he had in mind.

Pressure Groups

A wide range of sectional and promotional pressure groups chose to intervene in the 1980 campaign. Their activities fell into a number of categories, including publicizing and lobbying for particular issues, standing candidates for that same purpose, directly supporting either the government or the ALP, attempting to influence the selection of candidates by parties, and working for or against individual candidates.

Examples of pressure groups which promoted causes in a relatively even-handed manner included groups as diverse as the National Farmers Federation, whose primary concern for energy policy led them to be critical of the government parties, whom they traditionally support; the Australian Teachers Federation, which funded expensive media campaigns to highlight the problems of education; and the Royal Australian Institute of Architects which wanted to alert all political parties to "built environment" issues.

To publicize their cause some pressure groups decided to stand their own candidates for the Senate. The Call to Australia Party, the successor to the Family Action Movement, in New South Wales, led by the national spokesman for the Festival of Light, Rev. Fred Nile, pledged to "faithfully represent your family". Other pressure groups-cum-political parties included a pensioner lobby, the Retired Persons Federation of Australia, which fielded candidates in Victoria, and Jobless Action, a group concerned to assist the unemployed, who stood candidates in the ACT. Other groups chose to strongly support one or other of the major parties. For example, various parts of the trade union movement, including State branches of unions, State Trades Halls and ACTU spokesmen backed the ALP. One focus of this support was the October 17 Mobilisation Against the Government rallies and marches which were held in the major cities. The march and rally in Sydney was addressed by the new ACTU President. Employers' groups endorsed the Liberal Party through public campaigns for the "free enterprise" system. The major source of direct pressure group support for the government, however, came in the guise of full-page advertisements in the daily papers placed by so-called "independent" groups who variously described themselves as "a large group of concerned Australians", "realistic Australian individuals and organizations" or "a large group of business men vitally concerned with keeping a responsible Liberal Government in Canberra". The advertisements provoked allegations by the ALP that the Liberal Party itself was the force behind the advertisements, and the publishers of the *Sydney Morning Herald* would only publish one such advertisement on the condition that the word "independent" was deleted.

Attempts by pressure groups to publicly influence the preselection of major party candidates was less common, though each of the major sectional groups privately participates in major party preselection contests as a matter of course. Two clear cases of such action occurred in Victoria: ALP Senator, Jean Melzer, as a result of intra-party factional politics, was relegated to the number three position on the party's ticket, a position from which she was highly unlikely to be returned to the Senate. A vigorous but unsuccessful campaign for her to be raised to the number two position was waged, and was given its impetus by the participation of women's organizations. Secondly, delegates to the Liberal Party preselection in the electorate of Chisholm, meeting to choose a candidate to replace the retiring Minister for Posts and Telecommunications, were picketed by RTLA supporters who distributed a petition signed by 1,500 Chisholm residents. Prior to this some of the twenty candidates in the pre-selection had been interviewed by the local RTLA.

Support for or opposition to individual candidates, rather than emphasis on parties or general issues was a course adopted by numerous groups. It was this aspect of pressure group campaigning which aroused most controversy and criticism. Least controversial were women's groups, such as the League of Women Voters, which urged a vote for women candidates *per se* without concern for party divisions. Most controversial were "single issue" groups who concentrated on eliciting declarations from individual candidates on the issue in question, publicizing the responses and asking supporters to vote only for those candidates who gave the "correct" response. The technique was not new. It had been used by the temperance movement, for example, in the late nineteenth and early twentieth centuries.[33] But it had been revived in the early 1970s by WEL which popularized the method of sending a questionnaire to each candidate and then rating each of the candidates.[34] It is a technique which is formally nonpartisan, though groups can be accused of partisanship and of acting as a "front" for a major party as WEL was in 1972. Numerous pressure groups used variations on the method in 1980. They included major groups such as the Campaign for an Independent East Timor (CIET), RTLA, the Movement Against Uranium Mining (MAUM), and the Commission on Social Responsibility of the Uniting Church.[35] Candidates were thus bombarded by single-issue lobbyists. Once the responses had been collated, some groups such as RTLA and MAUM singled out certain candidates for intensified opposition or support. In the marginal suburban Melbourne electorate of La Trobe, the sitting Liberal member was one of those subject to a concentrated attack by MAUM, while his ALP opponent had similarly been singled out by RTLA.

Politicians of all parties were clearly apprehensive about these groups, and many would avoid, if possible, any declarations of either support or opposition for fear of alienating a section of the electorate. Reports from pressure groups indicated that LP candidates, in particular, were refusing to answer questionnaires.[36] The Victorian State director of the LP then revealed that the party had recommended to its candidates in Victoria not to respond. The Victorian secretary of the ALP pointed out that his party's position was similar. The issue was particularly sensitive in Victoria because of the apparent success of the RTLA in using these tactics at the State election only eighteen months before.

The Right to Life Association

The last two decades have seen a number of divisive debates in Australia over Federal and State policies towards the availability of abortion for women who desire to avail themselves of such a medical service. The arena varies as such policy is the responsibility of State Governments in each State, and the Federal Government in the ACT. The precise issue varies from conditions of availability, to restrictions on funding, to public or private provision of the service.

Public attitudes to this issue have altered markedly during the period in which it has been debated. While the issue is complicated, ten years ago it would appear that Australians increasingly supported reform of abortion legislation, and that by that stage a majority in the community wanted "fairly liberal abortion law reform" but with some controls.[37] Since then it would appear that the trend has continued so that only a very small percentage, less than 10 percent, of the population would not allow abortion to be legal in any circumstances. While less than a majority favour abortion being available in all circumstances, or easily, a large majority favour its availability under certain restrictions.[38]

Ten years ago opponents of liberal abortion unsuccessfully sought to defend the *status quo*. Contemporary conflicts have seen reformist groups now more or less satisfied with the *status quo*, defending current practice while opponents of reform seek to support more restrictive legislation. Usually legislation is introduced in the form of private members' bills rather than under government sponsorship, while it has become accepted for parties not to insist upon party discipline in voting but to allow individuals to cast a vote according to their conscience.

The issue has stimulated the growth of specialist promotional pressure groups of which the most prominent have been the RTLA and the Abortion Law Reform Association of Australia, and was one part of the reason for the growth of promotional groups with broader aims such as FOL. Sectional groups such as churches and women's organizations have taken public positions. Significantly, women's groups have divided over the issue. WEL was one of the groups which fought for early legislative reform; more recently conservative women's groups such as Women's Action Alliance have opposed law reform.

Federal Parliament debated several pieces of legislation of concern to these groups between 1978 and 1980. A bill was proposed in March 1979 by Stephen Lusher (NCP, Hume, NSW) which was to restrict the public funding of abortions. The motion was not voted on, after an amendment moved by Barry Simon (LP, McMillan, Victoria) had preempted it. Twelve months later, in March 1980, during debate over the Human Rights Bill, a Western Australian Liberal, John Martyr, attempted unsuccessfully to insert an amendment which would guarantee the "right" of the unborn "from conception". A subsequent amendment aimed at protecting children "before as well as after birth", moved once again by Simon, was passed. When the bill subsequently reached the Senate both the Martyr amendment (put by Senator Harradine) and the Simon amendment were defeated. The two actions were to make Simon the main target of the RTLA in October 1980.

The RTLA is active in all States and Territories. Two national organizations exist, Right to Life Australia, the creation of the Victorian RTLA, and the Australian Federation of Right to Life Associations, comprised of the ACT and all the State associations except Victoria's. Most public attention was focussed on the Victorian RTLA, the most professional and aggressive organization. Disagreement over tactics led to conflict between the two national organizations, when the Victorian RTLA chose to campaign not only in Victoria, but also in one electorate in Queensland and two in Tasmania.[39]

The Victorian RTLA was formed in 1973. It campaigned in the 1975 and 1977 elections, and the association's president, Margaret Tighe, stood against the Victorian Premier in the 1976 State election. Recently however, influenced by the tactics used by its American counterparts, the association's strategy has been refined. The new strategy focussed attention on the RTLA at the 1979 Victorian State election, when several defeated LP members claimed, with some grounds, that the RTLA had brought about their demise.[40]

The Victorian RTLA set out to "make abortion the KEY issue of the elections" and to "defeat pro-abortion candidates by the promotion of abortion as the DISQUALIFYING factor re the suitability of candidates for holding public office".[41] To achieve these ends RTLA members took part in election activities of a general nature such as issuing press releases, writing letters to the editor, attending and being vocal at election meetings. More importantly, each candidate's "pro-life form" was rated by RTLA on the basis of replies to a candidate survey, the voting record of all sitting members as recorded in Hansard, replies to letters from individual RTLA members, and answers to questions at public meetings.[42] These replies were then published in the press prior to the election. In some electorates each candidate was rated in numerical order, while in others several candidates were given approval.[43] RTLA then chose particular candidates for special attention. In the case of the Victorian RTLA this usually meant intensive campaigns *against* candidates. All other RTLAs favoured the alternative and less provocative tactic of endorsing selected candidates. For the Federal election, the Victorian RTLA selected ten candidates as "special targets": the ALP candidates in Henty, Latrobe, Hotham, Burke, Bendigo and Deakin, the ALP member for Maribyrnong, the LP members for McMillan and Holt, and the NCP member for Murray. In addition, in two of these seats alternative candidates were actively supported: the LP member for Deakin and the LP candidate in Murray. The most intense campaigns were located in McMillan and Murray.

Extensive resources are at the disposal of the RTLA to wage these special campaigns. It has 7,000 members in Victoria and received $300,000 in donations in the two years prior to the election.[44] It is also able to draw on extensive institutional support from the Catholic Church. This support comes not just from those conservative segments of the Church, including members of the DLP and NCC, who were associated with the anti-communist campaigns of the 1940s, 1950s and 1960s, but from a wide cross-section of clergy and laity.

The RTLA campaign against Barry Simon in McMillan is an indication of the type of campaign the association can initiate.

Following the election, RTLA summarized its activities as follows:

- Establishment of 6 branches of Right to Life [one already existed], and a Federal Electorate committee to co-ordinate action.
- The holding of several home meetings and public meetings to teach the pro-life issue and to convince voters of the need to vote "pro-life".
- Several half page advertisements in the [six] main local newspapers explaining the facts on Barry Simon's pro-abortion role in Federal Parliament.
- Handing out pro-life material at Catholic and other churches in the electorate.
- Mailing to all householders in the electorate a brochure seeking voter support in ousting Barry Simon [c. 38,000 letters].
- Radio advertisements.
- Posters, letters and press releases in local newspapers and advertisements listing the names of 313 McMillan voters committed to voting pro-life.
- "How To Vote" cards.[45]

The RTLA estimated the cost of its campaign in McMillan at $19,000, certainly high by Australian standards. Its total budget probably approached $70,000–$80,000, of which about $50,000 was spent in Victoria. The RTLA's campaign among Catholics in McMillan was undoubtedly assisted by the intervention in the campaign of the local Catholic Bishop, Arthur Fox, a veteran of anti-ALP campaigns on behalf of the DLP in previous elections. Fox, despite Simon's personal attempts to explain his position on abortion to him, chose openly to condemn politicians whose opposition to abortion was restricted to supporting State laws. Simon was mentioned by name. On polling day, RTLA how-to-vote cards placed Simon fifth and last. The RTLA card, which was used in each of the targeted electorates read "How to Vote to Save Australia's Babies".

Simon had won McMillan in 1977 by a majority of nearly 6,000 votes over the ALP candidate after the distribution of the preferences of the AD and DLP candidates and one independent candidate. The swing required for the LP to lose the seat was 4.9 percent. Simon had been the member since 1975. The ALP had never held the seat. On this occasion there were again five candidates: LP, ALP, AD, DLP and an independent. The RTLA's first choice was the DLP candidate, who had polled 4.8 percent in 1977, when he directed his second preferences to the LP. On this occasion his preferences were directed to the ALP candidate, a Catholic father of six who was rated "fairly pro-life" by the RTLA and was their second choice. The ALP candidate had not, however, given the commitments required by the RTLA.

The second preferences of DLP voters were clearly likely to be crucial to the survival of Simon. In an open letter to DLP voters, he appealed to them, over the heads of the DLP State executive, for their second preferences. The issue Simon chose to stress was his opposition to communism, an issue which had traditionally determined the second preferences of DLP voters.

> I have strongly supported the Prime Minister and the Government in the condemnation of the invasion of Afganistan by the Soviet Union, and its support for the Vietnam regime currently in occupation of Kampuchea. The attempted boycott of the Olympic Games by the Australian Government had my strong support. Voters should recall that it was not supported by the ALP, and in particular by Mr Cunningham, the party's candidate in McMillan.[46]

Simon, and all other candidates singled out by RTLA, may have been assisted by the reaction of several pressure groups to the anti-abortion campaign. The resources devoted to the election by these groups was, however, immeasurably smaller. The Women's Abortion Action Campaign attempted to publicize its own survey, which it conducted to counter RTLA pressure. The survey, not inconsistent with what was known of public attitudes, showed 76 percent supported "abortion rights", 16 percent were non-committal and 8 percent were opposed.[47] Representatives of WEL appealed for support for Simon, in particular, as "a friend of women". Dr Bertram Wainer, operator of a fertility clinic and a well-known figure in Victoria, took advertisements in the press to warn "Abortion under Attack". He also stood as an independent in the suburban electorate of Casey. The National Association for the Repeal of Abortion Laws (NARAL) sponsored by Wainer, distributed its own list of "pro-choice/abortion" and "anti-choice/abortion" parliamentarians, based on the same voting records utilized by RTLA, to sympathetic groups around Australia. It also distributed leaflets, especially in the electorates of McMillan and Latrobe. According to NARAL, RTLA was "working to forbid freedom of choice for women". Voters were urged to "vote for a politician that can uphold his views despite attack from unpopular, radical, minority, lobby groups". Essentially the activities of each of these groups were last-minute *ad hoc* responses to a well-coordinated RTLA campaign which had been planned many months before.

Achievements

Once again, minor parties were significant in Australian Federal elections. Unlike previous elections it was the L-NCP which, on balance, suffered at their hands rather than the ALP. The Australian Democrats won additional Senate seats in Victoria, South Australia and Queensland to add to the two they already possessed. Reflecting the party's diverse origins the victorious AD candidate in Victoria had a long history of involvement with the AP. Together with Senator Harradine in Tasmania, reelected with 21.7 percent, the five AD Senators would have the numbers from July 1981 to enable them to join the ALP to pass opposition legislation in the Senate. Were Senator Harradine to support the government, the AD and ALP together would still be able to block government-sponsored legislation. In the election for the House of Representatives, in four electorates (McMillan and Ballarat in Victoria, Kalgoorlie in Western Australia and Barton in New South Wales) the leading major party candidate after the counting of the primary votes was defeated after the distribution of the second preferences of the minor parties' candidates and independents. The ALP benefited on three occasions out of four.

The AD suffered a loss of support in the elections for both the House of Representatives and the Senate. This was especially so in the former, where its level of support fell from 9.4 percent to 6.6 percent, a drop of almost a third. The party's second preferences favored the ALP by a significant margin (about 54:46 across the nation) with just enough variation from electorate to electorate for there to be always a chance of a first-preference lead to be reversed by them, although it occurred only in Kalgoorlie (won by the ALP). Support for the AD in the Senate fell from 11.1 percent to 9.3 percent. However, the vote held up in those States where it was possible for the party to win a Senate seat (see Table 6-1). And in the scramble in each State for the fifth Senate place, the AD benefited from the distribution of preferences. In Victoria and South Australia ALP preferences flowed to the party, while in Queensland the party received sufficient preferences from the LP and from the supporters of the disgruntled third-placed NCP candidate, Senator Ron Maunsell, to win narrowly. After a recount, the party failed to win the fifth seat in Western Australia by only 560 votes, and an appeal was lodged with the Court of Disputed Returns, the High Court, alleging that those LP advertisements which claimed that a vote for the AD was equivalent to a vote for the ALP were misleading under the Electoral Act.

The performances of the AD in two successive Senate elections are equivalent to the achievements of the DLP in elections between 1955 and 1970. The AD have now won Senate seats in four States which equals the performance of the DLP, as does their total of five Senators in the Parliament at one time. The regional variation in their support is less than was the DLP's. So they have greater claims to be a national party. This is not to say their future is any more secure. Just as the ALP, perceived as more moderate, ate into their support, so might a future, more moderate L-NCP, led by someone other than the present Prime Minister, do likewise.

TABLE 6-1
Australian Democrats: Senate support, 1977 and 1980

State	1977 (%)	Elected	1980 (%)	Elected	Total
New South Wales	8.3	1	6.9	—	1
Victoria	16.2	1	11.3	1	2
Queensland	8.9	—	10.0	1	1
South Australia	11.2	—	13.1	1	1
Western Australia	12.5	—	9.3	—	—
Tasmania	5.9	—	3.2	—	—
Australia Capital Territory	12.8	—	8.6	—	—
Northern Territory	8.2	—	9.8	—	—
Total	11.1	2	9.3	3	5

Source: M. Mackerras, Elections 1980 (Sydney: Angus and Robertson, 1980), p. 236; M. Mackerras, Australian General Election and Senate Election 1980 Statistical Analysis (Department of Government, University of New South Wales at Dontroon, 1981) p. 39.

Whatever the future of the AD there is no indication of the party's having anything but a random impact on House of Representatives elections. Unlike the DLP, the AD are unable to act as a vehicle carrying supporters of one major party via a vote for a minor party across to the other major party. On a smaller scale than in their heyday, the DLP was able to achieve this again in 1980. In the three seats chosen by the State executive, the party was apparently able successfully to direct their second preferences to the ALP (only in McMillan were they distributed). In these seats in previous elections an equivalent percentage had flowed to the LP. Corangamite was a safe seat; in Holt the swing to the ALP was such that the DLP second preferences were not needed; in McMillan they were decisive. The direction of the DLP preferences confirms the interpretation of those who have argued that the phenomenon of the DLP must be explained in terms of issues (communism in the 1950s, abortion in 1980) rather than in terms of socioeconomic class (Table 6-2).

TABLE 6-2
DLP second preferences, House of Representatives, 1980

| Electorate | DLP Preferences directed to: | | | |
	Coalition	ALP	AD	Ind
Ballarat[a]	26.9	13.4	59.8	
Bruce	60.7	15.8	23.5	
Deakin[b]	79.4	8.2	12.4	
Henty[b]	79.0	8.7	12.3	
Hotham[b]	56.4	24.7	18.8	
La Trobe[b]	60.7	9.8	7.0	22.5
McMillan[c]	16.3	72.1	11.6	
Total	48.5	28.7	21.2	1.6

Notes: [a] Donkey vote
[b] ALP candidates were opposed by RTLA
[c] LP candidate was opposed by RTLA
Source: M. Mackerras Australian General Election and Senate Election 1980 Statistical Analysis pp. 31–32.

Parliamentarians and parties demonstrated by the defensive reaction of so many of them to the campaign by the RTLA that they were not prepared to underestimate its impact. The NCP member for Murray, for example, instituted legal proceedings against the RTLA, and took out his own advertisements to answer RTLA allegations about his views on abortion.[48] The pressure group opponents of RTLA were also aware that 1980 was a test-case. Should the RTLA's campaign be judged to have been effective, warned NARAL, "no politician will use a conscience vote responsibly again". Following the election the RTLA were loud in proclaiming their success, including the defeat of Simon in McMillan, just as groups such as WEL were confident that the RTLA's campaign had been ineffective. Despite the claims and counter-claims, assessing the impact of the campaign is hedged about with imponderables. The construction of plausible scenarios, in the absence of detailed surveys, must be the aim of the analyst.

The net impact of the RTLA campaign in Victoria equals the total transfer of votes (first and second preferences) to the major party candidate supported by RTLA away from the major party candidate opposed by RTLA minus the backlash of "pro-choice" voters moving in the opposite direction. A rough estimate of this impact can be made by comparing the two-party-preferred swing in electorates where the RTLA supported L-NCP candidates with those seats where the RTLA supported the ALP. These two aggregate figures can then be compared with the two-party-preferred swing in electorates where abortion does not appear to have been an issue. This is done in Table 6-3. On average the three seats where the RTLA supported the ALP

TABLE 6-3
The RTLA and Two-Party-Preferred Swing in Victoria

	Two-Party-Preferred Swing to ALP	
Electorates (3) in which RTLA opposed LP-NCP candidates		7.8%
Holt	8.2%	
McMillan	6.2%	
Murray	8.9%	
Electorates (23) in which RTLA did not campaign		6.7%
Electorates (7) in which RTLA opposed ALP candidates		4.9%
Bendigo	6.9%	
Burke	1.2%	
Deakin	5.1%	
Henty	5.5%	
Hotham	5.7%	
La Trobe	3.1%	
Maribyrnong	7.0%	
All Victorian electorates		6.2%

Source: Calculations for individual electorates by Malcolm Mackerras, other calculations by the author.

candidate showed a two-party-preferred swing of 7.8 percent to the ALP. The seven seats where the RTLA opposed the ALP candidates showed an average two-party-preferred swing of 4.9 percent. The two-party-preferred swing to the ALP over the State of Victoria was 6.2 percent; in the twenty-three seats where abortion was not a major issue it was 6.7 percent. The implication of this calculation is that, ceteris paribus the net impact of an intense RTLA campaign was positive, and was perhaps worth between 1 and 2 percent of the total vote. This is far less than the 5 or 6 percent claimed by the RTLA, but it is still enough to make a difference in a very close contest, such as McMillan, where the ALP won by 1816 votes. While the swing away from the LP in McMillan was no larger than the average swing in all Victorian electorates, the performance of the DLP, supported by the RTLA, was better with one possible exception than in any other Victorial electorate.[49] McMillan was the only electorate where the DLP, without the benefit of top position on the ballot paper, gained a higher percentage of the vote than it had in 1977.

In each electorate, however, other factors were also at work and the performance of candidates supported by the RTLA varied markedly. In the two other electorates, Holt and Murray, where the RTLA opposed LP or NCP sitting members, the swing towards the ALP was greater than the State-wide average. This was also the case, however, in two electorates, Bendigo and Maribyrnong, where ALP candidates *opposed* by the RTLA achieved swings *towards* them significantly greater than average.

The precise mechanism by which the shift of votes occurs from one major party to the other may vary from one electorate to another. The transfer may occur directly, or via a minor party such as the DLP. What must be stressed is that this scenario can be no more than a plausible construction, a sifting of circumstantial evidence. What is known of public attitudes towards abortion in Australia, with probably 6 to 7 percent of the supporters of each of the major parties being opposed to abortion in any circumstances, suggests that there does exist fertile ground for RTLA campaigns. It is not implausible that a third of such voters might alter their vote for reasons associated with their stance on this issue and outweigh the impact of those voters willing to leave a major party in order to support a "pro-choice" candidate.[50] While the major parties choose to allow their parliamentarians a "conscience vote" on this issue and choose candidates for election with random views on the issue, then votes in Parliament will cut across party lines. Gains made by a major party because of the issue might be reversed at a subsequent election. Such successes are an unpredictable bonus, and not a basis on which to build a firm majority.

Notes

1 J. Hutchison, "The Senate" in Richard Lucy, ed., *The Pieces of Politics* (Melbourne: Macmillan, 1975), pp. 407–17.
2 P. Reynolds, "The Role of the Minor Parties" in Howard R. Penniman, ed., *Australia at the Polls: The National Elections of 1975* (Washington D.C.: American Enterprise Institute, 1977) pp. 164–5.
3 T. Matthews, "Australian Pressure Groups" in H. Mayer and H. Nelson, eds., *Australian Politics: A Fifth Reader* (Melbourne: Longman Cheshire, 1980) pp. 466–7.
4 A.L. May, *The Battle for the Banks* (Sydney: Sydney University Press, 1968); R. Murray, *The Split: Australian Labor in the Fifties* (Melbourne: Cheshire, 1970).
5 Matthews, "Australian Pressure Groups" pp. 466–7.
6 Matthews, "Australian Pressure Groups" pp. 466–7 (DOGS); H.S. Albinski *Politics and Foreign Policy in Australia: the Impact of the Vietnam War* (Durham, N.C.: Duke University Press 1970) (The Vietnam War); D. Hilliard and J. Warhurst "Festival of Light" *Current Affairs Bulletin* 50(9), February 1974, pp. 13–19, and J. Warhurst "Taking a few political lives: the 'pro-life' campaign" in P.R. Hay, I. Ward and J. Warhurst, eds, *Anatomy of an Election* (Melbourne: Hill of Content, 1979), pp. 236–40 (FOL and RTLA); H. Mayer, ed., *Labor to Power: Australia's 1972 Election* (Sydney: Angus and Robertson, 1973) pp. 169–97 and J. Mercer, ed., *The*

Other Half: Women in Australian Society (Melbourne: Penguin, 1975) pp. 395–426 (WEL).

7 The name chosen in 1974 was the Family Action Movement, K. Richmond "Minor Parties in Australia" in G. Starr, K. Richmond, G. Maddox *Political Parties in Australia* (Melbourne: Heinemann Educational, 1978), pp. 371 –373.

8 P. Reynolds, *The Democratic Labor Party* (Brisbane: Jacaranda Press, 1974), pp. 1–16.

9 K. Cole, "The Australia Party—An Historical Perspective" in R. Lucy, ed., *The Pieces of Politics*, pp. 226–7.

10 M. Walsh, "The Harradine Affair", *The Australian Quarterly* 40(2) June 1968, pp. 31–9.

11 Reynolds, "The Role of Minor Parties", pp. 159–61.

12 Reynolds, "The Role of Minor Parties", p. 164; Colin A. Hughes, "The Case of the Arrested Pendulum" in Howard R. Penniman, ed., *The Australian National Elections of 1977* (Washington, DC: American Enterprise Institute, 1979), pp. 320–1.

13 M. Edwards, "Minor Parties and Independents" in P.R. Hay, I. Ward, J. Warhurst, eds., *Anatomy of an Election* (Melbourne: Hill of Content, 1979), pp. 83–84.

14 The other communist party is the Communist Party of Australia (Marxist-Leninist) which is pro-China. See B.J. Costr" . . . And Then There Were Three: The 1971 Split in the Communist Party of Australia" in Lucy, ed., *The Pieces of Politics*, pp. 213–22.

15 P. Reynolds, "The Australian Democrats" in Penniman, ed., *The Australian National Elections of 1977*, pp. 125–40; P. West, "The Australian Democrats" in R. Lucy, ed., *The Pieces of Politics*, 2nd edn (Melbourne: Macmillan, 1979), pp. 99–110; K. West, "From Movement to Party: the NCP and the Australian Democrats" in Mayer and Nelson, eds., *Australian Politics: A Fifth Reader* pp. 340–4.

16 Reynolds, "The Australian Democrats", p. 127.

17 Reynolds, "The Australian Democrats", p. 129–30; P. West, "The Australian Democrats", p. 105.

18 Reynolds, "The Australian Democrats", p. 138.

19 Richmond, "Minor Parties in Australia", p. 364.

20 D. Aitkin, "Labor owes it to the young voters", *National Times*, October 19–25, 1980, p. 30.

21 Reynolds, "The Australian Democrats", p. 140.

22 West, "From Movement to Party: the NCP and the Australian Democrats", p. 344.

23 Australian National Political Attitudes Study 1979, conducted by D.A. Aitkin. The total sample was 3016, while the number of respondents who identified with the Australian Democrats was 59. I am grateful to Professor Aitkin for permission to draw on the results of this survey.

24 Trade unions have too much power: 93.1 percent of Liberals, 61.6 percent of Labor, 96.6 percent of Democrats; big business has too much power: 47.8 percent of Liberals, 77.4 percent Labor, 78.0 percent of Democrats.

25 Homosexuality shoud be legal: 55.3 percent of Liberals, 63.2 percent of Labor, 69.5 percent of Democrats; legalize marihuana for use and sale: 25.9 percent of Liberals, 41.8 percent of Labor, 47.5 percent of Democrats; no censorship: 35.2 percent of Liberals, 49.6 percent of Labor, 45.8 percent

of Democrats; abortion should be able to be obtained easily: 40.3 percent of Liberals, 48.5 percent of Labor, 55.9 percent of Democrats.

26 Uranium should stay in the ground: 11.5 percent of Liberals, 29.9 percent of Labor, 30.5 percent of Democrats; reduce taxes rather than spend on social services: 67.1 percent of Liberals, 50.2 percent of Labor, 55.9 percent of Democrats.

27 *The Australian Liberal* 22(6), July 1980, p. 1.

28 ibid.

29 *Australian*, September 29, 1980.

30 Senator Colin Mason, letter to the Editor, *Australian*, September 30, 1980. Mason calculated that while the Democrats and the ALP voted together 80 percent of the time, 61.34 percent of these votes were procedural, and that on matters of substance the Democrats voted with the government 59 times, against the government 86 times.

31 *Australian*, October 9, 1980.

32 *Australian*, September 23, 1980.

33 J.D. Bollen, *Protestantism and Social Reform in New South Wales, 1890–1910* (Melbourne: Melbourne University Press, 1972). I am indebted to Peter Loveday for this reference.

34 H. Glezer, J. Mercer and P. Strong, "WEL strategy, 1972: the methods of a protest lobby" in H. Mayer, ed., *Labor to Power: Australia's 1972 election*, pp. 177–80.

35 These, and other smaller groups such as People for Alchohol Concern and Education questioned individual candidates. Other groups such as the Australian Conservation Foundation, the Aboriginal Treaty Committee and the Australian Association of Independent Businesses used a similar technique at the party rather than the candidate level.

36 The Uniting Church reported that its survey of attitudes to unemployment (returns from all States except Queensland) had been completed by 87 percent of AD candidates, 50 percent of ALP candidates, 30 percent of NCP candidates, but only 8 percent of LP candidates. CIET reported that all LP candidates in South Australia had failed to respond to their questionnaire.

37 P. Wilson, "Public Opinion and abortion law reform" in T. McMichael, ed., *Abortion: the Unenforceable Law* (Melbourne: Abortion Law Reform Association of Victoria, 1972) pp. 35–8.

38 The question is framed in various ways, so comparison across surveys is not always easy. The 1979 Aitkin national survey found that 44.1 percent favored easily obtainable abortion; 46.9 percent under special circumstances only; and 5.3 percent not under any circumstances. Just before the 1980 election a survey conducted by Australian Public Opinion Polls (The Gallup Method), Poll no. 04/6/80, July 8, 1980 showed 29 percent favored legalizing abortion in all circumstances; 24 percent in cases of exceptional hardship, either physical, mental of social; 23 percent if the mother's health either physical or mental were in danger; 13 percent only if the mother's life were in serious danger; while 9 percent would not legalise abortion in any circumstances.

39 The Victorian RTLA campaigned against the ALP member, Doug Everingham, in Capricornia (Qld), and for the LP members, Michael Hodgman (Dension) and Bruce Goodluck (Franklin) in Tasmania. Hodgman and Goodluck are among the official patrons of the association.

40 Warhurst, "Taking a Few Political Lives: the 'pro-life' campaign", p. 238.

41 "Right to Life 1980 Federal Election campaign", mimeo.

42 Use was made of whatever information was available. The survey contained two questions derived from the bills debated in Federal Parliament. They were: "Will you commit yourself to voting for the cessation of the use of health care money for the destruction of Australian babies before birth by abortion? Will you commit yourself to voting for a measure which recognizes the right to life of the unborn child from the moment of conception?" Answers were to be Yes or No. Unwillingness to provide answers was to be taken as a negative reply.

43 For example, to extract two electorates from the RTLA guide:

Ballarat	McMillan
* **Cotter, J.F.**	4 Burke, S.M.
* **Gough, G.J.**	2 Cunningham, B.T.
4 Mildren, J.B.	1 **Handley, B.D.**
* **Short, J.R.**	3 McCracken, R.T.
	5 Simon B.D.

The names of approved candidates were starred and written in bold type.

44 The RTLA's income for the first five months of the 1980/81 financial year (July-Novermber 1980) was $107, 427. *Right to Life News* Nov–Dec 1980, p. 3.

45 "1980 Federal Elections—Right to Life Association Victoria: Resume and Ratings of Election Campaign", mimeo, p. 1. I am indebted to Mrs Margaret Tighe for supplying me with RTLA documentation.

46 *Australian*, October 9, 1980.

47 Sydney Morning Herald, October 14, 1980.

48 On the other hand, the CPA candidate for Melbourne was outraged at being given a favorable rating by RTLA!

49 The DLP vote in McMillan was 5.0 percent. While in one other electorate the DLP vote was higher (Batman, 7.4 percent), this tally included a substantial donkey vote because the DLP had the top position on the ballot paper.

50 In this context, it should be noted that Bertram Wainer polled 4.0 percent in the electorate of Casey.

The author acknowledges the research assistance of Gillian Evans, Vance Merrill and Gillian O'Loghlin.

7
Holding the Balance of Power? Women in Australian Electoral Politics

Anne Summers

Australia was the world's second country, after New Zealand, to enfranchise women although four American States—Wyoming, Colorado, Utah and Idaho—and two Australian States—South Australia and Western Australia—had earlier given voting rights to women.[1] At the time the vote was secured in the two Australian States, the Australian suffrage movement was still in its infancy. The great struggle for votes for women did not require in Australia the ardor and militancy it took to persuade the British government to enfranchise women although it is not true to describe the process, as some earlier writers have, as being merely a case of women being handed the vote "on a plate".[2] But the fight for the right to vote was neither as concerted nor as protracted in South Australia and Western Australia, as it was to become in other States, such as New South Wales and Victoria, where women did not obtain the suffrage until after they were already able to vote in Federal elections. In both the former States, after some initial resistance to the innovative idea of enfranchising women, conservative male politicians saw it as a means of enlarging the conservative electorate and supported the measure as an anti-working-class tool.[3] This was especially the case in Western Australia where, after the discovery of gold in the early 1880s, an influx of miners threatened to undermine the existing balance of power.

The early Australian feminists saw the vote as giving them the opportunity to inject moralism and decency into civic life and influence events, rather than participate directly in them.[4] Few of the women who threw themselves into the struggle for the vote took advantage of the ultimate victory to stand for elected office.[5] In the seventy-nine years from the first Federal election until the elections of October 1980 only seventeen women had been elected to Federal Parliament. Of these, four had abbreviated parliamentary careers, serving only one three-year term. Only three women have ever achieved ministerial ranking[6] and while two of the three occupied Cabinet posts, one was not allocated a portfolio and was a Cabinet Minister at a time in Australian politics when all ministers were members of the Cabinet.[7]

The 1980 elections appear to have been a watershed for women. a record number of female candidates contested the election and a record number were elected. There had never before been more than two members of the House of Representatives at any one time (and that occurred only for a brief three years after World War II) following the 1980 elections there were three. While before the elections there were six female Senators—itself a record number—following the elections, there were nine. Shortly after the elections a male Senator died and a woman was selected to replace him, bringing the total number of female Senators to ten, and the total number of women in Parliament to thirteen—almost as many as have served since its inception. It is important to note that included in the statistic of seventeen women having been elected before 1980 were six women currently in the Parliament. Of these one was defeated in the 1980 poll, two were reelected and three were not facing election. When these women are added to the women elected on October 18, 1980, their total number—thirteen—outstrips the total of eleven women who gained office in all the years since Federation.

The impending success of women in the elections was unheralded and caught both party organizations and political commentators by surprise. The party affiliations of the new female parliamentarians is instructive in this respect. Of those elected (including those reelected), seven were members of the Australian Labor Party (ALP), one a member of the National Country Party (NCP), one a member of the Australian Democrats (AD), and only one a member of the majority governing party, the Liberal Party. The latter, Senator Dame Margaret Guilfoyle, who has achieved the highest status of any woman in Australian politics (she is a senior Cabinet Minister) was reelected. (See Table 7-1 and 7-2.)

In other words, the women elected for the first time all came from the minority parties and only one, the NCP member, Florence Bjelke-Petersen, became a member of the government. As will be discussed below, her election was one of the more controversial aspects of the entire campaign because she is the wife of the Premier of Queensland, Joh Bjelke-Petersen, and her preselection was seen in all quarters as being a piece of intraparty political maneuvring, rather than being a win for women as such.

The ALP fielded the most candidates, endorsing twenty-three women for the House of Representatives; however only five were preselected for seats which were "winnable", that is, needed a swing of less than 5 percent. The Liberals endorsed five women, in each case for seats that were blue-ribbon (or safe) Labor. The minority party, the Australian Democrats, endorsed thirty-one women, none of whom had any chance of gaining election since the preferential system of voting ensures that only major parties can win lower house seats. One of the most surprising aspects of the ALP effort was that it gave party endorsement to two women for safe Senate seats. (Another ALP woman, Senator Susan Ryan, was reendorsed for the seat she had previously occupied.) What has in the past been characteristic of all the major parties—that they will endorse women for certain Senate election but expect women to perform the near impossible in winning marginal lower house seats—was repeated, and accentuated, in the 1980 campaign.

Only one woman has ever won party endorsement for a safe House of Representatives seat: Dame Enid Lyons was elected to Parliament after her husband, the Prime Minister, died in 1943. Apart from this special case, women have never had the opportunity to win safe seats and 1980 was no exception. The three women elected to the House of Representatives in 1980 all occupy marginal seats and will have to fight hard to retain them if there is any swing back to the coalition parties at the next elections. Thus, the 1980 gains do not, of

TABLE 7-1
Women Members and Senators of the 32nd Australian Parliament, 1981 –

	Liberal	ALP	NCP	AD	Total
House of Representatives	—	3	—	—	3
Senate	4	4	1	1	10
Total	4	7	1	1	13

Notes: Includes three Senators who did not have to face election in 1980 and a woman selected to replace a deceased Senator in May 1981.

TABLE 7-2
Percentage of Women Members and Senators of the 32nd Australian Parliament, 1981 –

	House of Representatives	Senate
Total members	125	64
Percentage of women	2.4	15.6

themselves, guarantee that women are about to become an integral and permanent part of the Australian political scene. The gains could turn out to be merely transitory unless significant changes are made by all the major parties in their attitudes to preselection. The success of the female candidates in 1980 may, however, encourage this. An analysis of the results obtained by the women indicates that they were able to gain, on average, a slightly larger swing than the State average. The overall swing to Labor in the elections, on a two-party preferred basis, was 4.2 percent; the ALP's female candidates averaged a swing of 4.6 percent.[8] This result, together with the emerging evidence that the gap in numbers between men and women who vote for Labor is closing, may encourage all parties to pay greater attention to female voters, and to female candidates, in the future.

However, it is by no means guaranteed that the political parties will follow such a rational course; to explain this seemingly pessimistic prognosis, it is necessary to examine two factors more closely: the far greater success women have in winning safe Senate seats; and the women who were elected in 1980.

Preselection

Traditionally, it has been easier for women to win Senate seats. While the total numbers are small, the point is borne out by reference to Table 7-3 which shows that of the twenty-four women ever elected to Parliament, seventeen won Senate seats. Only one woman has held a House of Representatives seat for more than one consecutive term (and, as already pointed out, Dame Enid Lyons was a special case). One of the women elected in 1980, Joan Child, had previously won the same Victorian seat in the 1974 elections. She lost the seat in 1975, contested it again unsuccessfully in 1977 and won it back in 1980; this record indicates that it is far from being a safe Labor seat.

TABLE 7-3
Women Members and Senators of the Australian Parliament, 1901–81

	Liberal	ALP	Others	Total
House of Representatives	2	5	—	7
Senate	9	6	2	17
Total	11	11	2	24

Note: Includes those elected at Federal elections, October 1980 and a woman selected to replace a deceased Senator in May 1981.

Until 1975 when the L-NCP opposition used its majority in the Senate to defer approval of the Labor government's Budget, an action which eventually led to a constitutional crisis and the dismissal from office of the Prime Minister, Gough Whitlam, the Senate was not perceived as a powerful chamber. Although in the decade before 1975 some younger Senators had tried to make the Senate's committees function in an aggressive and investigative manner, similar to the committee system of the US Senate, they had not succeeded in raising the power or status of Australia's second chamber.

The Senate was not perceived, therefore, as the route to a serious career in politics. The Prime Minister is always drawn from the House of Representatives, the only chamber with the power to initiate money bills. Most ministers are also drawn from the House of Representatives. Only one Prime Minister, Sir John Gorton, began his political life in the Senate and his accession to the top position was unforeseen, precipitated by one of the most bizarre episodes in Australian political history: the disappearance of Prime Minister Harold Holt while swimming in December 1967. Gorton assumed Holt's job as Prime Minister and his house of Representatives seat simultaneously, after the Liberal Party had decided he would succeed the dead former leader.

The Senate has been an easier route into politics for women simply because there was marginally less competition (politically ambitious young men have always sought to enter the lower house) and because both the responsibilities, and the chance of advancement, were less. Senators represent entire States and do not have the heavy burden of electoral duties which fall to members of the lower house in their single-member constituencies. This makes it somewhat easier for women to consider a Senate career, particularly if they have families to look after. These factors, together with the traditional reluctance of the major political parties to withdraw preselection from a sitting member, have meant that women, having won Senate seats, had a high probability of retaining them for more than one term (see Table 7-4). One of the upsets in the lead-up to the 1980 campaign was the demotion at a sitting Senator, Jean Melzer, from a safe position on the ALP's Victorian Senate ticket to a virtually unwinnable slot. She was defeated.[9]

However, the factors that throw light on why it has been somewhat easier for women to gain Senate seats should not be exaggerated. They have relative merit only—as a means of trying to explain why the discrepancy between women's representation in the two chambers exists, why there has often been at least one female Senator whereas for vast tracts of time the House of Representatives has been an all-male chamber. Whatever the advantages of the Senate for women, they are slight, particularly when it is realized that since Federation there have been almost 360 Senators and only 17 of them have been women.

Of the women elected in 1980 for the first time, none can be assured a long-term parliamentary career. The three female members of the House of Representatives will have to fight hard to retain their seats although one, Ros Kelly the member for Canberra, is probably assured of a reasonably long tenure because she gained a large swing, putting her seat into a less marginal category. She is also young enough to be able to have serious political prospects, providing she can consolidate her hold on the seat.

The same cannot be said for the Senators. Of the four elected for the first time, three were aged fifty-nine or sixty at the time of election and can only expect to serve one six-year term before being required by their parties to make way for younger contenders, while the only young Senator is a member of the Australian Democrats, a minority party whose fortunes may have waned by the time she seeks reelection. She may gain preselection from her party in 1986, but at the time of writing it is difficult to predict whether the AD will still be a potent political force. The history of minority parties in Australia,

TABLE 7-4
Women Parliamentarians: Length of Service, 1901–80

Name	Party	Service	No. of times elected
Senate			
Breen, Marie	Lib.	1962–68	1
Buttfield, Nancy	Lib.	1955–65 1968–74	3
Coleman, Ruth[a]	ALP	1974–	2
Guilfoyle, Margaret[a]	Lib.	1971–	4
Martin, Kathryn[a]	ALP	1974–	2
Melzer, Jean[a]	ALP	1974–	2
Rankin, Annabelle	Lib.	1947–74	5
Robertson, Agnes	Lib./CP	1950–62	3
Ryan, Susan[b]	ALP	1975–	3
Tangney, Dorothy	ALP	1943–68	5
Walters, Shirley	Lib.	1975–	2
Wedgwood, Ivy	Lib.	1950–71	5
House of Representatives			
Blackburn, Doris	Ind. Lab.	1946–49	1
Brownbill, Kay	Lib.	1966–69	1
Child, Joan	ALP	1974–75 1980–	2
Lyons, Enid	UAP, Lib.	1943–51	3

Notes: [a] Subject to reelection at double dissolutions in 1974 and 1975.
[b] Subject to reelection every three years or whenever a House of Representatives election is held.

especially those born in splits from the Liberal Party, as was the AD, suggests this grouping will have a comparatively short life.

Early in 1981 the Liberal Senator for the Australian Capital Territory, John Knight, died suddenly. There are no provisions for by-elections for Senate vacancies caused by death or retirement; instead the government of the State from which the Senator was elected is obliged to appoint a person of the same party to fill the vacancy. In May 1981 a joint sitting of the two chambers of the Federal Parliament appointed Margaret Reid to replace John Knight (there being no State Parliament in the ACT). Senator Reid is comparatively young and provided she again gains Liberal endorsement, she must be seen as having the prospect of several terms in the Senate.

The net gain in 1980 of women with long-term prospects was, therefore, not great. Of the six already serving, two have already achieved considerable success and a third has prospects. Senator Dame Margaret Guilfoyle is already a Cabinet Minister, Senator Susan Ryan already a Shadow Minister, and Senator Kathy Martin has already served as a deputy whip for the government and could conceivably enter the Ministry in a post-Malcolm Fraser Liberal government. Of the remaining three, Senator Jean Melzer was defeated, and the remaining sitting Senators, Ruth Coleman and Shirley Walters, would probably not be considered young enough or sufficiently involved in the political mainstream of their respective parties to have any hope of promotion.

These should not, however, be the only criteria for evaluating the significance of the female parliamentarians. The very fact of their presence in such numbers will be exemplary and instructive. (In the first few weeks of the new Parliament, government ministers had constantly to correct themselves when answering questions from female members, after initially referring to them as "Honorable Gentleman", and to learn to say "Honorable Member".) So, while it is unlikely that many, or any, of the individual women elected in 1980 will go on to great political prominence, the mere fact of their election could prove to be trailblazing in encouraging other women to seek preselection, and in prodding parties to adopt less discriminatory preselection practices than in the past.

The Political Parties and Women

Until the 1980 elections, the conservative parties had elected the greater number of women. This is partly because representation of women is institutionalized within the Liberal Party. When the party

130

was established by Robert Menzies (later Sir Robert) in 1949 he recognized the need to attract women in order to augment the conservative vote. Using similar tactics to those adopted by conservative governments in giving women the right to vote, Menzies ensured that a strong women's organization was established within the party and women were given guaranteed, albeit token, representation on the party's major decision-making body, the Federal Executive. The party rules have always provided for one its two Federal vice-presidents to be a woman. Traditionally the Liberal Party has always had a higher proportion of female members than the ALP—about 50 percent compared with the ALP's 25–30 percent. Women's representation in Parliament in no way matched their representation in the party, but did appear to have the effect of prodding the Liberals to ensure that they always had at least one woman as Senator.

The Labor Party

The wins of Labor women in 1980 have evened up the representation tally and processes currently underway within the ALP may lead to greater, and guaranteed, representation of women in the future. Senator Susan Ryan, Senator for the ACT since 1975 and, having won election three times, Labor's most senior-ranking female parliamentarian, has argued on the basis of ANOP polls that if women had voted Labor in the same proportion as men in the 1977 and 1980 elections, Labor would have won government.[10] She argues that female voters are less attracted to Labor because of its male-dominated image, an image she says is gained partly from ALP policies and partly from the solid male majority at all levels of the party organization. Senator Ryan has analyzed opinion poll data, collected prior to the last four Federal elections, to argue her case and also to demonstrate that women's traditional anti-Labor bias is declining.

She has pointed out that while in 1974 there was an 8 percent difference in the Labor vote between men and women, a gap which narrowed only to 7 percent in 1975 and to 6 percent in 1977, there has been substantial improvement since then. Before the 1980 elections opinion polls showed that the difference between men and women intending to vote Labor had narrowed to 4.5 percent.[11]

Following the 1977 elections and a very poor result for Labor, the ALP established a Committee of Inquiry to review the party's structure and to make recommendations about how it could instigate reforms to enhance its electoral appeal. When the committee reported in early 1979, one of its most important, and controversial, findings concurred with Senator Ryan's assessment.[12] The committee recommended that in order to try and overcome the traditional image of the ALP as being male-dominated, the ALP introduce for a specified, limited term a policy of affirmative action. Under that policy, women would be guaranteed representation at all levels of party organization in proportion to their membership of the party. The committee stated that the policy ought also apply to party preselections, a radical move which, if it were adopted, would eventually guarantee that women for the first time could gain preselection for safe seats.

The recommendations have caused considerable controversy within the ALP but have prompted a serious soul-searching about how more women could be encouraged to vote Labor. The attention to party structure is only one element of this soul-searching, and it can be expected that great care will be put into evolving policies attractive to women before the next elections. A sign of the more conciliatory attitude of party chiefs towards the claims of women came when the National Executive of the ALP, the party's main decision-making body, voted to allocate $5,000 towards the traveling expense of women attending the first-ever National Conference of Labor Women, a large gathering held in Sydney in January 1981. At that conference, a large number of motions proposing policy changes were adopted and under party rules had to be considered by the main policy organ of the ALP, the National Conference, at its policy meeting in 1982.

The ALP had set aside its 1981 Conference to determine how much of the Committee of Inquiry recommendations ought to be adopted. Although only State branches of the party have the necessary power to implement most of the changes, their endorsement at the national body would mean a greater chance of local success. At the time of writing it appeared that at least a modified version of the affirmative action proposals had a good chance of being supported by the National Conference. They had been endorsed by the leader of the opposition, Bill Hayden, and several State conferences had given them sympathetic approval. Were they to be approved by the 1982 National Conference, the way would then be open for a greater number of female candidates' gaining preselection for safe seats than at any other time in Australian political history. The ALP's female members hoped that the changes in the party's structure would also have a favorable impact on the electorate, particularly the female electorate. A party structure that was nondiscriminatory towards women would presumably mean that women have a greater say in policy-making and would be likely to aid the process of generating polices attractive to women. (The mere fact of a party structure that did not discriminate against women would have only a marginal impact on the electorate.)

If the optimum aims of the ALP women were realized—increased numbers of women as candidates and policies more attractive to women—it could conceivably tip the balance in favor of a Labor victory in 1983. The election of three women in 1980, together with some earlier data, indicates that female candidates are not electoral liabilities in House of Representatives elections. There is some evidence to indicate that women may in fact possess electoral advantage, by attracting female voters—and not alienating male voters —that could outweigh party affiliation in closely contested seats.

During 1980 the ACT branch of the ALP employed a market research firm, Australian Nationwide Opinion Polls (ANOP), to survey the two ACT electorates. At the time the two sitting members were men—one ALP, one Liberal—but an ALP woman, Ros Kelly, was attempting to topple the Member for Canberra. She needed a swing of just over 1 percent to do so. The ANOP survey found that putting up a woman as candidate could attract female voters:

> An important finding suggests that when Labor fields a credible, high profile woman candidate then its vote amongst women is higher than amongst men.... There were in fact two percent more women voting Labor than men ... suggesting that Ros Kelly may be losing a few votes amongst men but gaining more than she loses amongst women.[13]

The survey also commented on the question of the candidate's being a woman appearing to outweigh party considerations:

> Women consider her to be a good Labor choice more so than men (fifty-four percent versus forty-four percent)—a significant finding reinforcing our earlier comments about the doubt that one must cast on the theory that women won't vote for women candidates. The overwhelming majority of Canberra voters were of the assessment that the sex of the candidate made little difference to their vote or to the performance of the elected representative. To a completely bland question we received an eighty-six percent indication to the "doesn't matter" attitude with the remaining fourteen percent split evenly between the minority views that either a man or a woman made a better member of Parliament.[14]

As there is no similar survey for the Australia-wide electorate, no body of evidence exists that could prompt political parties to preselect female candidates as a means of wooing votes from women. There has been little impetus for the conservative parties to do so, in any case, because of their continued electoral success. Since its wartime government was defeated in 1949, Labor has governed for only three of the intervening thirty or more years. Thus, the motivation to attract more votes from women now exists in Labor; however, it has taken a long time for that party to concede, at last, and still grudgingly, that this may be the way to government.[15]

It cannot be said that any of the major parties consciously set out to attract the women's vote by selecting female candidates in 1980. Labor found itself, to its surprise, with twenty-three women as candidates. The surprise was due to the fact that candidates gain preselection at electorate level and the national organization cannot directly influence the process; it was not until only a few months before the elections that the ALP national organization and the parliamentary leaders learned of the record number of female candidates. It then sought to turn this to advantage. Early in the campaign, on September 22, opposition leader Bill Hayden, and New South Wales Premier and national president of the ALP, Neville Wran, hosted a well-publicized breakfast for female candidates at Sydney's Wentworth Hotel. Invited to attend were representatives of all prominent women's organizations. But this event, important as it was, was hastily arranged—a product of the late realization that Labor might unwittingly have found itself a useful political means of attracting female votes—and it did not have the necessary complementary backing of policies thought out specially for women.

Apart from a discussion paper on women's issues launched and endorsed by Bill Hayden, no party developed special policies for women, although Labors' health program was presented as being mainly benefiting women. Labor promised free medical care for all children and for women during pregnancy and confinement. Following the election, this policy was attacked by Senator Ryan who, only three months after the election, told a conference of Labor women:

A Labor health insurance policy that offers free medical cover to women only during pregnancy and confinement is a policy that fails to take account of the fact that of the 7.2 million women in the Australian population only 1.2 million are of average child-bearing age, [i.e. aged 25–35] and the rest including the two million who pay tax (but excluding the 1.9 million under 15 and therefore covered) are not covered for the vast range of health problems, including the notorious health problems of working class women. Further, as the average family size has declined to 2.0 [children], a health policy that seems to assume that we spend most of our lives pregnant is one that women voters will not find irresistable.[16]

The Coalition Parties

The coalition parties, the Liberal and National Country Parties did not promote their female candidates as women. This was partly because they had few candidates but, more importantly, their most prominent female candidates were not running as women but rather as representatives of different sides in a particularly bitter coalition brawl.

Almost two years before the Federal elections the Queensland division of the Liberal Party decided, in principle, that it would field a separate voting ticket for the Senate elections. This was prompted by the fact that whereas at the Federal level and in every other State where the two parties work together in government or opposition, the Liberals are the majority and hence senior coalition partners, in Queensland they are not only a minority, but a downtrodden minority. The Liberal Party in Queensland has been extremely critical of many of the actions of its senior coalition partner, the National Party,[17] and particularly of its leader, Queensland Premier Joh Bjelke-Petersen. The Liberals have accused Bjelke-Petersen of undermining civil liberties by banning street assemblies, of bypassing the Parliament and governing by executive fiat, and of tolerating massive corruption amongst his National Party ministers.

The Liberals decided to take their campaign against Bjelke-Petersen at the State level into the Federal arena, via the Senate campaign. It had been expected that a State election in Queensland would precede the Federal elections and that the coalition infighting could be contained within the State. However, Prime Minister Malcolm Fraser and his National Country Party Deputy Prime Minster, Doug Anthony, feared that such a State coalition fissure could cause damage to the Federal coalition and, after discussions with Bjelke-Petersen, opted to hold the Federal elections three months earlier than required—thus, before the State elections. The tactic backfired to some extent because the Liberals' State campaign, organized around the slogan "Give the Liberals the Numbers", inevitably spilled over into the Federal sphere.

The importance of the coalition partners' running separate tickets for a Senate campaign can be appreciated when it is recognized that in all other States the ALP was competing against the coalition for the five Senate seats. When the coalition runs on separate tickets there is a three-way, rather than two-way, contest for the five seats and this creates the possibility that Labor will win three of the five seats—since the coalition vote will be split—or that the fifth seat will be won by a splinter party. The latter situation eventually prevailed in Queensland where the Australian Democrats won the fifth seat and the Nationals and the Liberals won only one seat each.

But the battle was fought out between two women. When the coalition partners join together for the Senate campaign they take turns, election by election, to take the majority of the three positions they hope to win. In 1980 it was the turn of the Nationals to have two of the three prime ballot positions as two of their sitting Senators were due for reelection, whereas the Liberals had only one. However, the Liberals boldly endorsed their Senate team, giving first position to the sitting Senator, Neville Bonner (Australia's only Aboriginal politician) and giving the winnable number two position to Yvonne McComb, then State president of the Liberal Party. Yvonne McComb, a dynamic fifty-nine-year old, was seen as electorally appealing because she was well known through her political campaigns against the Nationals.

The Nationals held out for some time, hoping that Anthony and Fraser could secure a reversal of the decision. When it became clear that the Liberals would stick to their guns, the National Party endorsed Florence (Flo) Bjelke-Petersen, also aged fifty-nine and the wife of the Premier, to head their ticket. This caused considerable bitterness within National Party ranks because it meant that the two sitting Senators, Ron Maunsell and Glenister Shiel, were relegated to virtually unwinnable positions on the ballot and were in effect sentenced to premature retirement.

The decision to endorse Flo Bjelke-Petersen caused considerable comment, and not a small amount of ridicule, within and beyond Queensland. It was designated the "Joh and Flo Show". But it was an astute political move on the part of the Nationals. While at State level the Nationals reign supreme, in a Federal election Queenslanders were more likely to favor Fraser and the Liberals. The Nationals were worried that Yvonne McComb's endorsement could attract votes away from them unless they countered with the electoral magic of the name Bjelke-Petersen. In what was dubbed "the Battle of the Grandmothers", the two parties traded public and private insults about their respective candidates who became, in the process, symbols of the coalition bickering. Yvonne McComb, a widow, was a career woman who had earned political endorsement in her own right. Flo Bjelke-Petersen had had no direct political involvement on her own account until, after considerable arm-twisting by her husband, the Nationals nominated her for the number one position. Prior to that she had enjoyed a folksy image, being mainly portrayed in the media as a champion maker of pumpkin scones.

The whole episode did nothing to enhance the prospects of women seeking political careers since it was seen by most other politicians and commentators as a comic item. Both women achieved national notoriety, unlike other female candidates who were attempting to gain office and who remained largely in obscurity until after they had been elected. (It is interesting in this respect to note that one of the Labor women elected to the House of Representatives won a sub-urban seat in Brisbane, the capital of Queensland, and that she achieved a swing of 1.5 percent above the State average.) Neither Yvonne McComb nor Flo Bjelke-Petersen had a long-term political career in prospect if elected since neither could hope to serve for more than one six-year term, because of this ages. When the votes were counted, the fact of their being women, and prominent women, had little if anything to do with the results. The votes fell into predictable party lines with the number one candidate for both the Liberals and the Nationals being elected, Labor taking two seats, and the fifth going to the Australian Democrats. Thus Flo Bjelke-Petersen became a Senator and Yvonne McComb did not: it had nothing to do with their talents or political skills, and virtually nothing to do with their sex. It was all a matter of where they appeared on the party ticket.

The Queensland experience was not typical of what happened to female candidates elsewhere, but it was instructive in one respect: to win seats in the Federal parliament women require strong party endorsement. This can come only from their gaining preselection for "safe" or at least, "winnable", seats.

Conclusion

The general mood of the Australian electorate in 1980 was perceived by all parties to be one of "creeping conservatism". There was virtually no mention of the kinds of massive social reforms that had swept Labor into power in 1972. The Australian Democrats cam-paigned against nuclear power and the growing economic strength of multinational corporations but their catch-cry (and main electoral appeal) was "We'll keep the bastards honest", a threat that was directed towards both of the major parties. The AD attracted people who were weary or cynical of politicians of both parties and who hoped the AD could win sufficient Senate seats to hold the balance of power and serve as a check on the large parties. The ALP promised to "Raise the Standard" if it was elected and campaigned heavily with an attack on eroded living standards under the Fraser government. Its campaign was tailored to appeal to the so-called middle ground, that electoral tract of middle-class, young family groups living in swinging seats. This group had been identified as the one which had lost the most economic ground under the five years of the Fraser government's priority policies of fighting inflation through monetarist policies, of holding down wages, and allowing unemployment to rise. The government campaigned on its record at first, starting the campaign with the slogan "Lead on Liberal", but ended by concentrating its efforts at attacking Labor over a promised wealth tax and capital gains tax when opinion polls showed the government to be in danger of losing the election. In all of these approaches by the major parties there was virtually nothing directed specifically at women. If anything, the ALP and the coalition parties, by their stress on the institution of the family, ignored women by seeing them as being totally subsumed within their family roles. None of the female candidates thought it prudent to campaign as women but instead identified themselves strongly as party members. However, a record number of women won and, as argued earlier, the average swing to female candidates was slightly higher than the overall swing. The 1980 election campaign did not demonstrate conclusively whether female candidates have extra electoral appeal if they gear their campaigns towards female voters, but it is starting to appear that this may be the case; if so, then female voters could hold the balance of power in 1983, in what is expected to be a very close election.

Notes

1 New Zealand gave women voting rights in 1983. The earliest enfranchisement of women came in Wyoming (1869) followed by Colorado (1893), South Australia (1894), Utah and Idaho (1896), and Western Australia (1899). The other Australian States gave women voting rights after the Federal franchise had been achieved in 1901: New South Wales (1902), Tasmania (1903), Queensland (1905), and Victoria (1908). England gave the vote to women aged thirty and over in 1918 and extended full adult suffrage in 1928. The United States introduced the Federal franchise for women in 1920

2 See, for instance, Ian Turner, "Prisoner, in Petticoats: A Shocking History of Female Emancipation in Australia", in Julie Rigg, ed., *In Her Own Right* (Melbourne: Nelson, 1969), p. 20.

3 Norman MacKenzie, *Women in Australia* (Melbourne: Cheshire, 1962), pp. 35–8.

4 See Anne Summers, *Damned Whores and God's Police: the Colonization of Women in Australia* (Melbourne: Penguin, 1975), Chapter eleven, "Feminism and the Suffragists".

5 One of the few feminist campaigners for the vote who several times

sought Federal elected office was Vida Goldstein who, arguing that women should never subjugate themselves to party, stood five times as an independent candidate in Victoria between 1903 and 1917. She was never elected but polled extremely well in the first Senate elections.

6 Dame Enid Lyons was a minister without portfolio, occupying the position of vice-president of the Executive Council from December 1949 until March 1951 in the Menzies government. Senator Dame Annabelle Rankin was Minister for Housing from December 1967 until March 1971 under both the Holt and the Gorton governments. Senator Dame Margaret Guilfoyle was Minister for Education during the caretaker Fraser government which lasted from the dismissal of the Labor government on November 11, 1975 until the holding of general elections in December that year. Following the elections she was appointed Minister for Social Security, a Cabinet post and one which she held until the 1980 elections. In the Cabinet reshuffle following those elections she was appointed Minister for Finance, also a Cabinet position. In 1980 she had been appointed a Dame of the British Empire, like her two ministerial predecessors. It is most unusual in Australian politics to award imperial honors to men unless they are on the brink of retirement.

7 Robert Menzies began the practice of selecting a Cabinet from his Ministry in 1956, a custom which was abandoned by the Whitlam government of 1972–75 but has been resumed by the Fraser government since 1975.

8 Figures compiled by Malcolm Mackerras, cited in Marian Sawer, "Women and Women's Issues in the 1980 Federal Elections", *Politics*. v. 16 no 2 (Nov. 1981) pp. 243–9.

9 See section, "The Senate Count" in Chapter 9 for an explanation of elections to the Senate. In order to be certain of being elected, candidates must occupy the number one or number two position on their party's "how-to-vote" ticket. Senator Melzer was relegated to the number three position after the faction of the ALP to which she belonged withdrew its support from her. Despite a strong fight, and a concerted campaign by women's groups, she failed to be reelected.

10 Senator Susan Ryan, "Keynote Address", delivered to the First National Labor Women's Conference, Sydney, Australia, January 1981.

11 ibid.

12 Australian Labor Party National Committee of Inquiry, *Report and Recommendations to the National Executive*, March 1979, pp. 10–11.

13 Ryan, "Keynote Address".

14 ibid.

15 The newly elected member for Canberra, Ros Kelly, has also argued this position strongly to a national conference of the Young Labor Movement, held in Canberra, May 1981.

16 Ryan, "Keynote Address".

17 In Queensland the rural conservative party calls itself the National Party even though its Federal members in Canberra are deemed to be members of the National Country Party.

8

The Media and the Campaign

Murray Goot

In the space of two weeks, a "dull" contest became a "cliffhanger". Central to this transformation were, of course, the polls. They dominated the press coverage and the television news; caused the Liberal Party to revamp its campaign and redouble its advertising; and both directly and indirectly affected the vote. The polls symbolized the campaign as contest in its purest form.

It was the press, not television, that commissioned the polls. Though the daily papers are not as powerful as they once were, the metropolitan dailies still sell over four million copies across electorates in which more than five and a half million vote. Over and above its own influence on voters, the influence of the press on politicians and on other media continues to be felt in many ways.

This is the first Federal election study to attempt a systematic analysis of more than one or two of these papers. The two national dailies together with the four Sydney and three Melbourne papers account for most of the metropolitan circulation and it is on these that the analysis is focussed. They range from the serious press to the entertainment press and include papers whose coverage of politics falls somewhere in between; and they include papers from each newspaper stable: John Fairfax & Sons Ltd, Herald and Weekly Times Ltd and News Limited.

The study then investigates the differences between channels in the campaign's share of the news (including differences between commercial channels and the ABC), and so commerical news "networking". It also looks at the prominence of the leaders in news bulletins and at news time given over to the "horse-race and hoopla". Where it makes sense to do so, comparisons are made with the press.

While the first two parts look at media practices and at Liberal and Labor strategies to exploit them, the third section looks at the ways in which both parties organized their own newspaper and television campaigns and, more closely, at the market research that informed them.

Was the Liberal Party's advantage in the advertising stakes reflected in the size of the swing? Was its campaign on wealth tax crucial? If not, what was it that finally frightened voters back to the government? It is to these questions that we turn in section four.

The Dailies

Readership

Except for two or three of the quality papers, circulation figures for the metropolitan dailies in the second and third quarters of 1980 were down on the corresponding period for 1979 and falling (Table 8-1). Notwithstanding this decline—in part reflecting a decline in two-paper purchases—the proportion of voters who claimed to be "regular readers" of a daily paper and to read more than one paper remained remarkably high. In surveys conducted in 1967 and 1979, 94 percent classified themselves as "regular readers" of the press; about 23 percent claimed to read one paper regularly; 41 percent, two; and 31 percent, three or more.[1] Whether election campaigns affect the number of papers that are bought is unclear. But they certainly affect the amount of attention "politics" gets from readers, a by-product, no doubt, of the shift in emphasis that takes place within the press itself. In 1967, 43 percent claimed to follow politics in the paper they mentioned first as one they read regularly; but shortly after the 1969 election, 58 percent said they had followed the campaign in their first-named paper. In 1979 the number claiming to follow politics in their first-named paper was 48 percent (53 percent in either their first- or second-named paper), so in 1980 the proportion following the election in the press might have been as high as two-in-three.[2]

The Press: Top, Middle, and Bottom

What "following politics" means varies from paper to paper. The variation appears to be more marked in Australia than in Britain.[3] The morning papers, especially the quality press, devoted much more space to Federal politics during the campaign period than did the afternoon press. Over the five-week period, the *Australian* and the *Australian Financial Review* (the two national dailies) set aside over

TABLE 8-1
The Press and Its Readers (in percentages)

Title	Publisher	Days	am/pm	Sales ('000) and Trend	Readers per issue[a]		Occupation								Party Preference[b]	
					Men %	Women %	Exec/ Managers %	Prof/ Senior Govt Officials %	Bus Prop/ Self-Employed %	Clerks/ Sales %	Tech/ Skilled %	Semi-Skilled %	Manual/ Domestic %	Home Duties %	L-NCP %	ALP %
National																
Australian	News	M–F	am	127+			20	15	10	9	7	3	3	3	53	32
Aust Fin Review	Fairfax	M–F	am	61+			32	11	10	9	6	3	3	3	62	25
Sydney																
Syd Morning Herald	Fairfax	M–Sat	am	258–	33	29	44	50	36	27	26	19	25	28	53	32
Daily Telegraph	News	M–Sat	am	309–	40	26	36	25	32	40	49	45	46	21	33	53
Sun	Fairfax	M–F	pm	349–	44	41	53	41	42	54	45	42	43	38	44	44
Daily Mirror	News	M–F	pm	359–	39	35	36	26	34	45	46	49	47	35	36	48
					177	140	225	172	167	186	179	162	171	125		
Melbourne																
Age	Fairfax/ Syme	M–Sat	am	243	36	30	54	57	43	42	30	19	20	33	42	42
Sun News-Pictorial	H & WT	M–Sat	am	629–	64	57	48	45	42	65	72	68	62	60	40	45
Herald	H & WT	M–Sat	pm	393–	52	48	62	53	51	60	49	49	56	50	40	46
					165	141	209	175	162	181	158	138	140	153		
Brisbane																
Courier-Mail	H & WT	M–Sat	am	270–	72	64	65	54	49	46	43	41	34	42	48	39
Telegraph	H & WT	M–F	pm	154–	48	46	30	22	23	34	32	34	23	24	43	45
					138	118	138	102	85	91	87	81	60	90		
Adelaide																
Advertiser	H & WT	M–Sat	am	228–	72	68	79	76	74	69	62	65	63	68	36	48
News	News	M–F	pm	164–	61	50	63	47	63	67	60	68	64	48	31	56
					145	124	182	138	154	149	126	139	132	119		
Perth																
West Australian	H & WT	M–F	am	253–	80	74	86	78	74	76	75	75	80	73	56	35
Daily News	H & WT	M–F	pm	117–	52	44	68	51	51	63	56	50	58	38	53	40
					132	118	194	146	143	151	139	132	143	113		
Hobart																
Mercury	H & WT	M–Sat	am	56												
Canberra																
Canberra Times	Fairfax	M–Sat	am	44												

Notes: [a] Readers per issue, based on men and women aged 18+; city totals include sales of the Australian and Australian Financial Review.
[b] Party preference: 'Undecided' responses not distributed.

Sources: Audit Bureau of Circulation and John Fairfax & Sons, for sales figures; McNair Anderson and Associates, readership survey, August 1979–August 1980 (n = 2,824, Sydney; 2,347, Melbourne; 2,019, Adelaide; 2,021, Brisbane; 1,745, Perth); Morgan Gallup Poll no. 352, April–June 1980, for readers per issue and occupation; Morgan Gallup Poll no. 352, April–June 1980, for party preference.

100,000 square centimeters of text for Federal politics; so did the *Sydney Morning Herald* and the Melbourne *Age*.

In Sydney and Melbourne the middling papers managed less than 40,000 square centimeters, with the Sydney *Sun* and *Daily Mirror*, the bottom of the political market, managing less than half that. The argument for rejecting the usual quality/mass or serious/popular distinction in favor of a three-tier model is a powerful one.[4] At one end of the spectrum, the coverage given Federal politics was eight times that at the other (Table 8-2). Allowing for the size of type, these figures actually understate the difference.

If allowance is made for the size of newspapers—or, at least, the amount of paper not given over to advertising—the differences are not quite so great. Even so, the quality dailies devoted twice as much editorial space to Federal politics as the middle papers, and five or six times as much editorial space to Federal politics as the papers at the bottom. Again, the gap is narrowed if headlines are counted. Except for the *Australian*, the quality press gave half the space to headlines given by the middling papers and about a quarter that given by the *Sun* and *Daily Mirror*, in both of which the total text occupied no more than twice the space occupied by the corresponding headlines. (Both papers depend heavily on front pages and posters to attract the passing trade.) For the quality press, the ratio of text to headline was more like 7:1 or 8:1 (Table 8-2).

These differences were reflected in the prominence given to Federal politics. Thus, most of the front-page leads in the *Australian* (64 percent), *Australian Financial Review* (68 percent), *Sydney Morning Herald* (57 percent), and *Age* (67 percent) covered Federal politics; most of those in the *Sydney Daily Telegraph* (37 percent), the *Sun News-Pictorial* (13 percent) and *Herald* (17 percent) in Melbourne, and the *Sun* (20 percent) and *Daily Mirror* (8 percent) in Sydney, did not. The Brisbane *Courier-Mail* (40 percent) and Adelaide *Advertiser* (50 percent)—middling rather than top papers—did not give the election quite the prominence of the top papers, but they were ahead of their afternoon counterparts, the Brisbane *Telegraph* (28 percent) and the Adelaide *News* (16 percent). Only in Perth, did the afternoon *Daily News* (48 percent) give as much prominence to the election as its stablement, the *West Australian* (47 percent).

A similar pattern emerges when front-page stories other than lead stories are considered. The quality press—the *Australian* (with 73 such stories), the *Australian Financial Review* (42), *Sydney Morning Herald* (56), and *Age* (67)—averaged up to three a day; the *Daily Telegraph* (11) and Melbourne *Herald* (18) averaged less than one every two days; while the *Sun*, *Daily Mirror*, and *Sun News-Pictorial*, apart from one or

TABLE 8-2

Press Coverage of Federal Politics, National, Sydney and Melbourne Dailies, September 15–October 18, 1980

	Federal Politics as % total editorial space[a]	Total			News	Features	Editorials			Cartoons		Letters			Headlines[a]
		Item No.	Total item space sq cm	Mon–Fri avg sq cm	Space %	Space %	No.	Space %	Avg size sq cm	No.	Space %	No.	Space %	Avg size sq cm	Space as % of total item space
Australian	19.1	1,053	115,571	23,114	53.9	24.0	40	6.1	176	23	6.5	212	9.4	51	29.4
Fin. Review	25.3	783	103,869	20,774	60.3	26.5	23	6.0	272	27	4.2	31	2.9	97	13.8
SMH	20.2	977	111,611	18,579	53.9	23.9	39	9.8	280	30	5.2	183	7.1	43	12.8
Daily Telegraph	9.3	445	32,618	5,822	63.3	10.7	26	11.2	136	20	11.9	44	2.8	21	39.3
Sun	4.6	271	16,033	3,207	54.7	19.5	18	11.8	105	19	5.5	53	8.5	26	49.5
Daily Mirror	4.0	193	17,863	3,573	42.4	20.9	13	6.9	95	14	28.3	24	2.4	18	52.3
Age	19.4	1,122	128,342	20,944	45.3	38.8	29	5.6	253	61	4.9	329	5.5	63[b]	15.8
Sun News-Pictorial	9.4	544	36,203	6,102	82.3	9.9	1	0.3	135	33	6.0	33	1.5	16	28.5
Herald	7.2	373	37,883	5,541	40.1	34.1	12	4.6	145	36	14.6	53	6.7	48	26.6

Notes: News, features, editorials, cartoons and letters jointly constitute total item space; and proportions are of total item space.
[a] Calculated on the basis of a "constructed week": the first Monday, second Tuesday ... fifth Friday, except for the Sun News-Pictorial which lacks data for the first Monday.
[b] Excludes "Access Age".

two "flyers", ran none. Among the other dailies, the *Canberra Times* (52), *Mercury* (32), *Courier-Mail* (37) and *Advertiser* (34) easily surpassed the afternoon tabloids: the *Telegraph* (6), the *News* (4) and *Daily News* (12). It is true that papers with the fewest political stories were generally tabloids, and that headlines occupy a proportionately larger space in tabloids than in broadsheets; but as a comparison of two tabloids (the *Australian Financial Review* and the *Sun*) or two broadsheets (the *Australian* and *Herald*) makes clear, the differences are not reducible to differences in format. (See Table 8-3.)

Differences between the morning and afternoon press relate, to some extent, to the timing of political news: the first editions of the afternoon papers are often on the streets by mid-morning; and few stories written after noon have much chance of making the "Late Final Extra".

It is the morning papers, out on the streets after midnight, that report the main political news stories of the day, including those timed for the evening news bulletins. This may help to explain why, of all the afternoon papers, it was the Perth *Daily News* that gave most prominence to campaign stories. When it was midday on the southeast (where the principal protagonists spent most of their time), it was still only 10 am in Perth.

Differences between the top, middle, and bottom of the press reflect differences in audience composition.[5] The audience for the quality press is skewed toward business executives (in the case of the *Australian Financial Review*, very heavily), middle management, senior public servants, and professionals—toward voters best equipped to assimilate the information that a newspaper of this type has to offer; best placed, day by day, to exert influence on government; and, partly as a result, more likely to think that the outcome of an election matters. In Sydney and Melbourne, where the market is segmented, morning papers of the middle range drew a disproportionately large number of white-collar and blue-collar workers; in other cities, where the market is less segmented the class skew is not so marked. Except for the Sydney *Daily Mirror* (which had an occupational skew similar to the *Daily Telegraph*) afternoon sales were also fairly evenly spread in occupational terms (Table 8-1). But the sheer size of the lower middle-class and working-class audience ensures these papers a relatively low political content.

Differences in the audience and in the conception of the audience manifested themselves in the relative frequencies of leading articles or editorials, feature articles, cartoons (the down-market press was more inclined to run cartoons which assumed an audience low on partisanship and high on political cynicism and fatalism) and letters

145

TABLE 8-3
Subjects of Lead stories during Campaign Period September 15–October 18, 1980: Metropolitan Dailies

	15/9/80	16/9/80	17/9/80	18/9/80	19/9/80	20/9/80	22/9/80
Australian	NSW by-election	ALP industrial relations policy	Industrial relations policies	Call-up	Liberal strike ballot plan		War threat to oil
Australian Financial Review	(Hotels)	(Shares)	Myer's report	(Insurance)	Tax evasion		NSW local elections
Sydney Morning Herald	(Football)	(Medicine)	(Local govt.)	EEC	(NSW Budget)	B-52s	NSW local elections
Daily Telegraph	NSW by-election	(Fire)	(Askin)	Hayden denied VIP jet	(NSW Budget)	(US missile)	(Fire)
Sun	(Football)	(Star tragedy)	(Football)	Oil price rise	(Wran v. Caroline Jones)		Hayden's voice
Daily Mirror	(Storm)	(Crime)	(Crime)	(Wran v. Caroline Jones)	Tax evasion		Govt. swim scholarship
Age	(Housing finance)	ALP industrial relations policy	Drugs' Royal Commission	(Vic. Budget)	Liberal strike ballot plan	B-52s	EEC
Sun News-Pictorial	(US hostages)	(Football)	(Show)	(Vic. Budget)	Footballers taxed	(Crime)	(US missile)
Herald	Industrial relations policies	(Olympics)	(Crime)	(Lady Diana)	(Crime)	(Football)	Hayden's voice
Courier-Mail	(OPEC)	(Strike)	Drugs' Royal Commission	(Strike)	Tax evasion	(New fuel)	(Football)
Telegraph	(Strike)	(Strike)	(Rescue)	Call-up	Sales tax		(Football)
Advertiser	(OPEC)	Unemployment demonstration	EEC	(Gaols)	Drugs' Royal Commission	Airline agreement	(Strikes)
News	(Strikes)	(Development)	(Medical)	(Adamson, MP)	Takeover		(Crime)
West Australian	(Aboriginal health)	(State Cabinet)	Speaker warns Hayden	House suspends Liberal	(Show)	B-52s	EEC
Daily News	(Accident)	(Fire)	(Yachting)	House suspends Keating	(WA Governor)		Tax evasion
Mercury	Campaign opens	(Tas. Budget)	(Tas. Budget)	(Tas. Budget)	(Tas. Budget)	B-52s	Nuclear free zone
Canberra Times	(US hostages)	Oil	(Canberra Mall)	PS ceilings	Drugs' Royal Commission	(Lay-offs)	(War)

Notes: Non-campaign stories in brackets

TABLE 8-3 (Cont'd)

	23/9/80	24/9/80	25/9/80	26/9/80	27/9/80	29/9/80	30/9/80
Australian	(War)	(War)	(War)	(War)		(War)	Lib. v. AD
Australian Financial Review	Interest rates	(War)	War threat to oil	(War)		(Super-powers)	Fraser's rural policy
Sydney Morning Herald	(War)	(War)	(War)	(War)	Gulf force	(War)	(War)
Daily Telegraph	(Fire)	(War)	(War)	(War)	(Football)	(Plane crash)	Promises
Sun	War threat to oil	(War)	(War)	(Football)		(War)	(War)
Daily Mirror	(War)	(War)	(War)	(Football)		(Motor racing)	(Milk price)
Age	(War)	(War)	(War)	Gulf force	Gulf force	(War)	(War)
Sun News-Pictorial	(Football)	(War)	(War)	(Football)	Gulf force	Disaster	(War)
Herald	(War)	(War)	(War)	(Football)	(Football)	(Football)	(War)
Courier-Mail	(War)	(War)	(War)	(War)	'3-cornered' contests	(War)	(War)
Telegraph	(War)	(War)	(Brych)	(Brych)		(War)	(Crime)
Advertiser	(Education)	(War)	(War)	(Development)	Gulf force	(War)	(Gaols)
News	(Salisbury)	(Salisbury)	(War)	(Football)		Senate control	Fraser's policy speech
West Australian	(War)	(War)	(War)	(Football)	Murdoch's TV bid	(War)	(War)
Daily News	(War)	(War)	(Brych)	(Football)		(War)	Fraser's policy speech
Mercury	(Education)	(War)	(War)	(War)	Floating dock	Ballot draw	(Education)
Canberra Times	(War)	(War)	(War)	(War)	(War)	(War)	(War)

TABLE 8-3 (Cont'd)

	1/10/80	2/10/80	3/10/80	4/10/80	6/10/80	7/10/80	8/10/80	9/10/80
Australian	Fraser's policy speech	Hayden's policy speech	Cost of promises		Hayden's petrol policy	(War)	(War)	Labor's wealth tax
Australian Financial Review	Fraser's policy speech	(Old development)	Opinion poll			Opinion poll	(Oil co.s)	Share slide
Sydney Morning Herald	Fraser's policy speech	Hayden's policy speech	Opinion poll	Opinion poll	Opinion poll	Opinion poll	Opinion poll	Share slide
Daily Telegraph	Fraser's policy speech	Hayden's policy speech	(Murder)	(Qantas error)	(Fire)	Strike threatens elections	Share slide	Share slide
Sun	(Football)	Cost of promises	(Murder)		(Races)	(Azaria Chamberlain)	(Shooting)	Fraser's Senate strategy
Daily Mirror	(Torture)	(Azaria Chamberlain)	(Ali fight)		(Car races)	(Azaria Chamberlain)	Murder	Labor's wealth tax
Age	Fraser's policy speech	Hayden's policy speech	Cost of promises	Opinion poll	PM fights back	Defense push	Supply	Share slide
Sun News-Pictorial	Fraser's policy speech	Hayden's policy speech	(Bushfires)	(Ali fight)	(Fire)	(Lotto)	(Murder)	(Gold find)
Herald	(War)	(War)	Disaster	(War)	(Crime)	(Hattie)	(Crime)	PM's Senate fear
Courier-Mail	Fraser's policy speech	Hayden's policy speech	(Azaria Chamberlain)	Opinion poll	(Strike)	(Strike)	Share slide	(Drought)
Telegraph	(Accident)	(War)	(Strike)		(Strike)	(Strike)	Supply	PM's switch
Advertiser	Fraser's policy speech	Hayden's policy speech	(War)	Opinion poll	PM on attack	(Gaols)	(Gaols)	Share slide
News	(Crime)	(Azaria Chamberlain)	(Steve McQueen)		(Princess Caroline)	(Azaria Chamberlain)	(Pay/jobs)	(Millhouse)
West Australian	Fraser's policy speech	Hayden's policy speech	Aboriginal employment	(Farm income)	(Disaster)	(Drought)	(Hospitals)	Share slide
Daily News	Hayden's policy speech	Hayden's policy speech	Opinion poll		PM on attack	(Azaria Chamberlain)	Share slide	WA seats
Mercury	Fraser's policy speech	Hayden's policy speech	Aboriginal land rights	(Drought)	(Hospital charges)	?	(War)	(War)
Canberra Times	Fraser's policy speech	Hayden's policy speech	Liberal's ACT campaign	(War)	Parties change tactics	Defense	Public Service	Share slide

TABLE 8-3 (Cont'd)

	10/10/80	11/10/80	13/10/80	14/10/80	15/10/80	16/10/80	17/10/80	18/10/80
Australian	AD v. Hayden on taxes		(War)	Opinion poll	Labor split on uranium	Fraser's tax cuts	Opinion poll	
Australian Financial Review	Fraser's new push		Economic responsibility	Tax bonus for bush	Opinion poll	Stock exchange	Opinion poll	
Sydney Morning Herald	Fraser's new tactics	(Prisons)	Hayden cancels street walks	Murdoch's TV bid	Opinion poll	Leaders on polls	Opinion poll	How-to-vote card stopped
Daily Telegraph	Opinion poll	(Terror)	(Mine blast)	(Drug haul)	(Violet Roberts)	Tax cut bonus	Opinion poll	(Racing)
Sun	(Hostages)		(Murder)	(Violet Roberts)	(Tragedy)	(Violet Roberts)	Opinion poll	
Daily Mirror	(Killer)		(Shooting)	(Kidnap)	(Pin balls)	(Violet Roberts)	(Football)	
Age	Liberal campaign	(Wage case)	Public TV soon	Murdoch's TV bid	Opinion poll	Fraser's tax cuts	(Gulf force)	Poll
Sun News-Pictorial	Opinion poll	(Crime)	(Earthquake)	(Drugs)	(Fire)	(Accident)	Opinion poll	(Crime)
Herald	(Crime)	(Racing)	PM's election meeting	Pol Pot	Opinion poll	(War)	(Crime)	(Racing)
Courier-Mail	Opinion poll	(War)	(War)	Opinion poll	Opinion poll	Opinion poll	Opinion poll	How-to-vote card stopped
Telegraph	(Crime)		(Drought)	(Drugs)	Opinion poll	Labor march	Opinion poll	
Advertiser	Opinion poll	Liberal strategy meeting	(War)	(Wage case)	Pol Pot	Oil prices	(War)	Poll
News	(Hawkes)		(Rescue)	(Disaster)	(Education)	Tax cuts	Opinion poll	
West Australian	Campaign violence	(Water Board)	(Earthquake)	Murdoch's TV bid	PM on inflation	Opinion poll	Foreign investment	(Compassion)
Daily News	(Accident)		Liberal 'lies'	Opinion poll	Opinion poll	WA seats	(Crime)	
Mercury	Labor's tax cuts	'Reds under beds'	Floating dock	Opinion poll	Opinion poll	Opinion poll	Opinion poll	Poll
Canberra Times	Unemployment	Labor marches	(Earthquake)	Murdoch's TV bid	Pol Pot	(Business)	Campaign wind-down	Labor's program costs

and other correspondence concerned with the campaign.

The quality press ran editorials on Federal politics, regularly and at length. The *Australian* and *Sydney Morning Herald*, which run first and second leaders, averaged more than one editorial on the election per day. The rest of the press, with the exception of the *Daily Telegraph*, ran editorials much less regularly. These differences say something about the political traditions of the newspaper groups: the means by which they attempt to wield influence. In Fairfax's *Sun* and News Limited's *Daily Telegraph* the proportion of editorial space (though not of words) occupied by editorials was twice that in the quality press; in two of the Herald and Weekly Times papers—the *Daily News* and the *Sun News-Pictorial* (except for one on election day) no editorials at all were run.

Both audience composition and press economics (the two are clearly related) go a long way to explain the substantial difference between the quality and the nonquality press in the number of feature articles. Except for the *Herald*, it was the quality press in Sydney and Melbourne that had most features. Bolstered by higher advertising charges, they can afford to employ more political and economic specialists; and, at election times, it is newspapers like the *Age* that also hire more specialists.

The quality papers not only published four to eight times the features published by the other papers; but (with the exception of the *Australian Financial Review*) they published upwards of four times as many letters on Federal politics, and the letters they published were, on the whole, much longer. The extremes were represented by the *Age* (including correspondence accepted by telephone and published under the heading "Access Age") and the *Daily Mirror*: fourteen times as many items of correspondence were published by one as by the other and the letters proper were four times as long in the *Age* (Table 8-2). Although we do not know how many letters were received but not published, the differences are very much what one would expect. The art of letter writing and (in the case of the *Australian*, at least) access to a typewriter are more middle-class than working-class virtues; middle-class voters are more likely than working-class voters to think that what they have to say will change the world (in the language of political science, they have a higher sense of "political efficacy") and the influential (with their own conception of the audience) might reckon that on matters of politics a letter to the *Sydney Morning Herald* is worth any number to a paper like the *Sun*. Apart from anything else, papers that take elections seriously can expect to generate a greater correspondence.

Under Starters Orders

The Prime Minister announced the date of the election, October 18, on the evening of Thursday, September 12. Made, according to tradition, to government members at 7:30 pm and to the House of Representatives at 8 pm, the news came too late for TV's main evening bulletin. Apart from the announcement itself, and five weeks later the news of the result, only the formal campaign opening by the Prime Minister (on the evening of September 30) and the leader of the opposition (on the evening of October 1) were assured of being placed on the front page.[6] Even some of the serious papers did not think Doug Anthony's opening speech for the National Country Party (NCP) (October 1) or Senator Chipp's for the Australian Democrats (AD) (October 8) warranted that sort of treatment.

Unlike 1977, there was no editorial opposition to the calling of an election a month or two ahead of time; but only the *Australian* and its stablemate the *Daily Telegraph* positively welcomed the news. The decision, they argued, ended "the uncertainty and bickering which interferes with the progress of government".[7] The *Age*, while reiterating its preference "for Governments serving their full term", conceded that the election was "only two months sooner than necessary" and that the timing had "advantages for Government, Opposition and public alike". The public, in particular, would "be spared a protracted election campaign" and would "be able to settle back to normal life well before the Christmas season".

The idea of elections as an intrusion—as something extraneous to everyday life that ordinary citizens would (or should) rather be spared—was even more common in the less prestigious press. The *Daily Mirror* thought the "most gratifying aspect" of the campaign was that it would be "short and sharp". The *West Australian* suggested that, had the date been set any later, "the electorate probably would have been bored stiff by the time it got to the polls". "In the next five weeks", said the Melbourne *Herald*," a million words will go into one collective ear and out the other." According to the Melbourne *Sun* the number of elections was "fast reaching the stage" where, for many people, "the mere obligation to vote is obscuring what they're voting about".

Elections were something governments should be spared as well. Reflecting on the fact that this was the fifth State or Federal election in eight years, the *Herald* decided that an election was "good for democracy, but not necessarily good for good government". According to the Sydney *Sun*, four-year parliaments were "wanted and needed" because three-year parliaments meant that "we only have one year of proper government".[8] That the "good" or "proper" government papers such as these had in mind might mean nastier government for the bulk of their readers, neither paper admitted. For a different readership the *Australian Financial Review* invoked a different myth. Since elections only encouraged parties to seek to intervene in the "free market" on behalf of "special interests", "the first casualty of politics will be economic rationality". That the dominance of the "free market" depended on a certain kind of politics was something the paper preferred to let slide.

No doubt the editorials would have been different had the government, as in 1975, been one that the press wanted to be rid of. But while each of the editorial writers noted some government shortcoming, most found more than enough to admire. "Compared to most of its predecessors", said the *Australian*, the government had made "a good fist" of things. The *Daily Mirror*, as firm a friend of the coalition's as its stablemate, conceded that the government still had problems with inflation and unemployment, but argued that it had done better than most industrialized countries. Only the *Age* thought the key to the government's success lay, not in its performance on inflation and unemployment, but in its success "in lowering public expectations".

Although most papers would have been happy without an election, there was no escaping the importance of elections in legitimizing a liberal democratic system. The myth of electoral sovereignty, implicit in the prominence given to reporting the election campaign, found more explicit editorial expression as well. Some papers waited until the end before telling voters that their decisions really mattered, others said so from the start. The "policies to be decided on at this election *are* important," insisted the *Herald*. According to the *Australian*, voters were about to "determine the shape and future of our country for the next decade".

Some of the morning papers referred to their own role in this process. The *Age* would "try to identify the main issues and ask the opposing parties to explain their policies coherently". Though all governments had "their limitations and failures ... the people's choice at the ballot box still matters and should be made with knowledge and care". The *West Australian*, conceding both the "big responsibility" of the news media and the "superficial" nature of their coverage "in recent elections", promised that it would "help the voter cut through the politics of confrontation to the substance behind the personalities".

For the *West Australian* itself, the substance of the campaign would be determined by the parties. It expected the "central battleground" to be the economy. Though most editorials promoted their own ideas about what the election should be about there was not much disagreement. The *Sydney Morning Herald* was not alone in nominating "the management of the economy, the alleviation of unemployment, foreign policy and defence" as the issues upon which "the campaign should be concentrated". "If it is not," it added, "those to blame will deserve to be judged irresponsible."

In place of issues there was always the possibility that the campaign would focus on personalities. The Melbourne *Herald* was resigned to the inevitable: "Like it or lump it, personalities will count". But the quality press, in particular, showed more fight. The *Sydney Morning Herlad* summed up the sentiment when in counterposed "personalities, TV 'images', and so on" against "issues forcefully, lucidly and responsibly expounded and debated". It went without saying that since personality politics was linked to television and issue politics to the press, a campaign that concentrated on personalities boosted the influence of TV and diminished the power of the press.

Unemployment, the Economy, and Defense

In the end, a number of the issues the election was supposed to "decide on" were not widely canvassed by the press. And the issues that received greatest prominence did so because of events that neither the press nor the parties had foreseen.

Unemployment figures for August were released by the Australian Bureau of Statistics on September 12; they showed an increase over the corresponding figure for 1979. By announcing an election on the same day the government may have hoped to draw media attention away from the figures. Whether that was the effect is another matter; an election announcement could also heighten the value of such news. As with most issues the press's sense of news value was not uniform. Moreover, in different places, the figures could be used to tell different stories. Though no paper used the story as its lead, both the *West Australian* and the *Canberra Times* had it on the front page. In Western Australia it was headlined: "Increase in Jobless Hits Government"; in Canberra: "Number of Jobless in ACT down 700". The *Age*, hardly the government's greatest ally, had "Jobless up 6400 last year" on page five.

The figures for September were released on October 9. This time the *Age* and *Sydney Morning Herald* carried summaries of the press release at the bottom of page one, leaving a fuller account, with conflicting interpretations by the minister and shadow minister, for page three. The *Canberra Times* with "Poll Dispute over Jobless Figures" elevated the story to the front-page lead. Accordng to the ABS, the number of people wanting to work full-time but out of work was a postwar record. Yet only the Fairfax papers made room for the story on the front page. The *Australian*, with "Viner claims victory as jobless stays at 6 pc", placed the story in the "Business Australian"; the *Daily Telegraph* managed only four sentences on page two. In Sydney and Melbourne none of the afternoon papers breathed a word of it.

Clearly, the treatment of unemployment was not only affected by ordinary news values like the time-frame within which newspapers operate and whether or not an item is "news". It was also affected by the politics of the press. The *Sydney Morning Herald*, apart from giving the official statistics a prominence they lacked in the News Limited press, ran a series on "living on the dole", and the *Age* ran a series on poverty.[9] Coverage was also affected by notions of audience interest. Most readers were not unemployed; and although unemployment continued to rank as the most important issue in the polls, some newspaper managements—especially after the 1977 election—would have discounted this ranking heavily.[10] And because the parties themselves read the polls in much the same way for much the same reasons, unemployment was never the issue on the hustings that it might have been.

Nonetheless, in the two months leading up to the election, agitation by or on behalf of the unemployed left its mark. More articles on unemployment (200) were spotted in a selection of fourteen newspapers (mostly morning papers) than on other issues on which Labor was fighting—like family living standards (169), the price of petrol (108), health (87), or housing (87). The "general feeling" conveyed in these items (except in the editorials) was "that labor would do more about this problem than the government". On health and housing, the ALP probably had more coverage than the government but it was "generally projected as criticising the Government rather than as promoting its [own] policies". Had press coverage of interest rates been monitored, the conclusion would probably have been similar. On petrol, however, "both sides of the argument came through clearly". Labor's "best issue" appeared to be family living standards, where it attacked the "$16 a week cut" in family income under Fraser and promised a $3 a week cut in taxation.[11] It seems hardly coincidental that on its "best issue", Labor's basic propositions (however flawed) could be presented in simple, concrete terms that touched virtually everyone and held promise of immediate change.

Economic management issues of the sort the Liberal-NCP coalition wanted to run on lacked these qualities. So, like its record on unemployment, the government's record here was not well covered either. Again, this was partly a consequence of its own timing. The government had chosen to go to the people before the upward pressure of interest rates forced it to raise housing interest rates, before OPEC could lift the price of petrol, and before the release of the Consumer Price Index cast further doubt on its ability to lower inflation.

On development, the government had played its card in 1977. In the absence of big new projects it was difficult to generate any further news. In Western Australia the huge North-West Shelf oil project got the go-ahead during the campaign. But it was something on which the parties were apparently agreed (it was welcomed by Labor's spokesman on minerals and energy, Paul Keating); and, in any event, it was hardly big news for people living in the eastern States. Roxby Downs, the proposed site of a huge minerals industry, hit the headlines in South Australia but only because negotiations with the State Liberal government had foundered.

Defense and foreign policy also presented issues on which the government wanted to fight. At home, Fraser had fought hard to prevent Australian participation in the Moscow Olympics; abroad, he cut a figure as a Commonwealth spokesman. He had announced the election only a day after returning from the Commonwealth Heads of Government Meeting (CHOGM) in Delhi, a trip which took in Washington and the highly valued domestic prize of an hour with the President of the United States. Liberal Party surveys had earlier confirmed what everyone already knew: that on matters of defense and foreign policy, Labor might be vulnerable. But for an issue in this area to take off required a "clear and present danger", or at least some semblance of a threat.

It was the outbreak of war between Iran and Iraq that put the world back on the front pages. In the week before the policy speeches the war dominated the headlines. Comment by the Prime Minister or the Minister for Foreign Affairs, Andrew Peacock, and speculation that the Australian Navy might contribute to a "Gulf force" organized by the United States, became front-page leads. The "threat" to Australia's oil imports gave the government new grounds to argue the merits of its "parity" pricing policy for Australian crude and to get good media coverage for it. These were only the first issues to take off in ways that no one had anticipated.

The Campaign as Contest

Editorials calling for rational debate were not the best guides to how the press as a whole would report the campaign. Papers which likened the election to another event scheduled for October 18, the Caulfied Cup, proved the better bet. The race metaphor was not only invoked by the *Daily Mirror* but by the *Canberra Times* as well. The amount of space occupied by news items wholly devoted to things other than the issues (the polls, profiles of the swinging seats, lists of candidates and their qualities, and so on) accounted for nearly one-third of total election coverage in the Sydney *Sun* and over one-quarter of the Melbourne *Herald*, but about one-quarter of the *Age* and the *Sydney Morning Herald* as well. The papers with less coverage of such issues came from the top of the market and the bottom.

The race metaphor suffused the headlines and the reporting of campaign news generally was heavily influenced by it. In one sense this is not surprising: election campaigns are contests by nature. Moreover, many of the things that occur during an election campaign occur only because of the campaign; a description of the event, without an account of the reason, would strip it of its meaning. But it is also true to say that most journalists (not to mention many politicians) are less interested in policies for their intrinsic qualities than as moves in the game.[12] Certainly, it is easier to focus on the game; and for news organizations that are thereby under less pressure to employ specialist journalists, cheaper. There is also an audience to consider. Even a newspaper like the *Age* felt voters wanted to be spared a long campaign. One way to spare them was to interpret events as "developments" in an ongoing tussle; for this purpose, the *Age* even hired political scientist, David Butler, and psephologist, Malcolm Mackerras.

Since the quality press was the principal location for explicitly interpretive reporting and least rigid in its distinction between straight news reporting and interpretive reporting, it was the quality rather than the popular press where the tendency was most marked. The policy speeches provided journalists with a field day. Hayden set out "to the capture the family vote", Anthony to offset "rural unrest". Many opening sentences interpreted events in terms of what the journalists themselves had thought likely to happen, reasonable to try, certain to work, and so on. In the *Australian Financial Review* the account of the Prime Minister's policy speech opened with a description of it as a "surprisingly wide-ranging package"; Anthony's proposals were thought "remarkably generous". Opening sentences on the front page of the *Australian* were replete with assessments of each move posing as descriptions. Thus, a statement by the Prime Minister was "a major assault"; Hayden's reply was "slammed back"; the Government conducted an "all-out assault"; and the Opposition, a "major retreat". A narrow, yet apparently definitive set of consequences threatened to bury the news itself. Journalism of this kind did not necessarily diminish the campaign as an occasion for the serious arguing of policies (the quality press, after all, provided most of the solid analysis as well); but it hardly encouraged it either.

More important is the way the framework of a fight helps determine news coverage and news placement. Issues, events, and people that are of only marginal relevance to the outcome—or that are defined as such by the main parties or by journalists—are themselves marginalized. For example, had it not been for the simultaneous contest in the Senate, the Australian Democrats would have received considerably less media attention than they did. It was not only to counter the fear of the "wasted vote" that induced Chipp to take every opportunity to argue that the Democrats would hold the balance of power: except where they threatened to help dislodge a sitting member (as with the Right to Life campaign in La Trobe), the very small parties were almost universally ignored. A "feature" on half a dozen minor candidates, carried by the *West Australian*, might easily have been mistaken for half a dozen letters to the editor.[13]

Where's the Money Coming From?

The most predictable story in the entire contest was the clash over the cost of each side's promises. Battle had been joined as early as August 26, when the Minister of Finance, Eric Robinson, told Parliament that Labor was committed to spending an extra $2,500 million in six areas alone. On the first parliamentary sitting to follow the election announcement Hayden claimed that figures prepared by the Department of Prime Minister and Cabinet demonstrated that Robinson had overstated the figure by $1,375 million. Anticipating the attack, Labor had deliberately put together a package of promises that were relatively cheap; but even that could not preempt it.

Meanwhile the Liberal Party secretariat was preparing a fifty-page document, costing Labor's "300 promises", to be released by Robinson immediately after Hayden's policy speech on Tuesday, October 1. Sydney was chosen as the venue for the release in the expectation that the *Sydney Morning Herald* and the John Laws 2UE talk-back show would give the story a better run than the *Age* and the Derryn Hinch show on 3AW.[14] October 2 was chosen for a number of reasons: to counter the morning after impact of Hayden's speech and to create scepticism in the audience for that night's delayed telecast; to tie up news time on Thursday and talk-back radio on Friday (talk-back shows in Sydney and Melbourne were to be briefed for Friday morning comments and State Divisions of the Liberal Party asked to coordinate phone-in activity); and to push Labor into the weekend before it could organize its counterattack. Talk-back shows in other capitals were to be organized along similar lines early in the following week. The purpose was to switch the campaign agenda from Labor's promise of tax cuts to the Liberal's campaign on Labor's "negatives".

The plan was something of a flop. Since Fraser was also in Sydney, he attracted most of the media's interest. Another problem was that a number of senior journalists believed that in the original parliamentary exchange Fraser had set out to misrepresent Hayden's promise on pensions. More important, and unbeknown to Robinson (despite the party's considerable investment in the technology of instant intraparty communication), Hayden and NSW Premier Neville Wran had released a costing of the government's promises (prepared by the NSW Treasury) three hours in advance of Robinson's press conference. Whatever the merits of either set of figures, the press had no stomach for an argument that promised to be confusing and inconclusive. The *Australian*, acting throughout the campaign as if it were a Liberal party auxiliary,[15] carried the Liberal release—"Spotlight switches to cost of promises"—as its lead story, with a smaller story on Labor's costing immediately adjacent. But the *Age*, with "A paper war over promises"—the only other Sydney or Melbourne paper to mention it on the front page—captured the dominant response. Over the next few days, Fraser continued to run the line but without much encouragement from the press.

Announcing Policies versus Announcing Proposals

The parties set out to create hard news that was less predictable. For the government, of course, there was the opportunity to make announcements which meant something rather more immediate and real than almost anything the opposition could contrive. In the run-up to the policy speech the government got good mileage out of its refusal to let the leader of the opposition use a VIP jet to start his campaign; its presentation of a scholarship to Michelle Ford (the best known swimmer to have missed the trip to Moscow) tenable at its new national sports center; the visit of the Deputy Prime Minister to the EEC, reported to have resulted in concessions for Australian agriculture (the visit made the front page of the *Syaney Morning Herald* and *Age* on three or four days); and the Prime Minister's offer of Australian facilities for the staging of American B-52 aircraft through Australia. Late in the campaign came the announcement that Australia was withdrawing its recognition of Pol Pot.

Labor, on the other hand, had to be content with policy proposals. It promoted the most important of these through a series of "national policy launches", involving the parliamentary leader and the appropriate shadow minister, and by a parallel series of brochures and cassettes (the latter distributed through party branches). Labor's "health care plan for Australia's families", the first in the series, had been launched in November 1979, in anticipation of a similar move by the government. It was followed by the "family home ownership plan" (February); "a plan to create 100,000 jobs for those who need them most" (March); a plan for energy, notably for cheaper petrol (April); a policy on "family living standards" (May); and, in the wake of the Olympics and the shadow of the government-sponsored "Life-Be-In-It" campaign, a family sport and recreation policy (August). These policies were covered by the quality press but few, if any, made the front page.

Once the campaign was underway, the policy launches did significantly better; none more so than the launch of Labor's industrial relations policy, on September 15. While the coverage (front page in several morning papers) owed something to the subject itself, it owed a good deal more to Hayden's simultaneous announcement that the retiring president of the Australian Council of Trade Unions and Labor candidate for the safe seat of Wills, Bob Hawke, had been appointed Labor's spokesman on industrial relations.

The decision to have someone on Labor's front-bench who was not yet a member of parliament was made with an eye to the media.[16] From the end of July, when Wran had asked for and been given the job of party president (a nonvoting position on the party's Federal executive vacant because of the sudden resignation of Neil Batt), Labor had promoted the idea of a "triumvirate" (the Liberals dubbed it a "troika"), consisting of Hayden himself, Wran, and Hawke. Sustained as a public relations device to broaden the focus of media attention (Hawke and Wran were much more popular political figures with both the media and the electorate at large), to defuse stories of the Hawke–Hayden rivalry (campaign committee meetings had already become "Bill and Bob" shows) and to win votes (Hayden announced that Wran was worth 2 to 3 percent in NSW), pictures of the three grabbed a lot of press space, not to mention television time. Labor made sure that during the rest of the campaign the "triumvirate" were seen together at least twice a week.

Nothing so marked the dependence of the press on the leaders as their indisposition. Wran's voice had needed surgery early in August and after several weeks' recuperation he could still muster little more than a croak.[17] Hayden was silenced by a bout of laryngitis at the end of the parliamentary sitting and he was out of action for much of the following week. Chipp lost his voice for a while later in the campaign (as did Flo Bjelke-Peterson). When any of the leaders sneezed the press caught cold. The state of Hayden's voice was noted on the front page of the *Sydney Morning Herald* on three occasions. The third was a reference to Hayden's "relatively resonant performance in support of Labor's policy for women". For anything about the policy itself, readers had to turn to page nine.

But even the best reported policy launch had a short half-life. Just as Fraser refused Hayden a debate, so the government in general chose to ignore much that the opposition announced; only by an oversight were they likely to provide the government with ammunition. At the same time journalists chose not to chase up the issues; with a few exceptions, notably Ross Gittin's *Sydney Morning Herald* series on "The Plain Truth," this was true of issues in general. In the absence of an open clash, the issues were as good as dead.

Labor's Leaks

The half-life of a leak was likely to be longer. Documents in the possession of one party containing information the other party would not have released (that is, documents obtained by unauthorized means) demand a response and even then are likely to leave lingering doubts. They have an authenticity that other claims made by the parties often lack. The principal source of leaks during the 1980 campaign was the public service and the principal beneficiary, therefore, the opposition.

Labor's first leak was a document from the department of the Prime Minister and Cabinet, costing Labor's promises (see Chapter 3). Next day, in Parliament, Hayden claimed that Defence Department sources had informed him that a major study had been undertaken to lift to 250,000 the number serving in the armed forces and to do so by conscription. Ever since the Soviet invasion of Afghanistan and Fraser's determination to have Australia boycott the Moscow Olympics, Labor had worked to head off a "khaki election". (Only days before, Wran had been at work on young voters, arguing that Fraser intended to reintroduce conscription; in March, Labor's pollster had recommended an organized rumor campaign). Several of the morning papers printed Hayden's allegation and the denial of the Minister for Defence on the front page. Next day, the *Australian* carried an exclusive front-page report on "Project Manhaul". The report dismissed the project as "basically a schoolboy-type examination exercise carried out to test army reserve officers". Having served Labor's purpose, the story faded away.

In the last week of the campaign Hayden produced a confidential Treasury Department document which argued that, given the mineral boom, a resources tax might be justified. Hayden used the document to support ALP policy for a resource rental tax on coal and oil companies, a tax the government had rejected. The Treasurer, in response, pointed out that governments did not necessarily follow all the advice they received. The *Age* and *Financial Review* ran the story on the front page—something neither paper had done when Labor launched its policy on foreign investment and a resource rent tax two weeks earlier.

"Unforced Error": Fraser's Threat to Supply

Stories at least as big came from policy positions to which the participants openly attached their names: big because players on the same side and the media regarded them as damaging. In tennis, these "errors" would be described as "unforced". Publicity put the perpetrators under considerable pressure to retreat.

Fraser's pledge that "if circumstances existed as existed in 1975.... I would do everything I could to get rid of the government of that day", was a case in point. Given off the cuff, at a Journalists' Club lunch—in response to a question about what he would do if he again had the numbers in the Senate to prevent Labor governing for a full term—it astounded Liberal officials, drew an immediate response from Hayden, and was front-page news for half a dozen morning papers not controlled by News Limited. The *Australian Financial Review* announced that Fraser "might well have blown the election". But the story petered out: Fraser backed down, stressing among other things the entirely hypothetical nature of his remark. On that point he was right. Whatever the outcome in the House, the balance of power in the Senate would probably be held by the Australian Democrats, and they had sworn affidavits not to block Supply. In any event, it was beginning to look as if the Liberals would not even control the House. Even as Fraser spoke, press interest was shifting.

The Polls

The polls symbolized the campaign as contest (between parties and increasingly between leaders) and promoted it. Without them, the tempo of the campaign, the issues, and the way the campaign was reported would have been different. That the polls would become a feature of the news coverage once the campaign got underway was never in doubt. What was not anticipated was the pattern of results.

Polling, now dominated by the prestige press, is the principal source of campaign news not controlled by the politicians. The growth in the number of polls (there was only one prior to 1972; in 1980 there were six) owes much to the expansion of a tertiary-educated, business, and professional readership. Increasingly familiar with market research as a tool of business, government and social sciences, an up-market readership generated a market for a service of this kind, at the same time attracting advertising revenue to pay for it. (The only evening papers involved in the commissioning of a poll, were the Melbourne *Herald* and the Sydney *Sun*.) In campaign periods when news scoops are notoriously elusive, often unreliable, and inherently unpredictable, the polls provide a guaranteed flow of more-or-less exclusive reports.[18] Since the result of an election often turns on a swing that is within the bounds of the sampling error of the polls, and since successive surveys rarely produce identical results, every survey can be represented as a new and important development.

As scoreboards (at least in posting the final score) the record of the polls had been a good one: they had always picked the winner.[19] Although political observers were aware, at the time the election was announced, that the government's position in the polls did not guarantee its reelection, Labor's support was written down: a sign to the government that all was not well but not meant to signal any serious intention to vote the government out. Besides, there was not a great deal of other evidence to suggest that Labor was about to get the large swing needed to topple to the government. Despite the best efforts of the Labor secretariat to convince journalists that Labor's support in the polls should not be written off—and the widely quoted analysis by Anne Summers to the same effect—the mood in the press gallery remained sceptical.[20] Hardly any political observers expected the government to lose; most expected a fairly comfortable coalition win, though with the loss of a few of their seats. On the eve of the policy speeches, correspondents for the *Age* described the campaign as dull, the voters as "jaded and apathetic", the government as safe.

It was the Saulwick poll of September 27–8 that shattered the illusion. Published in the *Age* and *Sydney Morning Herald* on October 4 (after the policy speeches), it put Labor ahead by sixteen points. The Morgan Gallup Poll, conducted September 20–21 and published in the *Bulletin* (a business weekly) on October 1 had put Labor ahead by three points, the first time that Morgan had shown Labor ahead for several weeks; and an ANOP survey of marginal seats in the capital cities, conducted at the same time as Saulwick's and published on October 3 by the *Australian Financial Review*, had put Labor ahead by four points (or two and one-half points nationally). These had cracked the illusion. But a lead of the size indicated by Saulwick was something completely different.

In 1977, when the coalition had been returned by an unexpectedly large margin, the Saulwick poll had been closer than any other. In 1978, Saulwick had again predicted a landslide (to Labor) in NSW. In addition, Labor people were suspicious of the Morgan Poll (the Morgan Research Centre did most of the Liberal's private polling and the management had long been regarded as anti-Labor) and Liberals were suspicious of ANOP (partly because ANOP conducted Labor's private polls and partly because of what they considered the doubtful validity of polling in marginal seats, especially seats that were exclusively in the city). Saulwick was a clean-skin.

Though none of the subsequent polls gave Labor a lead anything like the size of Saulwick's, Labor stayed ahead. Saulwick's next poll, conducted October 11–12, cut Labor's lead to nine; a relatively small number of telephone interviews, conducted at random on the day the poll was published, October 15, did not warrant a change in these figures. The Morgan Gallup Poll of September 27–28, published in the *Bulletin* with the usual ten days' delay, gave Labor a lead of seven; that of October 4–5, published October 15, still had Labor ahead by six; but the final poll of October 11–12 (published, by prior arrangement, in the *Australian* of October 17) cut this back to two points— enough to suggest that the government might still get back.

Of the other polls, only McNair Gallup suggested a shift back to the government at any stage. McNair's first poll, conducted September from 27–28 to October 4–5, and published by the Herald and Weekly Times chain on October 19, put Labor eight points ahead on the first weekend but only two ahead on the second. Its poll of October 11, published October 17, however, put Labor five points ahead, and a series of reinterviews by telephone, conducted even before the earlier poll had been published, encouraged it to advance this figure even further to six. The Spectrum telephone poll for the *Australian*, which put Labor four points ahead on September 27–28 (published October 6), showed no change on October 11–12 (published October 15). The second wave of ANOP's survey, conducted by telephone on October 13–14 and published on election eve, suggested that Labor's lead had actually grown from four points to seven and one-half nationally.

From October 3 until election day itself, there were only two days in which a new poll, or a reaction to an old one, failed to make the front-page lead in at least one Australian daily. Of the front page leads on the election, every second one touched on the polls. And front-page coverage, as lead story or otherwise, was only a fraction of the total poll coverage.[21] In the last two weeks of the campaign no less than 15 percent of total editorial space in the *Age* (excluding head-lines) was devoted to poll-related stories: hard news stories, comment (including the comments of Fraser and Hayden), features (including interviews with the pollsters), editorials and cartoons. In a number of other Sydney and Melbourne papers the proportion was not much lower.

The *Australian Financial Review* advertised its specially commissioned ANOP series in other Fairfax papers and on its posters and gave each story lead billing. The *Sydney Morning Herald* and *Age* gave priority to the state of the race. The Saulwick polls on voting intention in the House of Representatives were front-page leads, with less prominence being given to the polls on the leaders, voters, expectations of the result, and voting intention in the Senate. Questions on issues were tucked inside. The *Australian* gave Spectrum front-page coverage, with Spectrum's final poll, and later Morgan's, given lead billings.

Although some afternoon papers gave the polls as much space as the morning papers, they gave the polls less prominence. This was partly because, for their front pages, they were only interested in those polls which reported on the state of the race; and partly because most polls, published in the morning (often by their stablemate), were likely to be regarded as old news by the afternoon papers, substantial differences in audience notwithstanding. Thus, the Brisbane *Courier-Mail* had ten poll stories to the *Telegraph's* two; the Adelaide *Advertiser* seven to the *News's* one; the Melbourne *Age* four, and the *Sun News-Pictorial* three, to the *Herald's* one; the *Sydney Morning Herald* nine to the *Sun's* three. The exception was in Perth where the *West Australian* had only two while the *Daily News* had seven.

Few papers were held back from "lifting" stories by an exaggerated regard for other papers' exclusives. It was the race figures that were most often "lifted". Sometimes the pollster was acknowledged; more often, the paper in which the fuller story was to be published. Morgan's results leaked out of the polling organization itself; others leaked out from the publisher. Most papers finished up with at least one front-page story built from leaks of this sort, some with more. Few stuck to their own. The most quoted polls were those which, unlike Spectrum, had a track record.

Shaking Up the Liberals While the polls stayed bad for the government, better polls might have been worse. Until the first of the Saulwick polls hit, the Prime Minister had refused to take the opposition or its leader very seriously; his speeches even included jokes about the ALP. Those in the private office who had cautioned against the complacency evident in the policy speech, counseled greater urgency in the costing of Labor's promises, or been driven to distraction by the soporific nature of Fraser's speeches on development, were now vindicated. While Fraser flew from Whyalla, in South Australia, to spend the weekend at Nareen entertaining Princess Alexandra, those in the private office worked through the night with the party's campaign director, Tony Eggleton, to reconstruct the campaign.

Until his visit to Whyalla, Fraser had not held a public meeting. This was about to change and with it would change his campaign style. His targets would be carefully chosen and his attack hard-hitting. Socialism and the ALP (in Melbourne, heartland of Labor's socialist left); defense preparedness (in Perth, where the sense of threat was always strongest); the unions (in Sydney, the center of Australia's manufacturing industry); and so on. Public meetings would get the crowds, the adrenalin, the demonstrators, and, of course, the cameras. Street walks or "walkabouts" would show the human face of liberalism through the press and on the screen.

Fraser's attack on socialism, delivered the next day, Sunday, October 5, to a Liberal rally at Pakenham, outside of Melbourne, was the turning point. In a number of Monday's papers it was front-page news. The polls, Fraser had told the faithful, should alert all Australians: "if we were to believe those polls...." In a speech that lasted all of twelve minutes, the phrase "socialist government" was used to describe the Labor Party nineteen times.

The Share Market Response   The polls also rallied investors. Hayden's insistence that it was the Treasurer's caution on the resources boom, not the polls, that had caused the slide on the stock exchange, fooled no one. On the other hand, had Hayden acknowledged the polls as the cause and gone on to suggest (supposing for a moment that he had wanted to) that what was good for investors on the stock exchange was not necessarily good for ordinary Australians, he would have put the party up against the bedrock assumptions of the press. Not that the media needed to create a set of assumptions among their audience; that was already done. What was needed now was to organize them.[22]

Share prices did not fall immediately but the initial shudder was enough for the *Age* to move its daily market analysis from its customary position to the front page. On Wednesday, October 8, the *Age* reported that the share market, in the wake of the Saulwick poll and in anticipation of another "pro-Labor" poll in the *Bulletin*, had taken "one of its sharpest falls this year"; that the 2.9 percent drop in the national all-ordinary index on Tuesday "almost matched the big fall in February". The main falls were in minerals and metals, especially uranium, down 3.8 percent; and oil and gas, down 4.2 percent. The *Australian Financial Review*, on its front page, said that prices had suffered a "pounding", with the "collapse of prices ... one of the biggest single day falls ever seen on Australian share markets". But toward the back of the paper the "slump" was described as "much more moderate" in "percentage terms" and "very modest" compared with other occasions on which Labor had seemed capable of winning office; so modest, indeed, as to indicate "either a remarkably confident attitude that the conservative coalition will still be reelected or that life under the ALP may make little difference...." Neither the *Australian* nor the *Sydney Morning Herald*, despite their substantial business readership, thought the story worth even the small space on the front page afforded it by the *Age* and *Australian Financial Review*.

Most papers shared this news judgement. The *Daily Telegraph* did not. Servicing a largely working-class readership in Sydney's western suburbs, the *Daily Telegraph* had struggled against News Limited's management for the right to report the election "straight down the middle". After the policy speeches it had even taken its Canberra correspondent—and with him, virtually all election news—off the front page. Now that the government was in trouble, management decided to bring the paper into line. Wednesday October 8, saw "PANIC AS ALP SURGES AHEAD" across the front page; above it: "Opinion poll rumours rock stock exchange". There was no by-line. The following day, the share slide was the lead story in almost all the morning papers. The *West Australian* with "shares down again but fall eases" chose a factually correct, relatively neutral headline. The Adelaide *Advertiser* and *Canberra Times* highlighted a statement of Fraser's blaming Labor for the slump. Others led with the fall itself, its grip, or its size: In that sense the *Daily Telegraph's* "MILLIONS LOST IN NEW PLUNGE" ($3,000 million was the figure the paper settled for) was comparable with the *Sydney Morning Herald's* "$2,000m. off shares after polls". What made the *Daily Telegraph* stand out, apart from the lack of a by-line, was the line above: "Mums and dads hit hardest, say brokers". Who the brokers were, the paper was not saying; they were certainly unknown to more authoritative papers. According to the *Australian Financial Review*, "most of the heavy selling pressure appears to have come from the larger private clients ... sharebrokers reported there was also some small institutional selling, which was not evident in the bid [*sic*] shake out earlier in the week". A day earlier the same paper reported that "most of the big sellers were larger private investors".[23]

The last two weeks of the campaign saw Sydney's *Daily Telegraph* and *Daily Mirror* devote about one-eighth of their entire election coverage to the vicissitudes of the stock exchange; and that figure excludes headlines. Compared to the *Australian, Sydney Morning Herald,* or *Age*—papers with a much higher proportion of investors among their readers—the two Sydney tabloids devoted four to six times the space.

"Unforced Error": Threatening the Wealthy

With the enemy thus engaged on one front, News Limited's flagship was opening up another. The story was broken by the *Australian* on October 8, a morning on which most other papers gave greater prominence to Fraser's statement on the Senate and Supply. Under the headlines, "Fraser draws a bead on wealth-tax plan", Russell Schneider (who was coordinating News Limited's election coverage from their head office in Sydney) reported that an "ALP proposal to introduce new taxes on wealth" was set to become the focus of the government's challenge "to the growing popularity of Mr. Hayden". Although it was conceded that Ralph Willis had earlier announced that it was "dropping a plan for a tax on capital gains of $200,000 or more, and if elected would carry out an inquiry into all forms of wealth",[24] Labor's spokesman on primary industry, Senator Peter Walsh, and industrial relations spokesman, Bob Hawke, had now "revived fears that the ALP would bring in such a tax". A tax on transactions of $200,000 or more, Schneider argued, "would hit many thousands of home owners" and "thousands of people who have invested in early-maturing insurance policies, or superannuation schemes".

The reference to Hawke remains obscure. The reference to Peter Walsh was to an interview on Thursday, October 3, on the ABC. Asked whether Labor would introduce a capital gains tax, Senator Walsh replied: "We've made our attitude quite clear on this. We will be holding an enquiry into the distribution of wealth in Australia and the Labor Party believes there ought to be some form of capital taxation. . . ." He went on to point out, as had Willis, that:

> Australia is the only country in the OECD that doesn't have some form of capital taxation. Sweden and West Germany who have the best economic record over the last couple of decades of any OECD countries in terms of growth rate, low inflation, low unemployment, all have both capital gains tax, inheritance taxes and wealth taxes. So they've got all the conceivable capital taxes that there are and it certainly hasn't done those countries any harm.

167

He agreed that Labor "might introduce death taxes and gift tax".

Peter Nixon, the Minister for Primary Industry, also taking part in the program, was less than satisfied by these answers. "I think you're wriggling too much Peter ...", he interjected. "The fact is that you are not prepared to state openly what you're going to do on capital tax." But Walsh persisted: "I'm not wriggling. Whether it will be a capital gains tax, a wealth tax, or a reintroduction of inheritance taxes which they have in the United Kingdom and the United States, is something which is yet to be determined".[25]

The statement was picked up in the Liberal Party's Melbourne headquarters and conveyed that evening to the strategy committee. If the campaign had been going the way the Liberals had expected, nothing would have come of it. Fraser would certainly have attacked Labor on capital gains tax, wealth tax, and so on, but there was nothing new in that; reference to both had peppered his speeches for days.[26] Now that the polls were running against them, however, the Liberals were desperate to highlight something new, and they knew the journalists were too. Someone was sent off to look through Labor's record for statements on capital gains and wealth tax; someone else, an observer at Labor's 1979 Conference, recalled Labor's commitment to: "taxing large accumulations of personal capital above a floor level that is reviewed regularly and takes into account the special circumstances of farmers, small businessmen and aged people, and excludes the normal holdings assembled over a lifetime by persons and family units."[27] A number of delegates had been distinctly nervous about it. He remembered Wran telling Hayden: "You'll have to face this".

Soon quotes from Labor's spokesmen were being tried out on journalists. More thinking and talking produced three or four pages of material which was pushed around the campaign network. By October 8 some of the material was finding its way into Fraser's speeches and into the media. At the end of the campaign almost every speech focussed on this new "threat".

Both sides recognized the potential of the taxation issue as a weapon in the campaign. Taxation could be made into a concrete, dramatically simple issue with immediate consequences for almost everyone. Hayden had deliberately delayed the promise of a $3 a week tax cut until the policy speech; and it was that announcement, predictably, which had grabbed the headlines. With their fortunes now flagging, Labor's idea of a wealth tax—turned on its head and promoted as an attack on the "*un*wealthy"—opened for the Liberals a most attractive prospect.

In Sydney, where high real estate values made Labor especially vulnerable, the Murdoch press excelled itself. Indeed the only dailies in Australia to make wealth tax their lead story on October 9 were the *Australian* and *Daily Mirror* (the *Daily Telegraph* giving its front page over to the impact of the falls on the stock exchange). The *Australian's* headline was "Bank accounts force Labor's tax inquiry" and in smaller type "Howard claims 'snoopers' will check on public"; the *Daily Mirror* had "SPECIAL POWERS TO SNOOP ON ALL" above "ALP PLANS CASH, TAX PROBE"—"WAGES, SAVINGS, ASSETS"; while in Adelaide, the *News* settled for "LABOR SNOOPS ON YOUR MONEY", as a front-page flyer. The Hobart *Mercury* with "Fraser warns of Tax War under Labor" was the only non-News Limited paper to run a front-page story with anything like the same slant.

News Limited had got the ball rolling; it would keep it rolling while the Liberal Party prepared new ads. In next day's press the front-page stories on "wealth tax" covered Hayden's attack on the News Limited's line. Liberal Party advertising and the controversy it generated helped put the tax issue back on the front page for the beginning of the last week of the campaign.

Fraser's Last Fling?

With the campaign drawing to an end and the polls still running against the government, Fraser came under increasing pressure to pull something out of the hat. "Qualitative" research commissioned from Quantum Market Research the day after the Saulwick poll and presented to the crucial strategy committee meeting of October 7, argued that swinging voters and those still uncommitted were waiting for the Government to do something to match Labor's appeal to their hip-pocket. If Fraser refused, scare tactics were the party's best hope.

The last big strategy meeting, held on the weekend prior to polling day, again canvassed a number of hip-pocket options, especially a boost in family allowances. But any immediate or substantial offer would have brought into question the Government's credibility as an economic manager. Moreover, there were some signs that a turn-around in the polls had begun to occur. The McNair Gallup Poll, published on Friday, had the Government 9 points behind on September 27/28, but only 2 points behind on October 4/5.

In the end, however, the pressure—not least from News Ltd— proved too much. Fraser openly admitted that the Government had made a tactical error by introducing its own tax cuts from the beginning of the financial year instead of waiting, as Labor had done, for the beginning of the campaign. He now accepted that the Government should promise to recycle any additional revenue it might receive from an increase in the price of OPEC petroleum.

On October 15, the *Sydney Morning Herald* reported that the Treasurer had held out 'a thinly veiled election carrot in terms of a possible income tax cut next year.' The Government would once again return any increase in the oil levy revenue 'by way of personal income tax cuts', he said. A similar comment, made by Fraser, was also noted by the *Financial Review*. But, it pointed out, 'Fraser did not go so far as to make a specific promise.

Next day, the *Sydney Morning Herald* reported that Fraser 'would continue to pass on to taxpayers any significant increase in the oil levy revenue through tax cuts or family allowances', but that 'the Government might well not see the significant increases in the price of oil that have occurred over the last couple of years. For this reason Mr Fraser has not attempted to promote tax cuts or possible increases in family allowances as an election sweetener.'

Not so for the News group. The *Daily Telegraph's* lead story, carried the headline 'TAX CUTS BONUS PLEDGE BY PM' with the strap-line 'Family boost from oil levy.' In bold type it announced that 'the Prime Minister last night promised tax cuts or increased family allowances to compensate for rising petrol prices'; and that Fraser had 'seized on the tax issue to try to regain the election campaign initiative from the Labor Party's promised $3 a week tax cut'; only later did it admit that while Fraser had only talked of returning 'significant increases' he did not expect significant increases to occur. Immediately adjacent, the paper carried an attack on Fraser by Hayden for 'trying to buy votes'. Fraser's promise, Hayden was reported to have said, would cost $3,000 million. This statement, intended to undermine Fraser's, made it look even better.

The rest of the News group followed suit. Posters were used as Liberal Party advertisements—a technique used on behalf of the Labor Party in 1972. The *Australian's* poster shouted "FRASER'S TAX CUT PLEDGE" and in smaller type "OIL TO FINANCE FAMILY BENEFITS". In Adelaide, the *News* led with "Bonanza! Tax Cuts or Family Bonus". Of the other papers that gave Fraser's "promise" front-page space, none played it this way; but perhaps none of them had the Prime Minister's ear.

Violence

Matters of high politics were not the only issues to attract media attention, especially in the News Limited press. Stories linking politics to disorder of some kind—even common or parliamentary rowdiness—make good copy. They usually allow a shift of focus from politicians to ordinary members of the public (only by being constituted as deviant, disruptive, and so on is the active participation of thousands of ordinary citizens in an election campaign actually covered by the media); they are visually interesting (television apart, every paper wants photographs for its front page); and they are slightly less predictable than the platitudes of politicians. But because they are represented as threats to various sorts of legitimized order, they are politically charged as well. Journalists and media management know this and politicians do as well. In the 1980 campaign the government had less reason to worry about the impact of violence on its electoral chances than had the opposition.

Decorum and the threat to it were newsworthy from the start: "House in uproar as Fraser sends country to the polls". The *Australian's* strap-headline was matched by the *Courier Mail* and the local *Canberra Times*. Every morning paper described the scene. The following week, the Parliament's last week of sitting, brought further headlines.

The politicians had hardly stepped on to the hustings when an unemployed man pushed and "verbally abused" the Minister of Employment, Ian Viner, before tipping a bucket of rubbish over him. The incident was made the front-page lead in the *Advertiser*, the local paper, and was featured on the front pages of four other papers as well, including the *Australian* and *Daily Telegraph*. Later that week the *Australian* carried a similar front-page story, this time about "rowdy demonstrators" (unemployed) who "shouted and jeered" as Fraser "tried to speak" at a ceremony to mark the official start to the building of the new Parliament House. In the accompanying photograph a young woman was shown being "escorted" from the ceremony by two policemen after demonstrators "refused to be quiet".

As rallies started to multiply the press was inclined to treat them as if they should have been picnics. On October 9, the Brisbane *Telegraph* had "Fraser Jostled in Demo."; the *Daily Mirror* "PM Jostled in City Crowd", this time in Melbourne; while the Adelaide *News* had "Fraser jostled in Melbourne walk". "Rowdier the better—Fraser" announced the Adelaide *Advertiser*. Some of his supporters took these words literally.[28] On October 11, Hayden had to abandon a walk through the Boronia shopping center in the Liberal Party's marginal seat of La Trobe, when a group of Liberal supporters moved in on him. Next day, at St Mary's, outside Sydney, anti-government demonstrators standing outside a rally had placards ripped from their hands, one of their number (a baby) was grabbed for Mrs Fraser to hold, and another bashed by a member of the Prime Minister's party. These incidents were reported on the front pages of four papers; the News group mentioned neither set of incidents anywhere.

The News group, however, did take notice of a march planned for the afternoon before the election by the October Mobilisation Against the Government; indeed the News group were the only ones to run it as front-page news. The *Daily Telegraph* had "Marchers plan to defy Hayden", a piece which outlined how "defiant officials" of the Victorian ALP had decided to march. The *Australian* ran "March ban lifted for Victoria", advising its readers that Hayden had given the Victorian ALP "special permission" to march. That Hayden had no authority to give or withhold permission is neither here nor there; likewise, the contradiction between the two tales. The important thing was to pounce on anything within the Labor movement that spelled division.

Television News

Viewers

While the proportion of voters who follow politics in the press is now greater than in the mid-1960s, the proportion who follow politics on television is much greater still. In 1967, only 34 percent said they followed politics much on TV; in 1979 the proportion was 60 percent, regardless of party preference. And the evidence of the 1960s suggests that the election might have done more to boost the audience for politics on TV than the audience for politics in the press. While 43 percent followed politics in the press in 1967 and 59 percent did so during the 1969 election, the proportion who followed politics on TV jumped from 35 percent to 63 percent.[29] Other things being equal, the proportion following the election through TV in 1980 may have been closer to 100 percent.

Almost all viewers watch both the commercial channels and the Australian Broadcasting Commission (ABC), with more "regulars" for the commercial channels (72 percent) than the ABC (48 percent). Regular commercial viewers are heavy viewers; and the heavier viewers are more likely to read papers with a relatively low political content. In Sydney, during October–November 1980, nearly half of those aged thirteen plus spent at least three hours a day watching commercial TV; about one in eight spent less than an hour a day. Of the heavy viewers (three hours a day plus) over 80 percent read the *Mirror* and/or the *Sun*, over 35 percent read the *Daily Telegraph*, less than one-quarter read the *Sydney Morning Herald* and less than ten percent read the *Australian* and/or the *Financial Review*. In Melbourne about half the viewers—light and heavy—read the *Herald*. But whereas less than one-third of the heavy viewers read the *Age* and over two-thirds read the *Sun News-Pictorial*, half the light viewers read the *Age* and only one-third read the *Sun*. Those who spent fewest hours watching commercial TV spent disproportionately more time watching the ABC.[30]

The Campaign Share of the News

Leaving aside the headlines and the weather, the main ABC news bulletin on week nights ran for about 24 minutes. Allowing for headlines, weather, and the ads, Channel 7 covered close to eighteen minutes, Channel 9 averaged about twenty minutes, and Channel 10 in Melbourne and Sydney (nominally a sixty-minute program) about forty. But those who watched the ABC did even better than these comparisons suggest. In Sydney, Channel 2 broadcast nearly twice as much election-relevant material as 7 or 9; more even than Channel 10. The time given to Federal politics on commercial channels in Melbourne was roughly the same as in Sydney. But in Adelaide and Perth—whether because more time was spent on State politics, whether because most of the main campaigning went on elsewhere, or whether because Federal politics was judged less important—the time given to Federal politics, including the campaign, was substantially less (Table 8-4). Everywhere, the time devoted to Federal political items varied with the campaign itself.[31] The leanest week for the ABC was the second week of the campaign, between the end of the parliamentary session and the policy speeches. It was a lean week for a number of other stations as well. Channels 7 and 10 in Adelaide managed only five items apiece. The channels that managed to devote more time to Federal politics that week did so not with more items but with longer ones.

The week of the policy speeches saw increased coverage by virtually every station. Some, in Perth and Adelaide, increased their output by a factor of three. Generally, the last ten days, especially the three days prior to the TV blackout of October 15—were the fattest of the lot.[32] The gap between the ABC and the commercials narrowed but except for Channel 10 in Sydney and Melbourne it remained substantial.

The ABC, at least in Sydney, devoted more time to Federal politics by running a greater number of items rather than by running items of greater length; the latter would have opened up the possibility of

TABLE 8-4

Coverage of Federal Politics, Main Evening Television News Bulletin, Week Nights, Campaign Period, September 15–October 15, 1980 (in minutes and seconds)

	Sydney				Melbourne			Adelaide			Perth	
	2	7	9	10	7	9	10	7	9	10	7	9
Sept 15–Sept 19	41.22	20.34	19.51	19.40	14.51	18.49	32.08	15.34	14.55	13.32	11.26	14.04
Sept 22–Sept 26	24.03*	14.29	14.59	26.31	12.00	24.30	28.46	4.36	17.03	6.25	10.49	14.15
Sept 29–Oct 3	39.22	20.26	20.54	26.24*	24.53	22.28	39.33	14.48	19.21	19.23	28.18	14.25
Oct 6–Oct 10	34.04*	23.39	19.33*	42.41	20.40	22.14	30.00	15.47	20.46	23.44	24.45	23.47
Oct 13–Oct 15	33.20	20.24	23.02	34.30	22.01	25.26	32.50	10.31		10.21	16.11	16.00
Total	172.11**	99.32	98.19*	149.46*	94.25	113.27	161.17	61.16		73.25	91.29	82.31
Daily Average	8.12	4.20	4.28	6.48	4.06	4.56	7.01	2.40		3.12	3.58	3.35
Avg per item	1.32	1.31	1.27	1.48	1.22	1.23	1.45	1.18		1.46	1.08	1.24

Notes: Except for Channel 10 in Sydney and Melbourne which ran 60-minute bulletins, all other news bulletins were 30 minutes. Wednesday, October 15 was the last day on which material relating to the campaign could be broadcast.

* Data for one evening missing.
** Data for two evenings missing.

pursuing subjects in greater depth. It was Channel 10, not the ABC, that averaged the longest items. Not that the differences were great. The ABC spent about one-and-one-half minutes per item—similar to the time spent by 7 and 9 in Sydney and only about ten seconds more than 7 and 9 in Melbourne and 9 in Perth. Channel 10 averaged one-and-three-quarters minutes. The shortest items—not much longer than a minute—came from Channel 7 in Adelaide and Channel 7 in Perth (Table 8-4). This goes some way to explaining why Adelaide and Perth gave Federal politics less time than Sydney and Melbourne, or at least it helps to recast the question.

As well as including more items on Federal politics, the ABC gave the stories somewhat greater prominence overall. About half its lead stories were campaign-related.[33] For Channels 7 and 10 in Sydney the figure was about one in three, with Channel 9 somewhere in between. In other State capitals, so far as one can judge, the commercial stations fell within a similar range with the skew again toward the bottom (Table 8-5). While the ABC did not give political stories as consistently high a rating as some of the quality dailies, the commercial channels judged the election more newsworthy than most of the afternoon press.

In terms of proportion of news (including weather) given over to Federal politics, TV generally did better than the press. The ABC devoted about 30 percent of its news time to Federal politics, a figure which compares more than favorably with even the *Australian Financial Review*. In Sydney and Melbourne, Channels 7 and 9 devoted about 20 percent. In Perth the figure for the commercial stations was less than this; with Adelaide's Channels 7 and 10, the figure fell below 15 percent, comparable with Channel 10 in Sydney and Melbourne. But a figure half as large as that achieved by the ABC was still in excess of the equivalent for the Sydney and Melbourne popular press.

Federal politics led the ABC news every night during the first week of the campaign, when Parliament was still sitting, and on each of the last three nights. In between, a campaign lead was more the exception than the rule. Except for the last three nights, election leads on commercial channels were also more the exception than the rule. But if the election was not odds-on to lead the news in Sydney it was still a goot bet for first or second. In other States, election stories were generally pushed a but further down the news.

The News in Sequence

Sometimes stories about Federal politics in general and the election in

TABLE 8-5

Lead Stories on the Main Evening Television News Bulletins, Week Nights, Campaign Period, September 15—October 15, 1980 (including city of origin of all campaign stories)

	15.9.80	16.9.80	17.9.80	18.9.80	19.9.80	22.9.80	23.9.80	24.9.80	25.9.80	26.9.80
Sydney ABC 2	ALP's industrial rel. policy —Melbourne	Parliament re costing of ALP policies —Canberra	Peacock's S. Korea protest —Canberra	Parliament disarray —Canberra	B-52s —Canberra	(War)	(War)	(War)	(War)	(War)
ATN 7	Viner demonstration —Adelaide	Fraser v Hayden on costs —Canberra	(NSW politics: drugs)	Drug inquiry —Canberra	(NSW politics: GMH)	(NSW politics: sand mining)	(War)	(War)	(War)	(Football)
TCN 9	(Storm)	Drought relief —Sydney	(Strike)	(Bushfires)	B-52s —Canberra	Customs corruption —Sydney	(War)	(War)	(War)	(War)
TEN 10	(Storm)	(NSW politics: Luna Park)	(NSW politics: Askin)	(Storm)	(Fire)	H's throat; women's policies —Sydney	(War)	(War)	(War)	(War)
Melbourne HSV 7		(Vic politics: 1988 Olympics)	Conscription —Canberra	Petrol prices	(Truck hijack)	H's throat: women's policies —Sydney	(War)	(War)	(War)	(War)
GTV 9	(Football)	(Vic politics: 1988 Olympics)	(Vic politics: budget)	Footballers tax —Melbourne	(Fire)	Customs corruption —Sydney	(War)	(War)	(War)	Broadcasting Tribunal: ATV-10 —Melbourne
ATV-10	ALP's industrial rel policy —Melbourne	(Vic politics: 1988 Olympics)	VIP jet; conscription —Canberra	(Murder)	(Truck hijack)	(Air disaster)	(War)	(War)	(War)	(War)
Adelaide ADS 7	Viner demonstration —Adelaide	(SA politics: Roxby Downs)	(Car crash)	(Kidnapping)	(Truck hijack)	(Weapons in gaol)	(War)	War; Fraser on oil —Canberra	(SA politics: Roxby Downs)	(Boat sinks)
HWS 9	(Oil find)	(SA politics: Robert Downs)	(Car crash)	(Girls found)	(Fire)	(Weapons in gaol)	(War)	(War)	(SA politics: Roxby Downs)	(War)
SAS 10	Viner demonstration —Adelaide	(SA politics: Roxby Downs)	(Car crash)	Petrol prices	B-52s —Canberra	(Weapons in gaol)	War; Fraser on oil —Canberra	(War)	(SA politics: Roxby Downs)	(Boat sinks)
Perth TVW 7										(War)
STW 9	(OPEC)	(Fire)	(WA politics: hold-ups)	(WA politics: new Governor)	(WA politics: air-fares)	Customs corruption —Sydney	(War)	(War)	(War)	(War)

Notes: Non-campaign stories in brackets.

	29.9.80	30.9.80	1.10.80	2.10.80	3.10.80	6.10.80	7.10.80	8.10.80	9.10.80	10.10.80
Sydney ABC 2	(War)	N/W shelf oil —?	Gulf force —Sydney	(War)	Opinion polls; Fraser's campaign —Brisbane		(War)	Opinion polls; shares—?	(War)	(Gaol seige)
ATN 7	(Car racing)	(Cost of milk)	(War)	(War)	(Air fight)	Hayden's campaign —Melbourne	Opinion polls; Hayden's campaign —Sydney	(Gold nugget)	Hayden's campaign	(Gaol seige)
TCN 9	(War)	Liberal policy preview —Melbourne	Gulf force —Sydney	(Petrol spill)	(Bushfires)	Fraser's campaign —Perth	Hayden's campaign —Sydney	Opinion polls; share—?		(Gaol seige)
TEN 10	(Bushfires)	Liberal policy preview —Melbourne		(Petrol spill)	(Crime)	(Sea drama)	Fraser's campaign —Sydney	(Gold nugget)	Fraser's campaign —Melbourne	(Gaol seige)
Melbourne HSV 7	(War)	Liberals interest rates —Melbourne	(Strike)	(Bushfires)	(Bushfires)	(Bushfires)	(Drugs)	(Gold nugget)	(Inquest)	(Girl found)
GTV 9	(War)	Liberal policy preview —Melbourne	(Tennis)	(Bushfires)	(Bushfires)	(Inquest)	(Murder)	(Gold nugget)	Fraser's campaign —Melbourne	(Girl found)
ATV-10	(Air disaster)	Liberal policy preview —Melbourne	(Drugs)	(Bushfires)	(Bushfires)	(Inquest)	(Murder)	(Gold nugget)	(Boy found)	(Gaol seige)
Adelaide ADS 7	(Bushfire)	(N/W shelf oil)	(Mitsubishi takeover Chrysler)	(War)	(Fire death)	(War)	(SA politics: prison enquiry)	Share market: Fraser's campaign —Adelaide	(Trial)	(Gaol seige)
HWS 9	(Bushfire)	Liberal policy preview —Melbourne	(Mitsubishi takeover Chrysler)	(Oil spill)	Opinion polls; Hayden's campaign —Adelaide	(Princess Alexandra)	(SA politics: prison enquiry)	(SA politics: hospital upgraded)	(Trial)	(Gaol seige)
SAS 10	(War)	Liberal policy preview —Melbourne	(Qld politics: coal-oil plant)	(War)	Hayden's campaign —Adelaide	(SA politics: ex-Governor dies)	(SA politics: prison enquiry)	Share market: Fraser's campaign —Adelaide	(Trial)	(Gaol seige)
Perth TVW 7	(War)	(N/W shelf oil)	Opinion polls —Perth	(War)	(No strike)	Fraser's campaign —Perth	(WA politics: business debt)	(WA politics: railway protest)	Election odds: share market: unemployment	(Workers killed)
STW 9	Hayden's campaign —Perth	(Road toll)	(Breath tests)	(War)	(Bushfires)	Fraser's campaign —Perth	(Drugs)	(Gold nugget)	Stock market: Keating	(Workers killed)

	13/10/80	14/10/80	15/10/80
Sydney ABC 2	Hayden: resource tax document —Sydney	Derecognition of Pol Pot	Opinion polls; leaders comment —Canb./Sydney
ATN 7	(Mine disaster)	Derecognition of Pol Pot	Blackout; Fraser —Sydney
TCN 9	(Earthquake)	(Fire)	Opinion polls; Fraser Comments —Sydney
Ten 10	Fraser's campaign —Melbourne	(Fire)	Blackout; Fraser —Sydney
Melbourne HSV 7	Fraser's campaign —Melbourne	Derecognition of Pol Pot —Melbourne	Opinion polls, leaders —Canb./Syd./Melb.
GTV 9	Fraser's campaign —Melbourne	Derecognition of Pol Pot —Melbourne	Opinion polls; Fraser comments —Sydney
ATV-10	Fraser's campaign —Melbourne	Derecognition of Pol Pot —Melbourne	(Fire)
Adelaide ADS 7	(Plane crash)		
HWS 9			
SAS 10			
Perth TVW 7	Liberals use of Gov.-Gen.?	Hawke's campaign —Perth	Opinion polls; Hayden's campaign —Canberra
STW 9	(Strike)		Opinion polls; leaders comment —Sydney

particular were grouped together, sometimes they were not. The number of stories had some bearing on this. When there were only two or three stories, these were more likely to be run end-to-end than when there were four or more; and on the ABC there were four or more on most nights. But the sheer number of stories was not the only factor that governed their distribution, nor the most important.

During the campaign period many items of Federal news were not defined as campaign news or, at least, not as campaign news primarily. Implicitly, campaign stories appeared to be defined as statements made or events taking place in front of the camera, involving one of the leading players in an attack on another, on something not directly relevant to anything else in the news; or alternatively, a meta-statement—an independent assessment of the state of the contest—usually a poll. Federal political stories which were not campaign stories in this sense were often—though certainly not always—placed elsewhere.

Thus, a Federal story that related to a nonfederal story was commonly placed immediately after the nonfederal story; on the ABC news of September 15, for example, Fraser's address to the International Petroleum Congress at the Sydney Opera House, came immediately after an item on the OPEC meeting in Vienna, which in turn came after the bulletin's campaign items. Most of the stories affected in this way were connected with the Middle East War. On the ABC, both Fraser's enunciation of Australia's attitude to the war and the clash between Carrick and Keating over the meaning of the war for Australian oil, followed on the heels of the war news itself. The taking of such items out of the campaign context, investing them with an immediate relevance to the real world, may have worked to the government's advantage.

Stories for which there was no picture were also likely to be separated. More important, of course, such stories were less likely to make the TV news at all; or, if they did, they were likely to be shorter. Labor had to "launch" its policies not for the press but for TV.

The coverage of demonstrations and protests, pressure groups, even State Premiers critical of the government, were often separately placed. What primarily defined these stories apparently was not their campaign relevance but the fact that they were initiated by secondary players in the game. During the entire campaign only one such story (the protest against Viner) was the news lead of any of the channels.

Stories emanating from the government, in the "ordinary" course of its business, or from bodies set up by and responsible to the government, were also likely to be hived off. Thus, Fraser's announcement of a drug inquiry (September 18), Staley's call for tenders for the government communications satellite (September 18), and the decision of the Australian Broadcasting Tribunal (ABT) (September 26) not to allow News Limited's takeover of Melbourne's ATV-10 (a decision for which the ALP had fought)[34] were widely treated as things apart.

National Coverage

Almost every day of the campaign, at least one Federal political story received "national coverage"; that is, coverage on at least one commercial channel in each of the four cities—Sydney, Melbourne, Adelaide, and Perth. Some involved the secondary players (demonstrations, twice; and a farmers' lobby area); three involved government or quasigovernment bodies [the Australian Bureau of Statistics (ABS) and the Commonwealth Employment Service (CES), with the unemployment figures; and the ABT]; and three were reports on the polls or the stock exchanges. The rest presented the party leaders, direct. On average there were two such stories each day, usually one from each side. None emanated from the NCP or the other smaller parties.

The ALP decided early that it faced an uphill fight and that its use of television would be vital. It started strongly. Four of its "policy launches"—on industrial relations, women, foreign investment, and small business—were covered coast to coast. The industrial relations launch, with Hayden and Hawke, led the ABC news and the Channel 10 news in Melbourne; and the women's breakfast, with Hayden and Wran, led the Channel 10 news in Sydney and Channel 7's news in Melbourne. The "troika" helped generate other national coverage as well, with Hawke (speaking on unemployment at the University of Sydney; leaving the ACTU; and visiting a confectionary factory in Melbourne) doing particularly well. Three of Labor's attempts to embarrass the government through the release of independent documents were also extensively reported: "Project Manhaul", a lead story in Melbourne on Channels 7 and 10; the Parliamentary Library's report on living standards; and the Treasury document on a resource rental tax, which led the news on Channel 2.

After Hayden's policy speech, Labor continued to do well with its carefully staged attempts to promote Hayden as a man with whom ordinary voters could identify: playing to voters the image they already had of the man. Journalists traveling with Hayden were told two or three days in advance what the "visuals" would be. One day Hayden was in Hobart, lunching in a soup kitchen with some of the unemployed; another day he was in Sydney flourishing a copy of his tax return and challenging Fraser to do likewise;[35] on yet another he was in Brisbane, venue for the 1982 Commonwealth Games, outlining Labor's policies on sport and recreation, in the midst (this time by chance) of a kids' sports carnival; and so on. Most made the TV news in two or three cities.

Labor stole the march on the Liberals by two weeks. It was not until after the Saulwick poll of October 4 that the Liberals began to coordinate a series of counter-attractions. In terms of television coverage, the maneuver was an instant success. Fraser's attacks on socialism at Packenham, his speech in Perth on defense, his attack on the unions at a lunch-time rally in Martin Place, Sydney—all in the space of three days—went to air in every city, as did the Melbourne rally on October 9 where he was jostled.

On the last three nights of the campaign, Fraser—like Hayden—got national coverage but on issues of his own making. On Monday October 13, there was a rally in Melbourne's city square. "This, ladies and gentlemen, is the authentic voice of the Australian Labor Party. This is the standard they want to raise", Fraser shouted against voices which tried to drown his out. On Tuesday, Fraser addressed the National Press Club. (Hayden's address to the Club received similar coverage the following day.) And on Wednesday there was another rally in Sydney Square, again with plenty of heckling and plenty of noise.

To what extent was there networking of news? Over the last three day of the campaign the only stories that were networked by the three commercial networks were Liberal stories: one on the Melbourne rally; the other, Peacock's announcement that Australia was withdrawing its recognition of Pol Pot. One has to go back to the preview of the policy speeches to find a Labor story that received comparable coverage. The only other stories to receive coverage of this kind were Fraser's address to the International Petroleum Congress, Labor's breakfast for women candidates and the ABT's decision on ATV-10.

Most of the political stories that went to air during the campaign were broadcast in one or two cities only; of 500 stories that went to air, less than sixty were broadcast in Sydney, Melbourne, Adelaide, and Perth. (Were we able to add Brisbane and Hobart, the gap would certainly be greater.) On eight occasions blanket coverage was not achieved by networking but depended on stories "missed" by some channels being picked up by others. Another six stories were only networked by Channel 10, so they did not reach Perth and could not have reached Hobart. On this definition of networking, that meant about forty stories. On the strongest definition of networking—the same story run for the same length of time in the same order by each of the associated stations—no commercial networking took place at all.

Networking may also be considered in terms of the amount of time spent on common stories. Adding up the amount of time has two advantages: first, not all stories are counted as equal; second, a single story covered by one channel in one city is not counted as equal to a single story covered by one channel in a number of cities.

As one would expect, most of the time was not spent on common stories. But a significant part of it was, the proportion varying from week to week and from channel to channel (Table 8-6). Perhaps because there were so many stories to choose from, the week in which networking was least conspicuous was the week in which the campaign was building to a climax. Channel 7, with over one-third of its time devoted to network stories performed fairly steadily. Channels 9 and 10 devoted less time overall but varied much more markedly.

Part of the reason the figures are not higher is the different time zones. Stories originating in Perth (two hours behind the eastern States) were often too late for the main evening bulletins in other States. About 15 percent of all Federal news stories originated in Perth. This undercut the networking potential of Channels 7 and 9, but not of Channel 10. And Channel 10 was no more likely to network its news than 7 or 9. If time played a role, it was clearly a small one. Over a period of thirty days each channel averaged a little less than one networked campaign story a night.

TABLE 8-6

Stories Covered by the Networks as a Proportion of Total Time Devoted to Federal Politics, Week Nights, September 15–October, 1980 (in percentage)

	Commercial Networks		
	7	9	10
Sept 15–Sept 19	37.7*	26.7	52.1
Sept 22–Sept 26	41.3	18.7	24.7
Sept 29–Oct 3	40.0	9.0	37.0*
Oct 6–Oct 10	29.0	0.0*	21.6
Oct 13–Oct 15	34.1	35.1	17.6
Total	35.8	17.9	29.9

Notes: Channels 7 and 9 include Sydney, Melbourne, Adelaide and Perth; Channel 10 includes Sydney, Melbourne and Adelaide.
* Date for one night missing

Clearly, individual channels retain considerable autonomy, either in feeding stories into the network or drawing stories off the network or both. Of all the Federal stories broadcast on week nights on commercial TV over 200—more than half—went to air in only one of the four cities. No doubt this represents a greater degree of "news sharing" than is evident in the press, but it may not represent more than is evident across the front pages of the press.

Although the party leaders stuck fairly close to Canberra (in the first week) and to Melbourne and Sydney, front-benchers travelled more widely; each city televised many stories (from 40 in Adelaide to 60 in Perth) that were its "own", and more of these stories used the minor figures of the campaign than did those stories televised to more than one city.

The city with the highest proportion of its own stories was Perth, with 38 percent across all week nights. The other cities managed between 26 percent and 30 percent. Without the time difference, the score for Perth would probably have been closer to that for the other cities. Certainly the figures do not suggest the dominance of the eastern States over the south and west. Though Adelaide (152) and Perth (162) broadcast fewer stories (and, as noted earlier, spent less time on Federal politics) than Sydney (189) or Melbourne (193), this was not because they were simply relay stations for stories from the eastern States. On the contrary, they appear to have been just as free—in Perth, even freer—to chop network stories and to substitute their own.

Whether TV in general, and networking in particular, made the Federal news in each metropolis more alike than did the news on the front pages of their respective morning papers, prior to TV, remains an open question. But TV networks have yet to transform Australia into an electronic Athens.[36]

Leaders

In the scramble to get party leaders onto the box—at a press conference, in a studio interview, or addressing a rally—honors appear to have gone to the ALP. In Melbourne, at least, Hayden's voice was heard more often than Fraser's and members of Labor's front-bench (plus Wran) were heard more often than members of the government's front-bench (Table 8-7).

Labor put the "troika" to good use but its advantage in the scramble for TV time was not as great as was sometimes imagined.[37] Certainly, on Melbourne's Channel 10, Wran, Hayden and Hawke and members of Labor's front-bench appeared thirty-two times (over thirty days) while viewers heard from members of the government's front-bench no more than twenty-five times; but on Channel 7, the margin was narrower (twenty-three to nineteen) and on Channel 9 nonexistent (twenty-eight each). The Liberal's effort to "neutralize" Labor's lead, by having ministers available at the right times and the right places, met with limited success. In the last two weeks of the television campaign, two or three more Labor than government spokesmen appeared on each of Melbourne's commercial channels. While the gap in favor of Labor was narrowed on Channel 10, on Channel 9 Labor actually went ahead.

The final balance had less to do with the efforts of the parties than with the constraints on the channels. Licensed by the state, TV stations are keenly aware of the need to provide not only "fair"

TABLE 8-7

Political Actors Heard on the Main Evening News Bulletins, Melbourne Commercial TV, and Political Actors Quoted on the Front Page of Melbourne Dailies, September 15–October 15, 1980

Affiliation	Name	TV			Press		
		Ch. 7	Ch. 9	Ch.10	Age	Sun News-Pictorial	Herald
Liberal	Fraser	13	17	17	19	1	6
	Mrs Fraser	1	1		1		
	Peacock	2	3	2	1		
	Howard	1	1	1	2		
	Carrick			2	2		
	Staley		2		1		
	Other ministers (8)		2	1	5		1
	Other (3)	2			2		
	Candidates (2)		3	2	1		1
	Total	19	29	25	34	1	8
NCP	Anthony	2	1	1	8		
	Nixon		1				
	Candidates (2)		1	1	4		1
	Total	2	3	2	12		1
Labor	Hayden	16	18	21	18		7
	Hawke	2	5	5	6		
	Wran	2	3	2	2		
	Keating	3	1	2			
	Bowen				3		
	Other front-bench (4)		1	2	2		
	Other (3)	1		1	1		
	Candidates (1)		2				
	Total	24	30	33	32		7
Democrats	Chipp	3	2	4	4		
	Siddons	1		2	1		
	Total	4	2	6	5		
Other		7	7	21	11		
	Total	56	71	87	94	1	22

Note: Data missing for Channel 7, September 15, and for Channel 10, September 20–21.

coverage (treating stories on their own merits) but "balanced" coverage (giving equal time to both sides).[38] In Melbourne, there were only two nights on which an opposition spokesman appeared on Channel 9 or 10 and no government spokesmen; and vice versa. Channel 7 was exceptional in giving greater weight to news values, as it saw them: eight nights with no government spokesmen, only two with no-one from the opposition.

The practice of assigning journalists to leaders ensured that most of the television coverage was coverage of the leaders. Having made the investment, the stations wanted the story; having run a story on each of the leaders, and thereby satisfied the demand for both coverage and balance, anything else that got in had to do so on merit; and there was not much space left for it anyway.[39] What was true of TV was true to some extent of the press. Political stories on the front pages of Melbourne's dailies were more likely to be about the leaders than about anyone else. In this sense, what TV provides for one audience, the press provides for another.

Minor players get minor parts. Most government ministers and most of the Labor front-bench failed to appear; developments overseas accounted for the relatively frequent appearance of Peacock and Keating. Hardly any Liberal or Labor candidates were heard from. Channel 9 interviewed Joan Child (Labor) and Marshall Baillieu (Liberal), from the marginal seat of La Trobe. Barry Simons (Liberal) from the marginal seat of McMillan, and Mrs Tighe of the Right to Life Association were also interviewed (one by Channel 9, the other by Channel 10) in connection with RTLA's anti-Simon campaign.[40]

The NCP and AD also got small parts—smaller than their share of the vote warranted. Despite its longer news bulletin, Channel 10 interviewed only one other minor party candidate; but it provided more interviews with pressure groups than other channels. Channel 10 also had the only specialist commentator, David Butler. But the commentary, as with so much else of the coverage at the end of the campaign, was on the race.

All Horse-Race and Hoopla?

The idea that TV trivializes what might otherwise be an occasion for serious political debate is hardly a new one; it dates to the beginning of television itself. What is new are attempts by academic social science to measure the extent to which TV news is trivialized; that is, the extent to which TV news covers things other than the issues. In the best known of these studies, Patterson and McClure calculated that the time given during the 1972 presidential election by the three

American networks, to the candidates' stand on "key issues of the election" (16 to 25 percent of news time) and "the candidates' key personal and leadership qualifications for office" (5 to 10 percent of news time) dwarfed that given to "rallies, motorcades, polls, strategies", and so on, which ranged from 66 percent of news time on CBC to 79 percent on NBC. In the 1976 election 62 percent of network news was again given over to "horse race and hoopla".[41]

The 1980 election saw the first attempt to produce a comparable set of figures for Australia; and it yielded what appeared to be a remarkably similar set of results. According to Crofts, Boehringer and Bell, 18 percent of news time (excluding ads) on the main Sydney evening news bulletins was spent on the Australian election or on election-relevant material. But of this, only 4.3 percent was spent on issues; 13.8 percent, or 76 percent of total election coverage, was spent on what they called "the campaign".[42]

Content analysis is always problematic not least when qualitative distinctions are involved. Crofts et al. acknowledge that the campaign items "touched on many issues" but insist that "in all these items the campaign itself remained the principal focus"; items were only coded as issue-relevant, it seems, if they were not manifestly part of the campaign. While most of the coverage of Federal politics was generated by the campaign itself, it hardly follows that most of the coverage was of things other than the issues. To run the two together is to collapse two dimensions (campaign/noncampaign; issues/non-issues) into one. Consider for instance their treatment of "women's issues". Only one item on women in the entire campaign was coded as "issue-relevant": a report, prepared by Channel 10, on women's refuges in Sydney, threatened by a cut in State and Federal government funding. The Hilton breakfast for Labor's female candidates, at which "women's issues" were addressed and which was covered Australia-wide by each of the networks, was coded as campaign-relevant and, therefore, not issue-relevant. In the course of an analysis which, at other places, shows unusual sensitivity to the multidimensional nature of the news, this insistence on a one-dimensional view looks suspiciously like an attempt to fit the data to a preconceived theory.

The Sydney data can be reanalyzed but only if two conditions are met. Firstly, some statement needs to be made about which items are to be counted as nonissues. Secondly, some rule needs to be adopted for dealing with items that have both issue and nonissue components.

As nonissues, one can include the parliamentary brawls of the first week and demonstrations, the walkabouts, electoral tours, rallies, and book launches (of which there were five), reports on the state of the campaign, including polls and the share market, descriptions of individual seats and argument about the legality or etiquette of the ads. And where items can be classified under two or more headings it may be assumed that the amount of time under each head was equal. If these rules seem rough and ready, so are the data. Coding which purports to measure time to the nearest second (as do Patterson and McClure) or to calculate the proportion of time to the third decimal place (as do Crofts, et al.) ought to be treated with a large grain of salt.

Under these rules, most of the coverage no longer appears as horse-race and hoopla. Nonissue content accounted for about one-quarter of Channel 2's time, about one-third of the time on Channels 7 and 10, but nearly half the time of Channel 9. In the last ten days of the campaign the horse-race and hoopla was substantially greater than in the middle weeks. In the second last week every channel devoted about half its coverage to nonissues. In the last three days, however, differences among channels reemerged: Channels 2 and 10 dropped back to about one-third, while Channel 9 lifted its nonissue content to two-thirds.

Though the amount of space devoted to the horse-race and hoopla in the press also grew in the last two weeks of the campaign (judging from the space given to the polls and the share market in the national, Sydney, and Melbourne dailies) the press seems to have devoted less space to items wholly or almost wholly of this kind than did TV. Over the entire period, less space was given to "campaign activity" in the press—even in the popular press—than was given by TV—even the ABC. It is easy enough to show the newspapers are the better source for a "reasoning public" without having to exaggerate the deficiencies of TV.[43]

Advertising

From September 30, the day on which press advertising effectively commenced, more space was taken up by political ads in the non-quality press (in Sydney and Melbourne at least) than by Federal political news or comment. Ads on behalf or in favor of the Liberal Party occupied more than ten times the space occupied by ads for Labor.

Both ABC radio and ABC TV offered the four largest parties free time roughly proportional to their 1977 share of the vote: 135 minutes each to the coalition partners and the ALP and 30 minutes to the Democrats. Under Section 116(3) of the Broadcasting and Television

Act, which required that commercial broadcasters "afford reasonable opportunities for the broadcasting . . . of election matters to all political parties", the leaders' opening addresses were carried, free of charge, by all metropolitan commercial TV stations as well.

Parties also bought time; about the same amount as in 1972 (nearly 99 hours) and 1977 (nearly 103 hours), but much less than either 1974 (124 hours) or 1975 (over 161 hours)[44]. The coalition bought 14 hours on metropolitan TV at a cost of $858,753, Labor nearly 11 hours at a cost of $511,985, while minor candidates spend only $6,435. The coalition, which, according to information provided by the stations, paid out 62.4 percent of the total bought better time and more of it.[45] On country TV, where time was cheaper and advertising much heavier, the margin in favor of the government was greater still.

Most of the country radio stations relayed the leaders' opening addresses, but only a few of the metropolitan stations did so; and only a few offered the parties any other free time. Radio time was purchased, again, mostly by the coalition. In the metropolitan areas, the coalition purchased over 38 hours, Labor just under 20 hours and the Democrats a mere 3 hours. Purchasing a smaller proportion of advertising space in all media than their share of the vote, the minor parties were in effect priced-out.

Liberal Party

The first of the Liberal's national TV ads appeared on Sunday, September 28, two days before the Prime Minister's policy speech. Apart from some wariness about signalling its punches too early the Party doubted the value of money spent more than three weeks ahead of the poll. Any party that is ahead prefers a short campaign.

The first ads were intended to highlight a Liberal achievement—or at least a rhetorical aspiration: lower inflation than the rest of the OECD (vox pop interviews with travelers returning from Europe); resource development "to the advantage of all Australians"; Australia "as the best country in the world to bring up a family"; superior economic management; "lasting job opportunities" by "building a healthy economy"; and strength of leadership (photographs of Fraser and Hayden side by side, with Hayden's slowly fading away). Each ended with the graphic "Lead on, Liberal" and a burst of Mike Brady's song "Lead on Liberal, Lead on".

Except for unemployment, the ads covered issues on which the party's research put the Liberals ahead: economic management, inflation, development and leadership. On unemployment Labor was ahead; but the polls indicated that many voters blamed the unions or the unemployed themselves for unemployment, not the government. According to the party's own polls, the most popular prescription for reducing unemployment was government encouragement of industry and the promotion of training schemes, both of which it was already pursuing. There was little support for jobs created by the government direct. Clearly, the government's distinction between "real" and "phony" jobs had public appeal; and it was this that the party sought to push. Petrol prices, another issue on which the government might have been in trouble was not an issue that voters rated highly; "Foolium: Labor's miracle additive" never went to air.

The first phase of Liberal advertising emphasized the "positive"; but it did so on the cheap. Of their first five ads, three ("family," "resources", "jobs") were 10-second spots. They enabled the party to deliver reminders on a range of issues; to increase the proportion of the target audience exposed to an ad (its "reach"); and, more importantly, to increase the number of times members of the target audience were likely to see an ad (its "frequency")—all at minimal cost.[46]

Tuesday, September 30, saw the start of the Liberal's newspaper campaign—full-page ads announcing Fraser's policy speech. But with the Prime Minister carried "live" by television it was the party's cheapest night; except in Perth, no ads went to air. The following night, the Liberals resumed their advertising. A new 30-second spot, "Labor's inflation" featured a red, three-dimensional cut-out of Australia with a voice-over reminding voters of inflation under the last Labor government (Australia inflates), the subsequent Liberal government (Australia deflates) and a possible Labor government (Australia rapidly inflates, finally bursting with a loud bang leaving the screen completely red). On Thursday, October 2, the night of Hayden's delayed telecast, the Liberals introduced a new one on inflation: "Could Australians afford the cost of Labor's Bill?" Here, Australia sank under the weight of Labor's extra spending promises.

The first response to the adverse polls (because it required little lead time) was to drop ads. First to go were those that attacked Hayden. (Hayden had picked up well in the polls and the Liberals' own research suggested, much to their surprise, that the "troika" was working.) Next to go were the 10-second spots. Each of these had been spoken by Fraser; this was the last viewers were to hear from him. By Wednesday, D'Arcy-MacManus & Masius had drafted the first of the new ads. "Labor's making a lot of promises—but all they did last time was give us runaway inflation. So why risk something like 20 percent inflation?" The graphics, a series of thought balloons, were easy to prepare. On Friday and Saturday, October 10 and 11, this and another 30-second ad on inflation (the red cut-out of Australia) were the only Liberal ads to go to air nationally.

Meanwhile, the agency struggled to script, shoot, and distribute three new ads to run from Sunday until Wednesday evening, the last night of the electronic campaign. Alongside a warning against voting Democrat in the Senate (which had already gone to air) these would constitute the last phase of the national campaign. For the last four days of the campaign the agency had booked nine 10-second, twenty 30-second, and eighteen 60-second spots in Melbourne. But thanks to the ABT's 1977 ruling allowing political advertising beyond the normal maximum of eleven minutes in the hour,[47] (and perhaps to one or two corporate advertisers), it now extended its schedule. Instead of 47 spots or 19½ minutes, it actually used 117 spots or 91½ minutes. A similar set of rearrangements was made in other cities and, presumably, in the country.

The new ads were all haunted by the specter of "Labor's 20 percent inflation". The most controversial also raised the specter of a wealth tax:

> Labor calls it the "wealth tax" but it would really attack the un-wealthy.
> Labor's so-called "wealth tax" would hit hundreds of thousands of Australian families who own modest homes which have risen in value.
> Under Labor's 20 percent inflation, they would become a target for Labor's "wealth tax."
> Labor's new taxes!
> Where else *would* they get the money for all their promises?
> Lead on Liberal.

"Labor's Wealth Tax", was superimposed over a picture of a modern suburban home. As the announcer spoke the camera slowly pulled out to show that this house was "just one of many typical houses in a typical suburban street". At the request of the Federation of Australian Commercial Television Stations (FACTS), "would" was subsequently changed to "might".

Seen by many as a ploy to frighten home owners in Sydney, the ad actually went to air more often in Melbourne. The difference was not great (28 to 24) but its direction is significant. Some members of the Strategy Committee had not twigged to differences between the Sydney and Melbourne housing markets. Moreover there was some skepticism about the ad's pulling power; unlike the more familiar lines—milk, meat, and bread—it was a punt.

190

Since most political commentators only see TV at night they hardly noticed the ad that received the greatest exposure: a 60-second spot featuring a "series of heart warming and evocative child portraits, showing sequentially growth from a healthy 2-year-old to a 9-year-old", and a voice-over inviting viewers to "Let's make sure our kids grow up in a *growing* Australia...."

This was the Liberal party on the defensive—responding to the theme of the family in Labor's campaign, recycling some of its earlier ideas ("family", "resources", "jobs"), rising to the challenge set by Hayden's support in the polls, and ignoring Anthony's earlier advice that the election not be thought of as a contest for "Father of the Year". Among the final four, it was the only spot to feature Fraser. Designed primarily for daytime TV, it went to air no fewer than 66 times in Sydney and 55 times in Melbourne.

At the eleventh hour the party was appealing to women. On the evidence of the Party's private polls the Liberal's traditional lead among women was slipping. The third ad, therefore, was also made with women in mind:

Could your family afford Labor's 20 percent inflation?
Within three years a lamb chop could cost around 80¢.
A litre of milk 85¢.
A loaf of bread $1.15.
With Labor's 20 percent inflation a dozen eggs could cost $2.20.
Stay with the Liberal Government which *has* brought inflation
    under control and will keep it that way.

In Melbourne, where Senator Chipp seemed certain to win the fifth seat, the Senate ad was not used in the last week. In Sydney, however, where the fifth seat loomed as a three-way contest, the party kept running its Senate ad. In Brisbane, where a different Three-way contest loomed (Liberal, National, Democrat), the Senate ad stayed on. In addition, the State branch ran a 30-second ad in which Jim Killen, a Queensland MP and Minister for Defence, warned of the threat posed by Labor to 30 years of Liberalism. In Adelaide, Premier Tonkin advised a Liberal vote in the Senate. Western Australia, however, was the State that emerged with the highest proportion of its own ads. Indeed, in the final ten days, most of the Liberal ads in Perth were made especially for Western Australia. Chief among these was an ad for the Senate "Danger to the West", a 60 second commercial that went to air 61 times. In Adelaide, Brisbane and Perth "wealth tax" was completely overshadowed by ads specifically concerned with the Democrats in the Senate.

Press advertising started two days later than the TV ads and finished three days later. Print allowed the party to spell out ideas that a 10-second, even a 30-second spot, could not. The agency saw advantages in print—speed, reach to the ABC audience, duplication for commercial viewers—that Labor's agency did not. Almost all of its thirteen ads appeared once, in most of the metropolitan dailies. It believed in full-page ads and was prepared to pay for premium positions.

Once the campaign needed to be revamped the speed of the press was sometimes an advantage. "How will your pay packet stand up to Labor's 20% inflation?" appeared in one paper on October 8 and in a number of others by October 9, but its equivalent did not reach the screen until October 10. "Labor's wealth tax threatens the *unwealthy* family" made Saturday's *Age* and *Weekend Australian* before its first TV exposure on Sunday.

More often, press ads simply coincided with or followed TV. "Could your family affort Labor's 20% inflation", on TV on Sunday, was divided into three separate ads (eggs, milk, and lamb chops) for the press and appeared Tuesday to Thursday; "Mr Hayden 'won't retreat' from Labor's 'wealth' taxes that threaten the the unwealthy family", appeared in newspapers across Australia on the final Wednesday and Thursday. It was the only national ad to appear more than once. Placements were concentrated in the up-market dailies and, again, were heavier in Melbourne than in Sydney. Labor responded to the first of these ads by seeking legal advice. As a result, the National Secretary informed the media that the ad was in breach of section 161(e) of the *Commonwealth Electoral Act*.[48] The following day, October 14, the *Age* editorialized against the wealth tax ad and the ad which predicted "Labor's 20 percent inflation". Both ads had been run by the *Age*; but both "should be dropped". Later that day, the *Age* received two more Liberal advertisements: one on inflation, which "we decided did not breach the Act"; the other on "wealth tax", proclaiming that "Mr Hayden 'won't retreat' from Labor's 'Wealth' Taxes that threaten the *unwealthy*". "Won't retreat" was supported by quotations from Hayden in 1979. The *Age* noted that Hayden had "in fact recently retreated on a wealth tax and on a capital gains tax", and it refused to publish this recension unless the inverted commas around "won't retreat" were removed.[49] This the party agreed to do for the *Age*; but in every other paper it appeared unamended. On the eve of the poll, every daily carried two final ads: "Let's all make sure they grow up in a growing Australia", and "One final question before you vote tomorrow", followed, in smaller type, by "where would the Labor Party find the money to pay for its promises without inventing new taxes, sending inflation soaring, and cutting the buying power of your dollar?"

Ads were also inserted by State branches of the party (their own version of particular themes, or instructions on how-to-vote); by the Liberal premiers of South Australia, Victoria and Western Australia (seeking to mobilize support for the Federal coalition around the interests of their particular State); and by or on behalf of local candidates. These amounted to almost half as much again as that absorbed by the national campaign: the equivalent of about 45 broadsheet pages (compared to 80 authorized federally) plus about 23 tabloid sheets (compared with 77 federally).

Tasmania saw the greatest activity: 85 ads in the Hobart *Mercury* (including two full pages), most of them for those remarkable politicians, Bruce Goodluck and Michael Hodgman. In mainland cities, where the metropolitan press did not double so readily as a local press, there were fewer ads and their configuration was different. In Perth there were only 42 such ads but 17 were full page. Most of the big ads came in the last eight days when the polls indicated that the Democrats could win the fifth seat in the Senate. "Danger for the West!" with a sword (of Damocles) pointing down the page made eight appearances. The Premier, Sir Charles Court, (also used on television) weighed-in with "Threat to Western Australia". In Victoria, where the Liberals suddenly realized that they might lose a lot of their seats, both Premier Hamer, and former Premier, Sir Henry Bolte, rushed to the lists. Of the 16 full-page ads, inserted by the State Liberals over the last six days, eleven were authorized by these two. In South Australia, New South Wales and Queensland, State advertising was much less noticeable.

Friends of the Liberals The polls not only mobilized the party, they also mobilized its business base. Some rushed the party with donations; some dropped advice slips into the pay packets of employees; others put their money into advertising. Indeed, the last week saw party supporters buy more space in the metropolitan dailies than was bought by the State branches and local Liberal campaign committees combined. Across Australia, over 100 ads were placed, three-quarters of them full page.

This was not, of course, the first time that friends bearing ads had come to the aid of the party. The banks had done it in 1949, the insurance industry in 1974.[50] At the South Australian election of 1979, a business campaign, complete with advertising, had helped pave the way for the defeat of the Corcoran Labor government. It was the apparent success of that campaign that persuaded businessmen to try again.

The party and non-party campaigns involved complementary notions of the audience and the issues to be pushed. First, the non-party campaign was more heavily skewed towards the down-market press, read predominantly by Labor voters; the equivalent of 24.5 broadsheet pages and 52.7 tabloid pages was almost exactly the reverse of the way the Liberal State branches distributed their ads. Second, the non-party campaign focussed much more on jobs (45 full-page ads), on unions (13) and on petrol (18) than did the Liberals; only one or two of the non-party ads in Western Australia echoed lines already being run by the Liberals.

The campaign can be read as signifying a lack of confidence, among certain sections of business, in the party's ability to beat Labor: behind in the polls, advertising in the wrong places, running on the wrong issues. No doubt a number of influential Liberals were in touch with the party to voice such thoughts. Alternatively, the campaign can be seen as representing an agreed division of political work: the non-party campaign picking up arguments which the party preferred to see made independently, or at least sticking to issues which, the Party agreed, could do it little harm. Indeed it was party policy that, where possible, independent endorsements should be coordinated.[51] While the nature and extent of this coordination remain unclear, drafts of at least two of the ads[52] were sent to campaign headquarters and subsequently amended.

Within the business community itself, there was also coordination. Two of the most prolific advertisers, Nigel Buick and B.A. Harris, both from South Australia, put their names to very similar ads. Ads were not only published interstate but some involved interstate collaboration. Thus, an appeal to "women" sometimes appeared over the names of Buick and Gae Sorenson (of Sydney) and sometimes over the name of Sorenson alone. Finally, there were the similarities in the calling cards: "a large group of businessmen vitally concerned with keeping a responsible Liberal Government in Canberra"; and "a group of ordinary Australians concerned about keeping a responsible Government in Canberra", from two States.

Labor

TV ads for the Labor Party went to air on Wednesday, September 24, a few days ahead of the Liberals and a week ahead of Hayden's policy speech. By advertising first, Labor hoped to gain the initiative; by putting Hayden on after Fraser, it hoped to keep it. Not everyone associated with Labor's campaign had been in favor of TV spots. It was argued, for instance, that if the party were going to spend so much money (approximately $661,000 for air time alone) it should do it in less of a rush. In 1979, the party had explored the possibility of a "mid-term" campaign but had been forced to conclude that in terms of its likely cash flow it would not be able to support even a "minimally worthwhile" advertising campaign.[53] One member of Hayden's team (reputed to have made a million in the liquor trade without benefit of the "box") doubted the necessity of TV. Others argued that TV was worse than ineffective; that given the government's own advertising campaign—for the army reserve, fuel conservation and Project Australia—voters might be beginning to feel harrassed, even brainwashed.[54]

But the argument was easily pushed aside: TV might be a superficial medium, stronger on images than information; but the voters most likely to swing to Labor treated politics fairly superficially themselves and were precisely those most susceptible to the politics of the image. Far from suffering from a surfeit of nationalism, voters like these embraced it; and even if television were an ineffective or alienating medium, no campaign director, campaign committee or leader could take the risk of ignoring TV only to finish a few thousand votes from victory.

Labor built its commercials around three basic ideas: nationalism, development (on both of which it fell in with the government) and a declining standard of living. What it sought to communicate was "hope for a better future—both in terms of personal living standards and the development of a strong independent nation". It had to demonstrate "an understanding of the problems faced by typical Australians, an in-touchness which Fraser clearly lacked". It needed to be "moderate and responsible" keeping its message "simple and to a minimum".[55] Stressing the fact that the average viewer would see only fifteen ads in the whole campaign, and that repetition was the key to effectiveness, the agency had wanted to settle for two or three ads. In the end it ran more, with variants for different regions and seats. Its six "main theme" ads opened with a shot of an oil rig, followed by quick cuts to video for the opening lines of the campaign jingle:

We've got oil beneath the ocean
We've got mountains made of ore
Industry to build the future
Nature's bounty shore to shore
In our Australia.

They closed with video to match the rest of the jingle:

It's a golden wealthy country
Full of life and strength and might

> And the standard should be rising
> And the future should be bright
> We've got to raise the standard high.

With the last line the video dissolved to kids in a schoolyard flag-raising ceremony, dissolving again "through flag, as it hits top of pole, to slogan graphic: Raise the standard".

The party's new logotype, a stylized Australian flag, had been devised by the agency in 1978. At a time when nationalist sentiment was on the rise it was important, the agency argued, that the ALP not run the risk of appearing anything other than "truly Australian". Displayed for the first time at Labor's national conference in 1979 and subsequently adopted by all party branches, the flag gave the party, in the national secretary's telling phrase, a new "corporate image"; and they had "beaten the Liberals to it".

In its strategic Report of March 1980, ANOP argued that the "biggest single change" in what swinging voters said spontaneously about the future was their emphasis on "the need for an independent self-sufficient Australia". National pride was not just a matter of national jingles ("C'mon Aussie", "Have a go", "Raise a flag") but was becoming "accepted generally".[56] ANOP went on to suggest that the party also swing with development. In the outer States, at least, "development mania" was "very much part of the swinging voters' view of the future". The "central communications theme", in 1980, however "ideologically distasteful ... must include a rhetorical emphasis on an optimistic future and ... the embracing of a development outlook". The "Liberal strategy (make Australia great—development—independence overtones) is a sound one". Of six slogans tested "Liberal—Let's Make Australia Great" was "clearly the most effective and the most popular". Labor, by contrast, was considered "not as keen to pursue 'development' projects". In March, "Making Australia Great" became the working title for Labor's "main theme" commercial.

Each of the "main theme" ads attempted to reproduce the kinds of comments picked up by ANOP. After the opening lyric came a snatch of ordinary conversation around a particular theme, followed by a line of lyric, followed by Hayden's stating a Labor position in sympathy with the consensus that the conversation had established.

In one ad, nationalism and development were fused:

Man 1: It's a rich country, but who owns it?
Man 2: The minerals go east and the money goes west.
Man 3: Under Fraser, everybody gets rich off our minerals except us.

Lyrics: It's our Australia.

Hayden: We welcome mineral development, but overseas interests do better out of it than we do. We'll put more of
our resources to work for all of Australia.

In the others, however, nationalism and development formed a
sandwich with the third "key element" of the campaign—standard of
living issues—filling the space in between. The filling—petrol prices,
interest rates, health costs, taxation, and the cost of living—gave the
variety. In each of the conversations the ills of the world were sheeted
home to Fraser personally; Hayden, equally carefully, never mentioned him.

For the closing lyrics, the video included shots of Hayden appearing with Wran or Hawke (three times), or with Mrs Hayden or Lionel
Bowen (twice). ANOP's swingers thought Hayden "more impressive
on TV" than Fraser, so Labor was happy to have Hayden in every
spot. Had the sixth in the series (an ad on industrial relations) gone to
air, Wran and Hawke would have appeared again as well.[57]

More than ever before, the ALP's choice of issues, the style of its
ads, the solutions it offered (including the "family" wrapping,
something Whitlam had rejected) reflected the advice of its pollster.
The only substantial issue on which the party resisted this advice was
that of unemployment. Most of ANOP's "swinging voters" (16
percent of its sample) thought unemployment was going up and that
the ALP would do more than the government to bring it down. Yet
unemployment was categorized by ANOP as "a media issue—and a
politician's issue" not a voter's issue. "Swinging voters" (undefined)
were already convinced that Labor would "do something about
unemployment" and anyway, were "more concerned about their
own economic standard of living".[58]

ANOP's argument for "standard of living" issues over unemployment, like much else in its report was sustained by some rather
curious reasoning. The unemployed themselves (and their families)
might have been bemused by the distinction between a concern for
unemployment and a concern for one's "own economic standard of
living". The argument for concentrating on standard of living issues
largely derived from a question (not spelt out in the report) about
"government negatives"; unemployment was mentioned less often
than issues like prices, health insurance, and taxation. Since "standard of living" issues, *in toto*, were more important than unemployment, ANOP inferred that *every* "standard of living issue" was more
important than unemployment. The consequences of this error of
disaggregation were bizarre; for example, an issue like the price of

petrol (seen by only 5 percent of swinging voters as a "government negative") was given its own spot, while unemployment (seen by 22 percent as a "government negative") was not.

Ultimately, of course, decisions about which ads to make and which ads to run were taken not by the pollster or the advertising agency but by the party. The decision to run on petrol was the easiest. The day after the 1979 Federal Budget, the premier of South Australia, Des Corcoran, declared that Fraser had made "every petrol station a tax office" and called a snap election. The West Australian branch produced a car sticker: "I paid cash for the car, but the petrol's on H.P." In New South Wales, the party president and spokesman on minerals and energy, Paul Keating, worked tirelessly to talk up the issue; so did the State secretary, who thought a promise to cut the price of petrol (implied by the party's ads but not part of the party's policy) would guarantee victory.

The decision on unemployment was more difficult. ANOP's advice was rejected by Hayden. "Newsboy", a TV commercial, was subsequently scripted but did not reach an agreed form until September 24, nearly two weeks after the main batch. It depicted a succession of scenes and news posters—NEW HEALTH SLUG, PETROL PRICE SPIRALS, etc.; but of the nine posters only one was on unemployment and the voice-over failed to mention the issue.

The State secretaries decided which ads to put to air and when. In Perth, "newsboy" did not appear until October 2, and only went to air eighteen times; the "main theme" ads went to air 84 times. In other States the balance was fairly even, favoring the "main theme" ads by a small margin in Sydney (80:70) and Brisbane (57:52), and "newsboy" by an equally small margin in Victoria (48:42) and South Australia (60:56); roughly what one might expect, given the ideological complexion of the various branches. All the ads ran for 60 seconds.

The rhythm of Labor's advertising campaign was remarkably steady. The Sydney pattern was typical: 28 placements during the first four days (September 24–27); 31 placements during the last four days (October 12–15). Labor's TV campaign did not "die" (as many believed it did), but it did not finish with a flourish either. The decision not to respond to the Liberal ads, especially on wealth tax, reflected several considerations, not least the party's big overdraft. To have matched the Liberal's television advertising, even in the last four days, would have required an additional outlay of something in excess of $300,000. "Wealth tax" alone would have required over $60,000—almost as much as Labor's entire budget for this period in Sydney and Melbourne combined. The alternative, to substitute new ads for old, was also rejected. Firstly, although an attack over a capital gains tax had been talked about, Labor's strategists had nothing to counter it and were now uncertain about the damage it might do and how best to minimize it. Secondly, it was Combe's belief that a change of tack, mid-campaign, had in the past only worked when Labor was in government—Whitlam in 1974 and Dunstan in 1975. Thirdly, there was the danger that a shift in emphasis, from the issues of Labor's choosing to a new issue of the government's choosing, would leave voters with the impression of a campaign in disarray, especially since Labor's response to the issue did entail a shift of position.

Only in New South Wales, the center of the storm, did the party attempt to meet Liberal claims about a wealth tax. Full-page ads, charging that "Libs ads tell lies" and inviting readers to phone the party if they wanted to know "how the ALP's income tax cuts and oil price freeze will raise your standard of living" were published in the *Daily Telegraph* and *Sun* on October 15—the day the Liberals published theirs. Chosen to maximize "reach", Labor's ads in these two papers would have cost in excess of $6,000 or the equivalent of less than four 60-second placements on evening TV. A similar ad was prepared for other States, but "nobody was concerned at the time of the need to proceed with it".[59]

Labor's use of the press as a vehicle for its advertising—like its use of radio spots—had declined steadily since 1975. Two print versions of the "newsboy" ad were run, mostly in Sydney and Melbourne. Labor's other ads, not particularly numerous, were mostly inserted by State secretaries, usually to announce public meetings or to indicate how people should list their preferences in various seats. Labor's advertising agents saw the press as a secondary medium to be used only where TV had passed saturation; but they were not in favor of paying premium rates for "special" pages. Where complete coverage was needed in a single day (for example, to publicize meetings), press ads were more cost-efficient than TV; similarly, to reassure party activists (light viewers but heavy users of print) that the party was actually advertising. Otherwise the press was not used. In New South Wales, "Libs ads tell lies" may have been run as much to reassure the party faithful that the party was not ignoring the issue, as to reassure political waverers that Labor's intentions were not what the Liberals said they were.

The Swing Back

One thing the campaign confirmed, for most observers, was the power of advertising. Paul Keating's conclusion was widely quoted:

"What Labor needs is a couple of vicious and utterly cynical ad. men to do to the Liberals what they do to us. . . ."[60] With "wealth tax" (and inflation), the Liberals picked issues on which Labor seemed vulnerable; they "went to town" with their advertising; and Labor was eventually pinned back and passed. The inference seems obvious enough; the problem is to demonstrate it. There is, after all, at least one other explanation which does not entail the power of advertising: the persuasibility of the opinion polls.

Evidence from recent American presidential campaigns suggest that the power of paid-media as against free-media is considerably less than is often imagined. An analysis of the presidential vote in 1956 and 1960 found no relationship between media expenditure and voting patterns State-by-State: "both candidates have so much advertising and appear in all media so frequently that any difference between the two is normally not important".[61] A similar, if necessarily cruder, analysis of media usage in the 1980 Australian election actually suggests an inverse relationship between the amount of Liberal Party and allied advertising and the growth—from 1977 to 1980—in support for Labor.

Labor did best where, in terms of advertising space, it was most comprehensively beaten and worst where the advertising margin was narrower or even reversed (Table 8-8). In Melbourne, for instance, where the Liberal Party and other public-spirited citizens took out sixty-three full-page ads against Labor's seven—a wider margin than in any other city—the swing to Labor was greater than in any other city except Perth; and in Perth, too, 90 percent of the advertisements were anti-Labor. Conversely, in Brisbane, where the ratio of Liberal to Labor ads was 3:1—lower than anywhere else—the swing to Labor was relatively low as well; and in Hobart where Labor and its friends out-advertised the government, the swing to Labor was less than half the swing in Melbourne.

Television presents a similar picture. In Perth, where Labor was outadvertised by as great a margin as anywhere, the swing to Labor was 10.2 percent; in Sydney, where the Liberal's advertising lead was slight, the swing to Labor was only half as great. In Adelaide, the Liberals enjoyed a big margin in television time and the swing to Labor was lower than in any other metropolitan area; but this may be more coincidence than counter-instance.

It is possible that Liberal advertising helped turn the tide late in the campaign. In Sydney and Melbourne, where the Liberals outspent Labor, there clearly was a shift to the government; elsewhere, the survey data are not reliable. Even if Sydney and Melbourne were typical that would not clinch the case for advertising, unless one

TABLE 8-8
Advertising and the Vote

City	Advertising Coverage: Excess of anti-ALP over pro-ALP			ALP Support (in percentages)								Shift towards ALP (percentage points)
	Press ads (sq cm)	TV ads (minutes)		Sept 27/28	Sept 27/28	Sept 27/28 to Oct 4/5	Oct 4/5	Oct 11/12	Oct 11/12	Oct 11/12	Oct 18	From 1977 election to 1980 election
	Entire Period	Entire Period	Last Week	Morgan	Saulwick	McNair	Morgan	Morgan	McNair	Saulwick		
Sydney	78,262	12	55	49	51	49	48	46	49	49	46.6	4.1
Melbourne	104,914	54	55	52	59	53	53	49	50	51	49.1	9.0
Brisbane	28,720	39	58								47.1	6.8
Adelaide	59,089	96	81			BASE TO SMALL TO SPLIT					47.6	2.1
Perth	62,522	95	71								44.6	10.6
Hobart	50,918	-32	?								45.6	4.0
n				1065	2000	1873	2209	2409	2170	2000		

Sources: Metropolitan dailies and weekend newspapers for press ads; Bruce Tart Research and C.P.D. (Senate) March 31, 1981, p. 950 (for Hobart) for TV ads; Morgan Gallup Poll nos. 349, 351 and 353, Irving Saulwick and McNair Anderson computer reports for the public opinion poll data; and General Election for the House of Representatives, 1980: Analysis of result of count of first preference votes (Canberra: Australian Electoral Office, 1980) for the voting figures for each of the cities.

could separate the effects of advertising from the effects of the even more relentless nonadvertising campaign which ran parallel. The one postelection survey to address itself to the impact of the advertising, found that "swinging voters" in Melbourne (those who had indicated, in the Saulwick poll of September 27–28, that they intended switching from their 1977 vote) were "highly critical of party propaganda and sloganizing"; "the parties and their political messages", it concluded, lacked "credibility".[62]

In Western Australia the Liberal party spent over $50,000 (about $15,000 on the press and $35,000 on TV) advising voters of the "Danger to the West" which would result from the Liberal's failure to secure the fifth Senate seat. In no other seat did the party invest such treasure; the Liberal candidate, Noel Chrichton-Browne, won. Did money buy the 560 votes that made the difference? In the absence of quite specific survey data, it is impossible to say.

What of the "wealth tax" ads? The belief that these ads explain why Labor picked up more seats in Melbourne than in Sydney became so powerful after the election, that on the eve of the first New South Wales by-election, held in the Liberal marginal seat of Lowe, Bill Hayden persuaded the parliamentary Labor Party not to enlarge the scope of the capital gains tax beyond the rewriting of sections 26 (9) and 26AAA of the *Income Tax Act*.[63]

Nonetheless, evidence for the view that capital gains was Labor's undoing is not particularly convincing. As Table 8-8 shows, Labor was doing better in Melbourne than in Sydney *before* the policy speeches. Between the beginning of the campaign and the last week, Morgan's figures show a decline in Labor's support in Sydney but they show a decline in Melbourne as well; on Saulwick's figures the decline in Melbourne is much more marked than the decline in Sydney; while on McNair's figures there is hardly any shift at all. In both Sydney and Melbourne the election result corresponds almost exactly with the Morgan poll of the previous weekend. On Saulwick's and McNair's figures there was a shift away from Labor in the final week but it was not significantly greater in Sydney than in Melbourne.

Had the swing to Labor been affected by the threat of a capital gains or wealth tax, one would expect to find a dampened swing in areas of high income and high property values. In New South Wales and Victoria, seats classified by the Australian Electoral Office as "safe Liberal" did show a slightly below average swing but seats classified as "fairly safe Liberal" did not. Victorian seats classified as "marginal Liberal"—all won by Labor—actually showed a below average swing (5.7 percent of the two-party-preferred vote compared with 6.2

percent for the State as a whole); similar seats in New South Wales—few of which were won by Labor—showed an above-average swing to Labor (3.1 percent compared with 2.8 percent).[64] Yet, it was Melbourne where home prices were stagnant or falling, and Sydney where home prices were much higher.

There were, no doubt, substantial variations in income and home ownership both within and between electorates classified as "marginal Liberal". Only when it becomes possible to compare data from the 1981 census with data from the 1976 census will it be possible (if allowance can be made for changes in electoral boundaries) to explore these differences in detail. It seems unlikely, however, that these will change the picture substantially. At the 1976 census, Macquarie and St George (two marginal seats that Labor won from the Liberals) and Barton and Phillip (two it did not win) stood out as "more like Labor seats than Liberal seats on the income variable". In Phillip, where the swing to Labor was relatively low, almost half the dwellings were rented, not owner-occupied—twice the Sydney average.[65] It may be true that the people who were renting were looking forward (however unrealistically) to a home of their own and a large capital gain. But to suppose that the Liberals were able to create more fear among those without assets to tax is implausible.

The "hard" evidence of ecology is supported by the "soft" evidence of surveys. In an "exit poll' conducted outside selected polling booths in the marginal Liberal seats of Barton, Macquarie, Phillip, and St George, in Sydney, and in Henty, Hold, Hotham, and La Trobe, in Melbourne, 480 voters, including 206 Liberals, were asked why they had voted for that particular party. Even after probing (any other reason? anything else?) only one or two Liberals mentioned capital gains tax and no one mentioned wealth tax; of the twelve who had voted for some other party (or not voted at all) in 1977, none mentioned capital gains or wealth tax.[66]

On October 13–14, ANOP managed to contact, 1,003 of the 1,500 voters it had originally interviewed. All lived in marginal seats held by the Liberal party: those covered by McNair's exit poll, plus seats from each of the other States and Canberra. In the two weeks that had elapsed since their first interview, 8 percent said they had either moved between parties or out of the "undecided" category; most had switched to Labor or Democrat (ANOP being the only poll to show a further movement away from the government), a few to Liberal. The reasons given by those who had swung to Liberal were "diverse and difficult to group ... with no clear thrust apparent". The fear of wealth or capital gains tax figured as no more than one of several "sporadic references". The "wealth tax" issue had been on the agenda for five or six days, including one or two days as part of the Liberals' advertising campaign, and the Liberals ANOP interviewed (all being on the phone) were presumably better off than the rest of the sample. One of the four main reasons given for switching to Labor was the Liberals "negative campaign: Mudslinging. Distorting. Unfair". Part of the Liberals' campaign was apparently back-firing: on balance, wealth tax may have been doing the cause more harm than good. Again, one of the two main reasons given by voters who had switched to the Democrats was: "Campaign vitriol. Mudslinging. Attacks".[67]

According to the Liberal Party's telephone polls, Labor had gone into the last week of the campaign ahead on "tax" by 56 percent to 17 percent. The last of these polls, conducted in Sydney and Melbourne on the night of Wednesday, October 15, still had Labor ahead as the "best party on tax" by 51 percent to 23 percent. In an Australia-wide Morgan poll, conducted on the weekend of the election and into the following weekend, the only voters to mention tax in any form as an important consideration were those who had made up their minds in the last four weeks of the campaign. But whether any of these voters were thinking of wealth or capital gains tax is unclear; in any event, they comprised little more than 1 percent of the Liberal-National Country Party vote. When all those interviewed were asked what improvements they would like to see the ALP make, hardly anyone apparently suggested the dropping of a wealth or capital gains tax.

The assumption that like unemployment or inflation, a wealth or capital gains tax is something no party wishing to gain office would rationally advocate—the assumption which underlies most of the advice given to the Labor Party since the election—is certainly open to doubt. After the election the subscribing newspapers to the McNair Gallup Poll agreed to get some measure of public reaction to alternative tax proposals. McNair introduced the question to respondents by pointing out that in order to "keep personal tax down, the Federal government may have to introduce some new form of taxation". Interviewers went on to ask which form of taxation people would prefer—or, as McNair put it, would "dislike the least": a "wealth tax, whereby wealthier people pay more tax"; a "capital gains tax whereby people pay tax on the increase in value of their assets between when they are bought and when they are sold" (not what Labor's platform proposed); or a "value added tax, whereby a fixed percentage is added to the price of all goods and services"; or "some other form of taxation?" Wealth tax topped the poll. Despite the "anti-wealth tax" campaign, of six weeks before, wealth tax was supported by 47 percent, capital gains tax was accepted by 15 percent, VAT by 14 percent, and some other form of taxation by 8 percent; will 8 percent indicating no preference. A capital gains tax option, worded along the same lines as the wealth tax option, would presumably have drawn greater support; support for a wealth or capital gains tax might have exceeded 62 percent.[68]

So why the swing to the government in the last week or two of the campaign? What seems to be needed is an explanation which assumes a swing back across most of Australia, not just Sydney. Labor's 1980 gains correlate almost perfectly in every State, except South Australia, with the average increases in full-time unemployment per electorate; again, except for South Australia, the swing was strongest where there were Liberal or L-NCP governments, and weakest where there were State Labor governments.[69] As usual the swing in the campaign period itself—a shift to the government of no more than two or three percentage points—makes it impossible to draw positive inferences from the broad pattern of survey results. Without a panel of swinging voters to turn to, surveys cannot tell us very much and the only panel study in 1980, that conducted by ANOP, ended too early.

In the absence of a panel, one's hopes must lie with the day-of-the-election surveys. Unfortunately, however, the McNair exit poll made no attempt to distinguish those who had always intended to vote for a particular party from those whose minds had been made up only recently. The Morgan poll drew this distinction very precisely but the question with which it hoped to elicit the reasons for party support was poorly drafted. The high level of nonresponse (29 percent) and the absence of the category "always voted that way" (18 percent for Liberals and 26 percent for Labor in McNair's survey) suggest that the question left some voters misdirected and others mystified. The Melbourne University day-after-the-election survey included questions on when voters had made up their minds and why, but failed to report the results.

What does seem clear is that an unusually large number of voters made up their minds very late indeed. Of those interviewed by Morgan, no fewer than 12 percent (8 percent in 1977, 9 percent in 1975) said they had made up their minds within the last few days (4 percent), on the morning of the election (5 percent), or after they were handed a how-to-vote card (3 percent). Curiously, Morgan uncovered fewer late deciders among Liberal-NCP voters (9 percent) than Labor voters (11 percent). In the University of Melbourne survey, 44 percent of "swinging voters" had made up their minds less than a week before polling day (16 percent for stable voters) with 15 percent leaving the decision until polling day itself. That so large a number

205

decided so late does not mean necessarily that something quite unexpected happened to make them change their minds. In McNair's last preelection survey on October 11–12, 14 percent of those interviewed were not sure that they would stick with their current choice; and the figures in Sydney and Melbourne were virtually identical.[70]

Second thoughts may have been prompted by the polls. That people were aware of the polls and that most had accepted the interpretation placed on them by the media there can be little doubt. In the University of Melbourne survey "9 out of 10 . . . remembered that the opinion polls were predicting a Labor victory in the last week". Even four or five days before the election, in ANOP's panel study, 72 percent of respondents knew that the polls had indicated either a big swing (41 percent) or small swing (31 percent) to Labor since the 1977 elections. Those who were still uncommitted were slightly less likely to disbelieve the polls (39 percent) than the panel as a whole (46 percent). On the other hand, the proportion expecting the government to win remained steady. In March 1981 groups of Melbourne swinging voters interviewed on behalf of the Liberal Party hardly recalled the wealth tax ads; but they were keen to talk about the impact of the opinion polls.

How many votes were influenced by the polls? At the time of the ANOP study, October 13–14, 3 percent were prepared to say that the polls had influenced their choice. After the election, the University of Melbourne survey reported a much higher figure. Of those who had voted the same way in 1977 and 1980, only 4 percent indicated that the opinion polls had helped them decide. But among the swingers, those who had changed since 1977, 25 percent indicated that they had been influenced by the polls. In December the McNair Gallup Poll reported that about half of those interviewed thought the opinion polls had influenced the result; but put in that form the question was hardly worth asking.[71]

None of the surveys report the direction of the polls' influence. Some voters were probably reassured by Labor's improved standing: Labor is now so widely supported, they might have reasoned, it cannot be as doubtful a quantity as we had thought. ANOP, which found some evidence for both the impact of the polls and a swing to Labor, may have caught this process at work. For others, of course, Labor's improved standing might have given rise to concern; a fortiori among those whose initial "preference" for Labor was less an indication of serious commitment than of apparently safe protest. In 1980 there can be little argument as to which of the forces was the more important.[72].

In the McNair "exit poll" 23 of the 206 Liberal voters interviewed said they had not voted Liberal last time. Asked their reasons for voting Liberal this time, 17 percent mentioned the government's handling of the economy or its economic management (so did 12 percent of stable Liberals); 17 percent mentioned the government's success in keeping inflation down (12 percent for stable Liberals); while 26 percent (compared with 6 percent of stable Liberals) said they did not trust Labor, or did not think Labor could keep its promises. Together with the 22 percent (20 percent for stable Liberals) who thought the the government had done a good job, these were the main responses. Economic management, inflation, and distrust of Labor figured more prominently in the reasoning of those who had swung to the government (60 percent) than those who had stuck to the government (30 percent). Precampaign Liberal surveys had indicated that Whitlam—the memory and myth—still lingered.[73] When the Liberals took note of the polls and revamped their campaign the concerns in McNair's postelection survey were precisely the concerns they sought to stress. Not only in the ads but more especially in the press, on television news, and on current affairs programs, Labor found itself on the defensive, debating on grounds not of its own choosing and back-tracking.

Conclusion

The campaign-as-contest framed most media reporting; the polls, with their focus on party and leader support, constituted the major campaign initiative of the press. While the polls had their most dramatic impact on the Liberal campaign, the news and news practices of the media, especially of television, influenced the campaigns run by all the parties.

Though few depended on its entirely, most voters would have "followed" the campaign in the daily press. What voters followed, however, depended on what paper they read. The coverage of the campaign—proportion of lead stories, front pages, and news space in general, given over to the campaign, as well as the number of features, cartoons, editorials, and letters to the editor—was a function of where the paper ranked in terms of its coverage of serious news: at the top, somewhere in the middle, or at the bottom. It was at the top not the bottom that the electorate was seen as responsible: capable of processing information and forming its own judgement. Although few papers failed to endorse the government, the extent to which this support spilt over into ordinary news coverage varied from publisher to publisher. In their own, different ways, News Limited (despite some resistance from the *Daily Telegraph*), the more "balanced" Fairfax press and the low-key Herald and Weekly Times, all ran true to form.

The volume of campaign news varied with the state of the campaign. In Sydney and Melbourne, at least, it occupied a higher proportion of the news on television than in the press. If Sydney is typical, there was more campaign news on the ABC than on any of the commercial channels and it was on the ABC that the campaign received the greatest prominence. Channel 10, whose main news bulletin in Sydney and Melbourne ran for sixty minutes, ran items that were slightly longer than average but its total coverage of Federal politics was proportionately less. In Adelaide and Perth, where party leaders spent less time, coverage of the campaign was not as extensive as in Sydney or Melbourne. Media coverage, and not just TV coverage, was organized around the leaders: what they said to the media about their opponents was the archetypal campaign story. The leaders appeared on TV no more frequently than they were quoted on the front pages of the serious press.

About two stories a night were covered nationally, not always through the networks. The proportion of time on any of the networks that was common time varied greatly, day-by-day and week-by-week. About one-third of news time on the Seven and Ten networks was given over to common stories, nearly twice as much as on the Nine network: most news was not network news.

Some of the stories covered coast-to-coast were trivial in nature, as was much of the other coverage. A greater proportion of TV coverage could be described as trivial than press coverage, even at the bottom end of the market. But the argument that almost all the coverage was horse-race and hoopla is very much exaggerated.

The major advertising campaigns were organized, fairly uncritically, around market research. Labor's ads went to air first and would have gone even earlier had the party had the money to do so. They plotted a steady course around nationalism and development and declining living standards. Since it was geared to television, Labor's advertising finished on Wednesday, with the electronic blackout. The Liberals, at the start, felt like winners; they wanted a short, low-key campaign. Their emphasis, initially, was on leadership, economic management, inflation and development; once the polls went sour they concentrated on inflation and economic management, the family and Labor's wealth tax. At the same time they boosted their advertising budget enormously. Both nationally and at the State level they found plenty in reserve to take the fight right to the line.

On TV, radio, and the press the Liberal Party (helped, as previously noted, to an extraordinary extent in the press, by "third party" advertising) out-advertised Labor by a considerable margin. Whether, in the end, it did the party much good must be doubted. Everywhere the swing was to Labor and there is no evidence that advertising expenditure dampened this swing. On the contrary, the swing to Labor was greatest in those cities in which it was most heavily out-spent.

What of the last two weeks? The issue of wealth tax, spearheaded by the "wealth tax" ads, is generally accepted as the key to the swing back, especially in Sydney. But the evidence is against it. That the Liberals would do better in Sydney than in Melbourne was evident before any advertising was undertaken; moreover, the swing back to the Liberals occurred not just in Sydney but in Melbourne and probably across the rest of Australia as well. In the end, the swing to Labor in Sydney was slightly greater than the State's average in "fairly safe" Liberal seats and in the "marginal" Liberal seats Labor needed to win, but in Melbourne it was slightly less than the State average in the marginal seats Labor actually won. Few explained their vote by reference to wealth or capital gains tax.

Very likely, the shift in party support during the campaign was related to what voters read, heard, or saw as the news—or as commentary around the news—in the context of the polls. On inflation, economic management, and Labor's record, the media had not needed to create opinion; all that was necessary, through the operation of "ordinary news values", was to organize it.

Notes

1 Murray Goot, "Newspaper Circulation in Australia, 1932–1977", *Media Centre Papers*, no. 11) Bundoora: Centre for the Study of Educational Communication and Media, La Trobe University, 1979), for the decline and its causes; and 1967: Australian National University National Political Behaviour Survey, and 1979: Macquarie National Political Behaviour Survey, for readership figures. The figure for "regular readers" was put at 81 percent by the Saulwick poll in April 1976. *Age Poll Reprint Series* no. 18, p. 3.
2 D.A. Aitkin, *Stability and Change in Australian Politics* (Canberra: ANU Press, 1977), pp. 275, 286 for 1967 and 1969; and 1979 Macquarie National Political Behaviour Survey.
3 Colin Seymour-Ure, "Fleet Street", in David Butler and Dennis Kavanagh, *The British General Election of October 1974* (London: Macmillan, 1975), pp. 166–9.
4 Henry Mayer, *Dilemmas in Mass Media Policies* (Canberra: Academy of the Social Sciences in Australia, 1979), p. 24.

5 For the papers read by various "elites" in the mid-1970s see John Higley, Desley Deacon and Don Smart, *Elites in Australia* (London: Routledge & Kegan Paul, 1979), p. 214.

6 For press coverage of the policy speeches, see Geoff Pryor, "Media Monitoring by the Public", *Media Information Australia* no. 21, August, 1981, pp. 141–5.

7 As in 1977, the uncertainty had been created by Fraser himself who could have ended it all by foreswearing an early election. C.J. Lloyd, "A Lean Campaign for the Media", in Howard R. Penniman, ed., *The Australian National Elections of 1977* (Washington, D.C.: American Enterprise Institute, 1979), p. 233.

8 The only State with a four-year Parliament was Tasmania. In New South Wales a shift from three-year to four-year Parliaments was approved at a referendum on September 19, 1981.

9 Channel 10, however, also part of the Murdoch empire ran a couple of "special reports" on people in poverty. Unemployment was only mentioned in the news eight times. Geoff Speer and Peter Heldorf, "Eyewitness News, Unemployment and Poverty", *Media Papers*, no. 13 (Sydney: New South Wales Institute of Technology, September 1981), pp. 8–9.

10 A shift to selfishness in mass values during the 1970s is argued by the former managing editor of the *Australian Financial Review*, Maximilian Walsh, in *Poor Little Rich Country* (Ringwood: Penguin, 1979). For politicians' views, see Bob Carr "Unemployment Looks Less and Less Like and Election Issue", *Bulletin*, December 11, 1979, pp. 20–2.

11 Pryor, "Media Monitoring by the Public", p. 15; "Press Buries the Issues", *New Journalist*, no. 36, December, 1980, pp. 14–17.

12 See also Donald Horne, *Winner Take All?* (Ringwood: Penguin, 1981), ch. 6.

13 *West Australian*, October 11, 1980, pp. 27–33. For the assumptions underlying the treatment of the parties, see Henry Mayer, "Big Party Chauvinism and Minor Party Romanticism", in H. Mayer and H. Nelson, eds, *Australian Politics: A Fifth Reader* (Melbourne, Longman Cheshire, 1980).

14 Laws' audience was about 180,000; two-thirds, women over 45. For a confidential assessment of the *Age*, written in 1972, by the Federal president of the Liberal Party, see Alan Reid, *The Whitlam Experiment* (Melbourne: Hill of Content, 1976), p. 36; for an internal Liberal Party memorandum on how to handle Hinch, see *Commonwealth Parliamentary Debates* (hereinafter C.P.D.), (House of Representatives), April 8, 1981, p. 1463.

15 Murdoch had used his papers in this way before: for the Labor Party in 1972 especially and 1974; for the Liberals since 1975. Laurie Oakes and David Soloman, *The Making of an Australian Prime Minister* (Melbourne: Cheshire, 1973), ch. 19, for 1972; *Grab for Power* (Melbourne: Cheshire, 1974) for 1974; C.J. Lloyd, "The Media and the Elections", in Howard R. Penniman, ed., *Australia at the Polls* (Washington, D.C.: American Enterprise Institute, 1977), ch. 7, for 1975.

16 Although widely described as unprecedented this was not so. In South Australia, Don Dunstan appointed Len King shadow attorney-general in 1970, before the 1980 election. Neal Blewett and Dean Jeansch, *Playford to Dunstan* (Melbourne: Cheshire, 1971), p. 204. For the Federal precedent, see chapter 4, "Labor in 1980", note 8, in this volume.

17 Phillip McCarthy, "Neville's lost chords leaves a major gap in Labor's strategy", *National Times*, September 14–20, 1980, p. 3.

18 An ANOP poll commissioned by the *Australian* early in 1972, showing Labor in front, lifted that day's circulation from about 136,000 to 160,000. Personal communication from T.W. Beed, formerly managing director of ANOP, January 10, 1982.

19 For a fuller discussion of the record of the polls, their performance in 1980 and the reaction of the press, see Murray Goot, " 'Part science and a hell of a lot of human judgment': the polls and the 1980 election", *Newsletter of the University of Sydney Sample Survey Centre* 4 (December 1980), Special Supplement; Melbourne television's reporting of the polls is discussed in Ted J. Smith III, "Opinion polls, political demonstrations, and television coverage of the 1980 Federal election", *Regional Journal of Social Issues*, nos. 8/9, September 1981, pp. 19–26.

20 Anne Summers, "Labor writes itself off—but will the voters?", *Australian Financial Review*, July 18, 1980, p. 12–13, 18, 24.

21 In 1977 page-one mentions of the polls constituted only 17 percent of all poll mentions. Terence W. Beed, "The Uses of Public Opinion Poll Findings in the Australian Press", Institute of Statisticians Annual Conference, Trinity College, Cambridge, July 2–5, 1980, p. 30.

22 The distinction between creating opinion and organizing it is worked through in R.W. Connell, *Ruling Class Ruling Culture* (Cambridge: Cambridge University Press, 1977), pp. 193–4.

23 Compare this extract from speech notes prepared for Fraser on the same day: "Overseas investors are already signalling loud and clear what they expect if we were to believe the opinion polls, which I don't."

24 The reference was to a speech by Labor's shadow minister for Economic Affairs delivered in Sydney on July 5. Ralph Willis, "Taxation Policies In the '80's: The Labor Party View", in *Taxation Policies in the 80's* (Sydney: Taxation Institute Research and Education Trust, 1980), pp. 12–20. Unfortunately for Labor, Willis never distributed copies to the Canberra Press Gallery.

25 "Countrywide" broadcast, October 3, 1980, transcript, pp. 6–7.

26 Capital gains tax (not wealth tax) was listed under " 'ammunition' for use against ALP," in an early Liberal Party strategy document, reproduced in Anne Summers, "The Liberal blueprint to win the 1980 election", *Australian Financial Review*, November 12, 1979, p. 10.

27 *Australian Labor Party Platform Constitution and Rules as approved by the 33rd National Conference, Adelaide 1979* (Canberra; n.d.), p. 43.

28 One taxi driver alleged that he had been offered money by someone from Liberal Party headquarters to help disrupt a Fraser rally. See the interview with Derryn Hinch, "P.M.", broadcast October 10, 1980, transcript, pp. 5–8.

29 For sources, see note 2.

30 Information in this paragraph derives from McNair Anderson and Associates and from *The ABC in Review* (Canberra: AGPS 1981), vol. 3, Table 3.1.2 and 2.4.3.

31 This variation is ignored in Smith, "Opinion Polls ...", p. 16.

32 Under the *Broadcasting and Television Act* 1942 licensees are prohibited from broadcasting election matter after "midnight on the Wednesday, next preceding the day of the poll".

33 All figures relate to week-nights only. Comparisons between ABC and commercial news on the weekends were ruled out following the decision of those responsible for gathering the Sydney data not to monitor the "lightweight" weekend bulletins. Data from other States shows that this decision rested on a misreading of weekend TV. Unfortunately, it was not possible for us to monitor the ABC outside Sydney. For comparison between the ABC and commercial stations in Melbourne, and similar comments on weekend TV, see Smith, "Opinion Polls...."

34 *ATV-10 Melbourne—Control Investments Pty Ltd Share Transactions Inquiry Decision and Reasons for Decision* (Canberra: AGPS; 1980). This decision was subsequently overturned by the Administrative Appeals Tribunal. "Decision and Reasons for decision", handed down by Mr. Justice Morling, December 17, 1980 (mimeo).

35 Ironically, the one such event reported nationally was thought by some of Hayden's handlers to have been a mistake, since it fitted Fraser's description of him as "Whingeing Bill".

36 Findings broadly similar to these, calculated on the basis of items, not time, are reported for a nonelection period in Bruce Grundy, "Where is the News? A Content Analysis of a Week's Television News in Australia", in Patricia Edgar, ed., *The News in Focus* (South Melbourne: Macmillan, 1980), pp. 103–12.

37 On September 27–28, ANOP asked whether the ALP triumvirate would be "a help for the Labor vote on October 18 or not?"; 67 percent of "swinging voters" said it would. On the same weekend, in a telephone poll, Spectrum asked people's "opinion about the three-way leadership of the Australian Labor Party in the Federal election campaign"—a question guaranteed to get less favorable response; 40 percent were in favor, 45 percent against. Both surveys, in their different ways, assumed that a favorable attitude made a Labor vote more likely. So did Hayden, when he welcomed Wran as party president: "He will improve our vote in NSW by 2 to 3 per cent." The one thing that seems certain is that it did not. Anne Summers, "Trio stunning success", *Australian Financial Review*, October 8, 1980, p. 3; Spectrum Research; *Australian*, August 5, 1980, p. 3.

38 Given that politicians are "somewhat obsessed with numerical balance", the ABC keeps records to the nearest line and the nearest second. In 1980 the Liberal Party received 1157.00 minutes on ABC Radio, the NCP, 93.09, ALP 1154.20, Democrats 283.29, and others 50.06, including a government advantage of 20 minutes on radio current affairs programs AM and PM. On the television program "Nationwide" the government received almost an hour more than the opposition—something which produced a protest from the Australian Journalists Association and questions in Parliament. Letter from J.D. Norgard, Chairman of the ABC to David Combe, December 11, 1980; *C.P.D.* (Senate) May 13, 1981, p. 1954. This, of course, has nothing to do with "balance" in any other sense. For a broader attempt to compare the ABC and commercial TV, see Chris Duffield, "Bias and Television Coverage of the 1977 Election", *Media Papers*, no. 5 (Sydney: New South Wales Institute of Technology, 1980). A contradictory view is "Social Irresponsibility", *Quadrant*, July 1981, p. 66.

39 This is not to endorse the view of Crofts et al., that Sydney's TV coverage of party politics was "provided in lieu of coverage of general political items". It is clear, even on the figures from which this conclusion is

drawn, that there was considerable variation week-by-week in the ratio of "party political" to "political" material. The fact that the difference between "party political" and "political" is drawn on the narrowest possible grounds (the "leader of the opposition" is "political" while "the leader of the ALP" is "party political") is no doubt one reason for the variation. Stephen Crofts, Kathe Boehringer and Philip Bell, "Television News and the 1980 Federal Election", *Media Information Australia* no. 21 (August 1981), p. 11; the full version in Philip Bell et al., *Programmed Politics: A Study of Australian Television* (Sydney: Sable, 1982), ch. 2.

40 This campaign is discussed more fully in Marian Sawer, "Women and Women's Issues in the 1980 Federal Election", *Politics*, XVI, November 1981, pp. 243–9; and in chapter 6, "Minor Parties and Pressure Groups", in this volume.

41 Thomas E. Patterson and Robert D. McClure, *The Unseeing Eye* (New York: Putnam's, 1976), p. 41 for 1972; Thomas E. Patterson, "The Media Muffed the Message", *Washington Post*, December 5, 1976, p. B–1 cited in Harry Holloway and John George, *Public Opinion* (New York: St. Martin's Press, 1979), p. 250, for 1976.

42 Crofts et al., "Television and the 1980 Federal Election", p. 7.

43 Methods that produce exaggerated results are also used by Smith, "Opinion Polls . . .", p. 20.

44 Figures from the annual reports of the Australian Broadcasting Control Board (ABCB) and ABT cited in Ian Ward, "Big Spending On The Small Screen: Televised Party Political Advertising and the 1980 Campaign", *Politics* 17, May 1982, p. 87.

45 For details of station returns (TV and radio) see *C.P.D.* (Senate) March 31, 1981, pp. 936–54. Figures provided to the author by Bruce Tart Research indicate that Liberal Party ads went to air move often in Sydney (by about 27 minutes), Melbourne (16 minutes) and Perth (45 minutes) than station returns slow.

46 The agency had used 10-second spots for the South Australian election of 1975, their first assignment for the Liberal Party. Although, in 1976, the Australian Broadcasting Control Board recommended that no political ads on TV be shorter than five minutes, its successor, the ABT, recommended that the decision rest with political parties. Australian Broadcasting Tribunal, *Self-Regulation for Broadcasters* (Canberra: AGPS, 1977), p. 128.

47 For the original advertising schedule see Ian Ward "Party political advertising and the case for disclosure of electoral expenditure", *Regional Journal of Social Issues* No. 7, January 1981, p. 57; for the ABT's post-1977 ruling, see *Annual Report Australian Broadcasting Tribunal* (Canberra: AGPS, 1979) p. 15.

48 For a discussion of the subsequent High Court case, see chapter 9 in this volume and David Solomon, "Act no bar to false ads", *Australian Financial Review* March 19, 1981, p. 3. For a defence of the judgement, from the National Country Party's advertising agency, see Greg Daniel, "The home truths of political ads", *b & t advertising marketing and media weekly* April 9, 1981, p. 32. For party reaction, see *C.P.D.* (Senate) March 25, 1981, pp. 721–37. For the argument that political advertising is "necessarily full of deception, half-truths, exaggerations and falsities", see Henry Mayer "The Morality of Political Advertising", *MAC: Journal of Australian Marketing, Advertising, Communication*, no. 1, October 1980, pp. 9–13.

49 On the day of the election, the *Age* also "refused to publish the full page Right to Life advertisement because of the threatened writs arising from its publication the day before". Sawer, "Women and Women's Issues in the 1980 Federal election", p. 249, n. 4.

50 A.L. May, *Battle for the Banks* (Sydney: Sydney University Press, 1979), p. 100; Francis P. Power, *The Fight for "Life"* (Sandringham, Vic: F.R. Power, 1975), pp. 7–8.

51 Eggleton had first tasted trouble, in 1974, with John Singleton's ads. Oakes and Solomon, *Grab for Power*, pp. 455–6, 460.

52 "THE UNION TAIL WAGS THE LABOR DOG", authorized by B.A. Harris (an advertising man), Birdwood, South Australia and "LABOR IS ANTI-BUSINESS", authorized by M.R. Andrewartha, Kew, Victoria. Both argued the "collapse of investor confidence" on the stock exchanges.

53 "Report from the National Secretary and Campaign Director, David Combe, on the 1980 Federal Election" (mimeo), p. 14.

54 A view influenced by F. Emery and M. Emery, *A Choice of Futures* (Canberra: Centre for Continuing Education, Australian National University, 1975).

55 "Report from the National Secretary ...", p. 12. Many of Labor's ideas became known to the Liberal Party late in 1979, when campaign planning documents, in the care of Mullins, Ralph and Clarke (the then name of Labor's advertising agency), found their way to the Liberal Party. The Secretariat later released them to journalists in the Canberra Press Gallery. "ALP Campaign Planning", October 1979 (mimeo). Anne Summers, "Mullinsgate flushes out a political Judas", *Australian Financial Review* November 23, 1979, p. 3.

56 "Report from the National Secretary ...", p. 11.

57 At Labor's campaign committee meeting in March, Hawke thought industrial relations would be the number one issue. He also wanted an ad made on uranium; given his opposition to Labor's uranium policy, this was an intriguing request. The West Australian and South Australian branches believed uranium was not an issue which would help the government in their States. An ad was scripted but never used. Labor's failure to run ads on industrial relations and uranium in 1977 is detailed in Murray Goot, "Monitoring the Public, Marketing the Parties", in Penniman, ed. *The Australian Elections of 1977* pp. 206–15.

58 Compare: "we advertise not so much to change people's opinions but to reinforce those who have a pre-existing inclination to support us". "Report from the National Secretary ...", pp. 11, 21; ANOP "Voter Research 1979: Strategy summary and results", March 1980 (mimeo), p. 5.

59 "Report from the National Secretary ..." p. 8.

60 Maximilian Walsh, "How Paul Keating is taking on the left", *Bulletin*, February 2, 1982, p. 25. For an echo from the left, see Dennis Altman, "Election Reflection", *Nation Review*, November 1980, p. 11; from the Democrats, see Alan Hughes, "The Australian Federal Election, 1980", *Journal of Students of H.S.C. Politics*, vol. 8, March 1981, p. 14; from the right, see T.B. Millar, "Conservatives triumph on a slender base", *Round Table* no. 281, January 1981, p. 47.

61 Gary C. Jacobson, "The Impact of Broadcast Compaigning on Electoral Outcomes", *Journal of Politics*, vol. 37, August 1975, p. 781, The American evidence is reviewed in Michael J. Robinson, "The Media in 1980: Was the

Message the Massage", in Austin Ranney, ed., *The American Elections of 1980* (Washington, D.C.: American Enterprise Institute, 1981), p. 179.

62 Jean Holmes, "The 1980 Australian Federal Election", *Journal for Students of H.S.C. Politics*, vol. 8, March 1981, p. 10.

63 For example, on the right, Alan Reid, "Labor failed to win over 'little capitalists'", *Bulletin*, November 4, 1980, p. 34; on the left, Brian Abbey, "Post-election analysis: a broader view", *Labor Forum*, vol. 2, December 1980, p. 4. The Labor caucus decision was taken on February 3, 1982.

64 *General Election for the House of Representatives 1980: Analysis of Result of Count of First Preference Votes* (Canberra: Australian Electoral Office, 1980), pp. 27–30; Malcolm Mackerras, *Australian General Election and Senate Election 1980: Statistical Analysis* (Duntroon: Department of Government, Faculty of Military Studies, University of NSW, 1981), pp. 6–8.

65 Michael Poulsen and Peter Spearritt, *Sydney: A Social and Political Atlas* (North Sydney: George Allen & Unwin, 1981), pp. 13, 62, 142.

66 *Reasons for the Return of the Fraser Government: The Federal Election of October 18, 1980* (North Sydney: McNair Anderson Associates, n.d.), p. 8.

67 "The ANOP Marginal Seat Study" (mimeo). Also reported by Anne Summers "Fraser's Hopes Fade", *Australian Financial Review*, October 17, 1980, pp. 1, 3–4.

68 McNair Anderson Associates, "The Gallup Poll", press release 02/12/80 and computer sheets. On election eve Spectrum also had asked whether "There should be a capital gains tax on the sale of your personal property" and—not surprisingly—found only 10 percent in favour. *Weekend Australian*, October 18–19, 1980, p. 16. But a Morgan Gallup Poll, conducted June 26–July 3, 1982, found that 72 percent wanted a tax on profit from the sale of one or more of a number of items purchased within twelve months of resale (including property bought for investment), with 59 percent wanting a tax on profit derived from one or more such items held for longer than twelve months. *Bulletin* July 27, 1982, p. 39; Morgan Gallup Poll no. 447.

69 For the correlation with unemployment, I am grateful to David Peetz; for the possible influence of State Governments, see Neal Blewett, "Looking back on 1980: Forward to 1983. Some election reflections", *Labor Forum*, vol. 3, June 1981, pp. 4–5.

70 McNair Anderson Associates, "The Gallup Poll", press release and computer sheets.

71 McNair Anderson Associates, "The Gallup Poll", press release.

72 For the first process, see Elizabeth Noelle-Neumann, "The Spiral of Silence. A Theory of Public Opinion", *Journal of Communication*, vol. 24 1974, pp. 43–51; evidence for the second is noted in Robert M. Worcester, "Pollsters, The Press and Political Polling in Britain", *Public Opinion Quarterly*, vol. 44, Winter 1980, pp. 564–5.

73 Whitlam was one of Labor's best fund-raisers, but Labor's campaign directors instructed all branches that Whitlam not be invited to participate in the campaign in any way.

9
A Close-Run Thing

Colin A. Hughes

At the previous Australian national election in December 1977 the prophets had been discredited. It had seemed reasonable to expect that after the calamitous defeat of 1975 the Labor Party's fortunes would have to show an improvement in both votes and seats. In the event there had been a swing of only 1.1 percentage points to the ALP, and that swing was reflected in a gain of only two seats while the coalition government lost five in a slightly smaller House of Representatives.[1] In 1980 the prophets were more cautious—at least until the campaign was well under way and the opinion polls began to suggest a Labor victory. But until then, for those who looked at the broad picture, the ALP required a swing of 6.1 percent on top of its 1977 vote to win enough seats to have the barest possible majority in the House of Representatives. At the 1977 election the ALP had secured 45.4 percent of the two-party-preferred vote, but the bias of the electoral system (discussed below) added a handicap of another 1.4 percentage points to the 4.7 percentage points which would be required to give the party a *majority* of the two-party-preferred vote— but still not enough for a majority of *seats*. National swings as large as 6.1 percent had taken place in Australia in recent times; there had been a swing of 7.1 percent to the ALP in 1969 and one of 7.4 percent to the coalition more recently in 1975. But on both those occasions the government of the day, against which the swing operated, had obviously been in deep trouble by the time the election began. There were few signs in 1980 that Malcolm Fraser was in comparable difficulties.

In five of the six States and in the Australian Capital Territory the electoral boundaries were as they had been in 1977, making prediction somewhat easier. However, the House of Representatives had

216

been enlarged by one member since that election, the additional seat requiring a redistribution (redistricting) in Western Australia alone; the political effect was the creation of an additional constituency which was quite safe for the coalition, making Labor's task marginally more difficult. It should be added that the Fraser government, firmly in control of both the House and Senate was able to adopt the new boundaries for Western Australia without difficulty. In the future any proposed redistribution of seats will be more interesting for, if either house of the Federal Parliament rejects the new boundaries, under legislation in force since 1977, the next House of Representatives election for the State or States involved would return all the new number of members at large. As yet, there is no legislative provision as to how such an election should be conducted, although it would be a relatively simple matter to settle.

To return from speculation about 1983 to what was thought likely to happen in 1980, those electoral analysts who preferred building up their predictions seat by seat argued that a Labor victory would require one of two possible scenarios. At the 1975 election Australia had divided into two parts: the southeastern corner of the continent, comprising the states of New South Wales, Victoria, and South Australia plus the Australian Capital Territory, where the ALP's House of Representatives representation was now concentrated, and the rest of the country, comprising the States of Queensland, Western Australia, and Tasmania plus the Northern Territory, where the ALP had been virtually wiped out. At the 1977 election this division was substantially confirmed. In the southeast the coalition won fifty-five seats to Labor's thirty-four, but in the rest of the country the coalition's advantage was still overwhelming, thirty-one seats to a mere four. The ALP's previous electoral victory, in 1974, had been extremely narrow, sixty-six seats to sixty-one, but with relatively little difference between the two parts of the country as they came to be identified in the following year. In 1974 the southeast had supplied the Whitlam government's small majority with fifty ALP seats to the coalition's forty-three, offsetting the minimal advantage the coalition had in the outlying areas with its eighteen seats to Labor's sixteen. To regain a finger-tip grip on power on the same basis it had had in 1974, the Labor Party needed to pick up fourteen more seats in the southeast (which was just possible) and another thirteen in the outlying areas (which was quite unthinkable). Therefore, to compensate for what couldn't be done in the outlying areas, Labor had to do correspondingly better than its 1974 performance in the southeast, and that too was virtually unthinkable.

Accordingly, so the analysts argued, it would be best to dust off the predictions of 1977. Labor was likely to win some more votes and therefore some more seats, but could not hope to regain office on this occasion. The best it could hope for would be to get within striking distance of a victory in 1983, just as when the party under Gough Whitlam's leadership had struggled back from disaster in 1966 with a big swing in 1969 and then a second, smaller swing in 1972, to reenter office after twenty-three years in opposition. But if the swing were too small, then the party's new leader, Bill Hayden, would be discredited. A wide open struggle for succession to the leadership would be launched, and at the same time the possibility of improvement in economic conditions could set Malcolm Fraser on a career as Prime Minister which could rival Sir Robert Menzies' 1949–66 term for longevity. A rejuvenated and enlarged Labor opposition could press the Fraser government hard and keep up its momentum in 1983, but a second failure to get up from the canvas would raise the questions about the party's long-term chances of surviving which had been asked in the mid-1960s and then had been silenced by Whitlam's restoration of the party's fortunes. Another resounding defeat for the opposition would allow the Fraser government to continue administering the unpopular policies which it claimed were essential to economic recovery, and if these policies worked—or even if they merely coincided with a recovery really attributable to other causes— the association between coalition governments and prosperity might well be indelibly stamped on the electorate's mind.

As it happened the Labor Party did rather better than had been expected at the start of the campaign, although not as well as its supporters had hoped in some euphoric moments late in the campaign. The results will be discussed in more detail at the end of this chapter; in the meantime it should be noted that the ALP achieved a

TABLE 9-1
Safeness of House seats, 1969–80(%)

| Safeness Rating | Election | | | | | |
	1969	1972	1974	1975	1977	1980
Ultra-safe, Labor	4.0	4.0	7.1	0.8	0.8	4.8
Safe, Labor	19.2	20.8	17.3	10.4	14.5	16.0
Marginal, Labor	12.0	14.4	10.4	8.7	6.5	9.6
Ultra-marginal, Labor	12.8	13.6	17.3	8.7	8.9	10.4
Ultra-marginal, Coalition	14.4	22.4	17.3	15.7	13.7	24.0
Marginal, Coalition	16.8	11.2	10.4	20.4	23.4	12.0
Safe, Coalition	19.2	13.6	18.1	28.4	27.4	20.8
Ultra-safe, Coalition	1.6	0	2.4	7.1	4.8	2.4

Note: For explanation of method, see text, p. 219. Figures may not add to 100 percent because of rounding.
Source: Hughes, 'The Case of the Arrested Pendulum'', p. 311; Mackerras, ''Australian General Election and Senate Election, 1980'', pp. 12–13.

218

favorable swing of 4.2 percent, not quite what was required but still well past the half-way mark on a two-stage push back to office. However, in terms of seats gained its success had not been commensurate with the size of the swing. Labor had thirteen more seats, having won fourteen and lost one, for a total of fifty-one. It was still twelve seats short of the sixty-three necessary to eject the coalition and form a government. In terms of seats Hayden had barely halved the Fraser government's majority, despite the evidence of the opinion polls that Labor had been on the verge of wiping out that majority. Was half a victory no victory at all?

Competitiveness

One important consequence of a general election is the proportion of seats left teetering on the brink and vulnerable to the smallest shift of the electoral wind. Table 9-1 classifies the results of the Australian national elections from 1969 to 1980 according to the "safeness" of seats on the two-party-preferred vote at each election. The categories employed are: ultra-safe, in which the winning party receives 70 percent of the vote or better; safe, 60.0–69.9 percent; marginal, 55.0–59.9 percent; and ultra-marginal, 50.0–54.9 percent. The proportion of House of Representatives seats in each category is shown in the table.

Labor's gains in 1980 involved a slight increase in the number of its seats in each category of "safeness". Where previously there had been only one ultra-safe Labor seat, there were now six: three in New South Wales and three in Victoria. Ten of Labor's thirteen ultra-marginal seats were gained at the election; the other four gains moved immediately into the marginal column. At each of the previous three elections, just over half the seats in the House of Representatives were marginal or ultra-marginal. But whereas in 1975 and 1977 the coalition's safe and ultra-safe seats had greatly outnumbered Labor's—by more than three to one in 1975 and by two to one in 1977—by 1980 the two blocs of those seats were roughly equal. The advantage which kept the coalition in office in 1980 was to be found in the ultra-marginal category where it now held thirty seats to Labor's thirteen.

Following the 1977 election, the Prime Minister was able to form a ministry in which only four ministers held marginal seats and none were at the greater risk of ultra-marginal seats. After 1980 five coalition ministers including both parties' deputy leaders and the Treasurer occupied marginal seats and another four ministers were in the ultra-marginal category. While the attribution to a particular constituency of a safeness rating at any election may be the consequence of short-term forces and, therefore, can be misleading for the next election—the demotion of the normally blue-ribbon electorate of McPherson to the ultra-marginal category in 1980 being a good example of this—the altered situation of the ministry was one sign among several that the coalition had been seriously shaken.

About half the coalition's ultra-marginal seats of 1980 had never been won by Labor in that party's good years in the 1970s. Therefore, their occupants might feel less exposed than those in the other half, fearful that what their electors had done in 1972 or 1974 they might do again in 1983. Rather more than a third of these ultra-marginal seats were nonmetropolitan and therefore possibly somewhat more insulated against another swing to Labor. About half were situated in the outlying states (seven in Queensland, four in Western Australia, four in Tasmania, and the Northern Territory's one) which might be a good thing for the coalition if it could continue its special appeal in that quarter, but it could also quickly become dangerous if the strong-willed Premiers of Queensland and Western Australia began to attack Fraser's Canberra as vigorously as they had Whitlam's.

Writing with hindsight of the first six months of the new House of Representatives, it would appear that the Prime Minister's reputation for successful ruthlessness, forged in the turbulent months when the Whitlam government was brought down and its remnants scattered at the ensuing election, and then refurbished at the electoral victory of 1977, may have suffered some damage. The ancient political cry "But what have you done for us lately?" began to be heard, and displays of independence from various sections of the parliamentary Liberal Party suggested that members in the more marginal seats were beginning to worry about their newly exposed positions. In part this anxiety reflected a growing awareness that the 1980 election had been far closer than appreciated on election night, and that the size of the government's majority was more a product of the vagaries of the electoral system than a reflection of a comfortable margin in popular support separating it from the opposition.

Fairness

If the Australian electoral system had been scrupulously "fair" in converting votes into seats in strict proportion, in 1975 the ALP should have won another twenty seats, in 1977 another eighteen, but in 1980 only another eleven. If the electoral system was becoming less unfair, why was the change taking place? Earlier accounts of the Labor Party's problems in this series warned that the use of single-member constituencies to elect the House of Representatives imposed a substantial handicap on the losing party, and pointed to the "cube rule" formula. This states that when there are two parties, if the ratio of their votes is A:B the ratio of their seats will be $A^3:B^3$, and provides a rough-and-ready measure of the influence of the single-member constituency factor on the conversion of votes into seats. The difference between the estimated allocation of seats to the disadvantaged party, under the formula, and the party's actual share of seats, then has to be explained by other factors.[2] For 1975 and 1977 one could say that approximately two-thirds of the ALP's handicap came from the use of single-member constituencies; it would still be missing seven seats on both occasions. However, in 1980 when the two-party-preferred shares of the competing parties were extremely close and the multiplying effect of the cube rule formula was contained as a consequence, there was a minimal, one-seat difference between a proportionate and a cube rule allocation of seats, as Table 9-2 shows. It would appear that on this occasion almost all the ALP's handicap has to be sought elsewhere.

One possible explanation is that too many Labor voters are locked up wastefully in overly safe seats, although as we saw from Table 9-1 both parties hold approximately the same number of safe and ultra-safe seats. Nor would it appear on first examination that the size of enrollments in particular electorates—so that Labor wins the large-enrollment seats thereby wasting votes while the coalition wins the smaller-enrollment seats—matters much. If one takes the 10 percent deviation above or below State quota (average enrollment) permitted to the electoral commissioners drawing new electorate

TABLE 9-2
Two-party-preferred votes and seats, by State, House election, 1980

| State | Estimated Two-Party Vote | | Seats | | | | | |
| | | | Proportionate | | Cube Rule | | Actual | |
	L-NCP	ALP	L-NCP	ALP	L-NCP	ALP	L-NCP	ALP
New South Wales	49.6	50.4	21	22	21	22	25	18
Victoria	49.3	50.7	16	17	16	17	16	17
Queensland	53.1	46.9	10	9	11	8	14	5
South Australia	50.6	49.4	6	5	6	5	5	6
Western Australia	53.4	46.6	6	5	7	4	8	3
Tasmania	53.0	47.0	3	2	3	2	5	0
Australia	50.4	49.6	63	62	64	61	74	51

Source: Mackerras, "Australian General Election and Senate Election, 1980", pp. 6–11.

boundaries on a redistribution as a convenient measure of improper enrollment variations, at the 1980 election there were only nine more than 10 percent above—five won by the ALP, four by the coalition—and only two below—one each.

The electoral commissioners have a second major rule within which they have to work: it is that at the time when new boundaries are drawn, the enrollment of each and every electorate which exceeds 5,000 square kilometers in area must be smaller than the enrollment of each and every electorate which does not exceed 5,000 square kilometers in area. The provision was extracted by the National Country Party as the price for accepting the Liberal Party's retention of the 10 percent permissible deviation above and below State quota which the Whitlam Labor government had introduced in 1974. Between 1902 and 1974 the range had been 20 percent above or below quota; the advantage of being started off well below quota went to rural electorates plus a few others on the outskirts of the capital cities where enrollments were expected to grow rapidly because of urban sprawl. Once the permissible deviation had been cut down to 10 percent, another device was necessary to maintain weightage of rural electorates and their electors. The coalition's compromise solution was the 5,000 square kilometer formula and, given Australia's vast expanse, making some allowance for the area of the largest electorates has some attractions.[3] At the time of the 1980 election the top decile by area, thirteen in number, of House of Representatives electorates comprised 91.3 percent of the land area but contained only 10.4 percent of the national enrollment. All were larger than 50,000 square kilometers, and ranged downward from Kalgoorlie with 2,285,000 square kilometers and the Northern Territory with 1,347,500 square kilometers. This is why it is preferable to redraw the Australian electoral map, as has been done (see pp. 000–000), to compensate for the diversity in area. Indeed, the largest six electorates, all in excess of 400,000 square kilometers, cover 79.5 percent of Australia, leaving barely one-fifth for the remaining 119 electorates.

Table 9-3 sets out the average enrollments for the two classes of electorates, those above and those below the 5,000 square kilometer cutoff. The differences are negligible for New South Wales and Tasmania, slight for Queensland and Western Australia, and rather more substantial for Victoria and South Australia. However, the nine weighted electorates in Victoria still contain 8.6 quotas of enrollment, so it is difficult to attribute much political influence to the provision. In total, forty-one electorates in the States benefit from the formula; the Northern Territory is another large-area, small-enrollment electorate, but derives its advantage from constitutional status as a separate unit rather than from the coalition's amendment of the Electoral Act. Of those forty-one, in 1980 eighteen were won by the Liberal Party and eighteen by the NCP. Only five went to the ALP although these included two of the three largest in the country, Kalgoorlie and Grey. However, population, and consequently enrollment, growth takes place without regard to statutory prescriptions, and although the coalition's redistribution prior to the 1977 election started the electorates out with a handicap on the smaller, urban seats, the field quickly scattered. After barely three years, in New South Wales only six of the thirty-one small-area electorates had enrollments greater than the most populous (in enrollment) large-area electorate, Macarthur, while in Queensland just one of the nine small-area electorates had an enrollment larger than the enrollment of Fisher, a large-area electorate. Thus it is difficult to ascribe a definite influence to the 5,000 square kilometer rule in producing the Labor Party's handicap, though it would be hard to justify such an arbitrary restriction on the electoral commissioners' discretion when its supposed benefit is so short-lived.

Elsewhere I have tried to illustrate the distinction between equal representation of individual electors and fair representation of political parties.[4] The first can be measured for constituency enrollments by the Gini coefficient, a measure of inequality well-known in most of the social sciences, and the second may conveniently be measured by the difference in the percentages of the two-party-preferred vote required by each of the competing parties to win a bare majority of seats in the legislature. On the evidence of the 1977 results, the ALP required 51.5 percent of the two-party-preferred vote to win sixty-three seats in 1980. Once the results were known, that figure was slightly reduced, to 51 percent. However, on the 1980 figures it also appeared that the coalition could have retained the sixty-three seats

TABLE 9-3
Average enrollments of electorates larger and smaller than 5,000 Km²

| State | Area > 5,000 Km² | | Area < 5,000 Km² | |
	Average enrollment	No. of electorates	Average enrollment	No. of electorates
New South Wales	73,880	12	74,082	31
Victoria	69,792	9	74,381	24
Queensland	69,977	9	72,558	10
South Australia	74,698	3	78,151	8
Western Australia	67,269	4	68,601	7
Tasmania	54,752	4	54,467	1

Note: The Australian Capital Territory which is smaller than 5,000 Km² and the Northern Territory which forms a single electorate are not shown.

necessary to stay in office with only 49.1 percent of the two-party-preferred vote. Subtracting 49.1 percent from 51 percent gives 1.9 percent as the measure of bias between the parties, in this case in favor of the coalition. Table 9-4 shows both the Gini coefficients for enrollments and the bias measures for party competition in votes turned at the last six elections. Compared to 1972 and 1974 when the Labor Party won the election, its handicap in 1980 was somewhat less but still sufficient to set the party to thinking hard about reforms of the electoral system which might eliminate the current handicap, diminished though it might be compared to earlier elections.

One improvement might be the introduction of a system of proportional representation, abandoning single-member constituencies for multi-membered ones. A speculative exercise using the 1980 results subsequently reported that had the six States been divided up into one nine-member, eight seven-member, two six-member, and nine five-member constituencies, the result would have been an evenly-divided House of Representatives in which the Australian Democrats held the balance of power.[5] The Liberals would have lost four seats and the NCP eight, while the ALP would have gained seven and the Australian Democrats five (two in Victoria and one each in New South Wales, Queensland, and South Australia), producing a House in which the coalition had sixty-two seats, the ALP sixty-three and the Democrats five. Considering that the coalition had a slight lead over the ALP on the two-party-preferred vote and real first-preference votes alike, its supporters might question the equity of such a reform. Moreover, there are many varieties of proportional representation available for reformers to choose from. The scheme just described employed relatively large constituencies which would make it more likely that Australian Democrats could reach the proportion of votes necessary to win a seat. Also, it should be noted that in 1980 the Democrats' vote for the House of Representatives, where they had no chance of success, was consistently lower than

TABLE 9-4
Measures of enrollment equality and party-competition fairness, 1969–80

	Gini coefficient	Bias measure
1969	.059	2.9
1972	.076	2.9
1974	.086	2.4
1975	.095	2.8
1977	.045	2.8
1980	.054	1.9

Note: For an explanation of the bias measure see text.

their vote for the Senate where, in the States at least, there was a possibility of a Democrat candidate being elected; see Table 9-5. Proportional representation if it were introduced for the House of Representatives might increase the Democrats' vote. When the ALP unveiled the first version of its electoral reforms in July 1981,[6] the proposal was for relatively small multi-member constituencies, five-member in the capital cities and three-member in rural areas, which would limit the degree of proportionality possible and make it unlikely that more than one or two Democrats could win election—unless, of course, their vote were substantially stimulated by the change. Depending on how the existing constituencies were combined to form three- and five-member constituencies, the 1980 results became in three different sets, Labor fifty-nine or sixty, Liberals fifty-one or fifty-four, NCP eleven or twelve, the Australian Democrats nil or three.

During the 1920s one State, New South Wales, had operated just such an electoral system for State lower house elections: five-member constituencies in the urban areas and three-member in the rural areas. Few voters would remember that experiment; the much longer experience Tasmania has had with elections to its lower house from six- and subsequently seven-member constituencies tends to be written off as another peculiarity of a small and quaint State. Labor governments in two States, New South Wales and South Australia, recently were able to convert elections to their State upper houses to a list variation of proportional representation without much resistance; Victoria might follow suit for its upper house. The exact form proportional representation might take would presumably depend on whether a Labor government needed the support of the Australian Democrats to get the legislation through the Senate, and public opinion on the subject is still uncertain. There is, however, another electoral reform among the number of items in the ALP's July 1981

TABLE 9-5
Australian Democrats' share of House and Senate votes by States(%)

	House	Senate
New South Wales	5.7	6.9
Victoria	8.2	11.3
Queensland	5.3	10.0
South Australia	8.8	13.1
Western Australia	7.1	9.3
Tasmania	1.5[a]	3.2
Australian Capital Territory	5.6	8.5
Northern Territory	5.8	9.8

Note: [a] Only two of the five constituencies were contested.

program on which public opinion appears strongly favorable—modification of preferential voting as it applies with the present single-member constituencies.

Preferential Voting

The alternative vote, known in Australia as preferential voting, requires voters to express their "preferences" by rank ordering of candidates. As currently applied, preferences must be given for each and every candidate on the ballot paper. The ALP, which had usually been disadvantaged by its operation, was formally committed to a return of first-past-the-post (simple plurality) voting prior to 1974. During the election campaign that year Gough Whitlam altered the party's policy to "optional" preferential voting whereby voters would not be compelled to express a full range of preferences under pain of having their votes rejected if they did not. Subsequently, the Labor-controlled State of New South Wales implemented this change for its own lower house elections. A minor party like the Democratic Labor Party which sought to trade tightly-disciplined second preferences for policies wanted would never have agreed to such a change for the House of Representatives, but the Australian Democrats, having been ready to leave their supporters to make their own choices between the major contestants, could also be ready to let them abstain from that choice. A national survey in May 1979 showed 72 percent of voters (83 percent of Australian Democrats, 78 percent of ALP, 66 percent of Liberal, and 57 percent of NCP voters) in favor of a change to optional preferential voting, and only 26 percent wishing to retain the compulsory requirement.[7] A Labor victory in 1983 might well produce an end of the compulsory element in a system of voting that has lasted for more than sixty years. Should multi-member constituencies be introduced, the Labor discussion paper proposal is that voters would have to record as many preferences as there were vacancies to be filled plus one—thus at least six preferences in a five-member constituency and four preferences in a three-member constituency.

Table 9-6 shows the effect of preferential voting over the last six House of Representative elections. The decline of the DLP after 1972 temporarily lowered the number of electorates in which preferences were counted; the arrival of the Australian Democrats in 1977 brought the number of such electorates up again but at a lower level of impact on the final results.

In 1980 the results were changed in only six electorates. Three of

these were won by the coalition. One, Lyne, was a previously safe
NCP seat where the expected consequences of a State redistribution
dislodged two sitting members of the New South Wales legislative
assembly, one Liberal and one NCP, to seek a safer haven. They split
the coalition vote almost equally, and the NCP candidate then won
comfortably over his Labor opponent with Liberal preferences. In
Riverina, one of the most marginal seats in the nation, a tight
allocation of preferences (93 percent) from the Liberal candidate put
the NCP a whisker ahead of the sitting Labor member to provide the
coalition's one gain of a seat at the 1980 election. In the third
electorate, Barton, despite a slight edge to the ALP from Australian
Democrat preferences, an initial Labor lead of 0.59 percentage points
turned into a Liberal victory by 0.78 percentage points. The ballot-
paper had been headed by a right-wing independent whose votes,
swollen by the "donkey vote", put the Liberal incumbent ahead. The
donkey vote is reputedly cast by lazy or ill-prepared voters who mark
their preferences straight down the paper, with first preference going
to the candidate with the surname highest in alphabetic order.[8] The
three seats won because of preferences by the ALP were Kalgoorlie,
where their candidate benefited from the donkey vote and an
exceptionally large (64.5 percent) share of the Australian Democrat
preferences; Ballarat, involving the donkey vote and an even larger
(67 percent) share of Democrat preferences which included an unknown proportion of DLP third preferences; and McMillan, where an
edge in Australian Democrat preferences and an extraordinary 72
percent of DLP preferences (explained in Chapter 6) carried the day.
All three seats were Labor gains from the coalition.

TABLE 9-6
Seats affected by the distribution of preferences,
House elections, 1969–80

	Total Seats		Seats Won by the ALP	
Election	Preferences were counted	Preferences changed the result	Preferences were counted	Preferences changed the result
1969	40	12	5	0
1972	49	14	12	0
1974	33	10	9	1
1975	24	7	6	0
1977	46	4	11	0
1980	39	6	11	3

Note: The entries under "Preferences were counted" are total numbers of electorates where no
candidate won a majority on the first count and thus voters' preferences came into play in
subsequent counts. The entries under "Preferences changed the result" are total numbers of
electorates where the winner after preferences had been counted was not the candidate who
received the largest number of first preferences.
Source: Hughes, "The Case of the Arrested Pendulum", p. 318.

In both 1977 and 1980 the distribution of Australian Democrats' preferences had relatively little impact (see Table 9-7). Each time the advantage went to the ALP, in twenty contests to fifteen in 1977 and in twenty-six contests to thirteen in 1980. But what advantage there was remained slight; in 1977 there was no case of either major party obtaining more than 60 percent of Democrat preferences, and in 1980 there were only six such cases. One, O'Connor where there are three anti-Labor parties in the field, favored the coalition, the other five the ALP; only two of those led to Labor gains, Ballarat and Kalgoorlie. By avoiding the painful choice in House of Representatives contests between the two major parties, the Australian Democrats kept their supporters together. Their total House vote slipped from 9.4 percent of the national total in 1977 down to 6.6 percent in 1980 even though a few more seats were contested, but their Senate vote was still sufficient to gain the balance of power in the upper house after July 1, 1981—which had been the principal objective of their campaign.

TABLE 9-7
Distribution of Australian Democrat preferences,
House elections, 1980(%)

Electorate	Australian Democrat Preferences Going to:		Electorate	Australian Democrat Preferences Going to:	
	Coalition	Labor		Coalition	Labor
Barton	44.8	55.2	Mallee	55.2[a]	44.8
Eden–Monaro	58.3	41.7	Murray	58.0[a]	42.0
Lowe	46.2	53.8	Bowman	45.4	54.6
Lyne	50.1[a]	49.9	Brisbane	49.5	50.5
Macquarie	41.0	59.0	Fadden	38.9	61.1
Phillip	34.9	65.1	Herbert	52.1	47.9
Riverina	52.3[a]	47.6	Leichhardt	45.4	54.6
Ballarat	32.9	67.1	Lilley	42.0	58.0
Bendigo	45.5	54.5	McPherson	45.5[b]	54.5
Bruce	48.4	51.6	Petrie	48.3	51.7
Casey	45.8	54.2	Hawker	47.4	52.6
Chisholm	43.7	56.3	Kingston	43.5	56.5
Deakin	50.9	49.1	Canning	41.8	58.2
Diamond Valley	46.2	53.8	Kalgoorlie	35.5	64.5
Henty	44.6	55.4	Moore	50.6	49.4
Hotham	55.7	44.3	O'Connor	63.6[c]	36.4
Indi	58.3[a]	41.7	Perth	44.0	56.0
Isaacs	55.1	44.9	Stirling	33.7	66.3
La Trobe	43.0	57.0	Northern Territory	55.1	44.9
McMillan	42.3	57.7			

Notes: [a] Includes preferences given to both coalition parties.
   [b] Includes preferences given to Liberal and Independent (crypto-NCP) candidates.
   [c] Includes preferences given to both coalition parties and National Party of Western Australia.
Source: Australian Electoral Office, "General Election for The House of Representatives 1968: Result of Count of First Preference Votes and Distribution of Preferences".

Meanwhile the last third party to hold the balance of power in the Senate, the Democratic Labor Party, went even closer to the vanishing point. Confined to the one State, Victoria, where its share of the House of Representatives votes dropped from 5.3 percent in 1977, when it still contested every electorate in the State, to 1.1 percent in 1980, when it contested only twelve of the thirty-three, its dwindling band of supporters lost the last of their reputation as the reliable guarantors of coalition majorities which they had enjoyed in the 1960s. As Table 9-8 shows, in only two of the seven electorates where DLP preferences were counted did the coalition's share come close to 80 percent; the rule-of-thumb used to be that it would be a good 85 percent. In two electorates the coalition failed to hold even half of the DLP preferences: Ballarat, where the greater part went to the Australian Democrat and McMillan, where the ALP candidate received almost three-quarters of DLP preferences. Similarly, in the Senate vote in Victoria, when the time came to distribute the preferences of the DLP's leading candidate, 58.2 percent went to the Australian Democrats and only 36.3 percent to the coalition. And it was the success of the Democrats in the Senate election which may prove to be the most interesting consequence of the 1980 election in the ensuing three years.

The Senate Count

Under the Federal Constitution each of the six States is guaranteed an equal number of Senators, originally six per State with three places falling vacant at each triennial election, then ten per State since 1949 with five places vacated at each election. In the absence of any specific

TABLE 9-8
Distribution of DLP preferences, House elections, 1980

| Electorate | Percentage of DLP Preferences Going to: | | | |
	Coalition	Labor	Australian Democrats	Other
Ballarat	26.8	13.4	59.8	—
Bruce	60.7	15.7	23.6	—
Deakin	79.4	8.2	12.3	—
Henty	79.0	8.7	12.3	—
Hotham	56.4	24.7	18.9	—
La Trobe	60.7	9.8	7.0	22.5[a]
McMillan	16.3	72.1	11.6	—

Note: [a] United Christian Party.
Source: Australian Electoral Office, "General Election for the House of Representatives 1980: Result of Count of First Preference Votes and Distribution of Preferences".

provision for representation of the Federal Territories, and given their relatively small populations, when the Whitlam government legislated to elect Territorial Senators for the first time the decision was to allow only two Senators per territory and to tie their terms to the House of Representatives with which they would be elected and retire rather than to the Senate. Under the system of proportional representation which had prevailed for Senate elections since 1949 providing two Senators from a Territory meant one each for the major parties. Accordingly—apart from occasional idle speculation that the government could so irritate members of the Federal bureaucracy that the Australian Capital Territory would defeat its one Liberal Senator, an unlikely event requiring the Liberal vote to drop below 33.3 percent of the total—their fate is not of interest to the rest of Australia.

At the 1975 double dissolution all sixty places for the States had been vacated. The first five successful candidates from each State secured full terms, taking them to June 30, 1981; the other five won only abbreviated terms that ended on June 30, 1978, thereby restoring the cycle whereby half of the Senate retires at each triennial election. The first half-Senate election for many years in 1977 returned thirty senators who would continue into the second half of their six-year terms whatever might happen in 1980: sixteen for the coalition, twelve for the ALP, and two for the Australian Democrats. Because the other thirty State places coming up for election in 1980 (although they could not be occupied until July 1, 1981) were those currently held by the first five candidates selected in each State in 1975, the coalition was in an especially exposed position. One of the thirty was Senator Brian Harradine of Tasmania. Once a right-wing member of the ALP and now an Independent, his strong personal following in a State where the use of proportional representation over several generations at the election of the State House of Assembly had accustomed Tasmanian voters to making complicated decisions with elaborate ballot-papers virtually assured his reelection. The remaining twenty-nine retiring Senators comprised seventeen coalition supporters against only twelve from the Labor Party which had polled so badly in 1975 that it won only two of the five places in each and every State at a time when the coalition was winning three— except in Tasmania. In 1980 the Labor Party could reasonably expect to regain a three-to-two advantage only in New South Wales, a State with a normally high Labor vote where the party had done exceptionally well at the State election in 1978. The Australian Democrats, on the strength of their performance in the voting for the Senate in 1977, could aspire to seats from Victoria and South Australia. If the

other four States went sour along those lines, with the crucial fifth
seat going respectively one Independent, one ALP, two Australian
Democrats, the coalition still seemed assured of retaining the fifth
seat, and thereby a three-to-two advantage over the ALP or anybody
else, in Queensland and Western Australia. If they could do that, it
would mean the vacant places would be filled (now counting the
Territorial seats as well): sixteen for the coalition, eighteen for the
rest; the total Senate of sixty-four, including carryovers from the 1977
election, would be equally divided thirty-two against thirty-two. In
such a situation the combination of Labor, Democrats, and Senator
Harradine could block government legislation, although that coalition
could not be formed on every issue. On the other hand, in the rather
less likely event of the combination agreeing on some positive step
such as Senate-initiated legislation, the coalition could block it in the
Senate without having to resort to its expected majority in the House,
by which time the proposal would have had more unwelcome
publicity, and the chance of some coalition Senators' becoming
unsettled by a House-versus-Senate dispute would have increased.

That should have been the worst possible scenario for the Fraser
government had it not been for events in Queensland. Under the
single transferable vote system of proportional representation, which
has prevailed at Senate elections since 1949, it should have been
possible for electors to pick and choose among the candidates,
including those on the favored party tickets. Where a team of
candidates represented the coalition alliance, it should have been
possible to indicate preference as between the partners. However, in
practice since 1949 the coalition parties negotiated tickets and their
supporters honored the bargains with strict adherence to the coalition
"how-to-vote" instruction which went straight down the ticket. ALP
voters were equally well-disciplined. Table 9-9 shows how the

TABLE 9-9
Share of party's total of first preferences secured by leading candidate on ticket(%)

	Liberal	Coalition	NCP	ALP	Australian Democrats
New South Wales		98.5		99.3	96.6
Victoria		99.2		94.5	99.1
Queensland	91.2		81.6	98.6	97.1
South Australia	99.5		88.9	98.7	97.4
Western Australia	97.9		92.9	99.1	95.2
Tasmania	82.6		—	61.2	84.1
Australian Capital Territory[a]	99.2		—	98.1	97.6
Northern Territory[a]		97.3		97.9	94.9

Note: [a] Two candidates on ticket instead of three in the States.
Source: The Australian Electoral Office, "The Senate Election 18 October 1980: Result of Count of
First Preference Votes and Distribution of Surplus Votes and Preferences".

candidate placed at the top of his or her party's ticket can expect the overwhelming majority of first preference votes from the party, usually 98 to 99 percent except when the party is very small (the NCP in South Australia and, now, Western Australia) and except in Tasmania because of the independence of electoral judgement familiarity with proportional representation has brought. The exception to the record of coalition solidarity began in the 1950s in Western Australia, where the local Country Party started to run its own ticket, and usually collected the fifth seat which still went to swell the coalition ranks in Canberra. However, the Country Party vote in that State slowly declined. At the 1974 and 1975 double dissolution elections the National Country Party, as it was known by then, won only one Senate place out of ten, and at the 1977 election that place (when only five were being contested) was lost to the Liberals. In 1980 the NCP had split into two separate groups over State issues, and slipped even further from regaining a place in the Senate with the official branch winning 4.1 percent of the total vote, and the breakaways, known as the National Party of Western Australia, only 1.2 percent.

In Queensland bitter rivalries between the Liberal and National (as the NCP branch is known there) Parties had built up at the State level and occasionally spilled over into the Federal sphere despite the best endeavors of the Federal party leaders. The approximately equal electoral strength of the two partners had been reflected in a system of alternation whereby each party took it in turn to occupy the desirable third place on the coalition ticket and thus win the fifth seat. Admittedly at the height of the Democratic Labor Party's influence in the 1960s the fifth Senate seat usually went to the DLP candidate, but as it was never likely to go to the ALP the principle of alternation was maintained. In 1974 and 1975 when the sixth place on a ticket to choose ten Senators was less secure than third place on a ticket to choose five, the parties were fortunate that they did so well that their sixth candidate was returned and any unpleasantness as to whose candidate had suffered by being put sixth was avoided. When ordinary, five-vacancy elections returned in 1977, the three short-term Senators from the coalition were two Liberals and one National, that is the bottom half of the six elected in 1975, and the coalition ticket was composed accordingly. However, in 1980, when it was the National Party's turn to fill the first and third places on the ticket, the Liberal branch in Queensland repudiated the long-standing arrangement and decided to run its own separate ticket. For two accounts of the contest between the coalition partners in Queensland, see Chapter 5 and the section, "The Coalition Parties", in Chapter 7. As

Table 9-9 shows, Florence Bjelke-Petersen, at the head of the National Party ticket, won 81.6 percent of the ticket's votes, quite enough to give her a quota and immediate election, despite some media predictions that she would be hard-pressed to win a place at all because large numbers of National Party voters would resent her preferment over the sitting National Party Senators. Her share of the total National Party vote fell below 75 percent in only three of Queensland's nineteen House of Representatives' constituencies. (Table 9-10).

More significant for the long run than the displacement of two incumbent Senators by their party leader's wife, was the contest between the two tickets, Liberal and National. Although electoral contests between the coalition partners for seats in the State Parliament had spread more extensively around Queensland than ever before, there had never previously been an election, Federal or State, in which every coalition voter had had the opportunity to indicate which partner was preferred. On this occasion it was the National Party that won, with 53.8 percent of the combined vote, or by rather more than 40,000 votes in absolute terms. (At both the 1977 and 1980 State elections the Nationals outpolled the Liberals, but without a direct clash in each electorate it can only be conjectured as to which party has more support at that level of politics. Probably it is the Nationals.) Table 9–10 shows the National ticket's share of the combined vote in each of the nineteen House of Representatives constituencies. In six of the seven constituencies carried by the National Party in the House of Representatives ballot, they won more than two-thirds of coalition Senate votes, and in five of the seven constituencies won by the Liberal Party and all five of those won by the Labor Party, more than one-third. The Nationals' good showing in McPherson, a House of Representatives constituency they had

TABLE 9-10

Share of coalition vote secured by the National Party's Senate ticket in each House of Representatives constituency(%)

National-won		Liberal-won		Labor-won	
Maranoa	83.3	Herbert	52.2	Capricornia	70.2
Kennedy	82.4	McPherson	44.8	Griffith	38.0
Leichhardt	76.4	Fadden	41.6	Oxley	37.2
Dawson	75.3	Bowman	39.1	Lilley	36.7
Wide Bay	70.9	Petrie	37.8	Brisbane	34.7
Darling Downs	67.5	Ryan	32.2		
Fisher	58.5	Moreton	30.6		

Source: The Australian Electoral Office, "The Senate Election 18 October 1980: Result of Count of First Preference Votes and Distribution of Surplus Votes and Preferences".

held up to 1972 and which covered an area bitterly contested between the coalition partners in successive elections for the State Parliament, encouraged them into an exceptionally vigorous challenge at a House by-election a few months later, following the death of the sitting Liberal member. Despite a strong candidate in ex-Senator Glen Sheil, who abandoned the few remaining months of his term in the Senate in an attempt to move to the House, the National share of the coalition vote slipped slightly to 41.6 percent, which suggests that Flo Bjelke-Petersen was no liability to her party. Finally, her party's ability to win more than half the coalition Senate votes in the northern constituency of Herbert identifies a future flashpoint for coalition competition in Queensland should the cut-throat rivalry of 1980–81 continue.

The most important question of all following the collapse of the coalition alliance in Queensland was what effect it might have on the Fraser government's ability to control the Senate after July 1, 1981, and the answer of course depends on what happened in the other five States as well. In New South Wales the prediction of a Labor gain of the fifth seat was sound. On the final count the third Labor candidate already led the incumbent Liberal, Chris Puplick, by 64,000 votes, and received 72.7 percent of the Australian Democrat's preferences to win handsomely. Victoria had witnessed a low-key version of the Nationals' crisis in Queensland when an incumbent Labor senator, Jean Melzer, had been relegated to an unwinnable third place reputedly for her failure to remember her obligations in the complex factional arrangements that characterize the ALP in that State. (See also the section on "Preselection" in Chapter 7.) The party's feminists had been bitterly critical of the move, and Senator Melzer polled a large personal vote although it constituted only 5.3 percent of the total ALP vote, a much smaller protest vote than Senator Maunsell's 13.7 percent from National supporters in Queensland. On the penultimate count in Victoria, the Australian Democrat was already comfortably in front, and with 58.2 percent of the DLP preferences and then 89.6 percent of the third coalition candidate's (the NCP member of the ticket, which incidentally wiped out the party's representation in the Senate from Victoria) he defeated Senator Melzer easily. Similarly, in South Australia the predicted occurred: the Australian Democrat led on the last count and received 96.5 percent of Labor preferences to win easily. Western Australia nearly provided an upset in favor of the Australian Democrats, but the third Liberal candidate's lead on the final count was just big enough to withstand 96.2 percent of Labor preferences going to the Democrat, who ended up only 560 votes behind the Liberal. Tasmania also lived up to predictions with Senator Harradine winning a quota on first preferences. Some indication of the breadth of his support from adherents of the major parties was provided on the distribution of his second preferences, only 39.6 percent of which went to the second candidate on his personal ticket while 27.9 percent went off to the Liberals and 20.3 percent to Labor. By comparison, 94.1 percent of the Liberals' first candidate's surplus passed to their second candidate, and 96.8 percent of the Labor Party's surplus went straight down the ticket.

The coalition had retained the fifth seat from Western Australia, albeit by the narrowest of margins—and subsequently was able to withstand a legal challenge to the result (see below). For an evenly divided Senate, it had to win the fifth seat in Queensland as well. Both the Labor Party and the Australian Democrats did rather better than expected on first preferences, but both coalition tickets held together better than might have been expected: 93.1 percent of Flo Bjelke-Petersen's surplus went to her number two, Senator Sheil, and another 2.3 percent to her number three, Senator Maunsell, while 94.3 percent of Senator Bonner's surplus went to his number two, Yvonne McComb, and another 1.3 percent to the third Liberal candidate. Cross-ticket leakage was minimal, with only 2.6 percent of Flo Bjelke-Petersen's second preferences going over to the Liberals and only 2.3 percent of Senator Bonner's coming the other way. After the elimination of the various minor party and independent candidates, five candidates remained: the Australian Democrats' top candidate with 121,668 votes, followed by Yvonne McComb with 75,464 and Senator Sheil with 75,307, the third ALP candidate with 66,988, and Senator Maunsell with 46,347. Maunsell's exclusion brought Sheil up sharply: 83.9 percent of Maunsell's votes stayed with the National Party, only 9.8 percent drifted off to McComb, and the balance divided between the Democrats and the ALP. Labor votes strongly favored the Democrats who obtained 88.3 percent; 7.2 percent went to Sheil and 4.5 percent to McComb. At this point, the coalition still had a chance: the Democrat, with 182,649 votes could still be beaten by Sheil who then had 119,045 if Sheil could obtain at least 88.9 percent of McComb's 83,080. In the event he did not, receiving only 79.5 percent, and the fifth Queensland seat went unexpectedly to the Australian Democrats. A combination of the Liberals' attempt to grab the fifth seat for themselves, coupled with the leakage of one-fifth of their preferences to the Australian Democrats in the embittered atmosphere that their decision had created, had dealt the Fraser government a serious blow. Where it might have been able to manage the Senate by relying on Senator Harradine, now

235

it required his assistance merely to block a combination of the ALP and Democrats, and the pivotal importance of the Democrats had been enormously increased.

After the election, the Prime Minister sought to demote the Queensland Liberals' most influential Federal politician, Eric Robinson, from a Cabinet post to a less important portfolio outside Cabinet; he refused to accept the rebuff and withdrew to the backbenches. His sudden death after a heart attack (brought on, the Prime Minister's critics alleged, by chagrin at his treatment), caused an early by-election for McPherson where the strong National challenge forced the Prime Minister into a direct and open confrontation with the State Nationals led by Bjelke-Petersen on behalf of his own State Liberals, a position which he had previously avoided to the intense annoyance of the latter.

Campaign Expenditures

Previously it had been possible to dismiss the subject of campaign finance in Australia with the simple explanation that as controls were inadequate and not enforced in practice, it was difficult to know anything with any certainty. By the time of the 1980 election it was even easier to avoid the problem; those inadequate, unenforced controls had been abolished lest by some mischance they might actually operate and catch a transgressor. The rules contained in the Federal Electoral Act of 1946 had set permitted expenditure maxima of $500 for candidates for the House of Representatives and $1,000 for candidates for the Senate, and then required reasonably comprehensive disclosure of the sums expended. However, the maxima were totally unrealistic in their amounts, no maxima were set for Statewide expenditure on behalf of the teams of candidates, and prosecutions were never launched against candidates who filed returns that disclosed breaches of the Act or failed to lodge returns at all.[9] At the State level some States had never bothered to impose controls, and others of those which had done so subsequently repealed their legislation. One of those which still retained legislative provisions, rather like those applying to elections to the Federal Parliament but rather more realistic in the amounts permitted, was Tasmania. In July 1979 Tasmania had an election for the House of Assembly, and after it was over the Australian Democrats, who with a total of less than 3 percent of the vote had failed to win a seat, began to challenge the extent of compliance with campaign expenditure statutory requirements. Eventually a large number of candidates were subjected to nominal fines for various breaches of the State legislation and, more seriously, the results in one constituency were set aside, the seven members (including two ministers) turned out, and a fresh election required. Ordinarily, it should be noted, a vacancy in the Tasmanian House of Assembly is filled by continuing the counting of the general election results which usually, but not invariably, produces a new member of the same party as the previous member. Thus having to elect all seven members afresh was a completely novel experience and emphasized the seriousness of the matter. The Tasmanian government chose one solution: they raised the permitted maxima. Being a Labor government they naturally favored controls over the amounts well-endowed political parties might spend. The Federal government chose the other solution: it repealed the provisions of the Federal Electoral Act which might lead to a repetition of what had happened in Tasmania at the next Federal election. Their fears were not unreasonable for Senator Don Chipp, on behalf of the Australian Democrats, was already warning that his party had every intention of challenging results if a breach of the Electoral Act appeared to have taken place—and there was no way that compliance with the existing legislation was possible in the real world of current campaign methods. Thus, at the 1980 election, House of Representatives and Senate candidates were entitled, for the first time since 1902, to spend as much as they cared, and without any obligation to report on what they had done. The government's only genuflection to propriety was to appoint the former permanent head of the Attorney-General's department as a one-man inquiry to advise on what disclosure of campaign expenditure during the period of the campaign should be required—but with terms of reference which carefully precluded his touching on the subjects of disclosure of donations, expenditure prior to the campaign, or permissible maxima of expenditures, thus ensuring that his recommendations—when available, and if implemented—could have no adverse effect on the coalition's normal two-to-one advantage over the Labor Party in campaign spending. When, after the Federal election, the Labor government in New South Wales indicated that it would press ahead with the introduction of public funding of political parties along the lines it had been toying with for some time,[10] Prime Minister Fraser immediately denounced the proposal in the strongest possible terms on the ground that it was "corrupt" to take money from taxpayers and give it to political parties. Survey data suggest that Australian voters share Fraser's opposition to public funding of parties, but not his opposition to disclosure of the sources and amounts of private donations to parties and candidates.

Although the government had anticipated a challenge to the results based on breaches of the Electoral Act and blocked it by deleting the provisions which were certain to be breached, it had left another provision which prohibited electoral advertising "containing any untrue or incorrect statement intended or likely to mislead or improperly interfere with any elector in, or in relation to, the casting of his vote" (s. 161). After the election, the Australian Democrats applied to the Court of Disputed Returns to overturn the Senate result in Western Australia on the ground that Liberal advertising had warned electors that a vote for the Democrats was a vote for Labor (see Chapter 6). The Labor Party then joined the fray with petitions against a number of Liberal victories in marginal seats on the ground that Liberal advertising had misrepresented their taxation policy. Before the issue went to the Courts, it had been briefly canvassed in Parliament when Senator Chipp had queried an NCP advertisement in New South Wales which said in part "A vote for the Democrats is as good as a vote for Labor. Chipp has made it abundantly clear that he would prefer Labor to win the election ... a vote for the Democrats is a vote against the National Country Party." In its defense the government tabled opinions dating from 1919 and 1934 by two distinguished Solicitor-Generals, the highest nonpolitical legal advisers of the Federal government, which argued that to come within the prohibition statements would have to relate to the actual act of marking the ballot-paper rather than affecting the elector's judgement in deciding for whom to vote. Interpretation of the section was referred by the Court of Disputed Returns to the full High Court which agreed with the previous Solicitor-Generals. Any finding which had required the Courts to decide the truth or otherwise of campaign policy statements would have been virtually unworkable in practice, but the sense of grievance felt by both the Democrats and the Labor Party at misrepresentation of their position and policy respectively fueled their intention to set about electoral reform.

Candidates

Over the past decade or two, House of Representatives elections have brought out about 500 candidates, on average four per constituency. Two of the four represent the serious alternatives, the coalition and the Labor Party. (Competition between the coalition partners would inflate that figure slightly; there were, for example, eleven such contests in 1980, twelve in 1977, and sixteen in 1975.) The other two candidates in a typical constituency represent minor parties, such as the Democratic Labor Party in the past and the Australian Democrats in the late 1970s, which contest almost all seats, or the now fragmented Communist Party which contested relatively few, or are Independents even if running under some exotic label of their own choosing. More than half are new to the game, standing for the House of Representatives for the first time—52 percent in 1975, 59 percent in 1977, and 60 percent in 1980. Very few are veterans: in 1975 only eleven of the 482 candidates had first stood for the House of Representatives at the 1949 general election which had ushered in the long period of coalition hegemony, or earlier; at the 1977 election there were only five left in that category, and in 1980 only three. Those three among themselves nicely represented some of the major types of parliamentary candidacy—Sir William McMahon, the former Prime Minister, who had won a seat in 1949 and served continuously since then to become undisputed Father of the House in 1980; Sir Billy Snedden, the Speaker, who had first tried to enter the House from Western Australia where he also tried unsuccessfully for the State Parliament, then moved to Victoria where he ultimately won a seat in 1966 after five attempts spread over two States; and Ronald George Sarina, who began his career as a candidate in 1946 and has since divided his attention among the House, the Senate, and the New South Wales Legislative Assembly without ever getting elected to any one of them—a perennial independent candidate who in Sarina's case earned a niche in Australian electoral history by an early attempt to test the campaign expenditure provisions in the Courts.

Such veterans are exceptional. At the 1975 election only 22 percent of candidates had first stood for the House before 1970, by 1980 that proportion was down to 11 percent. The minor parties and the Independents inflate the proportion of brand new candidates at each election, but even for the major parties there is always a substantial infusion of new blood. The 1975 election, which came about on short notice, found 30 percent of Labor candidates and 46 percent of coalition candidates offering for the House of Representatives for the first time.[11] In 1977, with Labor out of office, the proportions were reversed: 48 percent of Labor candidates and 30 percent of coalition candidates were new; 1980 continued that pattern with 55 percent of Labor candidates and 35 percent of coalition candidates standing for the first time. But in comparison with the Australian Democrats, four-fifths of whose candidates in 1980 were new, the major parties are able to offer reasonably seasoned teams.

At the 1980 election there was a turnover of member slightly in excess of one-fifth of the House. Of the twenty-six members elected who had not sat in the previous Parliament, three were old Labor members winning their seats back after a time in the wilderness. Of the other twenty-three, one was elected for a freshly created constituency—in Western Australia; ten succeeded another member of the same party; and twelve won seats from the other side, eleven being Labor gains and one a NCP gain from Labor. Two of those who succeeded to safe party seats, both Labor, had tried for the House some years earlier and been unsuccessful then; two of those who won seats from their opponents had tried once before and one twice before. But eighteen of the twenty-six made it into the House on their first try. Nineteen of the twenty-six, the three returners and sixteen new members, would strengthen the opposition; only three Liberal and four NCP recruits brought new blood to the government which had been suffering from an embarrassment of surplus backbenchers ever since its triumph in 1975.

Some such figures of the rate of turnover in the composition of the House of Representatives are necessary to put into perspective demands that more adequate representation should be given women (discussed in Chapter 7), or any other group currently under-represented in the House. Table 9-11 shows the number of female candidates of various political persuasions at the last three elections, and the character of the constituencies they contested expressed in relative safeness for one or other of the major alternatives, coalition or Labor. The total number of female candidates rises steadily, from thirty in 1975 to forty-nine in 1977 and seventy-five in 1980, while the number nominated by the major parties rises even more steeply from ten, to eighteen, to twenty-eight. However, the coalition musters on average only four female candidates per election and, leaving aside the statistical anomaly of the weaker coalition partner nominating a woman in a seat that partner cannot win from its ally, there is only one case out of twelve where the coalition chose a woman who had any possibility of winning the seat. The ALP's record is somewhat better: the number of its female candidates rises steadily, and the proportion to be counted for the suicide squad in safe and ultra-safe coalition constituencies falls. But none were chosen for a Labor-held seat from which the incumbent was retiring, and three seats which were won by Labor women in 1980 reflect the outcome of the election rather than earlier money-in-bank certainties for their candidacies. As it happened there were only five Labor seats in 1980 where the incumbent retired voluntarily or otherwise. None were allocated to female candidates; in the eleven seats won by new Labor candidates, only two of these were women. Had both blocs of seats, the five already held by Labor and the nine won by new male candidates in 1980, been handed over to female candidates,

TABLE 9-11
Number of female candidates in 1975, 1977, and 1980 and the relative safeness of constituencies they contested

| | Number of seats | | | Number of female candidates | | | | | | | | | | | |
| | | | | Coalition | | | Labor | | | Democrats | | | Other | | |
	1975	1977	1980	1975	1977	1980	1975	1977	1980	1975	1977	1980	1975	1977	1980
Ultra-safe Labor	1	1	6	1	0	0	0	0	0	—	1	2	1	1[a]	2[a]
Safe Labor	14	18	20	2	2	4	0	0	0	—	4	3	3	0	2
Marginal Labor	10	9	12	0	0	1	0	0	1	—	1	2	0	1	1
Ultra-marginal Labor	11	10	13	1[b]	0	0	0	0	2	—	0	4	3	0	0
Ultra-marginal Coalition	19	18	30	0	0	0	0	2	6	—	2	8	3	0	4
Marginal Coalition	27	28	15	0	1[b]	0	1	5	7	—	2	5	3	2	1
Safe Coalition	36	34	26	0	0	0	3	7	7	—	10	6	6[a]	4	5
Ultra-safe Coalition	9	6	3	0	0	0	2	1	0	—	2	1	0	0	0
Total	127	124	125	4	3	5	6	15	23	—	22	31	19[a]	8[a]	15[a]

Notes: Safeness is determined by the result of the election at which the women candidates were standing, not the previous election
[a] Add one candidate to the figure because of two female candidates in one constituency.
[b] A NCP candidate in a Liberal constituency.

the resulting seventeen female members would have constitued one-third of the post-1980 parliamentary party. To achieve one-quarter representation in the parliamentary party, to correspond approximately to women's shares in the party's total membership, nine out of that total of fourteen seats would have been required. In 1980 there were another six female candidates in ultra-marginal coalition constituencies, one-third of the Labor candidates who narrowly missed election.

As long as the selection of candidates is decentralized to the State branch level, and involves as it does often the association of local and central organ delegates in balloting for particular constituencies, it will be difficult to match the requisite number of women to vacated and winnable seats to achieve an agreed target in the composition of the parliamentary party. After the election, the ALP Federal conference, to the surprise of most journalists and many of the party's supporters, adopted a target of 25 percent representation for women in State delegations to future conferences forthwith, and 30 percent in contingents to the Federal Parliament by the end of the decade. Achieving the latter target in the House of Representatives could be difficult: at the next three elections (presumably in 1983, 1986, and 1989) only seven Labor MHRs who held safe seats in 1980 are due to be past the age of sixty-five and compelled to retire; all of them come from New South Wales. Only two in marginal seats could be expected to step down over that period because of age. Thus affirmative action to the level proposed will require the removal of sitting members, or else a very high proportion of winnable seats being assigned to female candidates who then win them in sufficient numbers to assure continuous Labor governments from 1983 onward, or the acceptance of male domination in the House of Representatives and the trans-

TABLE 9-12
ALP share of two-party-preferred vote by State, 1969–80(%)

	1969	1972	1974	1975	1977	1980	Average 1969–80
New South Wales	51.6	55.5	54.9	46.8	47.6	50.4	51.1
Victoria	44.9	50.4	50.6	43.8	44.5	50.7	47.5
Queensland	49.9	49.5	45.4	39.8	42.0	46.9	45.6
South Australia	54.2	52.7	52.5	44.9	48.7	49.4	50.4
Western Australia	52.6	48.3	48.5	41.2	39.9	46.6	46.2
Tasmania	56.1	60.5	55.4	44.1	43.8	47.0	51.2
Australia	50.2	52.7	51.7	44.3	45.4	49.6	49.0
Range among States	11.2	12.2	10.0	7.0	8.8	4.1	5.6

Source: Mackerras, Elections 1980, pp. 213–214, and "Australian General Election and Senate Election, 1980", pp. 6–11.

formation of the ALP in the Senate into a predominantly female party. Moreover, the demand for more women in the parliamentary party is only the first of several to be raised; there are also strong cases for more recruits from immigrant backgrounds, whether first- or second-generation, and for the young, and perhaps even for repeal of party rules which force the retirement of Members of Parliament at the age at which most employees are compelled to stop work, thereby denying the growing number of pensioners and retired persons representation by their own sort of people.

Results

At the beginning of this chapter it was pointed out that on one calculation of what Labor would have to do to regain the narrow majority it secured in the House of Representatives at the 1974 general election—its last victory—it would need to win another fourteen seats in the south-eastern three States (plus the Australian Capital Territory) and another thirteen in the outlying three States (plus the Northern Territory). In the event its net gains were nine and four seats respectivity; as the two zones contained respectively eighty-nine and thirty-six seats this suggests a performance equally effective (or not) in both parts of the country. Tabe 9-12, which shows Labor's share of the two-party-preferred vote in each election since 1969, allows closer consideration of what actually happened. Labor's gains in the southeast varied considerably, from only 0.7 percentage points in South Australia and 2.8 percentage points in New South Wales, to 4.2 percentage points in the Australian Capital Territory (not shown in Table 9-12) and 6.2 percentage points in Victoria. Similarly in the outlying areas the range is considerable, from 1.3 percentage points in the Northern Territory (also not shown in Table 9-12), 3.2 percentage points in Tasmania, to 4.9 percentage points in Queensland and 6.7 percentage points in Western Australia. But if one looks at the bottom row of Table 9-12, it is noticeable that the 1980 results in the six States, expressed as two-party-preferred votes, are much closer together than at any of the five previous elections, or indeed at the four elections before those when the ranges extended from 9.0 percentage points in 1958 to 14.4 percentage points in 1966. State differences as expressed in votes cast were minimal in 1980, even though, as just noted, there were still variations of several percentage points in the swings to Labor taking place.

A second basis for grouping the States can be suggested in addition to what we have been using, the southeast versus the rest. An examination of the figures in Table 9-12, and especially of the averages for the period of six elections in the last column, shows that three States (New South Wales, South Australia, and Tasmania) have been marginally tilted to Labor and the other three (Victoria, Queensland, Western Australia) rather more tilted away from Labor. In the two elections since the debacle of 1975 the latter three have improved for Labor rather more than the first three: Western Australia by 8.0 percentage points, Queensland, 7.1 and Victoria, 6.9, compared to South Australia by 4.5 percentage points, New South Wales, 3.6 and Tasmania, 3.5. There has been convergence toward an Australia-wide uniformity. Tasmania, which had long been the best State for Labor in terms of the two-party-preferred vote, still lags below the national average, but Victoria has unexpectedly gone from being regularly anti-Labor to having the highest proportionate Labor vote of any State.

When previously, in 1972 and 1974, Labor had been able to win more than half the votes in Victoria it still failed to secure half the seats because of the vagaries of the electoral system—fourteen and sixteen respectively out of thirty-four. In 1980 votes were turned into seats more effectively than before, and for the first time since 1929 the Labor Party held more than half the House of Representatives seats for Victoria, traditionally the brightest jewel in the Liberal Party's crown and the source of all its postwar leaders except one, Sir William McMahon. Labor's considerable success in Victoria was probably influenced by some State factors, notably the growing unpopularity of the Liberal government headed by R.J. Hamer, who was forced into early retirement by his parliamentary colleagues, urged on by business interests a few months after the Federal election.

Labor's relative lack of success in New South Wales where it won only two seats while losing one on a 1977–80 swing of 2.8 percentage points in its favor is more mysterious. The State Labor government, led by Neville Wran, had won a quite remarkable victory in 1978 when the party's share of the State two-party-preferred vote zoomed up to 60 percent and Labor won seats in parts of Sydney for the first time ever. The opinion polls during the campaign had suggested that Labor was improving its position in New South Wales almost as much as in Victoria; for other States the subsample size makes such predictions less reliable. The swing of 2.8 percentage points that eventuated in New South Wales was much less than the polls had foreshadowed, although had that swing been uniform Labor would have done rather better in seats than it actually did with a new gain of four instead of one (retaining Riverina and winning Phillip and Macarthur as well). In the immediate) postelection period there was a tendency to attribute the failure of ALP hopes in New South Wales, and the Sydney metropolitan area in particular, to the government's counterattack against Labor's "wealth tax" and its likely impact on homeowners in the area where housing and land values had been inflating most rapidly. This explanation has been challenged within the party:

> What the Liberal propaganda on the "wealth tax issue" did highlight was the one apparent weakness in what appeared a well organized campaign viz. a certain lack of flexibility and responsiveness to advertising in the last days of the campaign. Moreover our policy on the "wealth tax issue" had sufficient content to generate fears, but was insufficiently specific to provide precise responses.
>
> While the "wealth tax issue" undoubtedly hurt Labor and was used unscrupulously to create fears in the community about the taxing policies of a Labor government, its impact has probably been exaggerated. As the Labor Party knows, it takes a long time and a lot of hard work to get even the simplest issues over to the public. Certainly, the use of the "wealth tax issue" to rationalise differences in swings between the states, or even between seats within one state, is unwise. Such explanations rest on assumptions about the political interest and political sophistication of the electorate which bear little relation to reality.[12]

Against this it could be argued that an association between a possible Labor tax and the average elector's biggest asset, the rapid appreciation of which regularly filled his newspaper's columns and dominated much of his neighborhood conversation, required the minimum of political interest or sophistication. An earlier Labor Prime Minister and Treasurer, Ben Chifley, coined a phrase which continues to be popular when he spoke of the voter's sensitive "hip-pocket nerve". The 1980 campaign, largely free from issues of foreign and defense policy and purged of the overtones of constitutional crisis which had affected the two previous elections, returned, as David Butler notes in Chapter 1, to an earlier style of campaign in which the party leaders offered shopping lists of benefits and costs to calculating-machine voters who, if not totally dessicated, at least were expected to be free of high ideological concerns. In such an atmosphere the "wealth tax issue" was a natural trump card, and the Prime Minister's ability to wrench his campaign strategy around into a U-turn so late in the day a considerable *tour de force* of political will. Labor, which has often looked and sounded disorganized and divided when new or revised issues were introduced late in the day in earlier campaigns, stuck to its original strategy. Quite possibly this is yet another handicap the Labor Party naturally suffers, and the avoidance of internal dissension during the campaign was as considerable an achievement on Hayden's part as abandoning one line of defense and opening up another of attack was on the part of Fraser.

The Labor Party continues to be confined very largely to metropolitan Australia. As in 1977 the swing to Labor was slightly smaller in rural seats than in the urban, and while gaining ten metropolitan seats (five in Melbourne, two each in Sydney and Brisbane, and one in Perth) there was a net gain of only three seats in nonmetropolitan areas. One of these was half of the Australian Capital Territory, the constituency of Canberra, which is definitely urban even if not metropolitan; another the huge mining constituency of Kalgoorlie in Western Australia, which balanced the loss of the somewhat similar seat of Riverina in New South Wales. Two in Victoria, Ballarat and McMillan, provided the only evidence of the Labor Party's ability to regain support outside the large State capital cities except in very special cases. Six of the twelve most marginal coalition seats, twelve being the number required to give the Labor party a majority in 1983 unless a redistribution alters the mathematics, are nonmetropolitan, as are four of the next twelve in order of marginality. It would certainly be possible for the ALP to win office without regaining significant representation outside the State capitals, apart from a handful of public service, mining, and heavy industry-dominated provincial centers. Perhaps the hostility to the Labor Party engendered in rural areas during the short span of the Whitlam government completed the erosion of Labor support outside the cities that had been going on for many years. If this is the case, then the significant dividing lines of electoral support in future Australian elections may be drawn within each State, rather than between States or even larger national regions.

Notes

1 Because the alternative vote (known in Australia as preferential voting) is used in elections for the House of Representatives it is possible to calculate a notional "two-party-preferred" vote for each constituency, for each State and Federal Territory, and for the country as a whole. Such calculations for recent Federal elections are to be found in Malcolm Mackerras, *Elections 1980* (Sydney: Angus and Robertson, 1980) and *Australian General Election and Senate Election 1980: Statistical Analysis* (Canberra: Faculty of Military Studies, University of New South Wales at Duntroon, 1981).

2 Hughes, "The Electorate Speaks", in Howard R. Penniman, ed., *Australia at the Polls: The National Elections of 1975* (Washington, D.C.: American Enterprise Institute, 1976), p. 286, and "The Case of the Arrested Pendulum", in Howard Penniman (ed.), *The Australian National Elections of 1977* (Washington, D.C.: American Enterprise Institute, 1979), p. 313. The "cube rule" formula's status as an iron law of electoral explanation has been vigorously attacked, but it still has its uses as a crude indicator of the effect of single-member constituencies.

3 The difficulties of representing large-area constituencies is also recognized by the payment of a larger allowance for electorate expenses: at the time of the election $16,750 for constituencies larger than 5,000 square kilometers compared to $11,500 for those smaller than that. Members with constituencies larger than 10,000 square kilometers also receive a special allowance with which to charter airplanes for travel about their electorates.

4 Colin A. Hughes, "Fair and Equal Constituencies: Australia, Jamaica and the United Kingdom", *Journal of Commonwealth and Comparative Politics*, vol. 16, November 1978, pp. 256–71.

5 E.W. Haber, B. Musidlak, and J.F.H. Wright, "Electing a representative House," *Australian Quarterly*, 53(1), Austumn 1981, pp. 46–55.

6 Senator Arthur Gietzelt, "Background Paper: Proposals for Change to Our Electoral System" (Sydney and Canberra: mimeo., 1981).

7 *Age*, May 28, 1979.

8 After the election an ALP member claimed that the donkey vote had worked to the advantage of the coalition with eleven of its members successful because of it, compared to only four Labor members; see Neal Blewett, "Looking back on 1980: Forward to 1983. Some election reflections", *Labor Forum*, 3(2), 1981, p. 3.

9 See Hughes, "The Case of the Arrested Pendulum", pp. 327–30.

10 See Ernest Chaples, "Public campaign finance: New South Wales bites the bullet", *Australian Quarterly*, 53(1), Autumn 1981, pp. 4–14, for details.

11 Figures in this section do not have regard to candidacies for other legislative bodies, whether the Senate or at the State level.

12 Blewett, "Looking back on 1980," p. 4.

10

The Anatomy of a Grievous Miscalculation: 3 February, 1983

Patrick Weller

At lunch time on February, 3 1983, Prime Minister Malcolm Fraser proceeded to the Governor-General's official residence in Canberra to ask for a dissolution of both Houses of the Australian Parliament, with the election to be held on March 5. That date was eight months before the three-year term of the Parliament expired and it meant that, of the three elections called by Fraser while he was Prime Minister, two had been early.

The decision was characteristic. Throughout his career Fraser had consistently taken advantage of any opportunities provided by the misfortunes of his opponents, whether they were rivals within his own Liberal Party or his official enemies in the Labor Party opposition. In 1968 he had played a leading part in the campaign that led to the accession of John Gorton to the prime ministership, after the sudden death of Harold Holt. In 1971 it was Fraser's resignation from Gorton's Cabinet and his personal attack on the Prime Minister's style of government that brought Gorton down. In February 1975 Fraser replaced Billy Snedden as opposition leader at the second attempt. In October 1975 he used the disarray into which the Labor government had fallen as an excuse to use the opposition numbers in the Senate to defer supply, initiating the constitutional crisis that led to Whitlam's dismissal by the Governor-General on November 11, and to Fraser's massive election win a month later. In 1977, arguing that he needed to bring elections in the Senate and House of Representatives back to a common polling day, he called an early election to ensure that Whitlam, by then seen as an electoral liability for the Labor Party, was still its leader; Whitlam had barely survived a challenge from Hayden in May 1977. Fraser's record was one of ruthless and successful opportunism, using the powers of the prime minister, the numbers when he had them and the letter of the constitution, to further his aims. He had won so often that he was credited with almost infallible political nous.

The decision to call an early election was no surprise. Fraser had considered calling one in December 1982, at the time when the December 5 by-election for the division of Flinders was actually held, but he had been dissuaded by the party organization and by his senior colleagues. That proved to be fortunate, for in November Fraser was admitted suddenly to hospital for an operation on his back and was forced to stay away from politics for almost three months. Yet in the by-election for the Melbourne suburban seat of Flinders, left vacant by the resignation of Phillip Lynch, a former deputy leader of the party, the government had done surprisingly well. The Labor Party only needed a swing of 5.6 percent to win and, given the high level of local unemployment and the expected anti-government swing normal at by-elections, everyone expected Labor to win. In fact Labor gained only a 2 percent swing and the Liberals retained the seat easily. Some local explanations could be provided: the Labor candidate was unimpressive; so was the Labor campaign. But the result also added to the pressure for an early election, as it was perceived to endorse the instincts of the Prime Minister that a quick poll could produce a victory.

In late January, when Fraser returned to work, Cabinet cleared the decks for an election, probably on March 19. A senior National Party (NP) minister, Peter Nixon, announced his retirement from politics, but was to be kept in his portfolio until the election. Then speculation grew that the Labor Party was considering a change in leadership, replacing Bill Hayden with Bob Hawke. Fraser decided to expedite the process of bringing on the election. It seems likely that he either hoped to lock Hayden into the leadership (since he clearly wanted to fight against Hayden rather than Hawke), or that he hoped to be running the campaign while Labor was in the middle of a bitter leadership struggle. Given that no Labor leader had ever been defeated in a leadership vote, and given Labor's long record of intra-party battles that were often suicidal, historical evidence supported his gamble.

For once his opportunism backfired. He badly underestimated his opponents. Labor was indeed in a state of depression. Its confidence had been built up gradually during a year of electoral success in 1982; but it was fragile and had been undermined by the defeat in Flinders. Hayden had visited the electorate frequently but he had not campaigned impressively. During the quiet summer holiday months of December and January, the leading members of the centre group in the party, who had remained loyal to Hayden when he was challenged for the leadership by Hawke in July 1982, began to have doubts. John Button, leader of the Labor Party in the Senate and one of the party's clearest thinkers, had a series of meetings with Hayden throughout January. Although a close friend of Hayden, Button became convinced that Labor could not win under his leadership. Lionel Bowen, the deputy leader, came to a similar conclusion. Other close colleagues argued that they were prepared to fight for Hayden in a caucus challenge but that if he did decide to stand down it should be done quickly.

On Thursday, February 3, a meeting of the executive of the parliamentary party was held in Brisbane. At that meeting, and with the prior knowledge of very few people, Hayden announced that he would resign the leadership of the party. The executive then decided that Hawke would be elected unopposed. Since all the possible contenders were also members of the executive, that effectively pre-empted the need for a ballot when the full caucus met to elect a leader during the next week.[1]

Hayden's resignation occurred soon after 11 am in Brisbane. Since Queensland had not gone onto daylight saving, it was 12 midday in Canberra. By that time, it seems, Fraser's appointment with the Governor-General had been made and the press tipped off to expect an early statement. Members of the Liberal Party had been informed that an election was imminent. The director of the Liberal Party was actually in Sydney, discussing campaign details with D'Arcy, Macmanus and Masius, the party's advertising agency.

In the following week, a report was leaked to the press suggesting that Fraser knew in advance that a change of Labor leadership was certain. That seems unlikely. Firstly, it was widely agreed within Liberal circles that if Hawke were elected, it would be better to allow the early honeymoon with the press to turn sour and to put him under pressure in Parliament, an arena which he did not appear to have mastered fully. But, secondly and more importantly, no preparations seem to have been made for a campaign against Hawke. After the election, Eggleton declared that, "Ironically, we began the meeting planning the campaign against Mr Hayden. We heard the mid-day news and found we were having a campaign against Mr Hawke. As one of the Masius (agency) men said 'It's more exciting than one-day cricket'."[2]

Fraser had called an election, expecting to fight Hayden or at least a divided party. In fact, due to Hayden's decision to stand down, he was faced with a united party led by a figure whom the polls had regularly seen as the most popular figure in Australia.

In the first rushed hour in which both decisions became known, Fraser appeared to have taken the initiative, calling an election while the opposition party was leaderless. But it soon became clear that Labor's coup had been so quick that it was Fraser who was put on the defensive. All his tactics were aimed at fighting a different, less popular leader. His miscalculation was all the greater because it had led to the result he probably wanted least—an immediate campaign against the popular Hawke. As a result Fraser started the campaign on the defensive and never recovered the initiative. Having lived by ruthlessly and successfully grasping opportunities, he was to lose everything by one major miscalculation. The style was typical; but for once his timing was very, very wrong.

It is interesting to ask why Fraser wanted an early election, even if it was against Hayden, and why both Fraser and the Labor Party believed that Fraser could win such an election. A survey of the political events of the previous two years shows a government that was scandal-ridden, divided and often ineffective, with an economic record that was poor, and an electoral record that was, with the exception of Flinders, one of almost continual disaster. Yet hardly anyone doubted that Fraser still *might* beat a Labor Party led by Hayden. To explain that is to understand much of the nature and psychology of Australian Federal politics.

The Liberal Party in Government : 1980–83

The Liberals' electoral victory of 1980 was narrow, even if the size of the majority in the House of Representatives was safe. It led to dangerous beliefs that the Prime Minister would be able to beat Hayden whenever he chose and that the director of the Liberal Party, Tony Eggleton, could always pull victory out of defeat. Perhaps the final victory also distracted attention away from the poorly run campaign and the degree to which it became necessary to adjust the party's advertising away from Fraser's personality.

After Fraser had won for the third time, his position appeared to be unassailable, even though in the last week of the campaign, when it was considered possible that the party might lose, quiet canvassing of alternatives had taken place. That had ended abruptly on election night. In the next week the ministry was reshuffled. Two junior ministers accepted overseas appointments and two others were dropped. At the senior level, two important changes were made. Eric Robinson, Minister of Finance and leading power in the Queensland branch of the Liberal Party, was offered a demotion to a minor portfolio outside Cabinet. This demotion was probably designed to appease the NP, for Robinson had been the main strategist in the Queensland Liberal Party's attempt to wrest majority status from their coalition partners. Robinson refused to accept demotion, strongly attacked the influence of the NP and retired to the backbench.[3] It was an early indication of the disquiet felt by many Liberals at Fraser's reliance on the three senior NP ministers.

The second change was even more significant. For the previous five years, Andrew Peacock, scion of the Melbourne establishment and for a long time regarded as an obvious successor and rival to Fraser, had been Minister of Foreign Affairs. He had good contacts with many overseas leaders and had been able to remain detached from the problems of the Australian economy. But he accepted what most observers believed: that if he was to become a serious contender for the Liberal leadership, he needed to gain experience in a domestic portfolio. To indicate the strength of his support, he decided to challenge Lynch for the deputy leadership; he lost by 47 votes to 35, but had polled sufficiently well to be able to demand a major domestic portfolio. He was given the highly sensitive position of Minister for Industrial Relations.

The other result of the 1980 election that was to have important consequences was the loss of government control of the Senate from July 1981. With the election of three more Australian Democrats, giving them five seats in total, Labor and the Democrats together were able to block government proposals. If they wanted to win motions or amend legislation, they also needed the support of the one Independent, Senator Harradine, an ex-Labor man elected in Tasmania.

If hopes of a continued and trouble-free Liberal government were high when the party was re-elected, they did not last. Very soon things started to go wrong and the government appeared to lurch reactively from one crisis to another throughout the next two years.

The first major crisis was the resignation of Andrew Peacock in April 1981. The nominal reason was the demand by the Prime Minister that Peacock's private secretary, Barry Simon, formerly a Liberal MP, resign after he had criticized the government's economic strategy. Under considerable pressure from the Prime Minister and senior Cabinet ministers, Simon did resign. Peacock was furious and, using a leaked story to the press about events that had occurred before the 1980 election as an excuse, he himself resigned on April 15. In his letter to the Prime Minister, he accused Fraser of "acts of gross disloyalty", of having "consistently allowed false and damaging reports to be published about me in my capacity of a senior minister".

He claimed that Fraser "had a dangerous reluctance to consult Cabinet and an obstinant determination to get [his] own way". Peacock declared his decision was "irrevocable".[4] When he explained his reasons to Parliament two weeks later, he spread his net of complaints far more widely. He used the same charges, and often quite deliberately the same language, that Fraser had used ten years earlier when he resigned from Gorton's Cabinet. He claimed that Fraser was "fracturing Cabinet government and the parliamentary system" by centralizing power around himself and an inner Coordination Committee of Cabinet; he complained that the Prime Minister had broken promises on several occasions, was guilty of frequent disloyalty to senior ministers and that he had kept Peacock, in his capacity as Minister for Industrial Relations, off important Cabinet committees, particularly the wages committee, despite promises to the contrary. He argued that the Department of Prime Minister and Cabinet had become so powerful that it had interfered between ministers and their departments; and he suggested that Fraser relied far too heavily on members of the NP. As an illustration of the Prime Minister's technique he provided a detailed account of the debate within the government about the withdrawal of recognition from the Pol Pot regime in Kampuchea. These events had occurred before the 1980 election, and six months before the resignation although they had been the subject of the press leak that nominally sparked the crisis. In adopting this course Peacock again followed Fraser's precedent, for in 1971 Fraser had used an example that arose some months before. Peacock's case was essentially personal: Fraser's style was inimical to successful *Cabinet* government; he was attempting to replace it with personal government. Peacock argued, "What I in fact have shown reveals the Prime Minister's determination to centralise power and satisfy a mania for getting his own way."[5]

Peacock declared he was not trying to bring Fraser down, but found it impossible to work with him. Unlike 1971, when Gorton's Cabinet was divided, Fraser ensured that all his ministers were drawn into a vote of confidence and many of them defended him in the ensuing vote of confidence that was defeated on party lines. Peacock was speedily replaced.

Yet the crisis was far from over, for all Australian prime ministers are extremely vulnerable. They are elected to the party leadership by the parliamentary members of their party, and become prime minister because they are party leaders. They must face re-election immediately after each Federal election and may in effect be challenged at any moment. The re-election procedure is likely to be a formality most of the time, for a winning prime minister is likely to be secure, but it is not always necessarily so. In 1969 John Gorton had to face two challengers whom he defeated fairly easily.

However, the procedure by which other challenges can be mounted may lead to considerable instability if the prime minister is unpopular, or is performing badly, provided there is an alternative candidate. It only requires a party meeting and a vote of no confidence for a challenge to be mounted. Compare the situation in Canada where a prime minister is elected by a vast party convention and can only be removed by convention, a procedure that leaves him almost invulnerable; or the United States procedure of fixed terms. Or the British system where the Conservative Party had only fixed opportunities for removing a prime minister and no chance in between. In those circumstances the prime minister may be safe from internal revolt. In Australia he is not.[6]

This method of electing and removing a leader has several consequences. First, every prime minister must retain continuous links with his backbenchers, particularly when things are not going too well. They elected him; they can remove him. Second, all prime ministers try to ensure that their leading rivals are either in Cabinet or out of Parliament altogether. Very seldom have they left rivals on the backbench or relegated them to it, because of the danger that, untainted by an unpopular government's errors, they could become a focus for discontent. In Fraser's case, when ministers had been forced to leave the ministry, the initiative had seldom been his. The leader of the party in the Senate, Reg Withers, had been sacked after a royal commission found him guilty of committing an "impropriety" in his dealings with an electoral redistribution. Others had resigned because they were involved in legal proceedings or because their personal affairs were under investigation. Now Peacock had resigned. Withers was an acknowledged "numbers" man and Peacock was a possible rival who could distance himself from many of the errors which the government made. The real dangers of such a combination on the backbench were soon to be illustrated.

The third consequence of this system of election was the tendency towards destabilization that could readily develop. If the leader is vulnerable, then rumor-mongering can be an effective means of getting a bandwagon rolling. Intrigue may become endemic in a dissatisfied party because it has a real prospect of success. If rumor can undermine a prime minster's credibility sufficiently for some supporters to waver, then a challenge may be mounted.

The year following Peacock's resignation illustrated all these consequences. There was no immediate challenge, but it was accepted that the question was *when* it would occur, not *if* it would.

In May 1981, Fraser's heavy-handed political tactics upset another important group with whom good relations were important: the non-Labor State premiers. At the Premiers Conference there had been hard bargaining for money, as there always was. The premiers were informed that on no account were any more funds available. On the evening that the Premier's Conference ended, Fraser and Howard gave a background briefing to two leading journalists indicating that they had been authorized by Cabinet to give the States $70 million more than the figure finally accepted by the premiers. The explanation of the briefing was, according to one minister, to show in the wake of the Peacock resignation that Fraser was still a tough politician capable of getting his own way.

The premiers were naturally furious. Sir Charles Court, the Western Australian Premier, strongly attacked Fraser and Howard. Once the story got out about the means employed, and then when Fraser's press secretary tried to stop it spreading, both Fraser and Howard were seen as being politically unwise and also less than competent in managing media (a skill at which Fraser was usually very good). The whole messy affair merely added to the impression of a bungling government.[7]

In September and October 1981, Fraser was faced with a return of the poor health that had occurred twice in the previous three years. At the same time the Commonwealth Heads of Government Meeting was lavishly held in Melbourne. It allowed Fraser to appear as the host and as a statesman, one who was particularly praised for his support of the independence of Zimbabwe and for his strident opposition to the policies of South Africa. But for much of the time that CHOGM was being held, the attention of the media was distracted by rumors that Fraser was seriously ill and about to retire, or that he was about to be challenged.[8] Nothing official was ever said, but it was probably more than mere gossip. In late 1981 the challenge came to nothing; but that had been merely a trial run.

At the same time Fraser was beginning to learn at first-hand the problems faced by a government that did not control the Senate. The Budget had provided for the imposition of a sales tax on a number of essential items including books, and the limited reintroduction of fees for second degrees in tertiary institutions. At first the Democrats declared that, although they opposed the sales tax, they would pass it because it was part of the government's Budget. Then they reversed the decision and voted with Labor to block both the sales tax and the fees for tertiary institutions. When the bills were presented a second time in the next session, they were again defeated. These defeats gave Fraser the official trigger he needed to call a double dissolution if he so wanted.[9]

The long-expected challenge from Peacock did occur, in April 1982. Following a massive swing against the government in a Federal by-election in New South Wales, and a morale-shattering defeat in the Victorian State election, it became evident that a challenge would soon be made. Before his opponents had an opportunity to marshal their forces, Fraser convened a party meeting to "settle the issue of the leadership". Up to the day before the meeting it was unclear what tactics might be used. Fraser could have arranged for a supporter to move a vote of confidence, or demanded an opponent move a "spill" motion declaring the leadership vacant; such a motion would have been put to a show of hands, requiring from all MPs a public show of allegiance. In the event Fraser stated that he believed there was a desire for a vote on the leadership, that he was prepared to stand down and then re-contest the position. He won easily by 54 votes to 27. At the same time the party elected John Howard deputy leader; his predecessor, Phillip Lynch, who had held the job since 1972, had stood down earlier that week (probably to avoid being pushed out). The opportunity to elect Howard as deputy leader satisfied those economic "dries" who wanted to maintain a check on Fraser and might otherwise have been persuaded to vote against him.

Peacock's vote was not so small that his reputation was destroyed, but neither was the margin narrow enough to permit thought of a second try. He publicly claimed that he would support the Prime Minister up to the next election, although he did not immediately re-enter the ministry. Peacock's time, it was argued, was still a long way away.

With the challenge defeated and a new deputy leader, it appeared that Fraser would have an opportunity to relax. But a week later another crisis exploded. One minister had, six months earlier, brought a colour television set through customs without paying duty on it. Whether he was asked to pay or not is debatable, but his customs declaration was clearly inaccurate. The Minister of Business and Consumer Affairs, who had held responsibility for customs, was almost immediately informed of the problem but took no action to ensure that all doubts were removed. It is possible that he was advised that there was no major problem. The customs officer who had questioned the procedure had pressure applied by senior officers to keep quiet.

In April the whole story reached the press. The two ministers, Michael Mackellar and John Moore, combined to release a statement explaining events. But the media demanded more. Editorials almost unanimously demanded that the ministers resign. The furore was probably all the greater because it touched on a matter that was easily understood by the public: a minister had improperly evaded customs duty and, like any other member of the public, should bear the consequences. On Monday, April 19, Cabinet met almost continuously, sometimes with Moore and Mackellar present, sometimes without them. Eventually it was decided that both should resign.

In theory these resignations followed the tradition of ministerial propriety and responsibility—Mackellar had improperly used his position, Moore had failed to ensure that his department had operated effectively, particularly after he became personally involved. The resignations were certainly explained in these terms. In practice the reasons were more prosaic. The costs of toughing it out and keeping the two in the ministry were regarded as greater than that of letting them go. It was a classic example of the practical application of ministerial responsibility, as explained six years earlier by another Liberal minister:

> It means today in practice that the Minister is responsible to Parliament for his Department to explain, and where error is shown, he takes corrective action. He will only resign if the Prime Minister believes it is for the good of the government but in most cases that simply admits error and, party conflict being what it is, admission of error is more serious than the error itself.[10]

In this instance it was easier to acknowledge the fault.

Two other scandals erupted within the next six months. The first was an ironic boomerang, a consequence of Fraser's desire to play politics hard. The Federal government and the Victorian government (at that time still in Liberal hands) had established a royal commission to investigate the Melbourne branch of the Ship-Painters and Dockers Union. The union had a history of bitter disputes and gangland murders; many of its members had criminal records. It was also, like many other unions, affiliated with the Labor Party. The royal commission was created to look into the affairs of the union and to examine its reputed links with organized crime. Those establishing the commission no doubt hoped that one by-product of the investigation would be some dirt that could be thrown at the Labor Party, particularly in Victoria during the approaching election campaign.

But the plan misfired. It is true that Costigan, the commissioner, found many links between the ship-painters and dockers and organized crime. But the unionists were often the frontmen for sophisticated white-collar operators of tax-evasion and tax-avoidance systems. The tax-evasion industry had grown rapidly in the previous seven years and several schemes had been declared illegal. Costigan uncovered a method that was colorfully called the "bottom of the harbor" scheme, by which companies with taxable assets were sold at inflated prices and thus became capital gains (not taxable in Australia); the records of the companies, subsequently transferred to dummy directors, men of straw who were often ship-painters and dockers, were notionally despatched to the bottom of the harbor.

What hurt the Liberal Party was that many of those involved in these schemes were members of, or close to, the Liberal Party. One man named in Costigan's report for his involvement with the scheme in Western Australia happened also to be chairman of the finance committee of the State branch of the Liberal Party and a government appointee to several bodies including the Australian Broadcasting Commission. At the Prime Minister's instigation, he was persuaded to stand down from these positions while his affairs were under investigation. Fraser's insistence on this action upset many of his backbenchers, who believed that the man was being effectively condemned without a fair hearing. There were other lengthy lists of people who were said to be involved in similar schemes. Since the Victorian government was the joint sponsor of the commission and was now in Labor hands, it was not possible for Fraser to suppress the reports.

Thus an investigation into the affairs of an insignificant if disreputable union developed into an exposé of the whole tax-evasion industry and immediately put the government on the defensive. In part, it was guilt by association; the main offenders moved in the same business circles. The amount of tax that had been avoided was variously calculated, with figures of $750 million being commonly used by Labor spokesmen while government spokesmen argued that it was much less.

The government was soon directly involved. The Costigan reports stated that in Western Australia the crown solicitor's office in Perth (part of the Federal Attorney-General's Department) had been very slow in pursuing tax evaders and that one of its officers had been running a call-girl racket from official premises. Demands for the resignation of the Attorney-General followed, on the (somewhat unfair) assumption that he should somehow have prevented such behaviour. The Treasurer was also attacked when it was revealed that the tax commissioner had recommended closing some of the "bottom-of-the-harbor" loopholes, but that nothing had been done. Such a series of devastating revelations about the incompetence of the bureaucracy, the slowness of ministerial reactions and the shady ethics of many of the business community, sent the government reeling. Further, there was always the fear that more was to come. One volume of Costigan's report was not published, leading to continued speculation about its contents, whether or when it might be leaked (particularly during the election campaign) and who would suffer if it was.

Fraser's proposed solution only added to his problems. He decided that new tax legislation would be introduced, making those who had avoided tax by using certain loopholes in the legislation retrospectively liable for the tax. Many members of the Liberal Party argued that the principle of retrospectivity was totally unacceptable and that some citizens who had been innocent of any guilty intent might suddenly find themselves liable to pay large tax bills. Public criticism from the conservative side of politics became common, particularly within the Western Australian branch of the party. The legislation passed the Senate only because it received Labor support. It was probably perceived as being electorally popular, and to an extent it blunted some of Labor's attacks, but it also exacerbated tensions within the Liberal Party.

A second royal commission report added to the government's problems. It had been learned the previous year that there had been a major meat substitution racket, with horse or kangaroo meat being exported as beef. Petty corruption among the meat inspectors was seen to be rife. Mr Justice Woodward, a judge who had just completed a term as the director of the Australian Security Intelligence Organisation (ASIO), was appointed to investigate. His report, issued in September 1982, roundly condemned the administration of the department of Primary Industry and argued that the NP minister, Peter Nixon, failed to correct known abuses. It said, among the other condemnations:

> I believe that the minister, having heard from a responsible source that there had been cases of bribery and abuse of power in his department, should have taken positive steps to investigate the matter.
>
> In my view he did not deal with this allegation in a manner that was adequate and effective.[11]

When the Attorney-General had explained why he refused to resign, he argued that the doctrine of ministerial responsibility required resignation only if the minister was personally involved. That, of course, had been the reason for Moore's resignation earlier in the year. Now, according to the royal commission, Nixon *was* personally involved. He offered his resignation; Fraser refused to accept it. Fraser argued that, on the basis of the evidence, there was no justification for the conclusions that Woodward had drawn about Nixon's behaviour. He quoted from the report selectively to support his conclusions, often using only parts of paragraphs and ignoring the fundamental comments at the end of the report. In the process he cast doubt on the use of evidence and the judgement of the man to whom, in previous years, he had entrusted Australia's internal security.

Clearly a double standard was being applied. When Senator Withers was condemned by a royal commission, there was no alternative, Fraser argued, except for him to resign. When Moore or Mackellar became involved in the colour TV affair, public opinion led Fraser to desert them. But when Nixon was involved, he fought hard to save the minister. The reasons were both personal and party. Fraser had always been close to the three leading NP members, Anthony, Sinclair and Nixon, all experienced politicians with a ruthless streak of opportunism. At times of crisis, he turned to them for advice, a fact which was one of the main complaints of Peacock and Robinson. To lose Nixon would have been disastrous. As Michelle Grattan wrote: "If Peter Nixon, one of Mr Fraser's closest confidants were dropped, the Prime Minister might as well announce that his government was sliding rapidly to its doom."[12] He chose instead to use the tried tactic of discrediting the accuser.

Moreover these ministers were, as NP members, beyond his direct control. Their resignation required the approval of the NP leader too. When in 1979 Ian Sinclair was committed to trial on charges of forgery, it was not until he was actually charged that he resigned. A Liberal minister in so much trouble would almost inevitably have been forced to stand down earlier. The double standard caused much comment among those who, like Withers, had been punished as a result of far less devastating criticism.

As a response to these attacks on administration, particularly when coupled with other emerging scandals about fraud in the payment of medical benefits and problems in the delivery of social security services, Fraser chose to set up a quick enquiry into the Public Service, the Review of Commonwealth Functions, headed by a leading businessman, John Reid.[13] As soon as Reid's name was announced, Hayden claimed that he too had been involved in tax-avoidance rackets; the intention of the attack was to tarnish all Fraser's choices. In fact, after Reid had stood down, the tax commissioner examined the charges and found that he did not owe any tax. For a time, then, as a result of an inadequately documented personal attack Labor lost the initiative and Hayden's tactics were severely criticized.

Then political activity effectively ceased for two weeks while the country stopped to watch the action of the Commonwealth Games in Brisbane. The standard of performance may not have been world-class and the level of media commentary often myopically nationalistic; but the total concentration on the games allowed Fraser to appear regularly on the news congratulating or embracing Australian winners and led to an enforced break in the attacks on his government.

Almost immediately, Fraser began to think of an early election again. On October 11 Lynch resigned from Cabinet and was replaced by Peacock who commented: "I would not have accepted this post if I didn't think that we could work cohesively together.... There has been a change (of view) on my part, but there has been a steady stream of discussions between the Prime Minister and myself."[14] He argued that the expansionary Budget introduced in August had met many of his earlier complaints and there was now a need to work together. It also seems that, once Fraser had defeated Peacock's challenge, he no longer felt threatened by him.[15] Peacock's return publicly suggested that the party was no longer so divided.

Lynch's resignation gave Fraser an alternative; he could either hold a general election or face the possible loss of Lynch's seat in a by-election. For a time Fraser appeared to favor the first. In early November Fraser finally, and reluctantly, decided not to call an early election which his advisers, particularly Tony Eggleton, believed would be disastrous. Instead a by-election for Flinders was set for December 5. Yet even if it was true that the Labor surge in September and October had been slowed by the rash attack on Reid, there was still nothing in the electoral or economic climate to encourage the Liberals to believe they could win a poll.

The Electorate

The results at all elections between the Federal poll of 1980 and the Flinders by-election merely confirmed the declining fortunes of the Liberal Party. In 1980 the Labor Party held office in New South Wales and Tasmania; by the time of the 1983 election Labor had won elections in four mainland States but lost Tasmania. Only Queensland had remained firmly in the grip of Bjelke-Petersen's National Party, with the Liberal Party as the junior and often ignored coalition partner.

Labor's upward progress had been consistent. In 1981 the New South Wales Labor government, headed by Neville Wran, increased its majority in the Legislative Assembly. The Liberal Party was in total disarray. Two months before the election it had replaced its leader; but the new man, Bruce MacDonald, proved to be no more effective. He made little mark in a campaign that was organized around Wran as an individual, with little attention to the party's record or to policy. MacDonald lost his own seat, leaving an ineffective and squabbling rump of the Liberal Party, which had the same number of seats as its NP partner. Each had 13; the Labor government had 69. Two years later, MacDonald's replacement was also removed, giving the Liberals the unenviable record of having had eight leaders in eight years. In the election Labor retained seats in areas that had previously been regarded as safely Liberal. It seemed that as long as Wran stayed leader, the party would be invincible in New South Wales.[16]

Other State Labor leaders had learnt from Wran's style which provided a model for success. He concentrated on consensus, on moving slowly, on cooperating with business, on providing an atmosphere of stability. Wran tried to ensure that the caucus was solidly behind the Cabinet; he wanted to avoid the impression of chaotic mismanagement that was believed to have pervaded the Whitlam administration. (Although it must be acknowledged that, as the Whitlam government recedes into history, so its reputed errors have grown. It often seems to be justification enough to say that an action is being taken to avoid recreating the problems of the Whitlam government.) Wran chose to move slowly if at all, to hold the middle ground, to allow business to feel comfortable with a Labor government.

Other States followed the Wran model in their choice of leaders. In Victoria the colorless Frank Wilkes, who had failed to win the previous election despite a substantial gain in votes and seats, was replaced by John Cain, whose father had been the last Labor Premier, 27 years earlier. In April 1981 the Cain-led Labor party had a landslide victory. Victoria had long been called the "jewel in the Liberal crown"; that jewel became very tarnished. The campaign seemed to concentrate as much on Federal issues as on the decaying reputation of a tired and scandal-ridden Liberal government. Cain won easily with a majority of seventeen seats in a House of 81 members.[17]

In September South Australia went to the polls. Its Liberal Premier had fallen into office when a new Labor Premier's decision to call a snap election had been undermined by a bus strike.[18] After three years the government had made little impression. The new Labor leader, John Bannon, was younger, persuasive and well-educated; he maintained a quiet approach to politics. Despite some internal divisions, the Labor Party received a swing of 5 percent and won five seats from the Liberals.[19]

In Western Australia the Liberal Party government had been considered to be as well entrenched as that of Victoria. In the previous 25 years the Labor Party had been in power for only three. But then a change of leader led to a resurgence. Brian Burke, a 35-year-old former journalist and son of a former Federal MP, replaced the older and uninspiring Ron Davies. In the Liberal government Sir Charles Court had retired after eight years as Premier. He had dominated his government with his hard-hitting and confrontationist style. His successor, Des O'Conner, was much less aggressive.

There were also severe tensions within that State's Liberal Party. Members of the State branch, including leading Federal backbenchers, had been openly critical of Fraser's determination to introduce retrospective taxation and of his "victimization" of those named in the Costigan report. The State government eventually called an election for February 19. When he announced the date the Premier declared that he hoped the election would be fought on State issues and he bluntly stated that Fraser would not be welcome. As it happened the Federal election was called two weeks before the State election was held, and State issues were entirely submerged. Fraser did not visit the west before February 19, but even so the State government was swept out of power with a massive swing against it of 8 percent.

The only exceptions to the trend against the coalition parties were Queensland—where a State election two months after the 1980 Federal poll easily returned the Bjelke-Petersen government—and Tasmania. Events in the latter were peculiar in the extreme. Tasmania is always short of industrial infrastructure and successive governments have attempted to attract investment by the offer of cheaper industrial electricity. This is provided by hydro-electricity schemes, often in the uninhabited south-western part of the island. The Hydro-electricity Commission is one of the largest employers in the island State and maintains its workforce by a continuing program of building dams. In the 1970s it flooded the picturesque Lake Pedder. In the 1980s it proposed to dam the Franklin River and flood what was declared to be "the last wild river in Australia". The Labor State Premier, Doug Lowe, was lukewarm about the proposal. He organized a referendum which, almost unbelievably, asked the Tasmanian population to choose between two dams. When Lowe wanted to add a "no dams" option to the ballot, a party coup replaced him as Premier with Harry Holgate. In the referendum both major parties supported the Franklin dam but opponents, led by the Tasmanian Wilderness Society, organized a "no dams" write-in campaign.

Almost 40 percent of the electorate cast informal "no dams" ballots. Next the Holgate government lost control of the House of Assembly when Lowe and one supporter resigned from the Labor Party. Holgate was forced to an election by defeat in a motion of no confidence. With the Holgate government seen as incompetent and faction-ridden, and with no major differences of policy, a Liberal government led by Robin Gray was elected with 19 seats in the 35-member House. Both parties supported the flooding of the Franklin.[20]

Even if this defeat was a set-back for the Labor Party, it was not too surprising as the Federal Liberal Party already held all the five Tasmanian seats in the House of Representatives. What rebounded to Federal Labor's advantage was the decision of the Tasmanian Wilderness Society to take their cause to a wider stage. It ran campaigns in two Federal by-elections and the Australian Capital Territory House of Assembly elections, asking voters to write "no dams" on the corner of their ballots. Although the "no dams" vote was never precisely counted, it was suggested that up to 40 percent of electors wrote in "no dams". The question of the Franklin, and of which major party would take action to stop the Tasmanian government from flooding it, became a major issue in national politics. The Federal Liberal government offered a variety of alternative schemes, but argued that, as the decision to flood the Franklin was within the State government's competence, the Federal government had no right to infringe the State's rights or to impose its will on the Tasmanian government. Labor categorically declared, in the face of opposition from its Tasmanian branch, that it would stop the dam.

Before Flinders there had been another significant Federal by-election. In late 1981 the former Liberal Prime Minister, Sir William McMahon, resigned from Parliament. He had held the seat of Lowe since 1949, on a number of occasions very narrowly. His timing could not have been worse for the Liberals. Labor replaced the left-wing woman who had run McMahon close in 1980 with a male member of the State Parliament. He was part of the dominant right-wing faction in the NSW branch; his State seat was within the boundaries of the Federal seat of Lowe. The decision caused an outcry from women in the party who declared that the party's policy of promoting women, adopted at the special conference six months earlier (see Chapter 7), was being ignored. The party's leaders believed that it was essential that the party win the seat and win it well; they believed that Michael Maher was the best candidate because he had many local contacts and had proved himself to be popular. Maher did win the seat easily, with a swing of such a size that government seemed to be within easy reach of Labor. When this was followed a few weeks later by the victory in the Victorian State elections, Labor's confidence was high.

Electorally there was no reason to doubt Labor's clear lead—until Flinders.

The Economy

The government's management of the economy gave the Liberal Party no more cause for electoral optimism. All the economic indicators suggested to the electorate that the Liberal economic policy was not working effectively. As Figure 10–1 shows, neither inflation nor unemployment had been kept under control. Whereas inflation had been reduced significantly after the change of government, it had risen consistently throughout 1981 and most of 1982; at the time of the

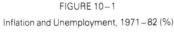

FIGURE 10–1

Inflation and Unemployment, 1971–82 (%)

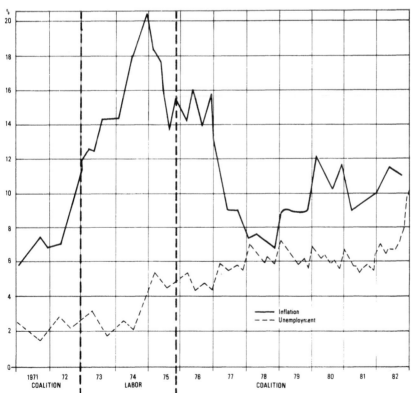

265

election, the rate of around 12 percent was considerably higher than that of most other equivalent OECD countries.

Unemployment was even more disturbing. At the beginning of the 1970s it used to be argued that no Australian government could survive with an unemployment rate of over 2 percent, and one of the causes of McMahon's defeat in 1972 was said to be a rate over that level. Under Whitlam it rose to 5 percent. Under Fraser it stayed around 6–7 percent from 1977 onwards, yet Liberal research suggested that although the electorate was concerned about unemployment, it was not perceived as an issue on which they were inclined to change their vote. But in 1982 the rate suddenly accelerated as the recession bit more deeply. Stories of firms closing and workers being laid off became commonplace. It was made more graphic when a group of miners and steelworkers, about to be put off, stormed through the doors of Parliament House in an angry demonstration. During the campaign the rate passed 10 percent, the highest figure since the depression of the 1930s. Although Fraser optimistically argued that such a figure would help the government's cause (quite how was not explained), such an explosion could only have harmed the government's chances. Public expectations of more unemployment—as measured by the Morgan Gallup Poll—which had been ranging between 60 percent (1976) and 73 percent (1978), shot up in the last quarter of 1982 to 88 percent, while the proportion of respondents expecting less unemployment dropped from between 20 percent (1977) and 10 percent (1978, 1979, 1981) to a mere 5 percent. Nevertheless, as Table 10–1 indicates, the Fraser government had been fairly successful in laying the blame for unemployment on one factor over which it had no control, the world economy, and on another factor which was linked to the Labor Party and which the government appeared to be attacking, the trade unions. It had been equally successful in keeping blame away from itself and from its natural allies, the employers, though cruel experience had substantially undercut the stereotype of the work-shy "dole-bludger", a stereotype which some pro-government newspapers had once run vigorously.

Interest rates climbed rapidly too. Even though home mortgage interest rates were protected from the worst effects of the market, increased repayments for housing loans hurt in the outer suburban electorates of the "mortgage belt", where voters were struggling to make ends meet in the face of increased monthly payments. The Australian dream of owning a home was threatened; those who had bought one, could barely afford to pay for it and those who wanted to could only see the prospects decline. And it was precisely in these

TABLE 10-1
Causes of Unemployment 1975–82 (%)

	1975	1976	1977	1978	1979	1980	1981	1982 Oct.	1982 Dec.
World economic pressure	32	25	30	32	36	34	35	52	52
Trade unions	36	42	43	42	32	30	34	43	46
Government	33	27	32	41	40	36	36	34	37
People not wanting to work	48	30	36	36	30	29	33	24	24
Employers	8	10	12	15	14	14	14	13	13
Others; no answer	3	6	6	5	9	7	7	5	5

Note: More than one answer possible.
Source: Morgan Gallup Poll, Findings No. 872, November 12, 1981 and No. 1013, January 11, 1983.

mortgage-belt areas that many Liberal MPs held their seats by small margins. Even though interest rates did come down marginally just before the poll, they were still at a worryingly high level.

Indeed it was in the field of economic management that the style of the Fraser government was most clearly epitomized. Activity was considerable; Cabinet met regularly and considered a vast number of submissions; the notional output of government was great. But such statistics can be misleading. Activity may not lead to purposive action; many of the submissions consisted of reconsidering what had already been analyzed once and then sent back to the bureaucracy for further detail. Too much almost certainly went to Cabinet, because the Prime Minister wanted to know what was going on and junior ministers were too scared to take decisions without Cabinet approval. Some businessmen complained it was difficult to get clear or prompt decisions out of government, while senior public servants described the procedures in Cabinet as a "desecration of the Cabinet system" and the "antithesis of good government".[21]

Rhetoric often hid the more prosaic reality. On the re-election of the government in 1980, the Prime Minister established a Cabinet committee to review government programs as an important means of reducing the level of government expenditure. Its report, when tabled in the House of Representatives, was, according to the Prime Minister, "the most significant and far reaching ministerial undertaking of its kind ever undertaken by a federal government".[22] But its contents were ideological in approach, it was never clear how far the recommendations would reduce public expenditure, and many of the proposals were subsequently abandoned.

In 1982 the government's Budget reversed many of its earlier policies. Acting against the Treasury's advice, it gave tax cuts and set out to expand the economy. It was widely regarded as an election

Budget, adding to the pressure for an early poll. But the shift was excoriated by the "dries" in the Liberal Party who argued that the government ought to remain true to its economic policy. It also made it difficult for the government to contemplate another Budget before an election, since that one would have to rein in the exploding deficit. In terms of economic management, it appeared that the Liberal government had a poor record on which to run.

Then, like pulling a rabbit out of a magician's hat, Fraser announced a wages pause, that is, the idea that all employees should forgo pay rises for a set period to allow the inflation rate to be reduced. The proposal was suggested by Sir Charles Court and had been organized by Fraser from his hospital bed; the pause was then effectively sold by two of his most competent colleagues, John Howard and Ian Macphee. A Premiers' Conference was called for December 7 (after the Flinders by-election), so the scheme could be considered by the State governments including the Labor governments in Victoria, New South Wales and South Australia. These had demanded a freeze on prices be included, but even before the conference Howard had rejected that notion. The Premiers' Conference still agreed to a six-months' freeze and that proposal was endorsed by the Arbitration Commission. Legislation freezing the wages of Commonwealth employees had been rushed through the Federal Parliament in November. The sole opponents were the unions, headed by the ACTU, and the Federal Labor Party, which, not surprisingly, had opposed a proposal that effectively required a cut in real wages.

Whether or not the wage pause would work economically, it seemed to have worked politically. The Labor Party was divided and uncertain about how to respond; its need to consult with, or even appear to represent, the unions was clearly shown. The initiative in the debate had returned to the government, even if it increased pressures for an early election before the promises of success could be tarnished by the possible failure of the pause to achieve substantial economic benefits. The result in the Flinders by-election seemed to justify the government's belief that, however mediocre its record of economic management, at least the electors prefered the known quality to the uncertain economic prospects of an apparently muddled Labor Party.

Labor 1980–83

During the 1980 election Bill Hayden had campaigned far more effectively than most observers expected. Since he only narrowly failed to become prime minister he was, not unexpectedly, re-elected unopposed as party leader. Nevertheless throughout the parliament, the media fuelled constant speculation about his relations with Hawke and the possibility of a change of leadership.

After the 1980 election Hawke was immediately elected to the parliamentary party executive, but he did not immediately adapt to the parliamentary environment. Nor did he seem to want to. He was in any case in an unenviable position. If he was quiet or ineffective, the media questioned his competence; if he made statements outside his shadow responsibilities of industrial relations, the media questioned his motives.

For a time, the potential leadership dispute stayed muted. In July 1981 a special National Conference altered the system of representation for future conferences; instead of being organized on a strictly Federal basis with equal representation from each State, the greater population of the larger States was recognized with representation for them being granted on the basis of size. The new conference would have 99 delegates.

The special conference also debated possible changes to the party's objective. In the end the objective remained the same, with both left-wing proposals to remove the qualifying clause and right-wing attempts to remove any reference to socialization being defeated. But to the objective were added 22 explanatory clauses which were to be used to interpret it, and these clauses effectively allowed the objective to be interpreted in almost any direction. The conference also confirmed the principle of increased representation for women.

Hayden's balanced and sensitive handling of issues and colleagues throughout the conference enhanced his reputation. Hawke intervened only once, in the debate on the objective, and then to launch an attack on the left, describing their arguments as "intellectual wanking". At the end of the conference, a headline in the *Australian Financial Review* declared "Hayden invincible, Hawke invisible"; the article argued it was not credible to suggest that Hayden could possibly be replaced by Hawke.[23]

In early 1982 Hayden still appeared to be firmly in the saddle. The Federal by-election of Lowe and the victory in the Victorian State elections suggested that the swing towards Labor was continuing. Hayden obviously felt confident; when he created a party strategy committee, Hawke was not selected to be on it, despite the fact that he had been one of the party's leadership triumvirate in the previous election.

In July 1982 the regular, and now enlarged, biennial National Conference met to settle the platform on which Labor would fight the next election. Although some serious issues were discussed, the whole week was dominated by the possibility of a challenge to Hayden. In a sense the whole affair was carefully played up in the media; talking about a challenge, often through carefully planned leaks, made the challenge a reality.

How little was at stake in policy terms between the two men was illustrated by the debates in the conference on the two major issues, a capital gains tax and the policy over uranium mining. Hawke had been chairman of the party's economic committee which brought to conference an amendment to the existing platform which suggested a limited capital gains tax. Hayden argued that to include any capital gains tax in the platform would be suicidal since he and others believed that it was that very issue which had lost the 1980 election in its final week. Hayden supported an amendment which promised to use existing legislation to pursue more energetically the tax cheats in the community. Two comments illustrate the nature of the debate. Hayden claimed:

> The argument is not about substance at all. It is about political presentation. It is aimed at maximising our capacity to attack effectively our opponents and not be put on the defensive.
>
> Why the blazes do we in the Labor Party so persistently go about doing things which can only be calculated to put us on the defensive?[24]

He believed that the Hawke proposal just could not be sold. Hawke's answer was: "If we cannot sell this proposition against Malcolm Fraser and what he has been doing to prop up the privileged and make the 95 percent pay what the 5 percent should have been paying, then we should not be in the bloody business of politics". As one commentator remarked, he left the audience in no doubt that "he was really saying: 'if you can't sell it, Bill, I can'".[25]

On the issue of the capital gains tax Hayden got the numbers and the amendment he supported was adopted by 54 votes to 43. It was seen as a vote of confidence in Hayden. On most other issues the two men agreed. They both supported the concept of a prices-and-incomes policy as the corner-stone of Labor's economic policy. Even more importantly, both supported changes to the uranium plank of the platform which had called for a moratorium of uranium mining and a repudiation of all existing contracts. Uranium is very much the symbolic issue of the left of the party which could be certain to oppose any weakening of that stand. The new policy listed a set of conditions under which mining could continue. Amid hectic demonstrations and threats to the preselection of some delegates, the new and softer policy was narrowly adopted by 53 votes to 46. Both Hayden and Hawke supported the change.

Nevertheless at the same time Hawke was giving interviews about Hayden's standings in the polls and expressing concern that the party was not doing better. He argued on television that there was no doubt that Labor could win under his leadership. His challenge was, according to respected columnist Michelle Grattan, "mounted almost exclusively on his very high rating in the public opinion polls and his argument that he can translate this into a near certain win for the ALP at the next election".[26] Some members of the left, disgusted with Hayden's stand on uranium, flirted with the idea of shifting their support to Hawke (despite that fact that he agreed with Hayden on the issue). If the left were to shift, then Hayden's position would become very tenuous. Under pressure Hayden followed Fraser's example and called a meeting of the parliamentary party to settle the leadership.

In the next week there followed an undignified and public squabble as the Labor Party often brawled in public. At one stage the leading members of the NSW left and right factions, Tom Uren and Paul Keating, publicly disagreed on radio about the processes that were going on. Keating finally threw the support of the NSW centre behind Hawke, after delaying a decision in the hope that the left might desert Hayden. It didn't. With the support of the left and of the centre votes led by John Button and Lionel Bowen, Hayden held on to win by a mere five votes, 43–38. Then, in a jovial press conference, he added Hawke to the strategy committee.

That narrow victory to Hayden was perhaps the worst possible result for Labor. It settled nothing. Hawke was proved to have considerable support in caucus, almost half of whom wanted a change. Had Hayden lost narrowly, his support would have dissolved, for some members of caucus may have supported him as a leader, but would not have supported him, once deposed, as a later challenger. Had Hawke lost badly, the issue might have died until after the next election. As it was, the challenge was merely on ice. Whatever assurances of support were given at the time, everyone knew that if Hayden consistently performed badly or if he made one major mistake, then everything would start again. Besides, the media were constantly probing, asking if it was on again.

For the next three months Hayden performed fairly well. He was of course given great ammunition by the series of scandals in government administration that were being uncovered. His speech attacking the government over the Woodward report was both very funny and devastating. But then the impetus was lost.

In part this change came as a consequence of the wages pause. Labor's reaction was ambivalent. On the one hand, to avoid being seen as negative, it had to either accept the general idea or present an alternative. But nothing so clearly articulated emerged. Initially the Federal Labor Party opposed the pause. But when Hayden and his colleagues met the executive of the ACTU the day before the Flinders by-election to discuss the prices-and-incomes package that was intended to be the corner-stone of Labor's economic package, they had little success. Nor did the ACTU strongly support Federal Labor's opposition to the pause. To the party's acute embarrassement the ACTU was considering accepting, in part at least, the argument for the wages pause. At the Premiers' Conference after Flinders, the Labor State premiers too acceded to a degree to the proposals. In January Hayden changed his position; he argued that the wages pause was a gimmick but that some attempts to make it work were desirable. But by this time the ACTU had decided to use industrial action to destroy the pause and in an angry meeting of the parliamentary executive, the ACTU line, espoused by Hawke, was preferred to Hayden's. Hayden therefore was forced to do a policy somersault, which did little for his public image. Yet at the same time it was made clear that no final agreement with the unions over a prices-and-incomes policy was likely to be achieved before March. Labor appeared to be unable to settle on an alternative economic package; an early election might find it without a policy at all.

At the same time Hayden's position was being gradually undermined. Hawke had been fairly quiet since the July challenge. On November 5 he publicly commented that the narrowing gap in the opinion polls must be "of concern" to the Labor Party; his statement was universally seen as ill-timed and, under pressure from the leading members of caucus, he wrote to all members of caucus denying that he was trying to launch a new challenge. But after Flinders there was mounting concern at Hayden's apparent inability to get the party's message across. It was expressed at a meeting of the party State secretaries in December, at a meeting of the national campaign committee, at a meeting of NSW candidates, and in caucus.

Finally, Hayden's two key supporters, Senate leader John Button and deputy leader Lionel Bowen, also became convinced of the need for a change. In a series of meetings throughout January, the case was strongly put to Hayden and considerable pressure, much of which has never become public, was exerted. Even though some supporters were still prepared to fight in caucus, Hayden could not win without Button's and Bowen's support.

The changeover was smooth and secret. Few members, even of the parliamentary executive, knew of Hayden's decision before the meeting, even though it was clear that Hayden's hold on the leadership was slipping when Bowen refused to endorse him publicly on television the night before. Nevertheless most people still expected Hayden to fight for his position. He chose to stand down, rather than divide the party just before an election that was almost certain to be held within the next six weeks. In going, he commented that he thought a "drover's dog" could lead Labor to victory.

Hawke was endorsed by the executive and immediately began to act as leader, even before his formal anointing by the full caucus the next week. He was not chosen for his skills in particular policy areas; indeed the industial relations policy (for which he had responsibility) had been cobbled together at the last moment at the previous conference. He was not chosen for his parliamentary performance, for at the time of his accession to the leadership it had been mediocre. He was chosen because he was a nationally popular figure with great skills of communication, with a known ability to dominate the media, with a deep if generalized belief in the process of reconciliation, and with a capacity to provide a message of hope. While his party colleagues put together most of the detailed ideas, Hawke was chosen to get them across. His great ability was Hayden's greatest failing: selling the party. Whatever happened after the party gained office could wait. Hawke, the party believed, was more likely to get them there.

Leadership and the Polls

When Hayden resigned he declared that: "I am not convinced that the Labor Party would not win under my leadership. I believe that a drover's dog could lead the Labor Party to victory the way the country is, and the way the opinion polls are showing up for the Labor Party." That view was justified. During 1980 and for the first months of 1981 there was little to choose between the parties, as indicated by voting intentions (Figure 10–2). But from mid-1981 a clear gap had opened between the two parties. On occasions the difference between the two parties was over 10 percent; on two instances it closed to within 1 or 2 percent. But most of the time the difference was considerable, with support for the Labor Party remaining firm at a level that was sufficiently high to ensure that Labor would confidently win an election. One of the two occasions when gap closed was during the Flinders by-election. Hayden had good reason to believe that the party would win under his leadership.

FIGURE 10–2

Voting intention 1980–83

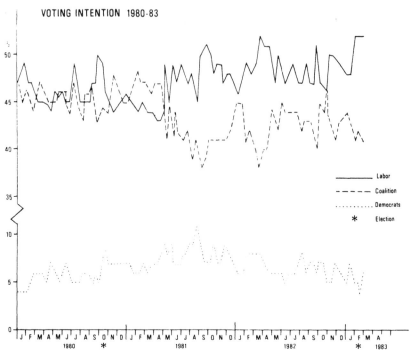

In terms of his approval rating, too, Hayden had some cause for comfort. Those who approved of his performance were always more numerous than those who disapproved (Figure 10–3). At times, particularly during the 1980 election and in the middle of 1982, over 50 percent approved of the way that he was doing his job. However in the last months of 1982 his approval rating declined and it is also possible to see a trend of rising disapproval.

Hayden's ratings provide an interesting contrast with those of the Prime Minister. With the exception of the period of the 1980 election, Fraser's disapproval rating was always higher than his approval rating (Figure 10–4). At times the latter sank below 30 percent while the former rose to almost 60 percent. The nadir of Fraser's rating occurred around the time of Peacock's resignation, with another trough occurring in 1982 during the Victorian State elections and the Liberal leadership challenge. There was an erratic but gradual increase in the last six months, but even so nearly 10 percent more disapproved of his performance at the end of 1982.

274

FIGURE 10–3

Aprroval/Disapproval of Performance of Lender of the Opposition 1979–83

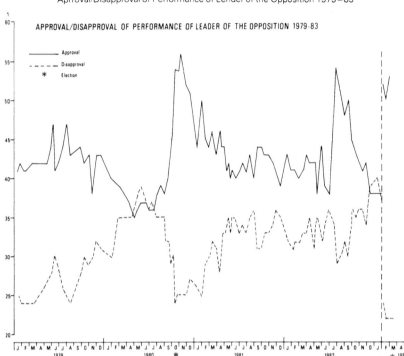

Such figures must, of course, be treated with caution. First, because almost 10 percent had no opinion on Fraser's performance; and 20 percent had none of Hayden, so the figures are not too easily comparable. Secondly, it is not clear in what way an approval rating may have an impact in an electoral contest. Fraser's performance after all, had never been highly rated, but he had still managed to win elections.

What undermined Hayden's position most of all was the question of who would make the best Prime Minister (Table 10–2). The opinion poll figures had been used by Hawke as one of the indicators that a change in the leadership was required. Fraser's consistent lead was obviously of concern to Hayden's supporters.

In itself such a rating might not have been significant. In Britain in 1979, far more people thought that Callaghan would make a better prime minister than Thatcher, yet Thatcher's party won. Similarly in Canada that year Trudeau was considered a more appropriate prime minister than Joe Clark, yet Clark's party won. Leadership approval

FIGURE 10–4
Approval/Disapproval of Performance of Prime Minister 1979–83

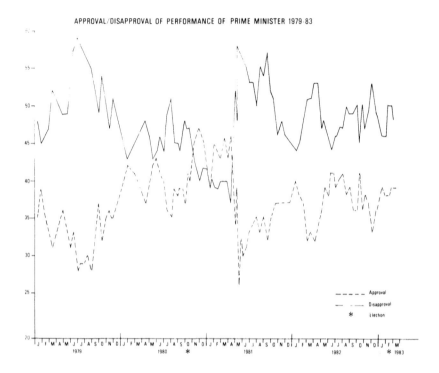

APPROVAL/DISAPPROVAL OF PERFORMANCE OF PRIME MINISTER 1979-83

TABLE 10-2
Who would make the better Prime Minister? (%)

	June 1982	July–Aug. 1982	Oct. 1982	Jan. 1983
Fraser	50	46	44	50
Hayden	31	38	38	38

Source: Morgan Gallup Poll, No. 486, January 1983.

ratings or perceived suitability for the prime ministership do not necessarily translate into votes for the party.

However, Hayden was faced with a problem that those leaders elsewhere did not have: an alternative leader whom the polls showed to be far more popular and an easy means of being removed. Hawke's standing was remarkable. From a time that even predated his entry to Parliament, he was preferred as party leader to Hayden (Table 10-3). What is more, Hawke's popularity was even higher among Labor voters than it was among all voters.

Further, while Hayden trailed Fraser, Hawke never did. When

TABLE 10-3
Preference for leader of the ALP in Federal Parliament (%)

	Aug. 1979	Oct. 1979	Aug. 1980	Apr. 1981	Oct. 1981	Apr. 1982	July 1982	Jan. 1983
Hayden	42	31	27	30	23	28	42	32
Hawke	41	53	57	57	65	56	49	56

Source: Morgan Gallup Poll, No. 1027, February 15, 1983.

electors were asked who they felt would make the better Prime
Minister, they opted for Hawke (table 10-4). Although the question
was not asked often, the results seemed clear.

TABLE 10-4
Preference for Prime Minister (%)

	March 1980	July 1982	Feb. 1983
Fraser	36	42	40
Hawke	53	49	50

Source: Morgan Gallup Poll, No. 486, January 1983.

The general picture provided by the polls suggested that while the
Labor Party was in the lead, its incumbent leader trailed both the
Prime Minister and the alternative within the party. Even if this may
not have been translated into votes, Labor's performance had been
sufficiently limp for those like Button, who wanted to make sure of
electoral victory, to add Hawke's distinctly greater popularity to the
party's firm support. If it was still possible that a drover's dog could
have won, they believed, in part on the evidence of the polls, that
Hawke's accession to the leadership might make it certain.

Explaining the Election

Given an array of unpropitious circumstances, why then did Fraser
and Labor believe that the election could be won by the government if
Fraser were faced by Hayden?

The Flinders by-election result is the obvious immediate cause.
Labor expected to win but failed. That led to considerable introver-
sion and to some scathing press comments. Michelle Grattan in the
Age declared: "Flinders has been an enormous setback to Bill Hayden
and the Labor Party. It is hard to overstate its psychological impact. It
will destabilise the party and produce a fresh crisis of doubt about the

leadership."[27] She argued that Labor members were shell-shocked. The *Sydney Morning Herald* claimed the party was in trouble because Hayden has failed "as a communicator and vote winner".[28] The defeat also left Labor without a credible economic policy. Even though the same issue reported Hawke's angry denial that he was planning a challenge, speculation grew. The lesson to be learned, according to Paul Kelly, was: "If Labor cannot successfully appeal to the electorate on the strength of its policy then it can only resort to appealing through the personality profile of its leader".[29]

These were typical reactions to Flinders. Whether or not Hayden was to be blamed for the defeat the demoralization that followed was an indication of how fragile the self-confidence of Labor was. Despite a series of clear victories in State politics and a consistent lead in the voting intention polls, it only took one defeat to destroy the feeling that the next election could be won.

Flinders, too, boosted the morale of the Liberals and almost certainly added to Fraser's reputation. He, after all, had argued for a general election at the time when Flinders was held; the result, whether or not it could have been translated into national terms, appeared to endorse his instincts. It also seemed to give added weight to the demands for an early poll while the initiative could be maintained.

The various attitudes that led to the events of February 3 probably go much deeper and are much less tangible. In part they are directed by the development of myths within the small elite that operates in or around Parliament House, in the rarefied air of high-level Federal politics. There reputations are made and unmade on the basis of actions and symbols that are hidden from most others. Fraser had the reputation of an instinctive political tactician, with a ruthless streak of opportunism, a record of almost unalloyed success; in Labor circles, it was believed that in any fight, at almost any time, he had the measure of Bill Hayden. Tony Eggleton was seen as the ultimate election organizer, at the head of a well-oiled, heavily funded professional machine, and with the capacity to come from behind to win. To an extent the Liberals too subscribed to these myths. Hence the Labor fears, stoked by Flinders, led to the change of leader—a change whose impact and timing was even more effective than the party could have hoped.

Yet finally the timing of the election was the decision of one man, Malcolm Fraser. In part an understanding of the decision is assisted by an appreciation of Fraser's approach to politics. In a recent article, "Fraser and Fraserism", Graham Little has skilfully used the tools to psychoanalysis to explain Fraser's approach. He argues that Fraser's appreciation of politics was narrow. Although he expressed an "exaggerated concern with propriety", that was within strictly conventional understandings of the way the system worked. Little claims that politics to Fraser is about competition, about ensuring that all other forces are kept strictly under control; as Little puts in, "Fraser's politics is based on competition under rule, contest-and-control". The result, he argues, is that Fraser's approach is always divisive; he rejects any ideas of conciliation and consensus as indications of weakness. "His thinking is always dichotomous, sharpening contest and legitimising control".[30] An obsession to gain a reassertion of an electoral mandate and to take advantage of Labor's weakness can readily be understood as a consequence of this competitive approach to politics. With Flinders a hopeful portent, such a chance to maintain control might not recur.

There were, perhaps, good political reasons for an early election, particularly if the economy were to get worse. Yet Fraser's frequent flirting with the idea of an early poll in the later months of 1982 and the calling of one in 1983 can best be understood by his own style, his desire to control the political environment, to keep demoralized enemies down. His ruthlessness had succeeded in the past; his timing had often been correct. This time he miscalculated. The result was the end of his political career.

Notes

1 For an account of the events leading to Hayden's dismissal, see *National Times*, March 13–19, 1983. For accounts of the election, published in the same month as the election, see Craig McGregor, *Time of Testing: The Bob Hawke Victory* (Melbourne: Penguin, 1983); Robert Haupt with Michelle Grattan, *31 Days to Power: Hawke's Victory* (Sydney: George Allen and Unwin, 1983); and Anne Summers, *Gamble for Power* (Sydney: Nelson, 1983).
2 *Sydney Morning Herald*, March 10, 1983.
3 For an account, see Russell Schneider, *The Colt from Kooyong* (Sydney: Angus & Robertson, 1981, pp. 86–88). Robinson had earlier resigned from the Cabinet, announcing reputedly that he would not work with "that big bastard" any longer. He was persuaded to reconsider his decision and rejoined the Cabinet before Parliament met and any public statements were made. See Don Markwell, "The Politics of Ministerial Resignations", in Patrick Weller and Dean Jaensch (eds) *Responsible Government in Australia* (Melbourne: Drummond, 1980), pp. 86–92.
4 For the letter, see *Age*, April 16, 1981.
5 *Commonwealth Parliamentary Debates*, April 28, 1981, 1607–1614.
6 For a more detailed account, see Patrick Weller, "The Vulnerability of Prime Ministers: A Comparative Analysis", *Parliamentary Affairs*, 36 (1),

Winter 1983, pp. 96–117.

7 See, for instance, *National Times*, May 10–16, 1981.

8 Colin Seymour-Ure, "Rumour and Politics", *Politics* 17 (2) November 1982, pp. 1–9, for an account of the events.

9 For a discussion of the decision to call a double dissolution, see below p. 318.

10 R. V. Garland, "Relations between Ministers and Departments", ACT, RIPA, *Newsletter*, 3 (3), August 1976, p. 24.

11 Quoted in *Australian Financial Review*, September 22, 1982.

12 *Age*, September 22, 1982.

13 The report of the committee *The Review of Commonwealth Administration* was published in February 1983.

14 *Age*, October 12, 1982.

15 ibid.

16 See Richard Lucy, "Wran Acts: The N.S.W. Election of 1981", *Politics*, 17 (1), May 1982, pp. 100–10. Of the eight Liberal leaders, one retired after ten years as Premier, two lost their seats in elections and four were removed in party room coups.

17 See Brian J. Costar and Colin A. Hughes (eds), *Labor to Office: The Victorian State Election of 1982* (Melbourne: Drummond, 1983).

18 Blair Badcock, "Was the South Australian Labor Party Struck by a Bus", *Politics*, 17 (1), May 1982, pp. 77–84.

19 Dean Jaensch, "The South Australian Election", *Politics*, 18 (1), May 1983.

20 Graham Smith, "The Tasmanian House of Assembly Elections of 1982", *Politics*, 17 (2), November 1982, pp. 121–7.

21 Patrick Weller and Michelle Grattan, *Can Ministers Cope?* (Melbourne: Hutchinson, 1981), p. 95.

22 Ministerial Statement, *Review of Commonwealth Functions* (Canberra: AGPS, 1981), p. 1.

23 *Australian Financial Review*, July 31, 1981.

24 *Age*, July 8, 1982.

25 *Australian Financial Review*, July 7, 1982.

26 *Age*, July 8, 1982.

27 *Age*, December 6, 1982.

28 *Sydney Morning Herald*, December 6, 1982.

29 ibid.

30 Graham Little, "Fraser and Fraserism", *Meanjin*, 21 (3), September 1983, pp. 293, 306.

The author would like to thank Virginia Cook for her help in finding material for this chapter.

11
An Election About Perceptions

Colin A. Hughes

Once it was known that there would be an election and that it would be held in only four weeks' time, the next question asked was how closely would it resemble previous Federal elections. Throughout the campaign commentators were preoccupied with such comparisons:

> the spectators watching this race, particularly the professionals, politicians, party workers, pollsters and journalists, largely see it as a rerun of the 1977 and 1980 election races. It is as though Australian elections with Labor trying to depose Malcolm Fraser have fallen into a fixed pattern, clearly established, and that 1983 must also fit the pattern. The pattern ... is that Labor launches the campaign with gusto and looks a winner. For a brief period in 1977, Gough Whitlam headed Fraser but he was run down at the end of the first week. Then in 1980 Bill Hayden bolted with a big lead, thought it was won, played safe, and lost it right on the line.[1]

After the 1982 Budget, the polls had suggested that the Liberals were only about 2 percentage points behind Labor. During the 1980 campaign Fraser had regained 4 percentage points. Such calculations encouraged the enthusiasm for an early election late in 1982,[2] and they were very much in evidence throughout the 1983 campaign. Moreover, to a limited extent they proved sound in the event. The gap did close in the final week of the campaign, as discussed below; the trouble for the coalition parties in 1983 was that the gap had been exceptionally large and it had started to close too late in the campaign.

In a frank postmortem interview, the Liberal campaign director, Tony Eggleton, agreed that he would have preferred the election later

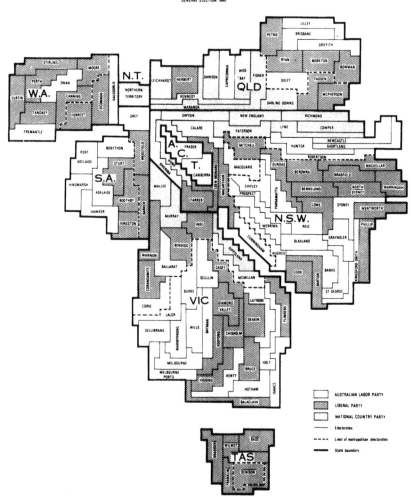

AUSTRALIAN HOUSE OF REPRESENTATIVES
GENERAL ELECTION 1980

AUSTRALIAN LABOR PARTY
LIBERAL PARTY
NATIONAL COUNTRY PARTY
Electorates
Limit of metropolitan electorates
State boundary

282

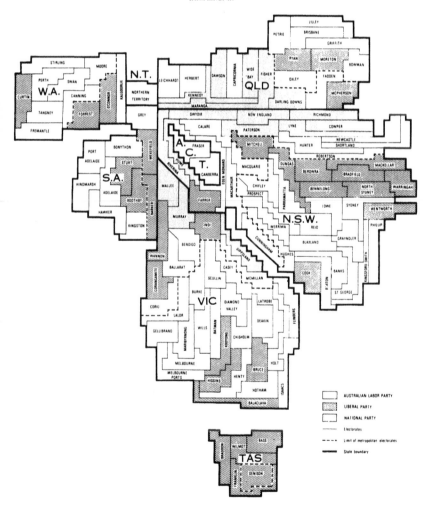

AUSTRALIAN HOUSE OF REPRESENTATIVES
GENERAL ELECTION 1983

AUSTRALIAN LABOR PARTY
LIBERAL PARTY
NATIONAL PARTY
Electorates
Limit of metropolitan electorates
State boundary

283

in 1983. Most of the preparatory work done in 1982 was no longer relevant once the ALP changed leaders and a strategy for beating Hawke had to be rushed together, developed as the campaign proceeded. Another six months would, so Eggleton thought, have allowed the time necessary to cut Hawke down to size, while even another week of campaigning time could have saved some seats, though probably not enough to have won the election. The campaign had been characterized by volatility: "Things always change during an election but they changed more in this campaign than I have ever known".[3] Somewhat paradoxically the Labor campaign team found itself less handicapped by the sudden replacement of Hayden with Hawke. All its preliminary planning was in hand, and only some changes in emphasis had to be made.[4]

One consequence of the speed with which the election was called was that the electoral rolls were automatically closed by the issue of the writs for the election of members of Parliament at the end of the day following the Governor-General's agreement to the dissolution. Enrollment is compulsory in Australia, as is voting, but normally there is a gap of days if not weeks between firm news that an election is about to be held and the issue of writs and closing of rolls. During that time tens of thousands of electors get onto the rolls for the first time, or modify their enrollments following changes of address. It is impossible to say how many new voters were prevented from getting on the rolls, though the media spoke vaguely of hundreds of thousands. As the Morgan Gallup Poll surveys during February showed the ALP doing about 10 percentage points better with the under-35 age group than with the over-35s, and as the under-35s would have been more affected by the sudden closing of the rolls, it is reasonable to assume that the ALP was disadvantaged. It is most unlikely that this was a consideration in the Prime Minister's mind when he rushed through his double dissolution. A challenge was mounted in the High Court to have the rolls reopened, resting on the plaintiffs' ability to secure enrollment on State electoral rolls in the meantime and the constitutional guarantee that anyone entitled to vote at a State election is entitled to vote at a Federal election. This, the High Court held, had been intended to cover a transitional period while the federation was being established, and the application failed.

Campaign Machinery

In the main both major parties quickly re-established the same sort of campaign organization that they had employed at previous elections. The Liberal headquarters was located as usual in Melbourne and Labor's as usual in Sydney; Liberal staff numbered about thirty, Labor about twenty. For the fourth consecutive election the Liberal advertising agency was D'Arcy, Macmanus and Masius, already involved in the Western Australian State election campaign, and on this occasion the party employed four separate research organizations. There was more use of telephone-polling than ever before, especially to keep up with swinging voters in the four capital cities where most marginal seats were at risk. The element of the Liberal organization that attracted most interest was the elaborate arrangements for monitoring the media on an hourly basis to record and analyze and try to pick up slips and contradictions from the Labor camp. In 1980 such monitoring, then on a smaller scale, had spotted a casual statement by an ALP shadow minister about a capital gains tax, and the party had used that statement with such effect that it was credited by some with saving the election.[5] As will appear, the Liberal and Labor campaigns in 1983 were exceptionally interactive with a variety of issues, often relatively trivial in substance, unexpectedly erupting, being pursued for a day or so, and then dropped. One journalist called it "space invaders" and "the politics of zap", and reflecting on the campaign afterwards the ALP Federal secretary, Bob McMullan, wondered about

> the style of our opponents who had so much electronic gear, so many people monitoring it, so many people with input that those at one end of the line had no idea what those at the other end of the line were doing. Our opponents seemed to know more about what our people were saying than we did. They seemed to be dominated by their technology. They were waiting for the technology to tell them the answers with this super monitoring.[6]

As usual the ALP had less money to spend, probably about $2 million by the national organization with the State branches spending a similar amount. Estimates for the Liberal national budget ranged between $3 million and $5 million, with additional expenditure by the party below the national level and by the National Party. At least 60 percent of advertising expenditure would have gone to television, where costs had risen by half since the last election in 1980, perhaps 25 percent on print advertising and the balance on radio. One new campaign technique tried by the Liberals was a personalized letter, produced by computer, from the Prime Minister to all electors in eight marginal divisions in New South Wales and Victoria. Its cost was estimated at $120,000–150,000 in New South Wales alone, and as the

Liberal Party lost all eight seats its future in Australian campaigns may still be doubtful. A rather more rewarding use of the computer for Liberals in New South Wales has been as an adjunct to fund-raising; within a week of the election announcement the State branch had sent out 14,000 letters seeking financial support.[7]

Television is now the most trusted and the most credible medium for politics in Australia.[8] Its importance had a substantial effect on the conduct of the campaign, with suitable events managed to provide action for the early evening news programs. Evening meetings which twenty years earlier had featured prominently in campaigns have now virtually disappeared because they fall outside network time.[9] Editorial comment in newspapers was relatively low key. A survey of press opinion at the end of the campaign reported one major daily, Melbourne's *Age*, supporting the ALP, the small circulation but influential *Financial Review* neutral, the *Sydney Morning Herald* "by a fine margin" for the coalition, and all other capital city morning papers for the coalition.[10] It was noticeable that the Murdoch group of papers became much cooler in their support of the coalition as the campaign progressed and the government's cause appeared less encouraging. A similar reading of the omens may have encouraged some journalists to be increasingly blunt with the Prime Minister in public, and this in turn led Fraser himself and other government supporters to be more critical of the press, culminating in a number of exchanges during the Prime Minister's last appearance during the campaign at a televised National Press Club luncheon.[11]

Only Four Weeks

Normally an Australian national election campaign runs for three weeks, preceded by a period of less formal politicking of uncertain duration. Theorizing about recent elections identified the latter part of the second week of the three as critical, the point at which the swing back to the government of the day began when its previously disgruntled supporters began to weigh the alternative and find it wanting. In 1983 there was only one week preceding the launching of the campaign; that was dominated by the new leader of the ALP who drew virtually all media coverage. During that week the Liberal strategists hastily re-examined their needs, and decided to shape their campaign around three themes—economic management and responsibility, union power, and leadership. When the party had been contemplating an election after the 1982 Budget, its private polls had suggested that although unemployment was rated as the most serious problem facing the nation, high taxes and high interest rates were seen as the issues most affecting respondents personally.[12] By the beginning of 1983 the employment situation had conspicuously worsened, and some action would be expected from a government seeking re-election. This was embodied in the first slogan the Liberals unveiled, "We're Not Waiting for the World" (subsequently incorporated in a campaign song), which was intended to show that despite previous suggestions that a turn-around in the Australian economy would be dependent on improvement in the economies of the world's major trading nations, notably the United States, initiatives could and should come from the Australian government.

Such overt campaigning as there was during that preliminary week began with Hawke's speedy withdrawal from a position that he had previously used to denigrate Hayden's campaigning capacity, the need for a capital gains tax. Hawke stated that he now accepted the party platform and was persuaded that it would work. Adequate enforcement of existing provisions of income tax legislation would tax speculative capital gains effectively. When Fraser held a press conference to launch some preliminary attacks on Hawke's credibility, he was pressed to say whether his government would pursue the sales tax bills which constituted nine of the thirteen bills that had justified the double dissolution. His answers were evasive; subsequently he stated that if sales taxes were introduced, the tax burden would be offset by income tax reductions; and later still he abandoned the measures completely. Such responses enabled Hawke to claim that either the Prime Minister had lied to the Governor-General when he asserted in his first letter seeking the double dissolution that the bills were "of importance to the Government's budgetary . . . policies", or else he was lying to the public now in promising to drop them. The episode was an early indication that Fraser was unable to shape the campaign to his own wishes, and that Hawke would be able frequently to turn attacks back onto Fraser. Scoring of that week went definitely in Hawke's favour.

The first week of the critical three-week campaign began with the policy speeches delivered by Fraser on Tuesday, February 15 and by Hawke on Wednesday, February 16. Even before then Hawke had engaged in something of a dry run. A substantial policy document entitled "Quality of Government" anticipated ALP proposals for machinery of government questions, while a series of policy meetings displayed Hawke, the articulate spokesman, flanked by appropriate shadow ministers. Finally, in company with his two principal economic policy shadow ministers, Paul Keating and Ralph Willis, he announced the ALP's "National Recovery and Reconstruction Plan", a document whose compilation had been under way for months.[13] Its cautious tone undercut Liberal counter-attacks which attempted to saddle Hawke with the record of the Whitlam years, for example in a full-page advertisement captioned "OH, NO, THE HAWKE SHOW IS A WHITLAM REPLAY!", illustrated by an old photograph of a grinning Hawke seated behind the former Labor leader with the warning: "Labor wants to spend money our country hasn't got. So you'd have to pay again for their promises. Don't risk it with Labor".

Fraser's policy speech on February 15 picked its way gingerly around explanations of what had gone wrong with the economy, and in passing tried to attach as much blame as possible to Hawke:

> Since 1975 our policies have done much to rebuild Australia. Because of our policies, Australia was one of the last countries hit by the world recession ... When the world recession finally hit Australia, its effect was greatly worsened by two things. The drought is one of the worst in Australia's history. And in the last year or two Australia has suffered a totally unjustified wages explosion, brought about by ACTU policies laid down when the present leader of the Labor Party was its president. The world recession would have done Australia far less damage if the unions had not pushed their demands for higher wages and shorter hours beyond the endurance of industry.
>
> This election will decide whether Australia goes the Labor way, with rampant union power, soaring inflation and worsening unemployment; or whether Australia puts the recession behind it and gets back on the road of more jobs and rising living standards.[14]

One newspaper wrote that, as a policy speech, it was "vintage Menzies", the striking feature being "its modesty, both of claims and of promises ... a promise to continue to muddle through, without too much change and without the certainties of behaviour which a Labor Government would threaten".[15] The government's difficulty, as the same paper's editor wrote subsequently, was that it had "to stand on and defend a record which is a sorry story of political trimming, abandoned principles, failure to cope with external changes, and bungling".[16] One of the Liberals' three themes, economic management and responsibility, was a two-edged sword, but nevertheless they dared not abandon a weapon that successive Liberal leaders had always relied upon.

Hawke's own speech the following day was not very much more substantial, though a promise of modest income tax cuts benefiting all but the wealthiest handful (those with taxable incomes over $60,000 per annum) and the promise of more jobs, especially for the young, held out some hope of better times. Much of the speech's emphasis was on where things were going wrong: the proportion of home-owners was falling; living standards were falling; economic growth had stopped and gone into reverse, and the Australian rate was well behind the average for the industrialized West. A fatal blow was dealt to the Liberal slogan—"There's no question of not waiting for the rest of the world. The rest of the world has left us behind!"—and an ALP television commercial hammered home the point, showing a person labeled "Australia" backing down an escalator whilst those bearing other OECD labels went steadily up.[17] Central to Labor's economic proposals was the immediate holding of "a national economic summit conference, fully representative of Australian industry, the Australian workforce and the Australian people through their electoral governments". Such a proposal had been around for some time, and both the ALP and the trade unions had tried unsuccessfully to press it on the Fraser government. Fraser and most of his senior ministers were deeply suspicious of "the Melbourne Club" of employers' organizations, trade unions and public servants involved in industrial relations who, they felt, inclined to Keynesian rather than monetarist strategies and were too quick to buy industrial peace at the price of wage rises. Hawke, whose working life had been spent in the atmosphere of tripartism, was naturally drawn to an extension of arrangements which he had mastered in the industrial sphere to a wider, macroeconomic realm. But as a proposal, it could be argued, the summit was no more than a promise of talk, not of specific action. There would have been scope for a vigorous coalition attack on Labor policies, or lack thereof, at this point in the campaign, but nature intervened.

On Wednesday, February 16, disastrous bushfires in a number of areas of South Australia and Victoria took seventy lives, rendered thousands homeless, dealt the economies of the two States a serious blow, and dominated television news for several days. Amid such a national disaster the continuation of party politics would have appeared indecent. The Prime Minister turned his attention to the part the Federal government could play in assisting the two State governments to provide relief to fire victims, and for four days removed himself and the coalition campaign machine from the stage. Hawke was equally constrained, though he lacked a useful alternative role to which he could turn. Commentators differed as to the likely effect of the fires: would they show Fraser standing above party and doing worthwhile things, or would they encourage the feeling of national solidarity in a time of crisis which Hawke was trying to cultivate? After the event it seems more likely that the fires damaged Fraser's campaign by preventing an immediate counter-attack on Hawke and costing him momentum which he badly needed to overtake Hawke's substantial lead. With only 31 days from dissolution to election, the loss of four days mattered.

Before the policy speeches were delivered Liberal advertising had retained some positive elements. For example, full-page advertisements on the day Fraser would deliver his speech still carried the banner "We're not waiting for the world", listed known iniatives and promised more to come that evening, and concluded: "The return of the Fraser Government, with its proven economic management and experience will see Australia pressing ahead ..." Re-appraisal of the situation suggested now that the only way to narrow the gap, which might be widening and was certainly not closing, was to hammer away at ALP credibility on economic management and union control. Early attempts to portray Hawke as untried and unpredictable and to point out the record of industrial disputes during the period he had been president of the ACTU had never really taken off. What had seemed a windfall when Hawke was photographed accepting a $50,000 campaign donation from the left-wing Amalgamated Metal, Foundry and Shipwrights Union and its leaders, Laurie Carmichael and John Halfpenny, was lost when Hawke produced a Liberal solicitation of funds which ended "All donations totally confidential". Moreover given that Hawke's record in trade union affairs had often been characterized by clashes with left-wing unions, it would be difficult to convince anyone familiar with industrial matters that he would be a willing or an easy victim of the left. The weekend after the fires another consequence of the decision to hold the election early damaged Liberal hopes still further. When the Western Australian Premier, Ray O'Connor, called a State election for February 19, he made it very clear that he did not wish the Prime Minister to take any part in the campaign. The Victorian Liberals had been equally inhospitable with their State election early in 1982, but Fraser's abstention had not prevented a calamitous loss. Having a Federal election overlaid on a State election, coupled with the injection of a popular ex-native son in the shape of Bob Hawke to reinforce a new State leader of the ALP, produced a swing of 8 percent to Labor, probably larger than would have been the case had there been no Federal election called. Converting the State voting figures to Federal divisions indicated that four, possibly five, House of Representative seats would be lost. That gloomy news fed damagingly back into the Liberal's national campaign.

Resuming campaigning after the bushfire moratorium, Fraser

sought again to drive home the theme of union power over a Labor government by releasing the text of the agreement Hawke was about to put to a meeting with the ACTU to seal the party's agreement with the trade union movement for an incomes policy. An earlier attempt to exploit industrial disputes had come unstuck over documentation; when the Prime Minister asserted that a strike by storemen and packers affecting pharmaceutical supplies had caused a shortage of vital drugs in Victorian hospitals, it was quickly established that there were no such shortages. Now his accusation of the improper surrender of government responsibility to the unions, based on the text he released to the press, collapsed when it was shown that the final three pages of the original document, omitted from the Liberals' version in circumstances which were never satisfactorily explained (though a boobytrap by Labor was postulated by some), had promised equal consultation of employer groups by a Labor government. Hawke when he subsequently met with the unions to ratify the agreement warned them:

> We as a government will certainly not be your handmaiden and this historic document makes it clear you do not expect that. In regard to every one of these issues, wages, tax, health, immigration, you have understood, agreed and take it as proper ... that there will be just as much opportunity for consultation with the employers as with you.[18]

The Liberals continued to try to press the point, sometimes with doubtful effect as when the Prime Minister on the day of Hawke's meeting with the unions issued a press release which read *in toto*: "This is the day Mr. Hawke has to go to his union masters to announce his policy". Even so constant a supporter of the government as the Adelaide *Advertiser* could merely head such a story: "20 words from Fraser, with a hint of panic".[19] Indeed the whole campaign was turning into something quite unlike any recent Australian election. Social welfare issues had receded so far into the background that when the Australian Council of Social Service (ACOSS) issued its pre-election appraisal of the alternative policies, the document was entitled "It's Obvious They Don't Care". ACOSS complained that both parties were providing more to middle and higher income groups through concessions such as tax cuts and assistance to home buyers than they were giving the poor by way of support.[20] Foreign affairs and defense, which had been for the coalition what social welfare normally was for the ALP, were equally quiet, in large part because of the extent of bipartisan agreement.[21] There was an early, and unsuccessful, attempt to show that Hawke would have to recall Australian troops from the Sinai peace-keeping force (with a view to reducing his popularity with Jewish voters for his strong pro-Israel stand). There was an equally unprofitable attempt to extrapolate from Hawke's statement that he was prepared to review the ANZUS treaty, by ignoring his proviso that this would depend on agreement from the United States and New Zealand, the proposition that he would tear up the American alliance. The media ignored the story. Eventually, late in the campaign, the Minister of Defence claimed than an ALP move to restrict access to Australian ports to US ships that were nuclear-powered or carrying nuclear weapons, a matter on which Hayden had been caught off balance previously, could reduce the opportunity for money-saving offsets on defense equipment Australia bought from the United States. It, too, dropped like a stone.

By the end of the second week of the campaign proper, Liberal strategists began to feel that the central issues they had wanted to run were getting lost. They tried to revive ancient fears of Labor extravagance with full-page advertisements showing Hawke's face twisted in an exceptionally demonic expression beneath captions like "OVER-NIGHT THIS MAN HAS GONE ON A MULTIBILLION DOLLAR SPENDING SPREE. Don't risk it with Labor" and "HAWKE'S UNION GOVERNMENT AND WILD SPENDING! You would pay for it. Don't Bankrupt Australia with Labor." The Treasurer, John Howard, had originally estimated the cost of Labor promises at $4,100 million; that figure, issued on February 21, was revised on March 3 by the addition of a further $200 million; the Liberals' own promises were costed at a mere $567 million. But the ALP put out its own figures which set the bill for its promises at a mere $1,500 million and the coalition's at $6,000 million, and (apart from some attempts to get closer to the truth tucked away in the back pages of the more conscientious newspapers) the battle of where the money was coming from failed to confer obvious advantage on either side.

What was to prove significant, though much later, was amplification Howard had provided on February 21 when fixing the cost of Labor promises at $4,100 million. Such a sum, he warned, would push the budgetary deficit up to $10,000 million, and that would damage private capital inflow into the country, damage private competition in the loan markets and adversely affect interest rate expectations.[22] Like most Western countries, Australia had heard a lot about the monetary benefits of a balanced Budget and the dangers of deficits in recent years. After all Mr Micawber who had first contrasted "result happiness" and "result misery" in such matters subsequently settled and prospered in Australia. It was said in the days preceding the election decision that one of the factors pushing the government towards an early election was the certainty of a huge blow-out in the 1983–84 deficit, a figure of $7,000 million being mentioned, but then the matter had been forgotten. Suddenly in the middle of the final week of the campaign Hawke began to drop hints that there was something odd about the deficit figures which, in the light of the widely held belief that the 1982 Budget had been forced on an unwilling Treasury Department by a government motivated by political considerations which had started to backslide from fiscal rectitude, raised suspicions that leaking was under way.[23] By that point Hawke was sufficiently certain of victory to wish to free himself from overly firm commitments, and the deficit would provide an admirable excuse:

> If we get into Government and we have the national economic summit conference and the people of Australia find out that Mr Fraser and Mr Howard haven't been telling the truth—that the budget deficit is very much higher . . . and there is consensus out of the summit that there would have to be some modification of our programmes, then obviously we would accede to that.[24]

After the election, one of the first acts of the incoming government was to call for up-to-date figures on the 1983–84 deficit. It then became public that the bureaucrats' expectation was $10,000 million, and that figure had been known to the former Treasurer over the period when the ALP was being blasted for extravagant promises which he said would produce that size deficit. It was alleged, and not denied, that when the figure had come into Howard's hands, he had wished to release it, but had been directed not to by a member of the Prime Minister's staff. Though Howard tried to distance himself from the Prime Minister in the affair, the episode left his political reputation as "Honest John" the worse for wear. On the assumption that Howard's close association with Fraser and his policies would have been a handicap sufficient to deny him succession to the Liberal leadership after Fraser retired even without the deficit scandal, the long-term importance of the concealed figure is the excuse it gave Hawke to re-examine expensive promises. Following the 1972 election Gough Whitlam had insisted that each and every element in Labor policy was covered by the mandate, a firm commitment for the government to implement it and an obligation on the opposition to accept it; even before election day it was unlikely that Hawke would be making such a claim for the policies of 1983.

In the final week of the campaign, the Liberal attack concentrated on union power and economic management. Observers agreed that the Prime Minister displayed an effectiveness which had previously been missing, and that his last public appearance before the statutory blackout (a requirement which he had always defended) prevented the electronic media carrying political news, at the National Press Club luncheon, was a positive performance that ought to have been tried much earlier. Despite the evidence of the polls, commentators were unwilling to suppose him defeated, mainly because of past recoveries but partly at least for the tenacity he was still displaying:

> Fraser cannot be written off because he never stops fighting. The man can no more stop fighting than he can admit mistakes. He ploughs on regardless, refusing even to contemplate defeat let alone admit it. Fraser is not just a bastard. He is a heroic bastard in the Australian tradition because he always ends up fighting alone—totally alone as he was this week. Lesser men were keeping their distance.[25]

Somewhere during the campaign "We're Not Waiting for the World" had been quietly dropped in favour of "Don't Bankrupt Australia With Labor". Advertising tried to particularize the threat, for example warning of "Labor's $16 a week grab" by calculating "the extra burden every Australian household would carry to pay for Labor's $4,000 million worth of promises is $15.91 per household, per week", to which had to be added the additional costs of higher inflation, higher interest rates and higher taxes.[26] Fraser had to backtrack on some of his attacks on Labor's economic integrity, for example when he first claimed that a Labor advertisement promising tax cuts was a "fraud and a cruel deception" because at least 2.5 million taxpayers would pay more under the proposals. He had ignored the proposed change in tax threshold which made the Labor promise correct. The point was taken, and the final Liberal advertisement, responding to Hawke's new temporizing about what Labor might do, warned: "He's started off promising tax cuts. Now he's talking higher taxes. Even his proposed tax scales would tax average Australians more on every dollar earned. How can you trust what he promises?" The attack had shifted to the marginal operation of the ALP's proposed revision of tax scales.

A much more damaging example of overkill was his response to a comment by the shadow Treasurer, Paul Keating, about the way that bank holdings could be used to finance a government deficit. Fraser had touched on the subject once before, in a radio program, without its attracting interest. Then on February 22, in the second week of the campaign, in a talkback show in response to a caller (subsequently identified as a campaign worker at ALP headquarters) who pressed him as to how a Labor government could "touch" her savings in the bank, he replied that a government could pass laws to give directions to the banks. Even while the repercussions of that statement were starting, he flew from Sydney to Melbourne and at a street rally responded to hostile interjectors with a stronger version. Would Hawke undertake not to reimpose death duties, expressed dramatically as a threat to "tax the savings of the dead"? Moreover, the Prime Minister warned, those who thought their savings were safe in the banks should think again: "Well, under Labor it'd be safer under your bed than it would be in the banks. They would be robbing the savings of the people to pay for their mad extravagant promises. Whichever way they did it, it would up interest rates, it would send businessmen bankrupt and cause massive increases in unemployment."[27] A spokesman for the banks sought to reassure depositors that their money was safe and ended up in a lengthy telephone discussion with the Prime Minister. The text of their conversation was subsequently released in an attempt to establish that what had been said was not untrue, but its effect was to show how hard the Prime Minister could lean on someone who got in his way. Several Liberal backbenchers publicly criticized Fraser's handling of the incident, and Hawke once again found ridicule the most effective weapon by asking how money could be put under the bed when the Communists were already there. Fraser remained publicly unrepentant. The Labor platform said that the party should "take the necessary steps to ensure that the Labor Government has sufficient control over the share of the country's savings required for funding priority programs", and that made it perfectly plain "that the Labor Party is looking for the savings of the people to fund their programs". The word "rob" he had used was correct; it was graphic, and only by using such language had he caught the attention of the media to a serious matter. The Treasurer, who called the language "colorful", backed as far away as he safely could, and even Murdoch's *Australian* condemned the statement in unusually forthright terms.

In marked contrast with the hard slogging, and frequent mistakes, of the Liberal campaign, the Labor Party floated along in a different world suffused in a rosy glow. Gaffes such as those which plagued the government from beginning to end of the campaign could be numbered on the fingers of one Labor hand. The shadow minister for tourism condemned high "penalty" rates for overtime which handicapped the tourist industry, which might have given offence to the relevant unions. If it did, they stayed silent. The deputy leader, Lionel Bowen, made encouraging noises about the possibility of growing sugarcane in the north of Western Australia, even though the party's rural policy for the campaign had specifically rejected the idea. Electors in marginal seats in cane-growing northern and central Queensland might have taken offence, but didn't and the ALP won the two seats in which it had had prospects. Paul Keating got himself into hot water by saying, with complete honesty, that Labor intended to go for economic growth "with a positive incomes policy and all I can say is that if we are elected we'll do our best to make it work. I'm not sure we can make it work but we're going to give it a good shot." Immediately the Prime Minister was holding an airport tarmac press conference to denounce such a state of affairs: "Two and a half years putting together a policy and they are not sure they can make it work". The next day Andrew Peacock told the same radio interviewer who had got Keating into trouble: "I don't know that any politician has said, 'We can honestly guarantee that our policies will work'", and the crisis had passed. Journalists who had once been sceptical of Hawke's calibre as a potential Prime Minister—when he had challenged Hayden in 1982 a number of harsh assessments and unflattering comparisons had been published—increasingly warmed to him as the campaign progressed, and his crowds were larger and more enthusiastic than any new national party leader could have reasonably expected.

Specific policies or undertakings mattered little compared to the sharp contrasts between the alternative prime ministers and their ideological positions. One journalist asked: "How are we to choose between a party ruled by a man obsessed with order and a party inspired by a man possessed of a vision?"[28] and subsequently elaborated the distinction:

> Mr Fraser assumes that Australians must be intimidated, frightened, into supporting his party ... Mr Fraser's claim is that only the Liberal-National Party coalition stands between civilisation and chaos. A corollary of this view is that human beings are selfish, egoistic and competitive and should submit, for their own good, to the rule of superior governors ... Mr Hawke, on the other hand, assumes that Australians will respond to encouragement, that they are essentially optimists who can be persuaded to modify the egoistic pursuit of self-interest ... Mr Hawke is appealing to a very Australian tradition—the tradition of self confidence combined with mutual responsibility.[29]

However, despite interest in the sharply opposing views of the two leaders, the media rarely applied the label of "corporatist" to Hawke's vision of a reconciliation of capital and labour embodied in an economic summit which would lead on to permanent machinery, etc. An exception was one editorial in the market-disposed *Financial Review* which expressed concern at the likely stifling of competition and initiative within such a corporatist consensus.[30]

The Liberal organization's postmortem report concluded that after five years the coalition was perceived to have failed to meet expectations held of it, while Hawke offered a fresh approach: "It was an election about perceptions rather than about platforms and policies".[31] A certain amount of evidence exists as to what voters thought about issues which derive from platforms and policies. It indicates considerable stability in voter perceptions and so could be a useful corrective for any suggestions of a substantial change in public opinions apparent in the preceding pages. Survey data for the two elections discussed in this book, 1980 and 1983, are available; the stimulus was a card listing a number of issues (21 in 1980, 20 in 1983) and voters were asked which of those would be most important to them personally. Nevertheless the two sets of figures in Table 11-1 confirm what was fairly obvious during the campaign: unemployment and interest rates mattered more in 1983 than in 1980. Unemployment had already been the most important issue in 1980, but its lead over inflation as an issue widened considerably in 1983. Increases were uniform for the three groups of voters on unemployment, just as they were in respect of concern about interest rates which moved from being a fairly unimportant issue in 1980 to fourth most important in 1983. What is more surprising is that the wages freeze, which had appeared so significant in the run-up to the Prime Minister's decision to hold the election and was reputed to have

TABLE 11-1
Main Election Issues 1980, 1983 (%)

| | Voting Intention | | | | | | | |
| | 1980 | | | | 1983 | | | |
	All	L-NP	ALP	AD	All	L-NP	ALP	AD
Reduce unemployment	41	35	48	40	55	49	63	55
Reduce the rate of inflation	26	28	26	24	31	35	30	28
Be tough with unions with bad strike records	21	33	13	14	26	40	15	29
Reduce interest rates	6	6	6	7	21	22	21	22
More for the needy and aged	20	15	24	15	20	17	21	22
Reduce personal income tax	17	19	16	17	18	17	19	17
Cost of health insurance	17	14	18	25	17	15	20	15
Assistance to families and children	12	9	14	11	13	13	14	11
The price of petrol	16	14	17	18	11	10	13	13
Control/freeze wages and salaries	14	20	9	13	11	16	8	9
Develop Australia's mineral resources	12	17	8	15	9	13	6	10
Spend more on defence	12	16	10	8	7	9	6	12

Source: Morgan Gallup Poll, Finding No. 760, September 1980 and *Bulletin*, March 2, 1983.

worked so well in the Flinders by-election, rated on a par with the non-specific issue of controlling wages and salaries in 1980. Perhaps the freeze was an idea whose time had already passed two weeks before the election; possibly it had never mattered all that much to the electorate and the media enthusiasm for anything new had blown it up unrealistically. Some issues, moral causes almost in the way they used to be presented, which had helped the coalition in the 1960s—minerals development and defense—declined still further between 1980 and 1983. But overall one is left with a suspicion that electorate demand reacts slowly to the changing supply of issues coming from the political parties.

Much more important in determining the result of the 1983 election were perceptions about the major parties and their leaders. Here we do not have access to figures though the leaking of the Liberal report provides an insight as to what they showed:

> In summary, the research told us that: The electorate was disillusioned and doubtful of our capacity; the swinging voter had little or no perception of Government achievement—and cared less; the electorate was concerned about tomorrow, not yesterday; there was grave worry about unemployment—and this was increasingly seen as a *personal* issue as well as a national issue; the electorate was attracted by Labor's prices and incomes policy (they saw it as better and fairer than the wages pause); they were looking for some hope and light at the end of the tunnel; they found Bob Hawke an attractive proposition, but with some reservations; in almost all "issue areas" they believed Labor would perform better than the coalition Government; they didn't think the Fraser Government would improve its game; while a Hawke Government could be risky, it was probably worth a try after seven years with the coalition in Canberra.[32]

As the report's author, Tony Eggleton, said: "It seems fairly clear now that the electorate had made up its mind and indeed the emergence of Mr Hawke gave a focal point and a momentum was all that was required for people who thought it was time for the other side to have a go".[33]

Some Sideshows

To this point the account of the 1983 campaign has focussed exclusively on the two largest parties, Liberal and Labor, and almost as exclusively on the leaders of those parties, Malcolm Fraser and Bob

Hawke. That was how the campaign appeared at the time, and how it still appears in retrospect. The campaign really was a one-ring circus, and very little happened elsewhere to distract attention from what was taking place in the center of that ring. The Liberals' regular ally, the National Party, was exceptionally subdued even though its rural constituents in the eastern States had been hit hard by an extensive and protracted drought. (After the election, the incoming ALP minister for Primary Industry attributed up to 70,000 of the current unemployed to the effects of the drought, and loss of farmers' purchasing power cut demand in many sectors of industry.) However, the coalition offered little by way of special encouragement to farmers, a promise by the Prime Minister to extend drought relief for a recovery period after the drought had ended being a conspicuous exception.

The only other party certain of winning seats in the Common-wealth Parliament, though in the Senate rather than the House of Representatives, was the Australian Democrats. Its leader, Senator Don Chipp, seeing his old enemy hanging on the ropes and a personal friend on the verge of becoming Prime Minister, allowed himself to appear closer to the Labor camp than at previous elections. He openly predicted a Labor victory, and such anxiety as he express-ed about that event concerned undue influence by greedy unionists rather than Communists unionists. The truly minor parties, the Progress Party, the remnant of the once-influential Democratic Labor Party and the splinter Marxist parties, all stood candidates, and because the unusual features of the Australian electoral system make the disposition of their votes more interesting than would be the case in most other countries they are looked at in subsequent sections. But during the campaign they were virtually invisible.

The advent of one-issue groups in Australian politics at the 1980 election (see Chapter 6) promised more than actually happened in 1983. The one issue that seemed as if it were going to be important, the intention of the Liberal government of Tasmania to build the Gordon-below-Franklin dam, produced vigorous activity by the Tasmanian Wilderness Society in association with the Australian Conservation Foundation; $200,000 was reportedly spent.[34] The Tasmanian Wilderness Society also selected thirteen marginal coali-tion seats in which to hand out its own how-to-vote cards. These supported the local ALP candidate for the House and the Democrat team for the Senate, a combination which was both realistic in applying pressure to sitting government members and reduced the appearance of links with any one party. However, survey data suggest that the popularity of the anti-dam cause might not have converted readily into votes. Two ANOP polls in February 1983 showed only 23 percent of respondents in favour of building the dam and 55 percent opposed, with 11 percent thinking they had not heard enough to judge. But 50 percent thought the decision should be made by the Tasmanian government alone, only 43.5 percent believed the Federal government should override it. At the election the government lost all the seats in which the anti-dam campaigners worked except the one in Tasmania, Wilmot, and it was claimed that where different how-to-vote card recommendations distinguished voters who were following the Tasmanian Wilderness Society card from those following the ALP's own card, a significant minority appeared to be motivated by the dam issue. The extent of the Labor victory masked any contribution that anti-dam campaigners made to it, though it would be possible to pick one or two seats where it could have been crucial, the most likely being Flinders. At the December 1982 by-election the Liberal candidate had proclaimed himself anti-dam, but as soon as the by-election was over the Fraser government rejected overriding the State government as contrary to its federalist philosophy; in March 1983, the anti-government swing in Flinders was exceptionally large. Certainly coalition leaders Anthony and Howard regarded the dam issue as important, and Hawke thought it desirable to hold out a hand of reconciliation to the people of Tasmania on election night and to treat action to stop construction as a high priority once in office.

An old interest-group issue, one which had appeared to have been buried years earlier, threatened briefly to revive and damage Labor's chances. Provision of government funds to privately operated, mainly parochial, schools had been abandoned in the nineteenth century; its restoration in the 1960s had given the coalition parties, which were first to accept the change, a temporary advantage over the ALP.[35] A section of the ALP, mainly on its left, and teachers unions and parents' organizations involved with the State schools remained unhappy about paying Federal funds to private schools, especially those which were already well-equipped and attended by children from the wealthiest sections of society whose parents paid substantial annual fees for an exclusive and quality education. Throughout the population acceptance of State aid had grown somewhat. In 1955, 51 percent had been in favour of it and 41 percent against, by 1980 the figures were 66 percent and 22 percent respectively.[36] The ALP's education policy emphasized needs and foreshadowed withdrawal of support from the best-endowed schools. Although none of these were operated by the Catholic Church, it was the National Catholic Education Commission which publicly pressed opposition to the proposal. The ALP had to move carefully between the Church, some clerical and lay elements of which had seriously harmed Labor's electoral chances in the late 1950s and throughout the 1960s, and the State-school teachers' unions which were preparing to spend $750,000 on pro-Labor advertising during the campaign. The party had changed its shadow minister of education before the campaign began, and now reduced the impact of the offending proposal by promising to phase out the 20 percent of cost subsidy going to the richest class of schools over four years, thereby giving them more time to adapt to the loss. Opponents of the change were still not happy, but at least they remained silent for the remainer of the campaign.

The Polls

As Figure 10–2 (p. 274) has already shown, the ALP had established a substantial lead over the coalition before the decision to dissolve Parliament was taken. The gap which existed while the party was still led by Hayden widened further once Hawke became leader, and then displayed a remarkable stability throughout the campaign period (the month of February). Figure 11–1 illustrates the findings of the four polls whose results were published; all show a comfortable Labor lead right to the end of the campaign. The opening of the gap after Hawke's accession had been a major news story, advantaging the ALP, though as was so often the case during the campaign predic-

FIGURE 11-1
Voting intentions shown by the public opinion polls

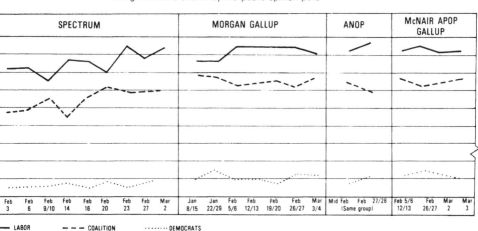

301

tions were qualified by past performances.[36] The maintenance of the lead continued the flow of such encouraging reports,[37] though minor perturbations in the trend line could induce uncertainty—thus a 1 percentage point decline in ALP voting intention, down to 52 percent, produced a story captioned: "Polls show Labor well ahead, but Govt closing".[38] Last minute polling (Thursday night and Friday before the Saturday poll) by McNair Gallup left the ALP and coalition exactly where they had been at the beginning of the campaign, at 51 percent and 43 percent respectively; the first preference results were 49.5 percent and 43.6 percent respectively.

The polls regularly predicted a Labor victory, and electors increasingly agreed with them. The ANOP recorded a fall in the proportion expecting a government victory from 35 percent in mid-February to only 17 percent by the end of the month, while the proportion expecting a Labor victory rose correspondingly from 51 percent to 73 percent.[39] The same ANOP surveys give some indication as to why voters might have expected the ALP to win. They were more likely to believe a Hawke Labor government would "do a better job in controlling wages and inflation" than a Fraser Liberal government—49 percent to 40 percent,—and they were much more likely to expect a Hawke government to control the unions and reduce the number of strikes, to lower the level of unemployment and to make the average income earner pay less tax. Asked whether they expected any personal benefit from a Labor win or a Liberal win, 50 percent identified a benefit expected from Labor, only 32 percent a benefit from the Liberals.[40] Given the choice between lower inflation, for which the parties rated equally, and less unemployment, which was strongly Labor's issue, 80 percent chose unemployment and 18 percent inflation.[41] In sum, dissatisfaction with the government's economic performance was critical in turning it out.

The Results

With Lowe already captured at a by-election, the ALP needed another twelve seats in the House of Representatives for the barest majority. In the event it won twenty-three, twice as many as were required: five more in New South Wales (Barton, Calare, Eden-Monaro, Macarthur, Phillip), six in Victoria (Bendigo, Casey, Chisholm, Deakin, Diamond Valley, Flinders), five in Queensland (Bowman, Fadden, Herbert, Leichhardt, Petrie), one in South Australia (Kingston), five in Western Australia (Canning, Moore, Perth, Stirling, Tangney), and the one territory seat it did not already hold, Northern Territory. As a consequence Labor now held 75 House seats to the Liberals' 33 and National Party's 17. In 1972 the Whitlam government had managed only 67 seats and in 1974, 66. The Hawke government was much better situated to survive the loss of some seats at the next general election and still retain office.

Labor secured 49.5 percent of first preferences for the House of Representatives compared to the Liberals' 34.4 percent and Nationals' 9.2 percent, an improvement of 4.3 percent compared with the Liberals' loss of 3.0 percent and the Nationals' gain of 0.2 percent— but that was with two more divisions contested. Some of Labor's improvement came at the expense of the Democrats, whose share of the national vote dropped from 6.6 percent to 5.0 percent.

The distinction between the southeastern corner of Australia and the outlying parts of the country which had been significant at recent elections (see p. 217) faded somewhat, although it was still noticeable. In the southeast Labor led the coalition by 56 seats ot 33, but by only 19 to 17 in the rest of the continent. Had Tasmania moved with the rest of the country, in which case all five of its seats would have gone to the ALP, then such a distinction would have disappeared and indeed the southeastern corner would have been slightly less Labor than the rest. The likelihood that the deviant Tasmanian results were determined by a single question, the Gordon-below-Franklin dam and its arousal of States' rights sentiment, suggests that the division which appeared in 1975 may prove to have been short-lived.

Examination of Table 11–2 which sets out the statewide swings in the two-party preferred vote between 1977 and 1980 and between 1980 and 1983 shows convergence on national electoral homogeneity. Traditionally anti-Labor Victoria, Queensland and Western Australia swing more to Labor. Tasmania's antipathy to the party that would prevent its dam-building restored a more normal electoral pattern in

TABLE 11-2
Statewide swings to ALP in two-party-preferred vote, 1977–80 and 1980–83 (%)

	1977–80	1980–83
New South Wales	2.8	3.8
Victoria	6.2	3.7
Queensland	4.9	2.7
South Australia	0.7	3.6
Western Australia	6.7	8.2
Tasmania	3.2	−4.2
Australian Capital Territory	4.2	7.4
Northern Territory	1.3	3.1
Australia	4.2	3.7

Source: For 1977 and 1980 figures Mackerras, "Australian General Election and Senate Election, 1980", pp. 6–11.

which at least one State goes against any national tide which might be running, and even in the States where there was a strong overall movement to the ALP there were odd seats which held back conspicuously. The most striking instance was Riverina in New South Wales where, despite such blandishments as Hawke's journeying to one of its principal towns to deliver Labor's rural policy speech and the promise of an interest-free loan of $4 million to a local cannery (one of the rare instances of pork-barrel politics in the campaign), the swing to Labor was only 0.1 percent compared to the statewide 3.8 percent. In 1980 there had even been a swing against Labor of 0.6 percent to make Riverina the coalition's only gain at that election, and over the period since its boundaries were drastically altered to bring in most of another, traditionally Labor, division, Darling, there has been a net loss of support for the ALP despite statewide movement to Labor of 6.6 percent and a national swing of 8.1 percent.

Generally though the swing of votes was sufficiently uniform as to confirm the pendulum model. Apart from the five Tasmanian seats which shifted in the wrong direction, there had been five seats vulnerable to a 1 percent swing, and all but one (Riverina) had been won by the ALP; eight seats vulnerable to a swing between 1 and 2 percent and all had gone; five seats to a swing between 2 and 3 percent and all had gone; four seats to a swing between 3 and 4 percent, and all but one (Dawson) had fallen to Labor. As if to compensate for the eccentric behavior of Riverina and Dawson, both mixtures of agricultural, pastoral and mining districts, two outer suburban seats had been won by the ALP with particularly large pro-Labor swings—Tangney in Western Australia with a swing of 8.6 percent, just above the statewide figure, and Flinders with a swing of 6.6 percent, considerably above Victoria's statewide figure. Flinders, requiring a swing of 5.7 percent to change after the 1980 election, proved to be the farthest victim of the swing to Labor. In addition to the five Tasmanian seats and Riverina and Dawson which were vulnerable to smaller swings than that, were three seats held by the Speaker (Bruce) and by two ministers (Sturt, Moreton) where sitting Liberals survived, due presumably to sufficient personal voting support in a very tight finish. Apart from Tasmania, a swing on the scale that actually took place ought to have shifted 23 seats, and as it happened 23 were won; the two that the pendulum had missed in that sector of its arc were compensated for by the additional gains of Tangney and Flinders.[42]

Late on election night Malcolm Fraser conceded defeat, announced that he accepted full responsibility for the decision to hold the election at that time and for the conduct of the campaign, and declared that he was standing down as Liberal leader forthwith. The following month he retired from the House of Representatives as well, producing the first by-election of the new Parliament. On March 11 the parliamentary Liberal Party chose Andrew Peacock to be its new leader. He defeated John Howard by 36 votes to 20, but Howard then retained the deputy leadership comfortably. The Liberals' former leader in the Senate stood down, and Liberal Senators elected a new one, reverting to an earlier practice of the upper house members' choosing their own leaders (whilst also voting for lower house leaders) which Fraser had stopped by insisting on nominating the Senate leaders himself. To most observers Peacock appeared the Liberal counterpart of, and response to, Bob Hawke—style rather than substance, an effective performer on television and careful cultivator of good relations with the media generally, but an unknown quantity on most policy issues. And, the observers agreed, Fraserism as the dominant strand of Liberal doctrine had ended with the career of its author.

Candidates

The total of 519 candidates in 1983 was the largest number ever offering for the House of Representatives. The ALP contested every seat, as it has done at every election for years. The Liberal Party contested 110, as it had done in 1980, and its National Party ally 31, two more than in 1980. The Democrats with 119 and the DLP with eleven were respectively two and one down on their 1980 totals, while the Progress Party dropped from seventeen candidates to only eleven and, largely as a consequence, its share of the national vote went from a mere 0.21 percent to a still tinier 0.08 percent. Even the supply of Independents declined slightly, 60 standing in 42 divisions compared to 63 standing in 47 divisions in 1980.

Accounting for the rise in the total number of candidates from 502 to 513 was a remarkable increase in candidates from the various small parties into which the Marxist tradition has fragmented in Australia (as elsewhere). As recently as 1977 there were only nine such candidates contesting eight divisions. In 1980, 23 stood in 15 divisions. By 1983 there were 52 in 40 divisions. Whereas in 1980 the Marxist candidates had been largely confined to New South Wales, fourteen candidates in eight divisions there, and three-quarters of the votes cast for Marxist candidates were recorded in New South Wales, in 1983 New South Wales accounted for a smaller proportion of the candidates and only half the national vote. However, a number of candidates standing in other States gave Sydney addresses which suggests the leading role of New South Wales-based elements in such parties. The great majority of the Marxist candidates in 1983 came from the Socialist Workers Party—38 of the 52; another six came from its Trotskyite sibling and bitter enemy, the Socialist Labor League. The Socialist Party of Australia, heirs of the Moscow connection locally, put forward only three candidates, well below its average for earlier elections when that version of the party predominated. The Communist Party of Australia combined the old party name with a Eurocommunist view of theory; it nominated five candidates.

One consequence of the sharp increase in the number of Marxist candidates has been an increase in the number of votes such candidates poll, up from 0.20 percent of the national total in 1977 to 0.43 percent in 1980 and to 0.72 percent in 1983, which is slightly over 1,200 votes per candidate. Closer examination suggests very strongly that such totals and averages are substantially swollen by the "donkey vote" (see p. 227), which advantages candidates placed at the top of the ballot-paper. In 1983 in New South Wales the five Marxist candidates at the top of the ballot-paper in their division averaged 4.3 percent of votes, but the nineteen not at the top averaged only 1.4 percent. In the other five States the nine Marxist candidates at the top of their ballot-papers averaged 3.1 percent, while the other twenty averaged only 0.9 percent. In fact Marxist candidates do not poll any better on average than the Independents, and corroboration of the belief that the total vote for the Marxist parties contains a substantial number that were cast at random comes from the three instances in which the second preference of Marxist candidates were distributed. In two the coalition parties received as many as the ALP did, and in the third, a quarter (of the 131 involved) went to non-Labor candidates.

One electoral reform planned by the incoming Labor government is placing party labels on the ballot-paper. This would remove a severe disability felt by minor parties which lack the members or supporters to ensure that their how-to-vote cards identifying their candidates and preferred patterns for the numbering of preferences are distributed at polling places spread all over the country—or even at all the polling places in the few divisions they are contesting. However, there may be cases in which the presence of a party label could be a disadvantage, and it is by no means impossible that candidates from the Marxist parties would suffer if they were clearly identified.

Another group of candidates whose numbers have been increasing is women who at last have begun to win seats. Figures for earlier elections from 1975 to 1980 have already been given (pp. 240–41). The increase in 1983 over 1980 (sixteen) was smaller than had taken place between 1977 and 1980 (26), but as the number of women in the House of Representatives doubled, from three to six, 1983 was still perceived as having been a good year for women in Federal politics. Admittedly the coalition parties put up only half the number of women candidates as stood for the ALP and only three of those eleven had even an outside chance of winning, but as the experience of the Labor Party has shown, it is easier to introduce a worthwhile number of female candidates into winnable seats when the party is in opposition. Then there is no male incumbent to remove first. The loss by the Liberal Party of so many seats which ought to appear recoverable at the next election should be a much better test of whether its leaders are going to respond to arguments advanced within the party after the 1983 election that its apparent lack of sympathy for women's issues had cost it votes.

Only one-third of female candidates came from the major parties, and in fact much of the increase since 1980 is to be explained by the extent to which the Socialist Workers Party nominated women—which also helps to explain the high concentration of female candidates in ultra-safe and safe Labor constituencies appearing in Table 11–3. With six of its 75 members of the House of Representatives now women, the ALP has hit 8 percent with a target of 30 percent by the end of the decade. Its Senate representation is much closer to target, with seven out of thirty, or 23 percent. Should (which seems sensible) the target be applied to representation in the Commonwealth Parliament as a whole, the figures are thirteen out of 105 or 12 percent. As the coalition parties re-elected their five female Senators and the Democrats their one, the upper house now contains thirteen women in a total membership of 64. The Liberals had a female Senator,

TABLE 11-3
Number of female candidates in 1983 and the relative safeness of constituencies they contested

	Number of seats	Coalition	Labor	Democrats	Other
Ultra-safe Labor	13	3	0	3	8
Safe Labor	24	3	1	6	9
Marginal Labor	17	4	3	4	3
Ultra-marginal Labor	21	0	2	4	5
Ultra-marginal Coalition	14	0	5	3	1
Marginal Coalition	18	0	5	3	4
Safe Coalition	15	0	4	4	0
Ultra-safe Coalition	3	1[a]	0	0	1
Total	125	11	20	27	31

Notes: Safeness is determined by the result at the 1983 election, not the previous election.
[a] A Liberal candidate in a National constituency.

Margaret Guilfoyle (Victoria), in their cabinet as Minister for Finance, and the Hawke government chose another female Senator, Susan Ryan (ACT), for its cabinet as Minister for Education and Youth Affairs. There was, however, some disappointment that a second woman was not elected by caucus to provide a female Minister in the House of Representatives as well. Runner-up for election to the Ministry had been a woman, Ros Kelly (Canberra, ACT), and another woman, Elaine Darling (Lilley, Qld), had polled well.

Overall the proportion of candidates standing for the House of Representatives for the first time at the 1983 general election was 56 percent, down slightly from the two preceding elections (see p. 239). Because the party had performed better in 1980, the proportion of new Labor candidates fell from 55 percent in 1980 to 45 percent; correspondingly the proportion of new coalition candidates rose, but only from 35 percent to 39 percent. The proportion of candidates with electoral records going back to before 1970 declined to 7.5 percent, but two of the three 1949 veterans were still in the field (see p. 239). Sir Billy Snedden, a former Liberal leader and Speaker since 1976, survived by the narrowest margins to become jointly Father of the House with Sir James Killen, and the indefatigible Ronald George Sarina, standing this time as a True Independent, polled 0.35 percent of the vote on his fifth unsuccessful attempt to enter the House of Representatives.

Only two new MHRs were added to the coalition side of the House compared with 30 to the Labor side. Twenty-two of the 30 won on their first attempt, four had made one previous unsuccessful attempt, three two previous unsuccessful attempts, and the thirtieth was a victim of the landslide of 1975 belatedly returning to the House after failing to get back in 1977 and 1980. In the main the Labor arrivals were replacing 23 coalition members who lost their seats. Three of these had parliamentary experience prior to 1972, including one minister who had been elected in 1969 only to lose his seat to Labor in 1972, chose not to offer again in 1974 and then came back in 1975. Ten, half of the remaining 20, dated from the great sweep of 1975; five had come into the House earlier, two in 1972 and three in 1974 and five later, two in 1977 and two in 1980. One was the unfortunate victor of Flinders who was now defeated without ever having taken his seat in Parliament—which had started on its summer recess before the by-election. A few of the twenty-three will probably trickle back into the House once the electoral pendulum has begun to swing the coalition's way again, though the certainty of a redistribution of electoral boundaries before the next general election will reduce the moral claim a former member has in respect of his old seat.

Preferential Voting

The alternative vote, or preferential voting as Australians invariably call it, has already been explained (at p. 226). As foreshadowed then, the 1983 election may prove to have been its last appearance in the form that has prevailed for more than 60 years. Within a few days of taking office, the minister responsible for electoral matters, Mick Young, was widely reported to be hard at work on a package of electoral reforms among which removal of the obligation to express preferences for each and every candidate figured prominently. Table 9–6 (p. 227) shows the impact of preferential voting on previous elections from 1969 to 1980. The 1983 election continued a pattern established since the decline of the Democratic Labor Party from the commanding position it occupied in the 1960s. Preferences were counted in 31 electorates in 1983, but in only two instances were the results changed thereby. In Cook, the ALP challenger had a lead of 137 votes over the Liberal incumbent, but 61.7 percent of the preferences of the third candidate, from the small right-wing Progress Party, favoured the Liberal who won by a margin of 148 votes in the closest finish of the election. In Gippsland, a safe National seat where the Liberals were now able to challenge because of the retirement of Peter Nixon, their preferences reversed the initial Labor lead. The ALP won a majority of the seats where preferences were counted, seventeen out of the 31, but in each instance their candidate had been ahead on the first count.

As in 1977 and 1980 the Australian Democrats' preferences mattered little; see Table 11–4. They were counted in fewer electorates than before, in only 26 compared to 35 in 1977 and 39 in 1980, and the advantage went to the ALP in a smaller proportion of cases in 1983, fifteen to eleven. Once again the advantage was relatively small in most cases; in only five divisions did one side or the other receive more than 60 percent of Democrat preferences. Twice the coalition was favoured. In Moreton a Liberal senior minister, Sir James Killen, was already almost 800 votes ahead; 63.6 percent of Democrat preferences meant that he was more than 2,000 votes ahead on the final count. In the safe rural seat of O'Connor, the Democrat preferences divided nearly equally among the four other candidates. The National Party of Western Australia candidate, strictly speaking not a coalition candidate like his National Country Party rival, received 14.1 percent of them, but as only one-fifth of his preferences went to the ALP on the subsequent count it still appears probable that more than 60 percent of Democrat preferences in O'Connor favoured the coalition ultimately. In the three cases where the ALP benefited

TABLE 11-4
Distribution of Australian Democrat preferences, House elections, 1983 (%)

Electorate	Australian Democrat preferences going to:		Electorate	Australian Democrat preferences going to:	
	Coalition	Labor		Coalition	Labor
Cowper	42.4	57.6	McMillan	29.4	70.6
Eden Monaro[a]	39.0	46.7	Bowman	51.4[b]	48.5
Macarthur	45.1	54.9	Fadden	47.8[b]	52.2
New England	50.9	49.1	Fisher	50.0[b]	50.0
Riverina	56.5	43.5	McPherson	49.6[b]	50.4
Bruce	36.3	63.7	Moreton	63.6	36.4
Casey	46.0	54.0	Petrie	50.5	49.5
Chisholm	43.4	56.6	Wide Bay	51.4	48.6
Deakin	43.2	56.8	Kingston	49.4	50.6
Diamond Valley	44.2	55.8	Sturt	40.3	59.7
Flinders	43.8	56.2	Forrest	53.2	46.8
Gippsland	54.5[b]	45.5	O'Connor	70.7[c]	29.3
Indi	53.5[b]	46.5	Northern Territory	26.7	73.3

Notes: [a] A further 14.3 percent went to an Independent candidate.
[b] Includes preferences given to both coalition parties.
[c] Includes preferences given to both coalition parties and National Party of Western Australia.
Source: Australian Electoral Office.

from more than 60 percent of Democrat preferences no common pattern appears. McMillan had been an especially hard-fought contest in 1980, and the Northern Territory is a law unto itself in respect of electoral behavior. Bruce, the most extreme instance of Democrat-preference advantage to the ALP among suburban divisions in Melbourne, was one of the electorates where the Tasmanian Wilderness Society campaigned against the government over the dam issue, and this may have had some influence on Democrat voters.

As for the Democratic Labor Party, its share of the total vote in Victoria, the only State in which it offered candidates, fell once again from 1.1 percent to 0.7 percent though its number of candidates was cut by only one, from twelve to eleven. Only one of the eleven had been a candidate for the party before, and that at the previous election in 1980, so continuity with the DLP which had kept the coalition in office so effectively was minimal. On the other hand, as appears in Table 11–5, the remaining handful of DLP voters reverted to solid allocation of their preferences to the coalition after a temporary lapse in 1980 (see p. 229).

Even more tightly disciplined were coalition voters. When Liberal preferences had to be distributed in Gippsland and Fisher, 93.2 percent and 93.5 percent respectively went to the National candidate. Correspondingly, when National preferences were allocated in Indi, McMillan and McPherson, 91.8 percent, 89.2 percent and 93.0 percent respectively went to the Liberal candidate. Considering that the first

TABLE 11-5
Distribution of DLP preferences, House elections, 1983 (%)

Electorate	Coalition	Labor	DLP preferences going to: Australian Democrats	Other
Bendigo	78.2	11.2	10.6	—
Casey	70.9	6.4	7.7	15.0[a]
Chisholm	85.9	8.0	6.1	—
Deakin	88.0	5.1	6.9	—
Diamond Valley	68.7	15.8	15.5	—
Gippsland	72.6[b]	13.8	5.5	8.1[c]
McMillan	87.3[b]	7.7	5.0	—

Notes: [a] Australian Christian.
[b] Includes preferences given to both coalition parties.
[c] Independent.
Source: Australian Electoral Office.

two of those seats had been taken by the Liberals from the National Party in recent years and the third had been fought over at a by-election two years earlier, coalition loyalty stood the test well. Even the breakaway National Party of Western Australia delivered 80.3 percent of its preferences in O'Connor to the candidates of the coalition partners.

Sixteen of the 125 divisions saw both Liberal and National candidates in the field, but in only three was there anything like an equal contest between them. In Gippsland the unexpected retirement of a National minister, Peter Nixon, allowed the local Liberal branches the opportunity they had long sought. On this occasion the Nationals repelled the attack, their candidate polling 31.5 percent of first preferences to the Liberal's 23.8 percent. In Capricornia the National Party nominated two candidates, one from each of the division's major urban centers, and the Liberal Party one, in a determined attempt to recapture the seat from the ALP. It had been held by the Nationals from 1975 to 1977, and their two candidates polled 25.3 percent of first preferences against the Liberal's 17.0 percent, leaving the ALP still firmly in possession. The third serious contest occurred in one of the most bitterly fought-over pieces of electoral territory in the country, McPherson. The Liberal incumbent won 35.9 percent of first preference votes compared to the National challenger's 23.5 percent, as a result not very different from the by-election held for the seat in 1981. In the other thirteen Liberal-National contests, only three of which were in ALP-held seats, the less successful coalition candidate failed to get as much as one-third of the combined coalition vote. It would appear that for the present there is little room for uncertainty as to which division ought to be contested by which

311

partner should alteration to the method of counting votes rule out competition between them at the next election.

The Senate Vote

The constitutional provisions for electing the Senate have been described previously (pp. 229–30). Because the 1983 election followed a double dissolution, all ten seats for each State, as well as the two Seats from each of the mainland territories, were at stake, and the advantage which one party might derive from the number of its incumbent Senators retiring compared with the number of its opponent's incumbents at risk was not a factor. In opinion surveys voting intentions are usually sought in respect of the House of Representatives only, and as the pre-election surveys showed support for the Australian Democrats significantly below their performance at the 1980 election it appeared possible that the party would have some difficulty retaining five seats and the balance of power in the Senate which it had enjoyed since 1 July 1981 (the date when the new Senators elected at the 1980 general election finally took their seats). All commentators expected the one Independent, Brian Harradine of Tasmania, to retain his seat. There was even some ill-informed speculation that he could carry a second Independent in on his ticket, but such speculation disregarded the evidence (see p. 235) that in 1980 over half of Senator Harradine's second preference votes had deserted his supporting candidate. But it was also the case that with ten vacancies per State the quota necessary for election had been halved, and it would be much easier for a minor party candidate or an Independent to be elected in 1983 than it had been in 1980. It was expected that the ALP would poll poorly in Tasmania, and it was considered unlikely that it would overtake the coalition vote in Queensland. In those circumstances it would be extremely difficult for Labor to win even half the 64 seats in the Senate, though it was even less likely that the coalition could regain the majority it had lost in 1980. That possibility had been the ostensible justification for holding the election at this time and under the double dissolution provisions, but it was a very long shot for the Prime Minister to attempt.

One handicap which was thought to affect the ALP's chances of winning a majority in the Senate was the considerably higher proportion of informal (not valid) ballot-papers in every Senate election. The proportion of informal votes recorded in each division has a strong positive correlation with the proportion of Labor votes, and it has always seemed plausible that the less well-educated, and nowadays the more recent immigrants who also tend to be concentrated in Labor electorates, experience difficulty in coping with the complexity of a Senate ballot-paper and are more likely to make errors which would render their vote informal. Although overall the number of candidates for the Senate corresponds to the number for the House of Representatives at roughly four candidates per vacancy, the requirement that every candidate must be assigned a number indicating the voter's preference, with no number duplicated and no sequential number omitted, is a formidable obstacle to equally effective performance on the two ballot-papers. Table 11–6 indicates the much higher rate of informal voting for the Senate and the extent of shortfall in the ALP's Senate vote. However, the explanation of Labor's shortfall is not simply informal voting, if that is an explanation at all. In Queensland many voters supported an ALP candidate for the House but gave their first preferences in the Senate to Senator Neville Bonner standing as an Independent; in Tasmania their equivalents backed Senator Harradine. A more widespread phenomenon would have been a vote for the ALP for the House and for the Australian Democrats for the Senate, the strategy advocated by the Tasmanian Wilderness Society. After making allowance for such matters, Labor politicians would argue that there is still a strong possibility that informal ballot-papers were cast by a disproportionate share of would-be Labor voters. Accordingly one of the central elements in the package of electoral changes the ALP began to assemble for early implementation is reduction of the voter's obligation to record as many preferences as there are candidates. If it were cut to twice as many preferences as there are vacancies to be filled,

TABLE 11-6
Number of Senate candidates, informal voting for the House and the Senate and ALP first preferences for the House and the Senate(%)

	Number of Senate candidates	Informal voting		ALP first preferences	
		House	Senate	House	Senate
New South Wales	62	2.2	11.1	50.1	47.4
Victoria	50	2.2	10.7	50.5	46.5
Queensland	42	1.3	8.6	46.1	39.6
South Australia	35	2.7	8.8	48.1	44.6
Western Australia	30	2.0	7.8	52.0	49.3
Tasmania	17	2.3	7.4	40.3	32.8
Australian Capital Territory[a]	8	2.2	3.3	63.9	55.4
Northern Territory[a]	6	4.4	4.5	46.6	46.0

Note: [a] Two Senators to be elected instead of ten in the States.
Source: Australian Electoral Office.

this would still entail ten preferences in an ordinary half-Senate election or twenty preferences following a double dissolution, and that would mean ranking three or four teams. The change would certainly reduce the number of mismarked ballot-papers, and it might effect a small improvement in the ALP's Senate vote, though on the 1983 figures it would be difficult to argue that more Senate seats could have been won by the Labor Party under a less demanding requirement.

Undoubtedly there will still be some voters who disapprove of the existence of an upper house, or dislike the particular one Australia has or regard it as relatively unimportant, and they will continue to spoil their ballot-papers deliberately, though such voters are probably few in number. There are certainly many more who see the existence of an upper house as an opportunity to work checks and balances and to produce an upper house whose political complexion differs from the lower house where it is determined which major party shall form the government. The DLP always performed better in Senate voting than in voting for the House; the Australian Democrats have done the same with the gap widening as their House vote has fallen. In 1977 the Democrats polled 9.4 percent of first preferences for the House and 11.1 percent for the Senate, in 1980 6.6 percent and 9.3 percent, and in 1983 5.0 percent and 9.6 percent. As the Democrats contested almost all House of Representatives seats at each of those elections, the influence of uncontested divisions on the House vote would be slight, and one can say that in 1983 approximately one Australian voter in twenty backed the Democrats for the Senate without thinking it necessary to support them in the House as well. In Victoria the Democrat's Senate vote was more than twice the share of their House vote, 12.0 percent against 5.7 percent, which may be attributed to Don Chipp's personal popularity, but everywhere their Senate vote was proportionately at least half as large again as their House vote.

Counting of Senate votes in 1983 was fairly uneventful, reflecting the substantial lead the ALP enjoyed over the coalition in most States, though the process was as protracted as ever and critics of the delay more vocal than usual. In New South Wales, despite the large number of candidates offering, the ALP had 5.2 quotas on first preferences, the coalition 4.2 quotas and the Democrats 0.95 quotas; in Victoria the comparable figures were 5.1 quotas, 4.2 quotas and 1.3 quotas; and in South Australia 4.9 quotas, 4.4 quotas and 1.3 quotas. Accordingly, three of the States each returned five Labor Senators, four coalition and one Democrat. The two Territories, as usual, returned one Labor Senator and one Liberal for the Australian Capital Territory and one Labor Senator and one National for the Northern

Territory, though the Liberal vote in the ACT was so diminished that for the first time the party lacked a quota on first preferences and additional counts became necessary. The Liberal team secured only 31.7 percent of first preferences in the ACT, reflecting Federal public servants' disenchantment with the Fraser Government and the consequences for the local economy of its haphazard attacks on public sector spending. In Western Australia the ALP received 5.4 quotas and the Liberals 4.5 quotas (the National Party and the National Party of Western Australia each ran a separate team and polled barely 10,000 first preferences between them), while the Democrats had only 0.75 quotas. The allocation of preferences eventually elected the Democrat's national president, J. G. Evans, as the first Democrat Senator to be elected from that State, making the State total five, four and one as in New South Wales, Victoria and South Australia.

In Queensland the Liberals' serious error of 1980 (pp. 231–34) in insisting on running a separate team against the National Party was nearly repeated by the decision to demote the Commonwealth Parliament's only Aboriginal, Senator Neville Bonner, to third place on their ticket. On the 1980 figures and any realistic reading of the coalition parties' support in Queensland, the best that could be hoped for was three seats for the National team and two for the Liberal. Instead of certain defeat as the Liberals' number three, Bonner chose an outside chance of survival as number one on his own ticket, and very nearly made it. The Labor team received 4.4 quotas which guaranteed it four places but no chance of a fifth; the National team, headed again by the State Premier's wife, Florence Bjelke-Petersen, received 3.2 quotas. But the Liberals could manage only 1.7 quotas, having obtained just more than half the number of primary votes the National team secured. That accounted for eight of the ten Queensland seats, four Labor, three National and one Liberal, and left a Liberal incumbent, Senator David MacGibbon, competing with the Democrats' Senator Michael Macklin and Senator Bonner for the two remaining places. The Democrat team began with 0.9 quotas to Bonner's 0.7 quotas, and in the final stages of counting Macklin pulled ahead to take the ninth vacancy. On the last count the distribution of surplus Labor votes followed the party's how-to-vote card which had been designed for simplicity and reduction in the number of spoiled ballot-papers and placed the Liberal team ahead of Bonner. MacGibbon was elected.

Because of the long experience Tasmanian voters have had in working proportional representation at elections for the State lower house as well as for the Senate, voting in Tasmania best illustrates the potential for voter choice under a system employing the single-transferable vote. Tasmanians use opportunities that the great majority of voters in the other States waive, and the count in that State will be used to illustrate Senate voting in 1983. It should be remembered, however, that Tasmania can be atypical in the extent to which party instructions are disregarded by voters.

Some 250,896 valid votes were cast, producing a quota of 22,809. The Liberal team polled 106,768 primary votes for 4.7 quotas; Labor only 82,343 primary votes for 3.6 quotas; the Democrats 17,089 votes for 0.7 quotas; and the two-member team of Independents led by Harradine 44,696 votes for 1.96 quotas. Three Senators could be elected immediately: the leaders of the Liberal and Labor teams and Harradine. Of the 53,287 surplus votes from the first Liberal Senator Peter Rae, 98.5 percent went to other members of the Liberal team, only 0.8 percent to the Democrats, 0.4 percent to the Labor team, and 0.2 percent to the remaining Independent. Similarly of the 35,106 surplus votes from the first Labor Senator, Don Grimes, 98.6 percent went to other members of the Labor team, 0.3 percent to Liberals, 0.8 percent to Democrats and 0.3 percent to the remaining Independents. But within each party bloc there was some evidence of independent choice; only 86.5 percent of Rae's surplus votes that stayed with the Liberals followed the official instruction to move to the number two, while among the better disciplined Labor voters, 92.4 percent of Grimes' surplus that stayed with the party went to their number two. Harradine's voters showed much more independence. Only 54.0 percent of his surplus votes went to the number two on his team, compared with 22.7 percent which went over to various Liberals, 17.9 percent to the remaining members of the ALP team, and 5.4 percent to the Democrats.

The second members of the two major parties' teams were now over the quota, and again their surplus votes stayed faithful to the ticket, 99.2 percent for the Liberals and 98.7 percent for Labor. By now the Liberals' large initial lead was affecting the symmetry of the count. Only a Liberal could be elected with more than a quota, and with 99.6 percent of his surplus remaining with the party a fourth Liberal Senator was elected next, again 99.7 percent of surplus votes staying loyal.

By this point an interesting situation existed. Of the original six Liberal candidates only two remained, with 14,081 and 5,378 votes respectively. But of the original six Labor candidates there were still four in the field with the third and fourth candidates on the ticket very nearly tied at 18,031 and 18,026 respectively, whilst the other two trailed with 1,644 and 2,511. Tasmania had been one of the States where the ALP Federal executive had decided to intervene and impose its own order on the Senate ticket, and the decision had mattered. Given the party's current unpopularity and the threat posed by a well-known Democrat candidate and by Harradine's drawing power for his companion's chances, even the fourth place on the ALP ticket was dangerous. The Federal executive demoted a relatively left-wing incumbent, Senator (and MHR 1972–75) John Coates, to that position, and Labor voters reacted by giving Coates 17.6 percent of Labor's primary votes. On the two counts when ALP surplus votes had been distributed, there had also been a small but significant leakage away from the next candidate on the party how-to-vote card and to Coates, 4.1 percent and 3.4 percent of those remaining with the party. With a relatively modest surplus to be passed down the Labor ticket its number four candidate had drawn almost level with its number three. The leading Democrat, Norm Sanders, a prominent anti-dam campaigner who had resigned the Democrats' only seat in the State lower house to contest the Senate, had 18,549 votes and the other two members of the Democrat team 280 and 351 votes respectively. John Jones, the other half of Harradine's team, trailed the field with only 12,381.

In successive counts the candidates with the fewest votes were excluded, and all their votes distributed, first two Democrats, then two Labor, then one Liberal. The only consequence of that was that Coates was now slightly ahead of his number three, Senator June Hearn, 20,580 to 19,482, whilst the remaining Liberal had 19,279 and Sanders 19,171. Jones' 12,721 votes were then allocated, and as had been the case with Harradine's primary votes—not surprisingly so because 11,593 of them had come to him from Harradine—scattered in all directions. Enough went to the Liberal (44.0 percent) to give him a quota and enough (24.6 percent) to Senator Hearn to put her ahead of Coates once more and with a quota as well. Sanders received 11.9 percent of Jones' votes and Coates the remaining 14.6 percent. Distribution of the small surplus of the fifth Liberal Senator was enough to produce a final result: 1,240 votes went to Coates to give him 23,678, over the quota, and 821 to Sanders to bring his total to 21,501. But as Hearn had also achieved a quota on that count, her even smaller surplus of 436 was allocated, 422 going to Coates, only fourteen to Sanders, making their final results 24,100 and 21,515 respectively.

With five seats the Democrats again held the balance of power in the Senate, now with only one Senator from Victoria instead of two, but with one from Western Australia to maintain the number. With thirty seats the ALP was still short of a majority in its own right, but with the support of the Democrats they could dispense with the services of Senator Harradine who, as one of his old opponents said gleefully, had become irrelevant. Although the firm commitment of the Democrats not to withhold supply from a government controlling the House of Representatives relieves the Hawke government of the anxieties that beset any Australian government lacking a majority in the Senate since the events of 1974–75, there is still one unpleasant consequence of the provisions of the Australian Constitution. To return to the regular cycle of half-Senate elections following a double dissolution, the ten Senators representing the States are divided into two groups, five who will serve a "full" term and five who will serve only "half" a term. By convention they are the first five elected and the last five elected respectively. But under Section 13 of the Constitution their terms in both cases date back to the first day of July preceding the election, in this case to 1 July 1982. Thus the Hawke government will have to hold an election for half the Senate, and because of the dangers of holding a Senate election by itself when the voters are likely to treat it as a gigantic by-election and vote against the government of the day to protest about whatever may be unpopular at the time, almost certainly an election for the House of Representatives as well, well before the middle of 1985, and quite possibly before the end of 1984.

The fact that the Fraser government, if re-elected, would be in the same fix had been put to the Prime Minister during the election campaign. It was a sensitive matter for Fraser because he had obtained an early election in 1977 to bring the two houses back into synchronization of their elections following the double dissolution of 1975—for which he was also responsible. In 1983 he had put them out of synchronization again, despite the arguments he had used in 1977 which included disregarding the defeat of a referendum proposal to compel synchronization. This might have embarrassed a lesser man, but then Fraser's behavior often recalled Speaker Cannon's observation about Theodore Roosevelt: "Roosevelt's all right, but he's got no more use for the Constitution than a tomcat has for a marriage license". He replied to the questioner that the constitutional amendment would be sought again, and would ensure that the Parliament being elected in 1983 would go a full term. His solution seemed very improbable, but more exciting game was afoot and the matter was not pursued during the campaign. After the election the Labor Party's commitment to amending the Constitution to prevent premature elections such as had taken place in 1977 and 1983 and establish fixed-term Parliaments took over center of the constitutional stage.

Notes

1 Paul Kelly, *Sydney Morning Herald*, February 18, 1983.
2 *National Times*, August 22–28, 1982.
3 Peter Bowers, *Sydney Morning Herald*, March 10, 1983.
4 *Sydney Morning Herald*, March 19, 1983.
5 *Courier Mail*, February 15, 1983.
6 *Sydney Morning Herald*, March 19, 1983.
7 ibid., March 5, 1983.
8 J.S. Western and Colin A. Hughes, *The Mass Media in Australia* 2nd edn, (St Lucia: University of Queensland Press, 1982), chap. 2.
9 *Age*, March 5, 1983; see also Max Walsh, "The Media: A Minefield for Politicians", *Bulletin*, March 8, 1983.
10 *Sydney Morning Herald*, March 4, 1983.
11 On Fraser's relations with the press, see Anne Summers, *Gamble for Power* (Melbourne: Nelson, 1983), pp. 128–38.
12 *National Times*, August 22–28, 1982.
13 Reproduced in Craig McGregor, *Time of Testing* (Ringwood, Vic.: Penguin, 1983), Appendix C.
14 Reproduced in ibid., Appendix A.
15 *Financial Review*, February 16, 1983.
16 P.P. McGuiness, *Financial Review*, February 24, 1983.
17 McGregor, *Time of testing*, Appendix B.
18 *Sydney Morning Herald*, February 23, 1983.
19 February 22, 1983.
20 *Canberra Times*, March 4, 1983.
21 Peter Robinson, *Financial Review*, March 2, 1983.
22 *Age*, February 22, 1983.
23 *Australian*, March 4, 1983.
24 *Age*, March 4, 1983
25 Peter Bowers, *Sydney Morning Herald*, March 5, 1983.
26 *Canberra Times*, March 2, 1983.
27 ibid., February 23, 1983.
28 Geoffrey Barker, *Age*, February 19, 1983.
29 *Age*, March 5, 1983.
30 March 3, 1983.
31 *Sydney Morning Herald*, March 28, 1983.
32 ibid,; emphasis in original.
33 ibid., March 10, 1983.
34 *Financial Review*, March 3, 1983.
35 See Henry S. Albinski, *The Australian Labor Party and the Aid to Parochial Schools Controversy* (University Park, Pa.: Pennsylvania State University, 1966), and M.C. Hogan, *The Catholic Campaign for State Aid* (Sydney: Catholic Theological Faculty, St Patrick's College, 1978).
36 For example, Max Walsh, "Labor Opens An Enormous Poll Lead", *Bulletin*, February 22, 1983.
37 For example, Bob Carr, "Gallup Poll: Hawke Looks the Winner", *Bulletin*, March 8 (but available before election day), 1983.

38 *Sydney Morning Herald*, February 26, 1983.
39 *Financial Review*, March 3, 1983.
40 Morgan Gallup Poll, Tabulation No. 497.
41 *Financial Review*, March 3, 1983.
42 Malcolm Mackerras, *Bulletin*, February 15, 1983.

APPENDIX A

A Summary of Australian National Election Results, 1977–80

Compiled by Richard Scammon

December 1977 Election Results, Australian House of Representatives

State	Total	Labor	Liberal	National[a] Country	Democrat	Other[b]
New South Wales	2,833,785	1,201,560	1,018,257	320,051	239,808	54,109
% of state vote		42.4	35.9	11.3	8.5	1.9
Seats	43	17	18	8	—	—
Queensland	1,175,663	443,221	326,135	305,275	77,169	23,863
% of state vote		37.7	27.7	26.0	6.6	2.0
Seats	19	3	9	7	—	—
South Australia	757,208	322,883	340,383	6,065	85,578	2,299
% of state vote		42.6	45.0	.8	11.3	.3
Seats	11	6	5	—	—	—
Tasmania	246,819	103,877	134,687	—	8,255	—
% of state vote		42.1	54.6	—	3.3	—
Seats	5	—	5	—	—	—
Victoria	2,127,526	791,083	842,545	120,032	250,943	122,923
% of state vote		37.2	39.6	5.6	11.8	5.8
Seats	33	10	20	3	—	—
Western Australia	632,024	205,793	307,699	25,559	70,590	22,383
% of state vote		32.6	48.7	4.0	11.2	3.5
Seats	10	1	9	—	—	—
Australian Capital Territory	115,091	57,823	48,190	—	8,544	534
% of territory vote		50.2	41.9	—	7.4	.5
Seats	2	1	1	—	—	—
Northern Territory	34,738	14,811	—	16,462	2,478	987
% of territory vote		42.6	—	47.4	7.1	2.8
Seats	1	—	—	1	—	—
Total, Australia	7,922,854	3,141,051	3,017,896	793,444	743,365	227,098
% of total vote		39.6	38.1	10.0	9.4	2.9
Seats	124	38	67	19	—	—

Notes: Vote listed is the first preference ballot count in each State and Territory. The party labels used here are those employed by the Australian Electoral Office in its official returns.
[a] National in Queensland and Victoria; National Country in New South Wales, South Australia and Western Australia; Country Liberal in the Northern Territory.
[b] Democratic Labor Party 113,271; Progress Party 52,767; Communist Party 14,098; Socialist Party 1,895; miscellaneous parties and Independent candidates 54,067.
Source: Australian Electoral Office.

October 1980 Election Results, Australian House of Representatives

State	Total	Labor	Liberal	National[a] Country	Democrat	Other[b]
New South Wales	2,928,454	1,357,556	1,044,191	307,400	166,144	53,163
% of state vote		46.4	35.7	10.5	5.7	1.8
Seats	43	18	16	9	—	—
Queensland	1,252,779	535,846	342,154	273,668	66,502	34,609
% of state vote		42.8	27.3	21.8	5.3	2.8
Seats	19	5	7	7	—	—
South Australia	784,204	348,649	348,981	10,937	68,857	6,780
% of state vote		44.5	44.5	1.4	8.8	.9
Seats	11	6	5	—	—	—
Tasmania	256,522	118,336	133,144	—	3,732	1,310
% of state vote		46.1	51.9		1.5	.5
Seats	5	—	5	—	—	—
Victoria	2,233,856	1,016,617	874,395	109,506	183,212	50,126
% of state vote		45.5	39.1	4.9	8.2	2.2
Seats	33	17	13	3	—	—
Western Australia	681,136	286,259	317,636	15,837	48,076	13,328
% of state vote		42.0	46.6	2.3	7.1	2.0
Seats	11	3	8	—	—	—
Australian Capital Territory	125,510	68,916	48,016	—	7,001	1,577
% of territory vote		54.9	38.3	—	5.6	1.3
Seats	2	2	—	—	—	—
Northern Territory	43,172	17,426	—	18,805	2,509	4,432
% of territory vote		40.4	—	43.6	5.8	10.3
Seats	1	—	—	1	—	—
Total, Australia	8,305,633	3,749,605	3,108,517	736,153	546,033	165,325
% of total vote		45.1	37.4	8.9	6.6	2.0
Seats	125	51	54	20	—	—

Notes: Vote listed is the first preference ballot count in each State and Territory. The party labels used here are those employed by the Australian Electoral Office in its official returns. The total House membership increased between 1977 and 1980 from 124 to 125 by the addition of a new constituency in Western Australia.
[a] National in Queensland and Victoria; National Country in New South Wales, South Australia and Western Australia; Country Liberal in Northern Territory.
[b] Democratic Labor Party 25,456; Progress Party 17,040; Socialist Labor League 15,045; Socialist Workers' Party 14,600; Communist Party 11,318; miscellaneous parties and Independent candidates 81,866.
Source: Australian Electoral Office.

December 1977 Election Results, Australian Senate

State	Total	Labor	Liberal/Nat'l Country[a]	Liberal	Nat'l Country[b]	Democrat	Other[c]
New South Wales	2,621,249	1,050,672	1,136,215	—	—	218,364	215,998
% of state vote		40.1	43.4	—	—	8.3	8.2
Seats	5	2	2	—	—	1	—
Queensland	1,098,872	380,418	564,190	—	—	98,165	56,099
% of state vote		34.6	51.3	—	—	8.9	5.1
Seats	5	2	3	—	—	—	—
South Australia	702,218	258,643	—	344,351	—	78,496	20,728
% of state vote		36.8	—	49.0	—	11.2	3.0
Seats	5	2	—	3	—	—	—
Tasmania	235,427	88,722	—	117,217	—	13,793	15,695
% of state vote		37.7	—	49.8	—	5.9	6.7
Seats	5	2	—	3	—	—	—
Victoria	1,990,436	680,673	833,477	—	—	322,493	153,793
% of state vote		34.2	41.9	—	—	16.2	7.7
Seats	5	2	2	—	—	1	—
Western Australia	600,158	196,781	—	278,413	36,619	74,912	13,433
% of state vote		32.8	—	46.4	6.1	12.5	2.2
Seats	5	2	—	3	—	—	—
Australian Capital Territory	114,200	49,374	—	43,897	—	14,561	6,368
% of territory vote		43.2	—	38.4	—	12.8	5.6
Seats	2	1	—	1	—	—	—
Northern Territory	33,647	13,593	—	—	15,463	2,766	1,825
% of territory vote		40.4	—	—	46.0	8.2	5.4
Seats	2	1	—	—	1	—	—
Total, Australia	7,396,207	2,718,876	2,533,882	783,878	52,082	823,550	483,939
% of total vote		36.8	34.3	10.6	.7	11.1	6.5
Seats	34	14	7	10	1	2	—

Notes: Vote listed is the first preference ballot count in each State and Territory. The party labels used here are those employed by the Australian Electoral Office in its official returns.

[a] Liberal/National Country group in New South Wales; Liberal/National group in Queensland and Victoria.

[b] National Country in Western Australia; Country Liberal in Northern Territory.

[c] Democratic Labor 123,192; Progress Party 85,170; Call to Australia 49,395; Australian Marijuana Party 44,276; Socialist Party 42,740; Australia Party 8,283; Workers' Party 3,033; miscellaneous 127,850.

Source: Australian Electoral Office.

State	Total	Labor	Liberal[a] Nat'l Country	Liberal	Nat'l Country[b]	Democrat	Other[c]
New South Wales	2,717,858	1,215,796	1,139,825	—	—	187,507	174,730
% of state vote		44.7	41.9	—	—	6.9	6.4
Seats	5	3	2	—	—	—	—
Queensland	1,157,330	445,277	—	266,407	309,622	115,429	20,595
% of state vote		38.5	—	23.0	26.8	10.0	1.8
Seats	5	2	—	1	1	1	—
South Australia	736,366	300,420	—	319,088	7,419	96,662	12,747
% of state vote		40.8	—	43.3	1.0	13.1	1.7
Seats	5	2	—	2	—	1	—
Tasmania	243,838	86,833	—	96,098	—	7,780	53,127
% of state vote		35.6	—	39.4	—	3.2	21.8
Seats	5	2	—	2	—	—	1
Victoria	2,039,716	877,468	831,703	—	—	231,113	99,432
% of state vote		43.0	40.8	—	—	11.3	4.9
Seats	5	2	2	—	—	1	—
Western Australia	630,504	244,729	—	283,429	25,937	58,538	17,871
% of state vote		38.8	—	45.0	4.1	9.3	2.8
Seats	5	2	—	3	—	—	—
Australian Capital Territory	124,704	63,280	—	46,267	—	10,663	4,494
% of territory vote		50.1	—	37.1	—	8.6	3.6
Seats	2	1	—	1	—	—	—
Northern Territory	42,078	16,384	—	—	19,129	4,113	2,452
% of territory vote		38.9	—	—	45.5	9.8	5.8
Seats	2	1	—	—	1	—	—
Total, Australia	7,692,364	3,250,187	1,971,528	1,011,289	362,107	711,805	385,448
% of total vote		42.3	25.6	13.1	4.7	9.3	5.0
Seats	34	15	4	9	2	3	1

Notes: Vote listed is the first preference ballot count in each State and Territory. The party labels used here are those employed by the Australian Electoral Office in its official returns.

[a] Liberal/National Country group in New South Wales; Liberal/National group in Victoria.

[b] National in Queensland; National Country in South Australia and Western Australia; Country Liberal in Northern Territory.

[c] Call to Australia 118,535; Harradine Group 52,247 (one elected in Tasmania); Democratic Labor 31,766; Australia Party 28,516; Australian Marijuana Party 28,337; Socialist Party 15,412; Progress Party 8,252; National Party of Western Australia 7,597; Jobless Action Community Campaign 4,001; miscellaneous 90,785.

Source: Australian Electoral Office.

APPENDIX B

A Summary of Australian National Election Results, 1972–75

Compiled by Richard M. Scammon

APPENDIX B

Example Showing the Application of Proportional Representation
(As used in Senate elections)

Say, 4 candidates to be elected; 610 votes recorded of which 15 are informal, i.e. there are 595 formal votes:

$$\text{Quota for election} = \left(\frac{595}{5}\right) + 1 = 120$$

Candidates	A	B	C	D	E	F	G	H	I	J	Total votes in count
First preference votes	30	10	20	320	5	150	40	..	10	10	= 595

D   1st elected with a surplus of 200 votes
F   2nd elected with a surplus of 30 votes

D's first preference votes are now sorted to continuing candidates, according to next available preference thereon (this is to ascertain the proportion in which surplus votes are to be transferred). Say they go:

A	B	C	E	G	H	I	J
..	300	16	..	..	..	..	4

Transfer value of D's surplus votes $= \dfrac{200}{320}$ (i.e. surplus ÷ 1st preferences) ∴ actual votes to be taken at random and transferred =

$$\left. \begin{array}{l} \text{to B } \dfrac{200}{320} \text{ of } 300 = 187 \\[2ex] \text{to C } \dfrac{200}{320} \text{ of } 16 = 10 \\[2ex] \text{to J } \dfrac{200}{320} \text{ of } 4 = 3 \end{array} \right\} = 200$$

F's 150 1st preference votes sorted to continuing candidates according to the next available preferences thereon. Say they go:

A	B	C	E	G	H	I	J
100	15	10	15	6	1	..	3

Transfer value of F's surplus votes $\dfrac{30}{150}$ (i.e., surplus ÷ 1st preferences)

∴ actual votes to be transferred:

$$\left. \begin{array}{l} \text{to A } \dfrac{30}{150} \text{ of } 100 = 20 \\[2ex] \text{to B } \dfrac{30}{150} \text{ of } 15 = 3 \\[2ex] \text{to C } \dfrac{30}{150} \text{ of } 10 = 2 \\[2ex] \text{to E } \dfrac{30}{150} \text{ of } 15 = 3 \\[2ex] \text{to G } \dfrac{30}{150} \text{ of } 6 = 1 \\[2ex] \text{to H } \dfrac{30}{150} \text{ of } 1 = 0 \\[2ex] \text{to J } \dfrac{30}{150} \text{ of } 3 = 1 \end{array} \right\} = 30$$

Tally sheet now reads:

Candidates	A	B	C	D	E	F	G	H	I	J	Total votes in count	Number of elected candidates' votes set aside
First preference votes	30	10	20	320	5	150	40	..	10	10	= 595	
D's 200 surplus votes transferred	..	187	10	1st Elected	..	2nd Elected	..	..	..	3	..	.. 120 } i.e.
F's 30 surplus votes transferred	20	3	2	1st Elected	3	2nd Elected	1	..	..	1	..	.. 120 } 2 quotas
Progress totals	50	200	32		8		41	..	10	14	= 355	

B 3rd elected with a surplus of 80 votes.

The 190 votes received by B from D and F now sorted to continuing candidates. Say they go:

A	C	E	G	H	I	J
..	..	..	..	187	3	..

Transfer value of B's surplus votes = $\dfrac{80}{190}$ (i.e. surplus votes ÷ votes received by B at the previous stage of the count)

∴ actual votes to be transferred:

$$\left.\begin{array}{l} \text{to } H \ \dfrac{80}{190} \text{ of } 187 = 79 \\[2mm] \text{to } I \ \dfrac{80}{190} \text{ of } \ 3 = 1 \end{array}\right\} = 80$$

Tally sheet now reads:

Candidates	A	B	C	E	G	H	I	J	Total votes in count	Number of elected candidates' votes set aside
Progress totals, brought forward	50	200	32	8	41	..	10	14	= 355	
B's surplus votes transferred	..	3rd Elected	..	..	..	79	1	..	.	120 (i.e. 1 quota)
Progress totals	50	3rd Elected	32	8	41	79	11	14	= 235	

No further candidate now having a quota, E with the fewest votes, is excluded and his 8 votes are transferred. Say they go:

A	C	G	H	I	J
2	..	..	..	5	1

Progress totals	52	32	41	79	16	15	= 235

J with the fewest votes, is now excluded and his 15 votes are transferred. Say they go:

A	C	G	H	I
..	..	..	12	3

Progress totals	52	32	41	91	19	= 235

I with the fewest votes, is now excluded and his 19 votes are transferred. Say they go:

A	C	G	H
..	..	9	10

Progress totals	52	32	50	101	= 235

C with the fewest votes, is now excluded and his 32 votes are transferred. Say they go:

	A	G	H
	12	10	10
Progress totals	64	60	111 = 235

G with the fewest votes, is now excluded and his 60 votes are transferred. Say they go:

	A	H
	55	5
Progress totals	119	116 = 235

A 4th elected.

Complete tally sheet would read:

Candidates	A	B	C	D	E	F	G	H	I	J	Total votes in count	Number of elected candidates' votes set aside
First preference votes	30	10	20	320	5	150	40	..	10	10	= 595	
D elected, 200 surplus votes transferred	..	187	10	*1st Elected*	..	*2nd Elected*	..	..	..	3		120
F elected, 30 surplus votes transferred	20	3	2		3		1	..	..	1		120
Progress totals	50	200	32		8		41	..	10	14	= 355	
B elected, 80 surplus votes transferred	..	*3rd Elected*	..		..		..	79	1	..		120
Progress totals	50		32		8		41	79	11	14	= 235	
E excluded, 8 votes transferred	2		..		*Excluded*		..	..	5	1		
Progress totals	52		32				41	79	16	15	= 235	
J excluded, 15 votes transferred	..		..				..	12	3	*Excluded*		
Progress totals	52		32				41	91	19		= 235	
I excluded, 19 votes transferred	..		..				9	10	*Excluded*			
Progress totals	52		32				50	101			= 235	
C excluded, 32 votes transferred	12		*Excluded*				10	10				
Progress totals	64						60	111			= 235	
G excluded, 60 votes transferred	55						*Excluded*	5				
Progress totals	119 *(4th Elected)*							116			= 235	

330

Example Showing the Application of the Alternative Vote
(As used in House of Representatives elections)

Let it be assumed that there are 5 candidates for which 610 votes were recorded and of these 10 are informal, i.e. there are 600 formal votes. For election a candidate must receive an absolute majority of the formal votes—i.e. 301 votes.

Candidates	Adams	Brown	Grey	Jones	White	Total
First preference votes	150	200	70	100	80	**600**

No candidate having received an absolute majority of the votes, candidate GREY, with the least number of votes, is excluded. His 70 ballot-papers are now sorted to continuing candidates according to the next available preference thereon. Say they go:

	Adams	Brown	Jones	White
	10	..	40	20

Tally sheet now reads:

	Adams	Brown	Grey	Jones	White	Total
First preference votes	150	200	70	100	80	600
GREY excluded—70 ballot-papers transferred	10	..	Excl.	40	20	
Progressive totals	**160**	**200**	..	**140**	**100**	**600**

No candidate yet having received an absolute majority of the votes, candidate WHITE with the fewest votes is now excluded and the 100 ballot-papers which were previously sorted to him are transferred to the next continuing candidates. Say they go:

	Adams	Brown	Jones
	15	30	55

This will give ADAMS (160 + 15) 175 votes, BROWN (200 + 30) 230 votes and JONES (140 + 55) 195 votes. ADAMS is now excluded and his 175 ballot-papers are transferred. Say they go:

	Brown	Jones
	60	115

Tally sheet now reads:

	Adams	Brown	Grey	Jones	White	Total
First preference votes	150	200	70	100	80	600
GREY excluded—70 ballot-papers transferred	10	..	Excl.	40	20	
Progressive totals	**160**	**200**	..	**140**	**100**	**600**
WHITE excluded—100 ballot-papers transferred	15	30	..	55	Excl.	
Progressive totals	**175**	**230**	..	**195**	..	**600**
ADAMS excluded—175 ballot-papers transferred	Excl.	60	..	115	..	
Progressive totals	..	**290**	..	**310**	..	**600**

Candidate JONES having received an absolute majority of the votes in the count is elected with 310 votes.

Examples of Ballots

(These 1975 ballots are substituted for the 1974 ballots reproduced in the Australian Electoral Office booklet.)

Form F

BALLOT-PAPER

(To be initialed on back by Presiding Officer before issue.)

COMMONWEALTH OF AUSTRALIA
STATE OF NEW SOUTH WALES

Electoral Division of SYDNEY
Election of One Member of the House of Representatives

DIRECTIONS:—Mark your vote on this ballot-paper by placing the numbers **1, 2, 3, 4** and **5** in the squares respectively opposite the names of the candidates, so as to indicate the order of your preference for them

CANDIDATES

☐ **AARONS, Laurence**

☐ **GIESEKAM, Merilyn**

☐ **MacNEIL, Roderick**

☐ **McMAHON, James Leslie**

☐ **WALLACE, Janis Joye**

Form E

COMMONWEALTH OF AUSTRALIA.

BALLOT-PAPER (To be initialed on back by Presiding Officer before Issue.)

STATE OF NEW SOUTH WALES — ELECTION OF TEN SENATORS.

DIRECTIONS.—Mark your vote on this ballot-paper by placing the numbers 1, 2, 3, 4, 5, 6, 7, 8, 9, 10, 11, 12, 13, 14, 15, 16, 17, 18, 19, 20, 21, 22, 23, 24, 25, 26, 27, 28, 29, 30, 31, 32, 33, 34, 35, 36, 37, 38, 39, 40, 41, 42, 43, 44, 45, 46, 47, 48, 49, 50, 51, 52 and 53 in the squares immediately to the left of the names of the respective candidates so as to indicate the order of your preference for them.

CANDIDATES

A
- JARVIS Helen Myfanwy
- ADLER Gordon Frank

B
- COTTON Robert Carrington
- CARRICK John Leslie
- SCOTT Douglas Barr
- BAUME Peter Erne
- LAJOVIC Milivoj Emil
- ROSS Dorothy Dickson

C
- BROWN Frieda Jessie
- NILE Frederick John
- HARRISON Kenneth Brian

D
- KELLY Ron
- KHOURY Robert Omar

E
- KANE John Thomas
- DALY Peter Francis
- McCOSKER Anne Therese
- CASEY William Denis
- KEOGH James Clement
- WESTMORE Peter Anthony

F
- GREEN Ross Winston
- WILSON Lyn

G
- MORGAN Terence Paul
- PAYNE Bill

H
- McCLELLAND Douglas
- McCLELLAND James Robert
- MULVIHILL James Anthony
- GIETZELT Arthur Thomas
- SIBRAA Kerry Walter
- RENSHAW Emily Anastasia

I
- HILL John Sinclair Leslie
- TIER Mark Douglas John
- O'SULLIVAN Susan Joan
- KENNARD Neville John
- GRANT John McDonald Falconer
- EDMONDS John Hanbury

J
- MASON Colin Victor James
- NEWMAN Robert Stanley
- McMILLAN Mavis Alexandra

(ungrouped)
- MARTIN Athol James
- ALLE Adrian Frederick
- HOWARD Neel Anthony
- POURSHASB Darius
- WOODS Lawrence William
- BURKE Kenneth
- BECHER Luciano George
- McPHERSON David Brian
- TABER Bruce Murray
- GUY Thomas Edward
- APPLEBY Reginald Thomas
- BOYTON Andrew Barclay
- STEUART Michael Gordon
- WOJESZLOVSZKY Michael
- BREEN-HEMINGWAY John Christopher Roc

NOTE.—The letter "A" or "B" or "C" or "D" or "E" or "F" or "G" or "H" or "I" or "J" appearing before the square immediately to the left of a candidate's surname indicates that that candidate and each other candidate who has the same letter appearing before the square immediately to the left of his surname have been grouped by mutual consent. The fact that no letter appears before the square immediately to the left of a candidate's surname indicates that the name of that candidate has not been included in any group.

APPENDIX C
A Summary of Australian National Election Results, 1983

Compiled by Colin A. Hughes

APPENDIX C

March 1983 Election Results. Australian House of Representatives

State	Total	Labor	Liberal	National[a]	Democrats	Other[b]
New South Wales	3,016,316	1,511,853	951,717	330,657	144,633	77,456
% of state vote		50.1	31.6	11.0	4.8	2.6
Seats	43	24	11	8	—	—
Queensland	1,346,389	621,146	328,530	319,647	62,637	14,429
% of state vote		46.1	24.4	23.7	4.7	1.1
Seats	19	10	3	6	—	—
South Australia	814,304	393,970	342,809	8,762	56,508	12,255
% of state vote		48.4	42.1	1.1	6.9	1.5
Seats	11	7	4	—	—	—
Tasmania	264,768	106,647	145.393	—	9,458	3,270
% of state vote		40.3	54.9	—	3.6	1.2
Seats	5	—	5	—	—	—
Victoria	2,340,951	1,182,247	869,413	114,065	133,183	42,043
% of state vote		50.5	37.1	4.9	5.7	1.8
Seats	33	23	7	3	—	—
Western Australia	728,630	378,545	304.677	5,999	29,273	10,136
% of state vote		52.0	41.8	0.8	4.0	1.4
Seats	11	8	3	—	—	—
Australian Capital Territory	128,631	82,189	41,213	—	—	5,229
% of state vote		63.9	32.0	—	—	4.1
Seats	2	2	—	—	—	—
Northern Territory	44,570	20,753	—	20,472	1,571	1,774
% of state vote		46.6	—	45.9	3.5	4.0
Seats	1	1	—	—	—	—
Total, Australia	8,684,559	4,297,350	2,983,752	799,602	437,263	166,592
% of total vote		49.5	34.4	9.2	5.0	1.9
Seats	125	75	33	17	—	—

Notes: Vote listed is the first preference ballot count in each State and Territory. The party labels used here are those employed by the Australian Electoral Office in its returns.
[a] National Country in Western Australia, Country Liberal in Northern Territory.
[b] Socialist Workers Party 46,073, Democratic Labor Party 17,318, Progress Party 6,652, Communist Party 6,398, Socialist Labor League 6,327, Socialist Party 4,165, National Party of Western Australia 3,686, miscellaneous parties and independent candidates 75,973.
Source: Australian Electoral Office.

March 1983 Election Results, Australian Senate

State	Total	Labor	Liberal National	Liberal	National[a]	Democrats	Other[b]
New South Wales	2,741,268	1,298,672	1,045,502	—	—	235,712	161,382
% of state vote		47.4	38.1			8.6	5.9
Seats	10	5	4			1	—
Queensland	1,247,321	493,424	—	187,495	363,462	98,997	103,943
% of state vote		39.6		15.0	29.1	7.9	8.3
Seats	10	4		2	3	1	—
South Australia	763,349	340,089	—	308,138	13,757	92,585	8,780
% of state vote		44.6		40.4	1.8	12.1	1.2
Seats	10	5		4	—	1	—
Tasmania	250,896	82,343	—	106,768	—	17,089	44,696
% of state vote		32.8		42.6		6.9	17.9
Seats	10	4		5		—	1
Victoria	2,137,934	994,471	816,106	—	—	256,402	70,955
% of state vote		46.5	39.2			12.0	3.3
Seats	10	5	4			1	—
Western Australia	685,058	337,417	—	280,878	7,689	46,626	12,448
% of state vote		49.3		41.0	1.1	6.9	1.8
Seats	10	5		4	—	1	—
Australian Capital Territory	127,246	70,433	—	40,292	—	15,141	1,380
% of state vote		55.4		31.7		11.9	1.1
Seats	2	1		1		—	—
Northern Territory	44,615	20,506	—	—	21,446	2,418	245
% of state vote		46.0			48.1	5.4	0.5
Seats	2	1			1	—	—
Total, Australia	7,997,687	3,637,355	1,861,608	923,571	406,354	764,970	403,829
% of total vote		45.5	23.3	11.5	5.1	9.6	5.0
Seats	64	30	8	16	4	5	1

Notes: Vote listed is the first preference ballot count in each State and Territory. The party labels used are those employed by the Australian Electoral Office in its returns.

[a] National Country in Western Australia, Country Liberal in Northern Territory.

[b] Call to Australia 96,065, Bonner ticket 83,602, Democratic Labor Party 47,206, Harradine ticket 44,696, Progress Party 13,012, Integrity Teams 11,234, Socialist Workers Party 9,352, Socialist Party 5,662, National Party of Western Australia 3,894, Social Democrat Party 2,304, Communist Party 1,058, miscellaneous 85,744.

Source: Australian Electoral Office.

Contributors

DON AITKIN is Professor of Political Science at the Research School of Social Sciences, Australian National University. He is the author of *Stability and Change in Australian Politics* (2nd ed. 1982), *Australian Political Institutions* (with Brian Jenks—2nd ed. 1982). His other books include *The Colonel, The Country Party of New South Wales* and a novel *The Second Chair*. He is currently working on the political diaries of the Hon. Peter Howson and a book on federalism.

DAVID BUTLER, a fellow of Nuffield College, Oxford, since 1951, has studied and lectured widely in the United States. He has written extensively on British politics and elections and is the author of *The Canberra Model*, co-author of *Political Change in Britain*, and co-editor of *Referendums*.

MURRAY GOOT is a senior lecturer in politics at Macquarie University in Sydney. He is the author of *Policies and Partisans* and co-author of *Women and Voting Studies* and *Australian Opinion Polls, 1941–1977*.

COLIN A. HUGHES is a professorial fellow in political science at the Australian National University. He is joint editor of half a dozen volumes of Australian electoral statistics and editor of a series on Australian state government. His most recent book is *A Handbook of Australian Government and Politics 1965–1974*.

MARTIN RAWLINSON is Managing Director of Australian Public Affairs Consultants Pty Ltd in Canberra. Between 1977 and 1980 he was Head of the Research Department of the Liberal Party's Secretariat. From 1975 to 1977 he was a federal public servant in the former Department of Urban and Regional Development.

KEITH RICHMOND was formerly on the staff of the Department of Politics, University of New England. He is currently employed by the Commonwealth Public Service. His research interests are in the field of Australian politics, especially parties, pressure groups, rural politics, and social movements. He has co-authored one book, *Political Parties in Australia*, 1978, contributed to a number of collections, and written numerous articles in professional journals.

ANNE SUMMERS is the Canberra Bureau Chief and Political Correspondent for the *Australian Financial Review*. In 1976 she won the Walkley Award for the best newspaper feature article. She holds a doctorate from the University of Sydney and is author of *Damned Whores and God's Police: The Colonization of Women in Australia*, 1975 *Gamble for Power*, 1983, is co-author, with Margaret Bettison of *Her Story: Australian Women in Print 1788–1975*, 1980 and author of numerous articles and monographs.

RICHARD M. SCAMMON, co-author of *This U.S.A.* and *The Real Majority*, is director of the Elections Research Center in Washington, D.C. He has edited the biennial series *America Votes* since 1956.

PATRICK WELLER is a senior lecturer in the Department of Political Science at the Australian National University. He is the editor of *Caucus Minutes 1901–1949* and *Federal Executive Minutes 1915–1955* and co-author of *Treasury Control in Australia, Politics and Policy in Australia* and *Can Ministers Cope?* In 1978–79 he was director of research at the Commonwealth Public Service Board.

JOHN WARHURST is a research fellow in political science at the Research School of Social Sciences, Australian National University. He is the author of *Jobs or Dogma?*, 1982 and *Anatomy of an Election*, 1979 and editor of *Politics and Government in Victoria*, 1982 and *State Governments and Australian Tariff Policy*, 1980.

AEI's *At the Polls* Studies

Australia at the Polls: The National Elections of 1975, Howard R.
Penniman, ed. Chapters by Leon D. Epstein, Patrick Weller,
R.F.I. Smith, D.W. Rawson, Michelle Grattan, Margaret Bridson
Cribb, Paul Reynolds, C.J. Lloyd, Terence W. Beed, Owen
Harries, and Colin A. Hughes. Appendixes by David Butler and
Richard M. Scammon. (373 pp., $5)

The Australian National Elections of 1977, Howard R. Penniman, ed.
Chapters by David Butler, David A. Kemp, Patrick Weller, Jean
Holmes, Paul Reynolds, Murray Goot, Terence W. Beed, C.J.
Lloyd, Ainsley Jolley, Duncan Ironmonger, and Colin A.
Hughes. Appendix by Richard M. Scammon. (367 pp., $8.25)

Britain at the Polls: The Parliamentary Elections of 1974, Howard R.
Penniman, ed. Chapters by Austin Ranney, Anthony King, Dick
Leonard, Michael Pinto-Duschinsky, Richard Rose, and Jay G.
Blumler. Appendix by Richard M. Scammon. (256 pp., $3)

Britain Says Yes: The 1975 Referendum on the Common Market, Anthony
King. (153 pp., $3.75)

Britain at the Polls, 1979: A Study of the General Election, Howard R.
Penniman, ed. Chapters by Austin Ranney, Anthony King, Dick
Leonard, William B. Livingston, Jorgen Rasmussen, Richard
Rose, Michael Pinto-Duschinsky, Monica Charlot, and Ivor
Crewe. Appendixes by Shelley Pinto-Duschinsky and Richard
M. Scammon. (345 pp., cloth $16.25, paper $8.25)

British Political Finance, 1830–1980, Michael Pinto-Duschinsky. (339
pp., cloth $17.95, paper $10.50)

Canada at the Polls: The General Election of 1974, Howard R. Penniman,
ed. Chapters by John Meisel, William P. Irvine, Stephen Clarkson, George Perlin, Jo Surich, Michael B. Stein, Khayyam Z.

Paltiel, Lawrence LeDuc, and Frederick J. Fletcher. Appendix by Richard M. Scammon. (310 pp., $4.50)

Canada at the Polls, 1979 and 1980: A Study of the General Elections, Howard R. Penniman, ed. Chapters by Alan C. Cairns, John Meisel, William P. Irvine, Robert J. Williams, John C. Courtney, Stephen Clarkson, Walter D. Young, Vincent Lemieux and Jean Crete, F. Leslie Seidle and Khayyam Zev Paltiel, Frederick J. Fletcher, and M. Janine Brodie and Jill Vickers. Appendix by Richard M. Scammon. (426 pp., cloth $17.25, paper $9.25)

France at the Polls: The Presidential Election of 1974, Howard R. Penniman, ed. Chapters by Roy Pierce, J. Blondel, Jean Charlot, Serge Hurtig, Marie-Thérèse Lancelot, Alain Lancelot, Alfred Grosser, and Monica Charlot. Appendix by Richard M. Scammon. (324 pp., $4.50)

The French National Assembly Elections of 1978, Howard R. Penniman, ed. Chapters by Roy Pierce, Jérôme Jaffré, Jean Charlot, Georges Lavau, Roland Cayrol, Monica Charlot, and Jeane J. Kirkpatrick. Appendix by Richard M. Scammon. (255 pp., $7.25)

Germany at the Polls: The Bundestag Election of 1976, Karl H. Cerny, ed. Chapters by Gerhard Loewenberg, David P. Conradt, Kurt Sontheimer, Heino Kaack, Werner Kaltefleiter, Paul Noack, Klaus Schönback, Rulolf Wildenmann, and Max Kaase. Appendix by Richard M. Scammon. (251 pp., $7.25)

Greece at the Polls: The National Elections of 1974 and 1977, Howard R. Penniman, ed. Chapters by Roy C. Macridis, Phaedo Vegleris, J.C. Loulis, Thanos Veremis, Angelos Elephantis, Michalis Papayannakis, and Theodore Couloumbis. Appendix by Richard M. Scammon. (220 pp., $15.25 cloth, $7.25 paper)

India at the Polls: The Parliamentary Elections of 1977, Myron Weiner. (150 pp., $6.25)

India at the Polls, 1980: A Study of the Parliamentary Elections, Myron Weiner.

Ireland at the Polls: The Dáil Elections of 1977, Howard R. Penniman, ed. Chapters by Basil Chubb, Richard Sinnott, Maurice Manning, and Brian Farrell. Appendixes by Basil Chubb and Richard M. Scammon. (199 pp., $6.25)

Israel at the Polls: The Knesset Election of 1977, Howard R. Penniman, ed. Chapters by Daniel J. Elazar, Avraham Brichta, Asher Arian, Benjamin Akzin, Myron J. Aronoff, Efraim Torgovnik, Elyakim Rubinstein, Leon Boim, Judith Elizur, Elihu Katz, and Bernard Reich. Appendix by Richard M. Scammon. (333 pp., $8.25)

Italy at the Polls: The Parliamentary Elections of 1976, Howard R. Penniman, ed. Chapters by Joseph LaPalombara, Douglas

Wertman, Giacomo Sani, Giuseppe Di Palma, Stephen Hellman, Gianfranco Pasquino, Robert Leonardi, William E. Porter, Robert D. Putnam, and Samuel H. Barnes. Appendix by Richard M. Scammon. (386 pp., $5.75)

Italy at the Polls, 1979: A Study of the Parliamentary Elections, Howard R. Penniman, ed. Chapters by Sidney Tarrow, Giacomo Sani, Douglas A. Wertman, Joseph LaPalombara, Gianfranco Pasquino, Robert Leonardi, Patrick McCarthy, Karen Beckwith, William E. Porter, and Samuel H. Barnes. Appendixes by Douglas A. Wertman and Richard M. Scammon. (335 pp., $16.25 cloth, $8.25 paper)

Japan at the Polls: The House of Councillors Election of 1974, Michael K. Blaker, ed. Chapters by Herbert Passin, Gerald L. Curtis, and Michael K. Blaker. (157 pp., $3)

A Season of Voting: The Japanese Elections of 1976 and 1977, Herbert Passin, ed. Chapters by Herbert Passin, Michael Blaker, Gerald L. Curtis, Nisihira Sigeki, and Kato Hirohisa. (199 pp., $6.25)

New Zealand at the Polls: The General Election of 1978, Howard R. Penniman, ed. Chapters by Stephen Levine, Keith Ovenden, Alan McRobie, Keith Jackson, Gilbert Antony Wood, Roderic Alley, Colin C. James, Brian Murphy, Les Cleveland, Judith Aitken, and Nigel S. Roberts. Appendix by Richard M. Scammon. (295 pp., $7.25)

Scandinavia at the Polls: Recent Political Trends in Denmark, Norway, and Sweden, Karl H. Cerny, ed. Chapters by Ole Borre, Henry Valen, Willy Martinussen, Bo Särlvik, Daniel Tarschys, Erik Allardt, Steen Sauerberg, Niels Thomsen, C.G. Uhr, Göran Ohlin, and Walter Galenson. (304 pp., $5.75)

Venezuela at the Polls: The National Elections of 1978, Howard R. Penniman, ed. Chapters by John D. Martz, Henry Wells, Robert E. O'Connor, David J. Myers, Donald Herman, and David Blank. Appendix by Richard M. Scammon. (287 pp., cloth $15.25, paper $7.25)

Democracy at the Polls: A Comparative Study of Competitive National Elections, David Butler, Howard R. Penniman, and Austin Ranney, eds. Chapters by David Butler, Arend Lijphart, Leon D. Epstein, Austin Ranney, Howard R. Penniman, Khayyam Zev Paltiel, Anthony Smith, Dennis Kavanagh, Ivor Crewe, Donald E. Stokes, Anthony King, and Jeane J. Kirkpatrick. (367 pp., $16.25 cloth, $8.25 paper)

Referendums: A Comparative Study of Practice and Theory, David Butler and Austin Ranney, eds. Chapters by Jean-François Aubert, Austin Ranney, Eugene C. Lee, Don Aitkin, Vincent Wright,

Sten Sparre Nilson, Maurice Manning, and David Butler. (250 pp., $4.75)

At the Polls studies are forthcoming on the latest national elections in Australia, Belgium, Denmark, France, Germany, Greece, Ireland, Israel, Jamaica, Japan, the Netherlands, New Zealand, Norway, Portugal, Spain, and Sweden. In addition, cross-national volumes on the first elections to the European Parliament, women in electoral politics, candidate selection, and parties of the left are under way.

See also the first volume in a new series of studies of American elections edited by Austin Ranney:

The American Elections of 1980, Austin Ranney, ed. Chapters by Austin Ranney, Nelson W. Polsby, Charles O. Jones, Michael J. Malbin, Albert R. Hunt, Michael J. Robinson, William Schneider, Thomas E. Mann and Norman J. Ornstein, Anthony King, and Aaron Wildavsky. Statistical appendix. (391 pp., $16.25 cloth, $8.25 paper)

Index

Abortion Law Reform Association of Australia, 112
Adermann, Evan, 93
Advertiser (Adelaide), 171, 291; political stories, 143, 145; polls coverage, 164; share market coverage, 166
Advertising, 1980 election campaign, see *Australian Labor Party; Liberal Party; National Country Party*
Age (Melbourne), 5, 48, 65–6, 90–1, 192, 286; election news coverage, 151, 156; feature articles, 150; issues, coverage of, 152, 153, 154; letters, 150; political stories, 143, 145; polls coverage, 162, 164, 165
agricultural sector, 2
Aitkin, Don, 19, 104
Annual Premiers' Conference, 2
Anthony, Doug, 81, 83–4, 85, 86, 90, 93
anti-dam cause, effect on 1983 election, 299–300
Anti-Vietnam War Groups, 99, 100
Australia Party (AP), 14, 98, 101–2
Australian, 47, 141, 158, 295; editorials, 150; election news coverage, 151; interpretative reporting, 156; issues, coverage of, 154; Labor leaks, 160; political stories, 143; polls coverage, 163, 164; support for government, 152; tax cuts, coverage of, 170; violence, coverage of, 171; wealth tax, coverage of, 167, 169
Australian Broadcasting Commission (ABC): election news coverage, 173–5, 175–9, 180–3; viewers, 172–3
Australian Conservation Foundation, 299
Australian Council of Social Services (ACOSS), 291
Australian Council of Trade Unions (ACTU), 99, 272

Australian Democrats (AD), 8, 11, 12, 14, 101, 102, 104–9, 116–7, 137, 157, 230, 299, 307, 314, 317; preferences, distribution of, 226–8; and Queensland, 235–6; support, 102–3, 105–6; weaknesses, 103–4
Australian electoral system, 3–4; fairness of, 220–6
Australian electorate, 11–31; political awareness, 27–30; volatility, 12–5
Australian Federation of Right to Life Association, 112
Australian Financial Review, 55–6, 269, 286; and Australian National Opinion Poll, 162; Fraser, threat to supply, 161; interpretative reporting, 161; Labor leaks, 161; political stories, 141, 143; polls coverage, 164; readership, 145; share market coverage; 166; tax cuts, coverage of, 170
Australian Labor Party, 1, 2, 4, 6–9, 55–77, 137–8; advertising campaign, 53, 72, 73–4, 188, 194, 199; capital gains, 27; election promises, costing, 47–8, 75; embourgeoisment of, 63; factional alignment, 61–2; Federal Executive, 58; gaffes, 295–6; gains in 1980, 219; headquarters, 285; identification with, 20–1; ideology and policy, 68–70; issues, 75–6, 197–8; leadership, 55–6, 64–8, 249, 269–73, 273–7; leaks, 160–1; Liberal Party advertising campaign, appeal to High Court against, 75–6; male-dominated image, 131–2; metropolitan areas, 246; national committee of inquiry, 59–60; National Conference, 59–60, 69–70; national planning committee, 71; organization, 57–60; policy launches, 159, 180; policy

345